Y

A Clinical Treatise On the Diseases of the Nervous System, Volume 2

A

CLINICAL TREATISE

ON THE

DISEASES

OF THE

NERVOUS SYSTEM

By M. ROSENTHAL

Professor of Diseases of the Nervous System at Vienna

WITH A PREFACE BY PROFESSOR CHARCOT

TRANSLATED FROM THE AUTHOR'S REVISED AND ENLARGED EDITION

BY

L. PUTZEL, M.D.

Visiting Physician for Nervous Diseases, Randall's Island Hospital. Physician to the Class for Nervous Diseases, Bellevue Hospital Out-Door Department, and Pathologist to the Lunatic Asylum, B. I.

VOLUME II.

NEW YORK

WILLIAM WOOD & COMPANY

27 GREAT JONES STREET

1879

CONTENTS.

CLASS VI.

NEUROSES ASSOCIATED WITH TREMOR AND DISORDERS OF CO-ORDINATION.

CLASS VII.

TOXIC NEUROSES.—POST-FEBRILE NERVOUS DISORDERS.— ANÆMIC AND REFLEX PARALYSIS.

CLASS VIII.

NEUROSES OF THE SEXUAL ORGANS.

CHAPTER XL.

CLASS IX.

DISEASES OF THE PERIPHERAL NERVOUS SYSTEM.

CHAPTER XLI.

CHAPTER XLII.

CHAPTER XLIII.

I.—DISEASES OF THE CRANIAL NERVES.

CHAPTER XLIV.

CHAPTER XLV.

CLINICAL TREATISE

ON

DISEASES OF THE NERVOUS SYSTEM.

DISEASES OF THE ANTERIOR PORTION OF THE CORD.

(ANTERIOR SCLEROSES.)

THE morbid processes occurring in the cortical cells of the brain in general progressive paralysis may also develop in the cord under the influence of various acute or chronic inflammatory affections. Degeneration and pigmentary atrophy occur in the multipolar nerve-cells of the anterior horns and in the fibres which unite these cells with the intra-medullary portion of the anterior roots and with the antero-lateral columns. From careful study of the affections of the anterior spinal nerve-roots we have become better acquainted with the influence of these delicate and important parts upon the motor and trophic functions, and a whole series of morbid types have been discovered which may be combined with various bulbar or spinal paralyses.

The anatomical data have so much the more importance with regard to the theory and clinical knowledge of the diseases in question, because nature herself, by isolating the lesions in certain nerve-cells, in certain groups of cells, or in certain bundles of the white substance, has furnished us with a positive and precise solution of all the problems which could be determined by experimentation. The most skilful and practised experimenter could never obtain equally positive results.

In the following section we shall first examine the rapid inflammatory processes occurring in the anterior horns (myelitis antica acuta) as they are found in acute spinal infantile paralysis and in that of adults; then, the chronic inflammatory processes in the anterior gray columns (myelitis antica chronica), which constitute the fundamental lesion of progressive muscular atrophy and its different forms.

CHAPTER XXIV.

A.—INFANTILE SPINAL PARALYSIS.

Pathological Anatomy.

THANKS to the attention which has lately been paid to lesions of the anterior gray columns of the cord, the nature of infantile spinal paralysis has become known for a short period.   Cornil (Comptes rendus de la Soc. de Biologie, 1864) relates the history of a woman, forty-nine years of age, who had suffered from paralysis of several muscles of the legs since the age of ten years.   The autopsy revealed *atrophy of the antero-lateral columns and the presence of abundant amyloid corpuscles in the anterior horns.*

But Cornil did not interpret these changes in their proper light.   Prévost and Vulpian (Gaz. Méd. de Paris, 1866) were the first to observe *atrophy and partial sclerosis of the left anterior horn and atrophy of the anterior roots,* with fatty degeneration of the muscles and their nerves, in a woman, seventy-eight years of age, who had had a deformity of the left foot since childhood.   In addition, the traces of a recent cerebro-spinal meningitis were present (without notable symptoms during life).   Then followed Charcot and Joffroy (Arch. de Physiol., 1870), Parrot and Joffroy (the same Archives), and Roger and Damaschino (Gaz. Méd. de Paris, 1871, 4. Observ.), who observed, in infantile spinal paralysis, *atrophy and deformity of the anterior horns,* increase of the connective-tissue network, fatty degeneration of the vessels, and atrophy of the nerve cells and fibres, with *partial sclerosis of the antero-lateral columns and anterior roots.*

Other observations of the same character have been recently published. Recklinghausen (Jahrb. d. Kinderheilk., 1871) reported a case of *atrophy of the cells of the anterior horns, of the anterior columns, and of the anterior portions of the lateral columns.*   M. Roth (Virch. Arch., Bd. 58, 1873) relates a case of *destruction of the right anterior horn* (visible under a low magnifying power), with atrophy of the nerve cells and fibres and of the anterior roots.   In addition there was *partial myelitis of the posterior horn and of the antero-lateral column.*   Finally, I have also had the opportunity of examining sections of the cord, after hardening in chromic acid, in a case of infantile spinal paralysis (*vide* Med. chir. Rundschau, Feb. Heft, 1872).   The appearances presented in these preparations were the following : atrophy and deformity of the anterior horn involved, rarefaction of the nerve-cells in certain places and amyloid degeneration of the cells in others, sclerotic enlargement with final atrophy, frequent absence of the nucleus, and complete disappearance of the cells, here and there, their place being occupied by a finely wavy connective-tissue.   The vessels were considerably enlarged and thickened, and the gray substance was very vascular.   There was atrophy with sclerosis of the antero-lateral column, corresponding to the lesion of the anterior horn.   Leyden has recently demonstrated (Arch. f. Psych., VI., 1876) that spinal infantile paralysis may be produced by various morbid processes (sclerosis, cicatrization, myelitis), whose sole common characteristic consists of their acute character and their situation in the anterior gray substance. According to Volkmann, the *paralyzed muscles*, even after the disease has lasted several years, merely present simple atrophy of the fibres, which have a finely granular appearance, with *increase of nuclei* and of the interstitial fatty tissue. According to Hayem, proliferation of the nuclei occurs in the perimysium and sarcolemma, and this accumulation renders the muscular fibres friable, without modifying the appearance of the striæ to any appreciable extent.

Etiology.

Infantile spinal paralysis occurs in the first three years of life, and usually between the sixth and fourteenth months. The children appear to enjoy good health previously, but sometimes have a delicate constitution, a pale color and a very irritable disposition. Nervous disorders are not infrequently present in the parents, especially in the mother. I have seen several cases in which the mother had suffered from *abdominal spasms*, and in which other children in the family had died of eclampsia or hydrocephalus. The action of cold is very problematical, and external influences (compression, according to Kennedy) do not appear to play any part in the etiology of the disease in question. According to Holmes Coote, among 1,000 children admitted to the Royal Orthopædic Hospital, there were 80 cases of infantile spinal paralysis, or 8 in 100. Among 192 cases of paralysis occurring in children, Heine, Jr., observed 158 of spinal origin, of which 84 were partial paralyses. Sex appears to possess no appreciable influence upon the frequency of occurrence of the disease.

Charcot and Joffroy consider *the primary atrophy of the nerve-cells of the anterior horns* as the point of departure of the disease. This lesion, together with secondary atrophy of the anterior roots, is sometimes the only textural change that can be discovered with the microscope upon transverse sections of the cord. The posterior horns and white columns of the cord are only affected secondarily and to a minor degree by the final development of the morbid process. Other French observers have arrived at the same conclusions. In opposition to this view, I desire to formulate another pathogenic theory of this disease, which appears to me to render the interpretation of the facts more simple and natural. If we examine transverse sections of different regions of the cord, we can readily distinguish, in the anterior horns which are most involved, very marked congestion, with dilatation and thickening of the vessels. The capillary network is also much more developed in the gray substance than usual.

These significant changes, and the abundant production of small nuclei around the vessels, demonstrate that the latter take an active part in the affection. We are, therefore, justified in believing that the disease begins with medullary hyperæmia and vascular exudation. The latter becomes more intense and more widely diffused, compromises the nutrition of the nerve-cells of the gray substance, and acts as the cause of the secondary proliferations and deformities. This inflammatory irritation, produced in the vascular system of the cord, should be manifested by the general symptoms of exudation and by febrile movement, and, in fact, these are the first signs which herald an attack of infantile paralysis.

If this vascular irritation is, at first, moderate in severity and extent, recovery is possible, provided that the delicate structure of the nerve-cells has not been compromised. It is probable that at least a portion of the temporary paralyses, described by Kennedy, belong to this category. Physicians frequently make observations which tend to demonstrate the possibility of the partial recovery of these vascular irritations ; we refer to the fact that, after the acute period of the disease, the paralysis, which often invades the trunk and limbs, abandons the upper parts of the body and remains localized in one or both lower limbs.

But if the vascular irritation is very severe at the outset, the nerve-cells, which present such a delicate structure in the infant, will become rapidly impaired. The morbid process then terminates in secondary proliferation and deformity of the nerve-cells, nerve-roots, and corresponding white columns. It appears that these vascular disturbances chiefly involve the gray substance, because, in the normal condition, it is richer in capillaries than the white matter, as has been demonstrated by injections. As the small nutrient vessels are not always situated on the same level as the nerve-cells which are affected, it sometimes follows that, in the microscopic preparations, we find manifest vascular changes without coexisting lesions in the cells, or, inversely, diseased nerve-cells appear side by side with apparently normal vessels. These facts justify us in the supposition that, in certain cases of infantile spinal paralysis, the lesions of the white substance may retrograde, while the gray substance of the anterior columns, on account of its more delicate structure and greater vascularity, undergoes profound changes.

Symptomatology.

Infantile paralysis was described as early as the last century by Underwood (Treatise on the Diseases of Children, London, 1784). Rilliet erroneously considered it to be an idiopathic paralysis, and Duchenne described it under the name of fatty atrophic paralysis of childhood. It usually begins suddenly. After one or several attacks of fever, accompanied by general symptoms of irritation (insomnia, convulsions, delirium, cries), but usually without disturbance of the intelligence, the parents or attendants notice, to their great surprise, when lifting the child, that he has been seized with paralysis during the night. The acute period only continues a short time, and is often entirely unnoticed. The paralysis then becomes evident, and frequently extends to the trunk and limbs. But it soon leaves the upper parts of the body, and remains permanent in one or two limbs, or only in certain groups of muscles. This circumscribed paralysis usually involves one of the upper or lower limbs. In the upper limbs the muscles affected, by preference, are the extensors of the arm or forearm and fingers; in the lower limbs they are the extensor of the thigh (psoas), but much more frequently the muscles innervated by the peroneal nerve, or the triceps muscle. Spinal infantile paralysis may assume the form of paraplegia, and very rarely of hemiplegia (the latter is almost always of cerebral origin). It may also affect the foot and hand upon opposite sides, or the muscles of the trunk (with secondary lateral curvature of the spinal column). In very rare instances, as in the following observation, the paralysis occurs in both upper limbs.

A boy, four years of age, had had, two years previously, after a short attack of fever, general paralysis of all the limbs, but which soon disappeared except in the two arms

Upon examination, I found the right upper limb markedly emaciated, the skin thickened and flaccid, the muscular tissue very much reduced in bulk. The shoulder was atrophied, angular, and was carried forward with difficulty. Extension of the arms and fingers was impossible, flexion was performed with difficulty, and the hand was emaciated and fixed in adduction. The deltoid responds slightly to the faradic current, but only in its internal fibres. The same phenomena are evident in the subscapularis and pectoralis major; the extensors of the arm and fingers scarcely react, the biceps very feebly. This also holds good of some of the muscular fibres of the atrophied thenar eminence. The galvanic excitability of the brachial plexus, of the nerves of the shoulder and arm, is very well preserved, and the paralyzed extensors respond to strong currents by slight contractions. The left upper limb is better nourished. It can be moved forwards and backwards with some effort; extension of the arm is slowly performed, flexion rapidly, and the fingers are freely movable. Electro-muscular contractility is preserved throughout, but is markedly weakened. I advised long-continued faradization of the muscles and galvanization of the nerves. When I again saw the child, at the end of about eight months, the right shoulder and hand had gained considerably in nutrition and power of movement, and the left side had almost completely recovered.

In certain cases motion is spontaneously re-established within one or two weeks, the electrical contractility of the affected muscles remaining but little or not at all affected. In other cases this recovery only occurs after the lapse of weeks or months. When the paralysis remains stationary, active movements and muscular nutrition gradually decline, and the limb atrophies and grows cold (after the disease has lasted several years, the temperature may become lowered from $5°-6°$ C.); the foot, especially, becomes livid. The disorders of muscular nutrition do not follow the same course as the paralysis, but are, on the contrary, entirely independent of them. The bones (epiphyses and diaphyses) of the atrophied limbs are also arrested in their growth, and the shortening may amount to two or three centimetres. According to Murray, the bones are thinned, and their nerves and vessels appear markedly atrophied. *Sensibility* is sometimes exaggerated at the outset, but, at a later period, it again becomes normal; this also holds good with regard to the reflex excitability. The antagonism of the muscles having disappeared, we notice the development of club-foot (genu valgum), of paralytic scoliosis or lordosis, obliquity of the shoulders, etc., in consequence of the weight of the diseased part, or of the labor imposed by severe exertions (Hueter). The epiphyses atrophy, and subluxations may even occur and permit unnatural passive movements (Laborde). The paralyses of the muscles of the leg and foot especially favor the development of secondary deformities, while paralysis of the extensor of the thigh (I have reported a case in which it lasted twelve years, with loss of electro-muscular contractility) only hinders walking to a slight extent when the muscles of the leg are intact. In these cases the gluteal muscles, in part, execute alternate movements of extension and rotation backwards, and then forwards. On the other hand, the thighs and condyles of the tibia, which are pressed against one another by the weight of the body, and the articular ligaments, furnish to the knee a firm basis of support during extension. It is only in taking long walks that it becomes necessary to employ an orthopædic apparatus.

The *faradic excitability of the muscles* may become weakened or may even disappear during the first weeks without proving an obstacle to the return of motion. As Salomon first pointed out (Jahrb. d. Kinderheilk., I., 1868), and as Eulenburg's observations and the case recorded above also prove, farado-muscular contractility may be abolished in the paralyzed muscles, although the galvano-muscular reaction is preserved for a long time. These facts cannot be doubted, but different interpretations are placed upon them by various authors. Some have maintained that though abolition of the farado-muscular with preservation of the galvano-muscular contractility is often observed in peripheral paralysis, the same fact is also noticed in paralyses of central origin. Clinical observation and the experiments of Erb and Ziemssen have shown that the faradic excitability of the muscles is very much enfeebled or abolished in peripheral paralyses, but that, on the other hand, the galvanic contractility is markedly increased at the onset or for a long time (this increase is even apparent with very weak currents). On the other hand, in central paralyses, in which the electro-muscular and galvano-muscular excitability sometimes disappear at a very early period, the galvanic contractility nevertheless lasts longer than the faradic. In such cases the faradic reaction disappears completely, but traces of galvanic excitability may still be detected with strong currents. This occurs in infantile spinal paralysis and progressive muscular atrophy. If we carefully examine the different muscular territories, we will find that the sound muscles react well to both currents, that, in the affected muscles, the reaction to both currents is weakened, and that, in the muscles which are most strongly affected, the faradic contractility has disappeared, but a weak reaction to galvanism (with a strong current) is still manifested. In completely atrophied and paralyzed muscles all reaction has entirely disappeared.

Diagnosis and Prognosis.

Infantile spinal paralysis, beginning with symptoms of irritation or fever, and involving one or two limbs during the night, is recognized as easily as the old forms, in which the diminution of electrical excitability, and the atrophy of the muscles and bones, furnish perfectly distinctive signs. There are, nevertheless, cases in which confusion with other analogous conditions is possible, if we neglect certain characteristic phenomena. *Paralyses secondary to acute cerebral affections of childhood* (apoplexy, encephalitis, eclampsia) assume the form of hemiplegia or paraplegia, in which one of the upper or lower limbs may be more profoundly involved. The children usually complain, for some days previously, of violent headache, heaviness and weakness in the legs, and then paralysis suddenly appears in the midst of general or partial convulsions, attended with loss of consciousness. Paralyses of this kind rarely disappear; in the majority of cases they only yield in part. The following circumstances may be taken into consideration in forming a diagnosis of an acute cerebral affection : loss of intelligence and speech; frequently coexisting paralysis of one-half of the face; frequent strabismus; dilatation of the pupils; normal electrical contractility, even after the lapse of several years; absence of disturbances on the part of temperature and muscular nutrition (intact fibres, even in markedly discolored and atrophied muscles : Cruveilhier).

The paralyses of the limbs, which occur in children in chronic cerebral affections (tumors, chronic hydrocephalus), may also lead to confusion with true infantile spinal paralysis. But these forms of paralysis are generally developed slowly and with fever. They are not infrequently accompanied by contractures which persist for a long time in the same position or reappear at certain intervals. We are justified in diagnosing a chronic cerebral disease. from the following signs: the appearance of cerebral symptoms of irritation (vomiting, convulsions, etc.); disorders of the intelligence and special senses: a more uniform wasting of the muscles; electrical excitability scarcely changed; paralysis of a hemiplegic type, and usually of slow development.

Progressive muscular atrophy presents great analogy to infantile spinal paralysis. But the latter appears suddenly, and partially retrogrades, while the former extends more or less rapidly, but in a continuous manner. Progressive muscular atrophy is exceedingly rare in children. Duchenne has, however, observed it in two children of the same family, aged respectively ten and twelve years, and I have also observed this affection in a boy nine years old (atrophy of the muscles of the left shoulder and arm, with loss of voluntary contractions and faradic excitability). The disease usually appears in children from the ages of five to seven years, and generally begins in the face, first attacking the orbicularis oris and the zygomatici (Duchenne). We then observe, as the first symptom, a peculiar immobility of the lips; they are separated from one another; the lower lip is dependent, and the naso-labial fold is effaced. The patient cannot purse the lips, and the face is unanimated during laughter. After a stationary period of several years, the upper limbs and trunk are involved in their turn, and, finally, the lower limbs. The peculiar, progressive course of the muscular atrophy, the preservation of certain muscles in the immediate vicinity of diseased parts, the atrophy of certain isolated portions of the same muscle, and the diminution or abolition of electrical contractility corresponding to the muscular degeneration, are characteristic signs which are useful in doubtful cases. The paralysis of *pseudo-muscular hypertrophy* is distinguished from infantile spinal paralysis by the following symptoms: the disease is apyretic throughout; in the beginning, motor power is only weakened; walking or the vertical position presents a staggering character, the vertebral column is sunken, the legs are separated; the paralysis only extends to the extremities and trunk at a late period; the electro-muscular contractility is preserved for a very long time; in a certain number of muscles the paralysis is preceded by an increase of volume. Finally, we can recognize the fact, even during life, that simple hyperplasia occurs in the adipose and interstitial connective tissue.

Delay in the development of co-ordination may retard the power of walking in children. We observe, in these cases, great weakness of the muscles and bones, and very marked relaxation of the ligaments. These children (from two to four years of age) can move their legs when sitting or lying down; they can even carry them to the mouth with the aid of their hands, but they are unable either to turn around or to walk. The intelligence presents no appreciable disturbances, the electro-muscular contractility is intact, and there are no convulsions or fever. All these symptoms are different from those observed in infantile spinal paralysis. The paresis of co-ordination diminishes as the children grow stronger under the influence of nourishing diet, the administration of beer or wine, and country air. I have seen a case of this kind terminate in complete recovery.

In *rachitis* we sometimes observe a condition of weakness and real paralysis of the lower limbs (the children are unable to walk, or even to turn about without assistance, and the legs are deformed). But we can usually recognize other signs of rachitis ; the electro-muscular contractility is normal throughout, and there are no symptoms of irritation or fever (tonic treatment, country air, and electrization of the muscles re-establish the motor power). A careful examination of the patient will prevent us from mistaking these cases for infantile spinal paralysis.

The *temporary paralysis of children,* described by Kennedy (after exposure or compression of the limbs), offers all the characteristics of a myopathic peripheral paralysis. We find no change in the reaction of the muscles to electricity, the nutrition of the muscles is not sensibly affected,.and the disease terminates in one or two weeks. By repeating the electrical exploration several times and by keeping the patient under observation for a certain period, we will be able to recognize the real nature of the disease.

The *prognosis* of infantile spinal paralysis depends upon the intensity and extent of the changes in the cells of the anterior horns. If the paralysis of the limbs soon becomes circumscribed and partially disappears, we may infer that the central lesions will follow a favorable course. The information which we obtain by faradization, concerning the existence or absence of electrical reaction in certain muscles, undoubtedly furnishes us with some idea of the condition of the muscular tissue.

The hypothesis of Duchenne, that faradization will lead to the development of new muscular fibres around others which have remained intact, has not been confirmed. Duchenne also maintained that the gravity of the prognosis is in direct relation with the nervous lesion which causes the atrophy, and that we are only able to judge of this lesion *by electrical exploration.* We cannot unreservedly admit the truth of this statement in all cases, as I have previously shown by several examples (Traité d'Électrothérapie, 2ᵉ édit., pp. 196, 197).

It appears, from some observations reported in the same work, that in certain cases of infantile spinal paralysis which have lasted six to nine months, the electrical excitability of the affected muscles may be wanting, although voluntary motion has returned. Thus, after this lapse of time, the absence of electro-muscular contractility, especially in robust children, should not induce us to make an unfavorable prognosis. Even in these cases we can produce a very favorable effect upon the nutrition, temperature, and development of the atrophied limbs by persevering in the electrical treatment. (This fact has been confirmed by several other observers.) If electrical excitability and motion have not returned within a year, all hope of recovery must be abandoned.

Treatment.

The *treatment* of infantile spinal paralysis should be begun, if possible, at the close of the second or third week of the disease, especially if no marked progress has been made towards spontaneous recovery. We obtain better results in this manner than if we decide to begin energetic treatment only at the end of several months.

Electricity, under the form of the galvanic current passing from the vertebral column to the nerves and muscles, constitutes the best means of treatment. We must continue this plan for several months, and afterwards combine it with local faradization. I have also seen good effects upon the nutrition and energy of the muscles from hydrotherapeutics (moist frictions, local packing of the extremities, followed by half-baths at 24.20° C., with mild irrigations to the vertebral column during the bath). The children should only be permitted to walk when aided by an attendant. Appropriate orthopædic treatment may be useful in order to confirm and correct the results of other methods.

B.—ACUTE SPINAL PARALYSIS IN THE ADULT.

In 1861, Duchenne, with his habitual clear-sightedness, observed that a disease sometimes occurs in adults which is very similar to infantile spinal paralysis. He located it in the anterior gray columns of the cord, and, therefore, called it general anterior spinal paralysis.

It was only after we had obtained some knowledge concerning infantile spinal paralysis that we were in a condition to thoroughly appreciate the acute anterior myelitis of adults. The first observation of this kind was published by Hallopeau (Arch. Génér., 1869), but was not attended with a microscopical examination. The patient was a woman, twenty years of age, who was suddenly seized, after confinement, with paralysis and pains in all the limbs. She recovered, little by little, with the exception of the left leg, the muscles of which atrophied and lost their electrical contractility. At a later period the left lower limb also improved, the patient was able to walk with crutches, but the electrical reactions remained absent. Ten months later the woman died of typhoid fever. At the autopsy, atrophy and degeneration were found, especially in the posterior muscles of the left leg and in certain muscular nerve-fibres. Some of the fibres of the anterior roots were also gray and degenerated. In the lower third of the dorsal region, *the two anterior horns were of a very marked deep gray color*, contrasting strongly with the hue of the gray matter, which had become transformed into pus. In the middle of the lumbar enlargement, *the anterior horns were softened and almost fluid*. This was, therefore, a case of central myelitis extending to the anterior horns, and which had presented, on account of the partial recovery of the paralyses, the same symptoms as infantile spinal paralysis.

A few years later Gombault published a very complete and clear observation (Arch. de Physiol., Jan., 1873). A woman was affected with paralysis of all the limbs, coming on within half an hour. This was followed by atrophy of the muscles with loss of electrical excitability; afterwards improvement progressed slowly for several months. The atrophy and paralysis were especially marked in the extensors of the forearm and in the interossei and muscles of the thenar eminence, the hand being slightly "en griffe." The patient died, within a year and a half, from intercurrent carcinosis. The autopsy revealed *pigmentary atrophy of the large ganglion-cells of the anterior horns*, especially in the cervical and lumbar enlargements. The anterior roots and the affected nerve-trunks had partially undergone fibroid degeneration ; the degenerations, to which we have previously referred, were found in the muscles.

In a very recent case, published by Cornil and Lépine (Gaz. Méd. de Paris, II., 1875), the patient, a man twenty-seven years of age, became affected with paralysis of the legs in consequence of exposure. Two years later the paralysis extended to the arms, attended with muscular atrophy, diminution or loss of electrical excitability, and preservation of sensation. The patient died of asphyxia, and the microscopical examination of the cord showed marked atrophy, and, in places, disappearance of the cells of the anterior horns, sclerosis of the gray substance, thickening of the vascular walls, general sclerosis of the lateral columns extending from above downwards, atrophy of the anterior roots, and granular degeneration of the muscles, the transverse striæ being still recognizable.

Bernhardt has recently published (Arch. f. Psychiatr., IV., Bd., 1873) three observations upon the same disease, occurring in adult males. I have myself seen a patient seized, after severe exposure, with paralysis of all the limbs, which became complete within a short period. During the entire course of the disease, which lasted several months, there were no fever, cerebral symptoms, spasms or disorders of sensation; the sphincters acted regularly. Marked muscular atrophy was manifested in the hands; the muscular contractility had disappeared at the end of several days, and reappeared very slowly and gradually. The galvanic excitability had suffered less, and, in the beginning, it was even increased. The voluntary movements then returned, but without keeping pace with the disappearance of the electrical symptoms. The patient could only walk after the end of a year, but he still manifested very great weakness and difficulty in executing the simplest movements. Cuming, Frey, Erb, and others have also published cases of this disease, which is also known as poliomyelitis anterior acuta (Kussmaul), or tephromyelitis (Charcot).

I have seen a case in which poliomyelitis anterior presented the characteristics of a cervical paraplegia, and terminated in recovery. A merchant, aged fifty years, was suddenly attacked with fever and diarrhœa, after severe exposure. These symptoms disappeared, but weakness of the legs supervened, followed, four weeks later, by paralysis of both arms. At the end of six months I found moderate paresis in the legs, whose galvanic excitability was merely diminished in intensity. Both arms and forearms were markedly atrophied and paralyzed, together with the hands, which were dependent, flexed and adducted, with very marked atrophy of the first interosseous space and of the thenar eminence. When the radial nerves were stimulated, the long supinators and flexors of the wrist alone responded. The faradic contractility had disappeared upon both sides in the extensors of the fingers (even in the left hand, in which active extension of the wrist was still possible). The galvanic reaction was present, but it was slow, and the contractions upon closure predominated at the anode. The muscles of the first interosseous space and of the thenar eminence had lost their excitability. Sensibility was intact, but the sphincters performed their functions properly. Under the influence of hydropathic and galvanic treatment, the lower limbs completely recovered at the end of several months, while two years passed before the upper limbs recovered sufficiently to enable the patient to write. Nevertheless, the faradic and galvanic excitability were only incompletely restored.

All the cases which we have reported are characterized by their acute onset, the preservation of sensation, the absence of trophic disturbances of the skin (bed-sores), and muscular atrophy with loss of electrical contractility. These cases likewise agree in their principal characteristics with infantile spinal paralysis. Histological investigations also confirm the relationship of these two affections. They merely vary in certain peculiarities depending upon the difference in age (more rapid and complete atrophy of the nerve-cells in children). The form which has been recently described under the name of *subacute anterior spinal paralysis* (the same symptoms, but following a slow and apyretic course) should be regarded as a variety of spinal paralysis of the adult.

CHAPTER XXV.

PROGRESSIVE MUSCULAR ATROPHY.

THE peculiar symptoms of this affection did not escape the attention of Charles Bell, the founder of nervous pathology. Other observations were afterwards published by Darwall, Abercrombie, Graves, Dubois, and Romberg. At that time the disease was supposed to be a local process in the muscles. Aran (Arch. Génér., Sept., 1850) was the first to call attention to the extremely characteristic appearance of these muscular paralyses, and has mentioned the following as the chief symptoms : the loss of nutrition, and, at the same time, of the functions of the muscles, and the extension of these phenomena to larger or smaller groups of muscles. To Duchenne is due the credit of rendering the diagnosis and prognosis of muscular atrophy more exact by his investigations with the faradic current, and of clearing up the physiological pathology of its symptoms. But full information upon the situation and nature of progressive muscular atrophy and allied affections has only been furnished by the recent advances in histology and the discovery of the degenerations of the anterior gray columns.

Pathological Anatomy and Experimental Investigations.

The data furnished by the older autopsies are as follows : the first observation is that made by Cruveilhier, who found, in one case (Arch. Génér., 1853), very marked atrophy of the anterior nerve-roots. Shortly afterwards, Valentiner (Prag. Vierteljschr., 1855) observed, in addition to atrophy of the anterior roots, a central softening of the inferior cervical and lower dorsal regions of the cord, with accumulation of granular cells in the white and gray substances. Leubuscher saw, in one case (Deutsche Klinik, 1857), the anterior and lateral columns transformed into an amorphous, doughy mass, of a whitish-gray color, with acute softening of the antero-lateral columns in the medulla oblongata. Analogous results have been published by Read and Thouvenet, and later by Menjaud, Bamberger, Grimm, and Joffroy. I have reported (Ber. Med. Centralzeit., 1871) an old observation (dating back to the year 1865), in which the autopsy revealed the existence of atrophy and whitish-gray coloration of the left brachial plexus, extending to the anterior roots of the thoracic nerves (the miscroscope showed amyloid degeneration of a portion of the nerve-fibres). In the following observations the degeneration chiefly affected the gray columns of the cord: Luys (Gaz. Méd., 1860, granulo-fatty cells in the anterior horns); Lockhart Clarke (several cases, *vide* Beale, Arch. of Med., 1861, and Med.-Chir. Trans., 1861, 1863, 1868, 1873); Bergmann (Petersb. Zschr., VII. Bd., 1865, small spots of softening in the gray substance); Hayem (Arch. de Phys., T. II., 1869); Charcot and Joffroy (eod. loc., 1869), chronic pigmentary atrophy of the nerve-cells of the anterior horns with atrophy of the lateral columns.

The atrophy of the anterior horns, or even of the posterior horns, was accompanied by dilatation of the central canal (central cavity filled with fluid, hydromyelitis) in the observations of Gull (Guy's Hosp. Rep., 1862), Schueppel (Arch. d. Heilk., 1865), and Grimm (Virch. Arch., 1869). Hydromyelitis appears to consist of a dropsical distention of the central canal, with partial retraction of the surrounding tissue. According to others, this dilatation of the canal is secondary to an old central myelitis.

The examples of atrophy limited to the anterior or posterior roots, or to the posterior columns (Virchow and Friedreich), refer to observations made twenty years ago, and, together with the negative results obtained, at the same period, by Oppenheimer, Hasse, Friedberg, Menyon, etc., have lost all value at the present time. These statements have been controverted by positive data, which are continually accumulating, thanks to the more complete methods of investigation of modern histology.

Some authors were led to explain the trophic disturbances by a sclerosis of the cervical portion of the sympathetic nerve (Schneevogt, Jaccoud, Duménil), but this theory has also lost its importance. In the first place, atrophy of the anterior horns was found three times, and softening of the cord once, in the cases which were relied upon to substantiate this theory; in addition, the more recent and complete microscopical examinations of Frommann, Hayem, Charcot, and Joffroy, and the older investigations of Friedreich have demonstrated the complete integrity of the sympathetic nerve and its ganglia in progressive muscular atrophy.

The tissue changes which the muscles present upon the cadaver correspond to the symptoms observed during life. Certain muscles preserve their normal red color; others, on the contrary, are pale or even of a grayish-yellow. Immediately adjacent muscles frequently present very different degrees of degeneration ; in the same muscles we may find intact fibres side by side with others affected with fatty degeneration. The apparently healthy muscles present a normal consistence, and show no changes under the microscope. Those which are slightly affected, have lost, to a greater or less degree, their transverse or longitudinal striæ, and contain cells or fatty drops, of variable number and dimensions, in the interior or in the interspaces of the fibres. The most seriously affected muscles are softened, gelatinous, and transformed into a transparent, amorphous fatty matter. According to Virchow, the fatty degeneration may either occur between the primitive fibres (parenchymatous form), or in the interfibrillary tissue (interstitial form); both forms may also coexist.

The progressive degeneration of the cells of the anterior horns, which constitutes the fundamental lesion of progressive muscular atrophy, may be *primary* and entirely independent of any other spinal lesion. On the other hand, it is secondary in very many cases. The lesions are then first developed in the columns of the cord, from whence they extend to the anterior part of the gray columns.

Among the morbid processes, whose pathological influence upon the secondary degeneration of the anterior gray columns of the cord and upon progressive muscular atrophy has been recently recognized, we may mention cerebral apoplexy, in which the sclerosis of the lateral columns may sometimes extend forwards (Charcot); labio-glosso-pharyngeal paralysis, in which the lesion of the bulbar nuclei may extend to the anterior part of the cord; central myelitis, in which the anterior part of the gray axis of the cord may participate in the degeneration either primarily or secondarily (traumatism, tumor); cerebro-spinal sclerosis, the sclerosis of the posterior columns in ataxia, and symmetrical sclerosis of the lateral columns (amyotrophic lateral sclerosis of Charcot), when they also attack the anterior horns; finally, meningo-myelitis in vertebral caries (Hayem), and hypertrophic spinal pachymeningitis (Charcot), which we have previously discussed, may produce compression-lesions of the anterior horns and roots.

Hayem (Compt. Rend. Ac. des Sc., LXXVIII., 1874) has experimentally produced progressive muscular atrophy in animals, by tearing out, or by simple incision of, the sciatic nerve. If the animals survived the experiment two or three months, they presented, at first, progressive muscular atrophy in the posterior limb upon the side opposite to the lesion. Afterwards it also involved the anterior limbs and the muscles dependent on the bulbar nuclei. The autopsy showed the presence of hemorrhagic perimeningitis and generalized central myelitis with intense hyperæmia of the gray substance, numerous extravasations and exudations into the central canal, and degeneration, advancing even to complete destruction, of the groups of anterior nerve-cells. By simple contusion of the gray substance of the cord, Vulpian has been unable to produce, in animals, atrophy of the muscles whose nerves originate in the wounded part of the cord.

Etiology.

Sexual excesses, especially onanism—upon which great stress has been laid by some authors—and exposure, give rise to only a small proportion of cases of the disease under consideration. The same may be said of acute diseases. Roberts, Gerhardt, and Nesemann have seen cases develop after typhoid fever, rubeola, and scarlatina; in one of my patients the disease appeared six months after an attack of variola. Acute articular rheumatism (Anstie, Friedreich), the puerperal condition (Charcot and Joffroy), and the typhoid form of cholera, are also mentioned as causes of progressive muscular atrophy. The influence of heredity has been observed in a certain number of cases; Roberts has noted it eighteen times in sixty-nine cases. In an observation which I published in detail (Wien. med. Halle, 1862), the disease was produced by a fall from a roof; the concussion (which had produced double fracture of the ribs in the neighborhood of the spinal column) had, undoubtedly, also produced lesions in the cord. Russel-Reynolds and Bergmann have each published a case of atrophy following traumatism.

The over-exertion to which certain groups of muscles are subjected in certain occupations exercises a very evident influence upon the development of progressive muscular atrophy. For this reason we find a large number of cases in the working-classes, and a much greater frequency of the disease in the upper limbs, and more especially in the small muscles of the thumb and other fingers. We can often recognize the evident influence of the predominant action of one-half of the body during work. Thus I have seen a laboring man, who removed considerable masses of earth with the spade and pick, and in whom the muscles of both shoulders were atrophied and paralyzed, to the exclusion of the arms and forearms, which were normal. In a weaver, who plied the shuttle with the thumb and index-finger of the left hand, these two fingers were first and most seriously affected by the atrophy and paralysis. A workman was employed in a brewery to hermetically close large bottles ; he wielded a heavy hammer with the right hand, and the muscles of the shoulder were first affected upon this side, while in the left hand, which held the bottles, the atrophy involved all the muscles of the fingers, those of the arm and shoulder remaining intact.

Males are more subject to progressive muscular atrophy than females, on account of their more arduous labors and great exposure to noxious influences. According to Friedreich's statistics, females only constitute eighteen per cent. of the whole number of cases. There is also a greater congenital predisposition in the male sex. The largest number of cases occur between the ages of thirty and fifty years; the disease has few victims above or below these limits.

Symptomatology.

Progressive muscular atrophy (atrophic progressive muscular atrophy of Cruveilhier, wasting palsy of the English) is usually characterized, during the first periods of the disease, by certain symptoms of irritation on the part of sensation and motion. In the beginning the patients frequently experience a sensation of a current of cold air, formication, numbness, wandering pains, and complain that the arm or hand is easily fatigued. Every exertion causes tremor; they suffer from spasms and tension in the muscles; the fingers become stiff, and remain applied to one another. As a rule, the muscular tissue first atrophies in the thumb and hypothenar eminence; the movements of opposition and abduction of the thumb are lost, the hand and fingers lose their agility, the latter become more and more curved, the interosseous spaces are markedly hollowed out. The atrophy and paralysis of the small muscles of the hand, and the greater tension of the antagonists, of the extensors and flexors of the phalanges, situated in the forearm, gives to the retraction of the hand (according to Duchenne) the appearance of a claw (griffe de la main: clasped hand, or claw-shaped hand). The forearm soon becomes more and more flattened (especially on the extensor side),

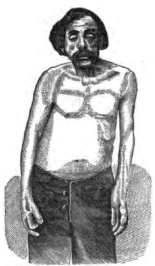

Fig. 16.—Progressive muscular atrophy, involving the muscles of the trunk and upper extremities.

and, during this time, the atrophy extends to other muscles, to the shoulder (which appears angular and oblique) and to the trunk (atrophy of the deltoid, trapezius, pectoralis major, muscles of the neck, back, and abdomen). Afterwards the atrophy and paralysis also extend to the lower limbs and ultimately to the respiratory muscles and to the tongue and pharynx. (Fig. 16.)

The affection does not always produce the same disorders in the upper limbs. The atrophy appears most frequently and runs its course most rapidly in the small muscles of the fingers, in those which move the wrist, in the muscles of the arm and forearm, and then in the shoulders. Paralysis of the rotators of the humerus backwards (infraspinatus and teres minor) is combined with that of the deltoid. If the latter muscle (the principal elevator of the arm) becomes paralyzed, the adjacent muscles of the shoulder (trapezius, rhomboid, serratus magnus) will supplement its action; but after a time they succumb, as have the others, to this unusual expenditure of force. The atrophy is generally bilateral, affecting symmetrical groups of muscles; but this rule is not without exceptions. More rarely the affection begins in the shoulder and extends upwards or downwards, or it has several points of departure at the same time.

Dull pains (but sometimes of a tearing or lancinating character) are soon added to the disorders of nutrition and motion. They are either diffuse, or follow the tract of certain nerves; they occur periodically, and are usually mistaken for rheumatism. The shoulders then become flattened, the scapulæ are often separated from the trunk, deflected, and limited in their movements, and this region becomes the seat of distressing neuralgic pains. Reflex excitability is not infrequently increased from the beginning. The motor symptoms of irritation consist, in the first stages, of clonic, sometimes tonic, muscular spasms. Fibrillary twitchings occur in the muscles at a later period, and either develop spontaneously, or after movement (in one case I observed them very distinctly in the tongue). In certain cases the shortening and retraction of the muscles produce contractures and subluxations of the knees and feet, or even scoliosis of the vertebral column.

The atrophy and paralysis do not always follow the same course. Paralysis may appear without notable change in the nutrition (we must take into consideration, in such cases, the proliferation of the interstitial connective and adipose tissue). On the other hand, markedly atrophied muscles may preserve their functions. But in the advanced stages of the disease the paralysis and atrophy of the muscles go on hand in hand. Baerwinkel and Frommann have noticed an elevation of temperature at the onset. At a later period, after the abolition of the muscular functions and the lowering of nutrition, the temperature falls 2°, 3°, and even 4° C. (Eulenburg, Duchenne, R. Reynolds, and Friedreich). (I have noted this fact in two cases by measurements in the axilla and upon different muscles.) For the same reasons, the amount of creatine, which is a product of intra-muscular nutritive changes, diminishes sensibly in the urine (analysis has shown this in three of my patients). These facts may be logically deduced from the continuous deterioration of muscular nutrition.

Interesting *oculo-pupillary symptoms* sometimes develop, as I have observed in several cases. In these instances, one of the pupils (usually that upon the most affected side) is contracted to less than half its normal size, and reacts slightly or not at all to light. The dilatation following the introduction of atropine only disappears after the lapse of ten or twelve days. The contraction of the pupils, caused by contraction of the radiating fibres, only appears when the affection extends as high as the cilio-spinal centre, or when the latter is under the influence of ascending lesions of the cervical cord. Schneemann, Voisin, Menjaud, and Bergmann have also reported analogous observations. In Menjaud's case (Gaz. des Hôp., Jan., 1866) contraction of the left pupil occurred with flattening of the cornea. The last pairs of cervical and the first pairs of dorsal nerves were found atrophied, more markedly on the left side (the central foyer of the fibres of the iris is situated in the corresponding portion of the cord). Cl. Bernard has made an experiment which confirms these pathological observations. After having divided the anterior roots in dogs, he saw contraction of the pupil soon develop, with flattening of the cornea, and sinking in of the eyeball, but without increase of vascularization or of the temperature. On the other hand, the latter symptoms were immediately observed after section of the ascending branch of the thoracic sympathetic, while the condition of the pupils underwent no change.

The following *trophic disturbances* have been observed: herpes (in one of my patients, along the radial nerve of the atrophied arm); the combination of the disease with fatty muscular hypertrophy (one observation by Friedreich, another by myself, with shapeless thickening, at first in the middle fingers and then in the others); finally, the very rare complication with hypertrophy of the bones (enlargement of the metacarpus, according to Remak), with concentric osseous atrophy (Le Gendre and Friedreich) and with arthropathies (noted by Patruban, Remak, and myself). The case which I observed occurred in a woman, fifty years of age, suffering from progressive muscular atrophy of both arms. In the third year of the disease, the lower limbs also became involved, and the right shoulder became swollen until it almost attained the size of a child's head, without the least pain or sign of inflammation; matters remained in this condition for a year. Towards the end of the fourth year, the paralyzed limbs were reduced to skeleton-like proportions. Incontinence of urine and fæces and bed-sores over the sacrum developed, and the patient died of intercurrent pneumonia of the right lung. An autopsy could not be obtained.

Finally, *electrical exploration* gives different results according to the stage of the muscular affection. The electro-muscular contractility is normal in the healthy muscles; in the affected muscles it is either diminished or increased. At a more advanced stage of the disease, voluntary impulse may still be transmitted by the nerves and produce contraction of certain muscles, although this can no longer be obtained by electrical irritation on account of its peripheral origin and of the intra-muscular changes. This abolition of electro-muscular contractility is soon followed by loss of voluntary motion. The galvanic excitability of the nerve-trunks is increased in certain branches; in others, on the contrary, it may be normal or even diminished. It may be preserved in the nerve-filaments nearest to the centres, and diminished in the peripheral ramifications.

This is due to the differences in the secondary changes in the various branches of the nerves. In mixed nerve-trunks, sensibility remains intact for a longer time than motion. The weakened galvano-muscular contractility may persist for a longer time than the previously affected faradic contractility. (For further details, *vide* the preceding chapter.)

Remak has called attention to the *increase of electrical reflex excitability*, and to the *diplegic contractions* produced by the stimulation of two distant parts of the muscles. The diplegic contractions may be obtained, according to Eulenburg, over the entire or larger portion of the surface of the body. These are true reflex contractions, whose origin must be sought in the reflex apparatus of the spinal cord and medulla oblongata, but they may also be observed in cases of exaggerated excitability of the muscles.

Progressive muscular atrophy generally runs a chronic course ; even when it is hereditary, the disease does not prevent the patient from attaining an advanced age. I have observed one case which lasted more than twenty years ; at other times the patients may die during the first years of the disease. Duchenne considers the affection less serious when it proceeds from the muscles of the trunk than when it begins in the hands and extends upwards. When the muscles of respiration and deglutition are affected at an early period, the danger may rapidly attain its maximum. But, happily for the patient, this does not generally occur until towards the close of the disease.

The Nature of Progressive Muscular Atrophy.

Since the clinical picture of progressive muscular atrophy has been completely unveiled, and pathological anatomists have devoted all their zeal to the solutions of the problems which this affection presents, the most diverse data have been accumulated, and have led to a very decided difference of opinion. Observers are divided into two camps, each of which numbers equally celebrated names among its adherents. Among the advocates of the theory of the central nature of the disease, we may mention Cruveilhier, Valentiner, Remak, Frommann, Virchow, Charcot and Joffroy, L. Clarke, Hayem and Duchenne. Among the defenders of its primary myopathic origin are included Arat, Meryon, Wachsmuth, Oppenheimer, Hasse, Friedberg, and Roberts. The latter theory has been recently supported with especial zeal by Friedreich (*vide* a long and interesting monograph by this author: Ueber progressive Muskelatrophie, etc., Berlin, 1873). If we examine the arguments advanced by this authoritative representative of the myopathic theory, we will find that Friedreich regards progressive muscular atrophy as an intra-muscular inflammatory process, which begins with hyperplasia of the interstitial connective tissue, and terminates in atrophy and separation of the muscular elements, in waxy or fatty degeneration, and, finally, in a fibrous transformation of the muscular fibres. Diffuse fatty degeneration often occurs as an accessory phenomenon. This progressive chronic myositis is capable of producing secondary disorders in the nervous system, by extension of the lesions to the intra-muscular nerves, and by neuritis, extending along the nerve-trunks, plexuses, and anterior roots, to the spinal cord.

In order to establish his theory, Friedreich calls attention to the similarity in the histological changes of the muscular tissue in atrophy and in other forms of muscular inflammation; to the tendency of progressive muscular atrophy to be arrested, in its extension, by the large articulations; to the variability of the lesions in different parts of the nervous system, as we find by several examples in medical literature; to the frequent predominance of the changes in the anterior roots as compared with those in the cord; to the negative results of examinations of the cord, noted several times in foreign observations and in his own (one of them was even complicated with bulbar paralysis); finally, to the fact that atrophy of the ganglion-cells develops, secondarily, as has been observed after amputations, in consequence of prolonged abolition of the muscular functions.

It appears to me that this full *exposé* of Friedreich's arguments can be responded to by facts equally well proven and well founded. We base our opposition upon the data furnished by anatomy and clinical observation. From the former point of view, we may refer to the fact that, in acute myelitis, we also observe nuclear proliferation of the sarcolemma, fatty degeneration of the primitive fibrillæ, and even, if the patients have survived the attack for a long time, considerable atrophy of the muscles. Progressive muscular atrophy is not always arrested at the articulations, and even when this does occur, it may be explained by the fact that muscles with synergic action are also limited by the articulations, and that their ganglion-cells probably form distinct groups in the cord. Since, moreover, the same group of cells may furnish fibres to different peripheral muscles, we can comprehend the leaps made by progressive muscular atrophy in its development, while a parenchymatous muscular inflammation should follow, in its course, the anatomical continuity of the organs. With regard to the inconstancy of the anatomical lesions in the different paths of the central nervous system, and to the cases in which negative results were obtained, it may be stated that all these facts relate to a former period, in which the methods of examination now at our command were unknown. We now find lesions of the gray substance more frequently and constantly ; the fact has also been recognized that degeneration of the anterior roots is not always proportional to the amount of change in the gray horns. Finally, the argument drawn from the analogy in the secondary atrophy which the cells present after amputations, is not well founded, for, according to Vulpian, Clarke, and Dickinson, we never find, in these cases, disappearance or deformity of the ganglion-cells or new-formed connective tissue, but merely a simple atrophy of the cells, with coexisting atrophy in the corresponding part of the cord.

From a clinical point of view, many symptoms indicate the spinal origin of the disease; the dorsal pains which sometimes appear at the onset; the neuralgia of the limbs; the frequency of spasmodic symptoms, and increase of reflex excitability; the peculiar reactions of the muscles and nerves to the galvanic current ; the paralysis of the sphincters and the impotence observed by Cruveilhier, Tardieu, and myself; the complication with bulbar paralysis, ataxia, and myelitis; finally, the trophic disturbances (rare, it is true) of the bones and articulations. In the same manner that excesses, onanism, and over-exertion produce, in predisposed subjects, the medullary degenerations of ataxia or myelitis, so also the atrophy and deformity of the cells of the anterior horns may be due to excessive use of certain muscles, which is sometimes added to bad habits of life as a pathogenic factor.

The myopathic theory is entirely incapable of explaining certain well-known forms of progressive muscular atrophy, which accompany diseases of an evidently central nature. In central myelitis of a rapid course, in the acute spinal paralysis of adults, in tumors of the gray substance, in sclerosis of the posterior or lateral columns extending to the gray substance, progressive muscular atrophy may develop, as we have shown above, both clinically and physiologically, from the extension of the degeneration to the cells of the anterior horns and the intra-medullary anterior root-fibres. The microscope, by clearing up the minute lesions of the anterior gray columns, has definitely fixed our information concerning various morbid processes of the nerve-centres, and from this alone we are able to thoroughly understand the pathogeny of the affection.

We therefore think, in view of the preceding arguments, that the attacks of Friedreich will be unable to shake the position of the nervous theory, which is daily becoming more solid and unassailable. Progressive muscular atrophy, in the larger number of its forms, originates in the central gray axis; the changes in the antero-lateral columns are rather secondary and accessory. According to the experiments of Hayem and the clinical observations which he has reported, there is only a very small number of varieties in which we are justified in assuming that myelitis of the anterior gray columns is secondary to irritation of the nerves and their roots. Among the causes of these rare forms of progressive muscular atrophy, we may mention meningo-myelitis and pachymeningitis, of which we have spoken in the beginning of this work, and the sclerosis of the anterior horns, complicating degeneration of the inner root-fibres, in ataxia.

Diagnosis and Prognosis.

In the clinical history of progressive muscular atrophy, the peculiar atrophy of the muscular system, the emaciation, the deformity of the limbs and trunk, and the electrical reactions, either in muscles still intact or in their remains, impress the disease with such a characteristic seal, that the diagnosis can almost always be made at the first inspection of the patient. There are, nevertheless, cases in which certain symptoms, of a different nature, may lead us to form an erroneous diagnosis. It will not be superfluous, in view of these cases, to refer to the principal elements in differential diagnosis.

In *spinal meningitis*, the unequal compression exercised, by the exudation, upon the nerve-roots may also cause marked atrophy of the limbs, paralyses, and abolition of electro-muscular contractility. But in these cases the active movements and reflex excitability of the nerve-trunks have already disappeared, in great part, at the end of some weeks, a fact which does not obtain in progressive muscular atrophy. In addition, the febrile beginning, the tonic spasms of the neck, the painful muscular stiffness extending throughout the trunk, and its almost always notoriously rheumatic origin, establish the differential diagnosis from spinal meningitis very clearly. (*Vide* page 188, Vol. I., for further details.)

Symmetrical *sclerosis of the lateral columns*, with degeneration of the cells of the anterior horns (amyotrophic lateral sclerosis, described for the first time by Charcot in Prog. Méd., 1874), is distinguished, according to this author, from progressive muscular atrophy, by its rapid course (one to three years), by the ultimate affection of all the limbs, the upper being more completely atrophied and paralyzed, the lower being simply paralyzed; by the almost constant extension of the lesions to the bulbar nuclei (while, according to Duchenne, among one hundred and thirty-nine cases of progressive muscular atrophy the bulbar nuclei were only involved thirteen times); by the prolonged preservation of electro-muscular contractility; finally, by the permanent spasmodic contractures of the paralyzed and atrophied limbs, which are fixed in a semi-flexed position, the upper limbs being pronated.

Infantile spinal paralysis has also many symptoms in common with progressive muscular atrophy, but the latter is very rare in childhood. We have given, in detail, the distinguishing features of infantile spinal paralysis in the preceding chapter.

In *spondylitis* of the upper segment of the vertebral column, paralysis and atrophy of one arm sometimes occur (a case of this kind is reported on page 216, Vol. I.), recalling the appearances of progressive muscular atrophy. The condition of the bodies of the vertebræ, the pains in the vertebral column during movements of rotation or flexion, excentric neu

ralgia developing around the diseased part, and the unilateral and circumscribed form of the disease, furnish the necessary differential data.

Paralysis and emaciation of one or both arms, with contracture of the
fingers, are also observed, at times, in *hysteria.* In such cases the disorders of sensation (especially anæsthesia), the diminution and disappearance of electro-muscular and electro-cutaneous sensibility, with slight alteration of electro-muscular contractility, and other hysterical symptoms,
form the basis of diagnosis.

General lead palsy of both upper limbs also resembles, in some points,
progressive muscular atrophy. But even in the more advanced forms,
the completely pendent hand is not flexed "en griffe," and we do not observe entire disappearance of the muscles of the thenar and hypothenar
eminences. They have preserved, in great part, their electrical contractility, and the supinators are generally intact. In the majority of these
cases we also find that the patients have worked in lead and have suffered
from lead colic; ulceration and coloration of the gums and obstinate constipation likewise occur.

The muscular atrophy and deformity of the hands, which accompany
rheumatismus nodosus, have the following characteristics: painful swelling
of the smaller and larger joints and of the epiphyses, frequent creaking
and ankyloses, and, even in old cases, intact condition of the electro-muscular contractility. These phenomena are not observed in progressive
muscular atrophy. *Traumatic lesions of the cervical and brachial plexuses* may also produce symptoms of progressive muscular atrophy, examples of which will be found in the chapter on traumatic paralyses. Cases
of this kind are distinguished by the following circumstances: the atrophy
and paralysis rapidly involve the injured arm; the disease chiefly attacks
the muscles supplied by certain nerves; there is diminution or loss of electro-muscular contractility in the affected parts; painful spots are felt
upon pressure over the plexus or certain nerve-trunks.

From the nature of the disease, to which we have referred in the previous section, we can readily comprehend that the *prognosis* of progressive muscular atrophy must be unfavorable in the majority of cases. In
the beginning, as soon as the first signs of alterations in the muscles are
manifested in the dorsum and palm of the hand, the patients should immediately abandon all pursuits requiring muscular exertion. In a case of
moderate atrophy of the left thenar eminence, of the first two interossei
and of the lower half of the forearm, with diminution of faradic reaction,
the patient abandoned his trade (weaver), took a long trip to the country,
and made a recovery, through the employment of faradization, which has
persisted for a year and a half. In a mechanic, treated by Duchenne
(Electrisation Localisée, 2ᵉ édit., Obs. 121), a large portion of the muscles of
the left arm and trunk were atrophied; the muscles of the arm recovered
their nutrition and motor functions, through the use of the faradic current.
The recovery has continued for ten years, although the patient has resumed
his manual labor. But these are merely fortunate exceptions. As a
rule, renewed efforts cause the muscles to lose the little which they have
gained, and motion and nutrition deteriorate more and more. In older or
more advanced forms, we may sometimes obtain marked improvement, or
an arrest of the disease for a certain length of time, especially in young
and otherwise healthy subjects. In the large majority of my cases there
was no marked or lasting improvement. The disease pursues its course
without remission, and despite careful treatment continued for a number of months. The circumstances which are of most importance are the

intensity of the central lesions and the extension of the degeneration to the trophic centres. When the latter are not seriously involved, when the atrophy of the muscles is limited to a part of the extremities, the disease may be arrested at a certain point or may even retrocede. But the situation is grave when an hereditary disposition is present, when the muscles are rapidly involved, and when the muscular atrophy proceeds from several points at the same time. If the atrophy and paralysis attack the respiratory muscles, the diaphragm and pharynx, very serious complications will develop, such as pulmonary hypostasis, bronchitis, and asphyxia.

Treatment.

Following Duchenne's example, we may begin the treatment of progressive muscular atrophy by means of the induced current. It should be very strong in the beginning, and, when the functions and sensibility of the muscles have improved, we should employ weaker currents in order that they may not be too exciting. If the disease is very extended, it is difficult to give all the muscles sufficient attention and the full benefit which may thus be derived from electrization. In treatment with galvanism, interrupted currents should be passed from the vertebral column and plexuses to the nerves of the affected muscles. In this manner we may cause the current to act upon entire groups of muscles. The descending current, which is preferably employed, should not produce too violent contractions. In more extended forms it will be wise to alternately apply the constant current to the nerves, and the induced current to the muscles. At the first appearance of disorders of respiration or deglutition, we must employ galvanization or faradization of the phrenic or hypoglossal nerves.

Remak recommends galvanization of the fibres of the sympathetic, which presents very marked sensibility in progressive muscular atrophy. But, in the first place, our knowledge of the sympathetic system is still involved in obscurity, and we must remember that, in applying an electrode over the upper cervical ganglion, the current will readily affect the brachial plexus; furthermore, the sympathetic has, at the present time, lost the importance which had been previously attached to it in progressive muscular atrophy; finally, I have employed this method several times without obtaining the brilliant results which some neurologists claim.

CHAPTER XXVI.

NEUROSES OF THE SPINAL CORD (SPINAL IRRITATION, NEURASTHENIA).

If we observe a large number of cases of nervous disease, we not infrequently find certain conditions which cannot be regarded as true spinal diseases, and which do not enter into the large and elastic category of hysterical affections. These diseases may even last several years, under very different aspects, without giving rise to the severe symptoms, the profound changes, or to the complications which are observed in consequence of changes in the tissues of the spinal cord. Nevertheless we cannot fail to recognize that medullary symptoms of irritation or depression constitute the most striking features of these mysterious morbid conditions. Without admitting the theoretical views hitherto enunciated concerning the disease in question, we nevertheless think that, from a practical point of view, it will be convenient to retain the symptomatic term of spinal irritation, in order to designate these morbid conditions whose exact boundaries and classification still remain to be drawn. We may even question whether such changeable and capricious symptoms will ever obtain an anatomical basis through the aid of post-mortem examinations.

Before entering into a description of the different forms of spinal irritation, we may remark that its complex symptoms do not always appear to be solely dependent upon the spinal cord; the frequent complication with psychopathic symptoms indicates that the cerebrum may also be involved. The clinical analysis of the forms which are included under spinal irritation shows, in addition, that symptoms either of depression or of irritation predominate in each case. But we also meet with mixed forms in which the two orders of symptoms are intermingled. I believe, however, that, from a practical point of view, we may distinguish, for the purposes of study and treatment of spinal irritation, a hyperæsthetic form and a depressive form (neurasthenia of several authors).

a. *Hyperæsthetic Form of Spinal Irritation.*

The symptoms of irritation predominate in this type. They are observed especially in females, and generally develop progressively. The first manifestations of the disease consist of frequently recurring mental uneasiness and a feeling of malaise in the back and limbs. Usually the patients complain of distressing rachialgia, which only appears, at first, intermittently and after exertion or fatigue, but soon becomes more persistent and intense. The pain is usually situated between the scapulæ or in the neck, and more rarely in the lower part of the dorsal spine; it almost always occupies several vertebræ, and is less subject to variations of position than of intensity.

The painful region presents acute sensibility (tenderness of the spine) even to slight mechanical, electrical, or thermic irritations (the contact of a sponge dipped in hot water). The spinous processes, and a portion of the transverse processes, cannot tolerate the slightest pressure, and when the hyperæsthesia is also present in the skin which covers them, the weight of the clothes or leaning against a piece of furniture, etc., produces intolerable pain. The dorsal pain also increases, according to the statements of the patients, during exertion, flexion of the trunk, the vertical position, ascending a flight of stairs, etc. The vertebral column is then hyperæsthetic and painful throughout a large part of its extent, and forms, in some sort, a centre, from which the pains radiate towards different parts of the body.

According to the height at which these phenomena of irritation are situated, certain symptoms will assume more importance. When the disease chiefly involves the cervical region, the spinal pain and sensitiveness are especially marked in the neck. We may then observe other concomitant symptoms : cephalalgia, vertigo, insomnia, nausea, vomiting, cervico-occipital or cervico-brachial neuralgia, pains radiating into the nerves of the face. We also notice dyspnœa, palpitation of the heart, and hiccough; the upper limbs feel heavy and sore.

If the dorsal region is affected, we often find, in addition to the vertebral pains in this region, brachialgia, intercostal neuralgia, gastralgia, and dyspepsia. Finally, if the affection occupies the lower dorsal and the lumbar region, lumbar neuralgias, pains along the crural and sciatic nerves, neuralgia of the abdominal walls, colic, ovaralgia, and vesical spasm are especially noticeable. In addition, the legs are usually weak and the feet are more often cold than warm.

The *pains* in the different portions of the body, to which we have referred, are either fixed or wandering and intermittent; they often follow the course of the nerves. They may be accompanied by formication, numbness in the limbs, sensations of burning, heat, and, sometimes, of cold. Generally, we do not notice true anæsthesias in these forms of spinal irritation.

More or less serious *motor disturbances* often occur. These consist, in the slight forms, of muscular weakness, diminished resistance to fatigue, and partial muscular spasms in the limbs.

In more severe forms the pains rapidly increase in violence, and may deprive the patients of the use of their limbs. They can only walk a few steps with marked effort, tremor, and vertigo. They cannot even use their hands in the simplest occupations, to perform any manual labor, to write, play the piano, etc., all muscular action producing pain in the back and limbs. The patient asks to be left quiet in the dorsal decubitus and in absolute muscular inaction. Nevertheless true paralyses do not occur.

The *mental faculties* are also changed, and present the symptoms of abnormal irritability. There is a condition of intellectual malaise, and a feeling of constriction in the head; the patient cannot speak or read a long time, as he soon becomes tired; the face readily reddens or pales. Insomnia usually occurs. These extremely sensitive individuals react very strongly to the impressions of the outer world. Slight functional disorders are sufficient to produce strong febrile movement and cephalic symptoms, followed by exhaustion.

Spinal irritation (the hyperæsthetic form) nearly always pursues a chronic course. The phenomena of irritation may disappear after having lasted several weeks or months, but exacerbations and relapses are frequent; they occur from slight causes, and often without any known provocation. A permanent improvement of the irritative symptoms has a favorable effect upon the general condition, since the patients, hitherto confined to the dorsal decubitis, may again rise; their movements increase in activity and duration, and digestion, sleep, and the mental condition improve.

The improvement may persist for a longer or shorter period. If it continues for a certain length of time, we may hope for recovery, under favorable conditions, and if the patients are properly treated. But frequently they retain some annoying spinal symptoms during their whole life. Sometimes the hyperæsthetic form passes into the depressive form, which we shall describe at a later period.

From an *etiological* point of view, we may remark that spinal irritation is much more frequent in women, especially from the ages of ten to thirty years. An hereditary predisposition to nervous affections often plays an important part as a pathogenic factor. Among the *exciting causes* we may mention all influences which produce stimulation or depression of the nervous system. Lively emotions, mental distress, unrequited love, excessive stimulation of sexual desires, over-exertion and night-work, constitute some of the most frequent causes. Morbid conditions of the blood (anæmia and hydræmia), contagious and miasmatic affections (acute exanthemata, typhoid and intermittent fever, etc.), hæmorrhages, seminal losses, and finally, traumatic and rheumatic affections, may also give rise to spinal irritation.

All that can be said at present, with regard to the *nature of spinal irritation*, is that it consists in an abnormal irritability of the nervous centres, usually hereditary, but also acquired under the influence of different diseases, of anæmia, or of prolonged mental excitement.

The rapid exhaustion and the excessive irritability of the vaso-motor apparatus contained in the cord plays a considerable part in the symptoms of spinal irritation. We may, at least, suppose that the exciting and debilitating influences to which we have referred produce an exaggerated shock of the vasomotor centres, giving rise to relaxation of the vessels and hyperæmia; if these centres recover with difficulty, the vessels, on their part, will occupy a long time before their normal tonus is restored. In other forms the extreme mental excitement gives rise to contractions of the vessels through irritation of the vasomotor centres; if this vascular spasm is often repeated, a rebellious and long-continued anæmia will result.

The *diagnosis* of spinal irritation sometimes meets with great difficulties, especially in the initial forms. But after watching the case for some time, we will observe the vertebral pain with circumscribed hyperæsthesia, the excentric pains, the irritability of the sensorium, the rapid exhaustion of the motor energy, the absence of manifest paralysis and anæsthesia, the variability of the coexisting nervous phenomena, and the slight gravity of the objective signs. The diagnosis may be made from this *ensemble* of symptoms, when we are able, at the same time, to exclude all other spinal lesions with analogous manifestations. The differentiation from *spondylitis* and *vertebral caries*, which are also more frequent in young subjects, has been established in the chapters relating to these affections. *Spinal meningitis* is characterized, in the beginning, by elevation of temperature and frequency of the pulse, by violent and diffused dorsal pain, by tonic spasms of the muscles of the neck and back which render all movements painful, and by the atrophic paralyses and contractures of the limbs with loss of farado-muscular contractility which follow this disease.

Myelitis is distinguished from spinal irritation by the early appearance of evident anæsthesia and paralysis; by the correlation of the disturbances of sensation with the distribution of the medullary sensory nerves; by the existence of girdling pains, and often of spasms and contractures. We also find other important diagnostic signs in myelitis, viz.: abolition. of the action of the sphincters; tenderness and pain upon pressure of the vertebral column usually less pronounced; no abnormal psychical irritability or fluctuation in the symptoms, such as is observed in spinal irritation.

The latter coincides with hysteria in the extreme susceptibility of the nervous system; but we do not find those profound changes in the psychical sphere, nor the convulsive or paralytic disorders of motion or sensation, with anomalies in the electrical reactions, nor the disorders of vegetative life, which belong to hysteria. Apart from these important symptoms, the other manifestations of nervousness in spinal irritation do not offer that tenacity and periodicity, nor the prognostic and therapeutic difficulties, which sometimes complicate the history of hysteria.

The *treatment* of spinal irritation should consist in removing, as far as possible, the pathogenic causes to which we have referred, and in improving the tone of the nervous system. The best stimulant and tonic effects are obtained by *abundant nutriment*, with light wines or beer; we may also administer small doses of *iron* and *quinine*. A long sojourn in the pure air of the *country*, preferably upon high mountains and in the midst of forests, usually exercises a salutary influence upon the nervous functions. But, in these conditions, we must not advise the patients to indulge in too much exercise; they should, on the contrary, rest often and long.

The *antiphlogistic* and *derivative* measures of former therapeutics are rarely employed at the present time. In robust and full-blooded subjects we may derive benefit from scarifications along the vertebral column, and from the application of leeches to the vulva or anus. The moxa and actual cautery are no longer employed. The cautious employment of blisters. and tartar emetic ointment may be sometimes recommended.

In order to quiet the distressing dorsal pains and the burning sensations in the legs and soles of the feet, the patient should wear upon the back a tube of india-rubber, filled with moderately cold water; the tube is kept in place by a bandage applied transversely in such a manner as not to prove annoying, and, if the vertebral sensibility is very acute, a layer of wadding may be interposed.

Good effects are sometimes produced by passing the ascending constant galvanic current along the spinal column (exposing the painful points to the action of the cathode). The current should be of moderate intensity, and the sitting of short duration. Nux vomica and strychnine are recommended by several authors. Finally, hydrotherapeutics may also prove successful in spinal irritation. At first, affusions should be made to the back (with water which is rendered cooler from day to day) in a half-bath of 24°–20° C.; later, we may employ wet packs, continued until the warmth of the body has returned, followed by lotions and irrigations of the vertebral column, while the patient is in a half-bath of moderate temperature. We may also recommend the patient to wear a moist cloth upon the back, covered with a dry one, and renewed two or three times daily. Cold applications and cold douches should not be employed; warm douches to the dorsal spine often prove advantageous.

b. *Depressed Form of Spinal Irritation (Neurasthenia).*

In this variety of spinal irritation, the most striking characteristics are represented by symptoms of spinal depression. We refer chiefly to this neurosis when we speak of "nervous weakness," and Beard, Rockwell, and Erb have proposed for it the term neurasthenia. Leyden has recently described cases of this kind under the title of "spinal irritation, following seminal losses."

Dorsal pain is almost always present in this form, as in the preceding, but it is neither so acute nor so persistent. The pain is situated sometimes in the lumbar, sometimes in the upper dorsal portion of the vertebral column. Some of the spinous processes are moderately tender on pressure, and the patient experiences in them a sensation of burning, compression, or tension. The dorsal pain increases after fatigue and exertion, after extensive movements of the vertebral column, and after exposure and excesses. We often observe, as coexisting symptoms, a feeling of oppression, dyspnœa, palpitation of the heart, and constriction of the head. Certain patients complain of annoying numbness or formication in the coverings of the cranium. But the phenomena which especially distress the patients are *weakness in performing movements* and *rapid exhaustion.* After a very short walk, motion becomes difficult, and the knees and lumbar region are the seat of a peculiar sensation of relaxation. The patients cannot stand, for any length of time, without supporting themselves or bending one of the knees. They are also almost always unable to stand upon one foot with the eyes closed, although they are able to do this with the eyes open. The upper limbs also take part in this exhaustion, although to a less degree.

Forced movements soon produce a sensation of heaviness in the legs, with muscular pains. A small quantity of wine, taken during repose, often produces strengthening and tonic effects. Other important disorders also appear on the part of the genital functions. In general the patients are easily excitable, but the erections and virile power are deficient; ejaculation of semen is often premature, and followed by distressing sensations in the back and legs. When the mind is occupied with erotic thoughts, and even after defecation or micturition, some drops of prostatic fluid (almost always without admixture with spermatozoids) frequently appear at the meatus. True spermatorrhœa only occurs at great intervals; chronic pollutions, on the other hand, are frequent, and, when they follow one another in rapid succession, they greatly aggravate the manifestations of the disease. In the majority of patients, the urethral canal presents, especially in the prostatic portion, an acute sensitiveness, even when a sound of small calibre (19 or 20, Charrière) can be introduced without difficulty. This operation may produce intense local pain, a burning sensation, and even convulsions. The functions of the bladder are usually normal; sometimes, however, a burning sensation is experienced after the passage of the last drops of urine.

The *psychical faculties* may be more or less affected. The intelligence is preserved, but memory and judgment are defective. The capacity for intellectual labor is markedly diminished, and the patients are deficient in will power. A hypochondriacal disposition is especially noticeable, sometimes with a tendency to weep, and with a peculiar dread of locomotor ataxia. The sleep is uneasy and frequently interrupted, and the patients complain of prostration and dulness upon rising from bed. Numbness and formication in the feet are frequently experienced. But the most disagreeable sensation of which the patients complain is coldness of the hands and feet, which only disappears slowly after the patient has become warm in bed; on the other hand, when covered too warmly, cerebral congestions readily occur.

The *nutritive functions* are almost always poorly accomplished. The patients complain of flatulence, belching, diminution of appetite, and constipation; the tongue is coated, and the patients are emaciated and anæmic; dilatation of the stomach is observed in rare instances.

Objective examination discloses no disorders of motion or sensation corresponding to the numerous subjective disturbances of which the patients complain. The most striking phenomenon in the disease is the want of persistence in the muscular activity. In the majority of cases the affection develops progressively and almost insensibly. It only reaches its culmination after the lapse of several months or even of several years. Nevertheless, in exceptional instances, the symptoms may appear more rapidly under the influence of emotions, fatigue, excesses, or repeated seminal losses. Recent and slight cases may recover after a few weeks. In old, chronic forms (lasting several years) the condition of the patient may vary a great deal; but we cannot hope for persistent improvement except after the lapse of months or years, even under the most appropriate treatment and habits of life. Relapses are not infrequent, and are often produced by slight causes; the patient is sad and melancholy, and flees the society of his fellows more and more. Under unfavorable conditions, excessive exertion, fatigue, and violent exposure may implant the first germs of organic lesions of the spinal cord.

The male sex furnishes a much larger proportion of cases of the depressed form of spinal irritation than the female sex, contrary to what occurs in the hyperæsthetic variety. The disease develops, with the greatest frequency, at puberty and during middle age. The influence of heredity is manifested by the coexistence of other neuroses in the same family. The disease is much more frequent among the better classes of society than among the poor.

Excessive excitement of the sexual functions constitute the most frequent and positive cause of this affection. This is especially true of masturbation, which young boys frequently continue in youth, and which, being then combined with greater hardships, develops spinal irritation. Onanism may lead to the same results in young girls. Sexual excesses also act in the same manner, especially those which are committed by weak young people at the age of puberty or shortly after marriage; this also occurs from prolonged and unsatisfied sexual excitement.

Finally, intellectual efforts, insomnia, miserable habits of life, and prolonged emotional disturbance, may, in predisposed subjects, lead to the outbreak of this spinal neurosis.

We can merely form hypotheses as to the *nature of the disease*. The prolonged action of the causes which we have mentioned, acting especially during youth, may produce excessive irritability of the medullary and vasomotor centres. This condition, becoming chronic, causes rapid exhaustion of the spinal nervous influx, and a slowing of the current of blood with passive hyperæmia, or a lowering of the temperature in the peripheral parts. The lumbar pains, the weakness of the legs, the circulatory disturbances in the same regions, and the disorders of the sexual functions, indicate anæmia of the lumbar portion of the cord, and the chronic character of this lesion accounts for the tenacity of the symptoms of depression depending upon it.

In forming a *diagnosis*, we must carefully examine the patient and take into consideration the previous history of the disease. A prolonged observation will often be necessary in order to exclude the onset of other spinal diseases.

Incipient *ataxia*, which is most readily mistaken for this variety of spinal irritation, is distinguished by the characteristic lancinating pains and sciatica, by the early disorders of sensation, the girdling pains, the pupillary anomalies, the pareses of ocular muscles, the oscillations which the patient experiences when he wishes to turn around with the eyes closed, and by the exaggeration of galvanic excitability. Incipient *myelitis* is characterized by the rapid appearance of vague neuralgia, manifest paresis and paralysis of the lower limbs, the prompt abolition of the various forms of sensibility in the same regions, the stiffness and difficulty of movements and the feebleness of the sphincters. The distinctive signs of commencing *vertebral caries* have been described in a preceding chapter. Finally, intense dorsal pain, acute sensitiveness of the vertebral column, neuralgia and pain during motion, are peculiar to the hyperæsthetic form of spinal irritation; while, in the depressed form, the predominant symptoms consist of the exhaustion of the motor energy, the sexual weakness, the seminal losses, the psychical changes, etc.

The *treatment* must consist at first of prolonged rest and isolation of the patient; he should abstain from emotional and sexual excitement and from intellectual labor. Benefit is derived from a trip to the country, either among the mountains or at the sea-shore, avoiding, at the same time, all fatigue and long walks. The diet should be substantial but easily digested, and a little wine or beer may be taken with the meals. Small doses of quinine or nux vomica, and light ferruginous preparations or waters often prove advantageous.

A trip to a chalybeate spring is indicated in anæmic, emaciated patients, who are very sensitive to cold or who suffer from painful twinges in the muscles. At a later period, when recovery has made some progress, moderately cool lotions may serve as a transition to *hydrotherapeutic treatment*. We may begin by making irrigations to the back in a half-bath of moderate temperature, which is gradually lowered; afterwards we may employ lotions with a wet cloth. We should avoid douches, full cold baths, etc. Sea-baths are also useful during convalescence.

Finally, electricity gives some good results. The moderate ascending continuous current should be passed through the dorsal spine, and may also be applied to the legs; faradic currents of great tension should not be employed.

CLASS IV.

HYSTERIA AND ITS CONCOMITANT NERVOUS DISORDERS.

CHAPTER XXVII.

HYSTERIA.

HYSTERIA must be regarded as one of the oldest products of civilization. It was described with great clearness by Herodotus and Hippocrates, and in the writings of Plato. Certain hysterical phenomena have played a sad part at other periods, as in the terrible history of sorcery which darkened the early period of Christianity. Hysterical patients affected with convulsions or catalepsy, and others who were delirious or ecstatic, were accused of intercourse with the devil, and many of these unhappy creatures died at the stake, as being possessed of a demon. Hysteria, combined with a condition of religious exaltation, also played a considerable part in the convulsive epidemics of the last century.

Symptomatology.

The numerous peculiarities of this morbid process do not permit a description of its symptoms in a strict chronological order. We shall therefore study separately the disorders of sensation and motion, of the sensorial functions and of vegetative life.

The *sensory disturbances* are characterized by hyperæsthesia, anæsthesia, and neuralgia.

Hyperæsthesia.—The skin is frequently the site of spontaneous pains; the lightest touch will also produce painful sensations. In a more severe form the hands cannot grasp any object, and the feet cannot tolerate the contact with the ground.

The hyperæsthesia rarely extends over the entire surface of the body. In a quarter of the cases of hyperæsthesia, observed by Briquet (Traité de l'Hystérie, Paris, 1859), it extended over one-half the body (usually the left), and was limited by the median line.

Upon the scalp, the hyperæsthesia is manifested chiefly at the occiput; it also occurs upon the back, thorax, and abdominal walls. Larger or smaller patches of hyperæsthesia are also found upon the limbs, and may readily pass unnoticed. Brodie first called attention to *hyperæsthesia of the joints,* usually involving the hip and knee. When it is accompanied by swelling and œdema of the neighboring parts, it may simulate arthritis. The real nature of these phenomena is rendered evident by the following circumstances: normal position of the parts (except when secondary contracture of the muscles has developed); passive motion preserved; peculiar sensibility of the skin to pinching, even in parts which are at a distance from the joint; no appreciable change in the nutrition of the muscles, even after the disease has lasted a long time; alteration in the affection at each menstrual epoch (Stannius).

In consequence of *muscular hyperæsthesia,* which is frequent in hysterical patients, superficial pressure, weak faradic excitation, or even the slightest movement, will produce intolerable pain, and the patients are condemned to absolute rest.

Hyperæsthesia of the special senses is a rare but very distressing symptom. The eye becomes extremely sensitive to light, the ear to the slightest noise, the nose to certain odors.

The hyperæsthesia usually occurs in consequence of emotional excitement, after an hysterical seizure ; it may be limited to one-half the body, while the other half is anæsthetic. Finally, hyperæsthesia constitutes a favorable sign in hysterical paralyses, which were primarily complicated with anæsthesia.

We may here mention the *abnormal increase of reflex excitability* sometimes present in hysteria. Stilling and Tuerck have noticed that pressure upon the spinous processes may give rise to convulsions. In other cases, deep pressure over the ovary or epigastric region (Schuetzenberger) produces analogous hysterical symptoms.

Anæsthesia.—Beau distinguishes two forms of anæsthesia: anæsthesia to contact and to pain (analgesia). The latter variety also occurs in hypochondria, cerebral apoplexy, spinal diseases, lead-poisoning, and in the first stage of ether and chloroform narcosis.

Hysterical anæsthesia rarely involves the whole integument. Hemiplegia of sensation occurs more frequently, and almost always upon the left side. This latter fact is owing, according to Briquet, to the greater sensibility of the skin to stimulation, and to the greater delicacy of the tactile functions, upon the left half of the body. The analgesia usually occupies the same limits as the anæsthesia; in exploration we employ the point of a pin or the electric brush. According to Charcot's recent observations (loc. cit.), hemianæsthesia, together with paresis and contracture of the limbs, appears to be connected with a bilateral or unilateral ovaralgia, and frequently changes its situation in the same way that the latter does. The anæsthetic region is sometimes interspersed with small spots in which sensibility remains intact. As a rule, the anæsthetic parts have also lost their sensibility to temperature and their reflex excitability.

Before continuing the study of hysterical disorders of innervation, I wish to relate an observation, which is interesting from several points of view, and which I have published in detail in the Wien. Med. Zeitung, 23, 24, 1871:

A girl, twenty-three years old, whom I had previously treated for hysteria and catalepsy, suffered a relapse in consequence of a violent blow upon the left breast. She complained of obstinate hiccough, alternating with epileptiform attacks. The latter were preceded by a subjective sensation of cold and discoloration of the hands and tips of the fingers. *The hands became very pale, the tips of the fingers and nails of a deep blue ; the patient experienced a disagreeable sensation of cold in the hands, and their temperature, which was* 33.4° *C. in the normal condition, sunk to* 30.6° *C.*, and the pulse dropped from 72 to 65 or 66. After the termination of the hystero-epileptic attack, the temperature of the hands again ascended to about 35.6°, the warmth returned, the fingers and nails became very red, and were the seat of an abundant perspiration: the pulse increased to 84 or 88.

During a few hours preceding the attack, the patient suffered from hyperæsthesia of the skin in various parts of the trunk; the muscles were also hyperæsthetic to pressure and to the contact of the bed, so that the patient was frequently obliged to change her position. *Marked elevation of temperature was observed upon the hyperæsthetic side of the body.*

When the pallor and cyanosis of the hand became manifest, the hyperæsthesia diminished, and gave place to anæsthesia of the hands, with a sensation of numbness in the fingers and toes. These signs infallibly indicated the approach of an attack.

Towards the close of the attack, if the fingers or hand were touched, *they were drawn away by a reflex movement, although consciousness was still abolished, and the pupils were insensible to light.* This condition having lasted about three months, an attack of fever suddenly developed, which quickly yielded to large doses of quinine. The menses then reappeared, and the hiccough, vomiting, and epileptiform attacks suddenly ceased.

It is evident that, in this case, the attacks were accompanied by manifest symptoms of spasmodic contraction, followed by dilatation of the vessels, which will justify us in the belief that the epileptiform attacks were caused by an extension of the spasmodic phenomena to the cerebral arteries. Analogous disorders of vaso-motor innervation probably caused the periodical return of the hyperæsthesia, since the latter always co-existed with a palpable elevation of temperature upon the affected side, and disappeared as soon as anæsthesia developed, with a fall in the temperature, pallor of the skin, and partial cyanosis.

Vascular dilatation and rise of temperature are due, according to the doctrines hitherto admitted, to paralysis of the vaso-motor nerves. According to Goltz's experiments (Pflüg. Arch., 9. Bd., 1874), on the other hand, these phenomena are due to exaggerated function of the vaso-dilator nerves, which are innervated from the spinal centre. Upon enclosing the sympathetic or sciatic nerves in spirals, formed of copper and platinum wire, O. Weber (Centralbl., 10, 1864) observed narrowing of the vessels, lowering of the temperature, and pallor of the integument, in the regions corresponding to these nerves. These phenomena persisted for several weeks, and were preceded by hyperæsthesia and often by spasmodic convulsions; nevertheless, when the experiment was carefully performed, no nutritive or inflammatory disorders were produced.

When the anæsthesia is more profound and extended, the *muscular tissue* becomes involved in its turn, the muscular power diminishing and the electro-muscular and cutaneous sensibility disappearing. The various *mucous membranes* may also be involved. Anæsthesia of the nasal mucous membrane causes *anosmia;* complete or incomplete *anæsthesia of taste* will develop, according as the buccal cavity and tongue have lost their sensibility to contact and pain throughout their whole extent, or only upon one-half. If a morsel is placed in the mouth, while the eyes are closed, and if the fingers are anæsthetic at the same time, the patients will not perceive the presence of anything in the mouth except by looking in a mirror, and only then will movements of deglutition commence.

The abolition of sensation may also involve the *larger and smaller joints* of the limbs and trunk as well as the bones. In certain cases I have observed lively resistance to passive movements, without knowledge or intention on the part of the patients (reflex contractions of the antagonistic muscles). When the anæsthesia is very marked, it also involves *the nerves ;* they will not respond to energetic pressure, or to strong galvanic or faradic currents.

Finally, *sight* and *hearing* may also become anæsthetic. In the first case, sight is confused, and the eyes soon become tired when the patient fixes them upon her work; anæsthesia of the retina, amblyopia or amaurosis are very rare; the latter is always associated with hysterical disorders of sensation and motion. After a certain length of time it subsides as suddenly as it has appeared. Hirschberg, Bouchut, and Galezowski have observed hyperæmia, and even opaque exudation and discoloration of the papilla, with partial dilatation of the retinal vessels, in these cases of hemiopia and chromatopsia.

Jaeger has noticed temporary bluish coloration of the optic nerve after attacks of hysteria. Anæsthesia of audition is usually incomplete, and is accompanied by roaring in the ears, a sensation of compression, and enfeebled hearing. These nervous auditory disorders usually occupy only one side, and disappear spontaneously or after appropriate treatment.

When the anæsthesia and analgesia are generalized (in the skin, muscles, and joints), a very curious disorder of innervation is produced, which was described for the first time by Duchenne, and of which I have also observed an example (Wien. Med. Presse, 5, 1867). When the eyes are closed, or during the night, these patients are incapable of performing any motions, although they imagine that they have executed the actions which they willed. They cannot bring their muscles into play, unless they look at the limb which they desire to move.

These observations led Duchenne to accept the doctrine of the existence of a special *muscular sense*, which, starting from the muscles, stimulates the brain, and determines the choice of the muscles which are to be brought into action.

But I think that we can resort to simpler and more natural explanations of this phenomenon. We know, in fact, that each sense has its special origin in the central organ, and may be hindered in its functions by various causes, either because its terminal apparatus has lost its sensibility to external influences, in consequence of a change in the peripheral nerves, or because there is some obstruction in the central conductors.

We must also consider another important circumstance. While the hysterical patients in question are unable, when the eyes are closed, to voluntarily excite the motor action of the nerves, in order to accomplish the desired movement, *the influence of the will upon innervation becomes much more effective when aided by the sense of sight.* When a healthy person attempts to seize an object (with the eyes closed), he uses an entirely disproportionate amount of force—sometimes excessive, sometimes insufficient. This *regulating action of sight* has a much greater influence when the muscles, articulations, and cutaneous nerves are completely anæsthetic.

Hysterical neuralgia.—Hysterical neuralgias sometimes occur along the course of certain nerves, especially after excitement or hysterical convulsions. They undergo rapid modifications with regard to their situation and intensity, and are accompanied by other characteristic signs of hysteria. *Cephalic* neuralgia is most frequent, occurring in the frontal, temporal, auricular, or occipital regions. *Hemicrania* is very frequent, especially on the left side; the *clavus hystericus* (Valentiner) usually occupies a circumscribed part of the sagittal suture, and radiates from this point.

We may also meet with *omalgia, brachialgia, mastodynia, intercostal neuralgia, lumbar neuralgia,* simple or double *sciatica,* and a pain in the coccygeal region, occurring either in the sitting or standing position, and described by Simpson, Scanzoni, and Hoerschelmann under the name of *coccygodynia* (hyperæsthesia of the branches of the coccygeal plexus).

The *rachialgia* is a spontaneous dorsal pain, almost always increased on pressure. It may be caused either by a neuralgia of the lumbar branches, or by irritation of the posterior branches which supply the skin and muscles of the dorsal region, or of the sensitive fibres which Luschka has discovered in great number in the vertebral veins and vertebræ. *Cardialgia* and *enteralgia* are observed at times. *Ovaralgia* is much more frequent, and has been especially referred to of late by Charcot (fixed iliac pain of Briquet). It occurs with or without appreciable enlargement of the ovary, compression of which may produce an hysterical convulsion, while energetic pressure will moderate and sometimes even suspend a convulsion.

The *motor disorders* consist either of irritation of the motor functions, as in spasms and contractures, or of diminution or even complete abolition of these functions, as in paresis and paralysis.

Hysterical spasms.—Almost all hysterical patients present an abnormal motor excitability, which appears, in the slighter forms, as vivacity and precipitation of movements. When this excitability is more intense, it gives rise to contractions of certain muscles or of entire groups of muscles, or may even assume the form of convulsions.

The spasms of the head observed in hysterical patients are: *spasmodic contractions of the muscles of the face and spasm of certain ocular muscles* (with convergent or divergent strabismus).

In the cervical region, spasms occur in the *sterno-mastoid* and *trapezius* muscles, and in the *pharynx, larynx,* and *œsophagus.* When the pharynx is affected, spasms develop in the apparatus of deglutition, and usually occur in a sudden and violent manner (contraction of the transverse muscular fibres of the pharynx and the upper third of the œsophagus, the contraction of which muscles, according to Helmholtz, very quickly follows their stimulation). The spasms in the muscles of deglutition may even compromise alimentation, as I have observed in two cases, in which galvanization always caused immediate cessation of the spasm. Contraction of the thoracic portion of the œsophagus may also occur and may be propagated to the constrictors of the pharynx, and prevent the introduction of the œsophageal sound. The *globus hystericus* (sensation of a ball rising) is merely a sensory irritative symptom. In certain forms of spasms of deglutition, the constriction of the muscles of the lower part of the œsophagus, and perhaps, also, of the circular fibres of the cardiac extremity of the stomach, gives rise to regurgitation and vomiting of food.

The *spasmodic contraction of the laryngeal muscles* appears, in the lighter forms, as *hysterical laughter*, which may last a quarter of an hour at a time, and is sometimes followed or interrupted by *convulsive weeping.* At a more advanced stage, *convulsive cries* make their appearance, under the form of barking, howling, and sneering. At other times the sounds simulate the cries of different animals, and may exercise a contagious effect upon predisposed subjects, so that epidemics of hysterical cries may be produced. *Spasm of the glottis* occurs in rare cases from the reflex effect of hyperæsthesia of the laryngeal mucous membrane, from irritation of the recurrent nerve. Guisan and Dubois mention cases in which death from asphyxia occurred, and Bell and Briquet report others in which the danger was only averted by resort to tracheotomy. To this category also belong *hysterical asthma* (perhaps from spasm of the bronchial muscles) and *hysterical cough* (irritation of the superior laryngeal nerve). Hysterical *yawning* results from spasmodic movements of inspiration, and is accompanied by other spasmodic phenomena.

The *spasmodic phenomena which are observed on the part of the abdomen* consist of sobs, eructations, borborygmus, and spasms of the genito-urinary apparatus. The *sob* (or hiccough) is a clonic spasm of the diaphragm, with noisy penetration of the inspired air through the glottis, retraction of the epigastrium and hypochondrium, followed by expiration. Hiccough frequently appears as the precursor of an hysterical or cataleptic convulsion, or may develop, on the other hand, at the termination of such convulsions. *Hysterical eructations* consist in the expulsion of gas from the stomach, with very marked deglutition of air. *Borborygmus* is due to movement of the intestinal gases; the intestinal contractions are sometimes appreciable to the sight and touch.

Spasm of the vagina (vaginismus) is a painful contraction of the constrictor cunni, which prevents sexual intercourse and even hinders the introduction of the finger. *The sphincters of the bladder and anus* are also sometimes affected with spasmodic contraction. *Goose-flesh* is a very frequent phenomenon in hysterical patients, and is due to spasmodic contraction of the muscular fibres contained in the skin.

Tonic spasms occur in the neck, limbs, and abdomen under the form of *contractures*, with abnormal positions of the limbs. These contractures usually appear after emotional excitement or hysterical convulsions. They generally involve the knee, wrist, and the phalangeal joints of one hand (Fig. 17); in rare cases, spasmodic club-foot is developed. The contracture is situated, by preference, in the adductors and flexors of the hand and fingers, and is characterized by the fact that it is not only associated, in the majority of cases, with paralysis of the antagonists, but is also accompanied by a simultaneous abolition of the functions of certain other muscles, by anæsthesia, and more rarely by hyperæsthesia.

FIG. 17.—Hysterical contracture of left upper limb.

Certain forms are complicated with symptoms of irritation on the part of the nerve-centres. I had under observation a young girl who suffered from hystero-epileptic convulsions for several years. These were followed by *contracture of the right upper limb* at the elbow and wrist, with *continual vibrations of the right arm ;* the same phenomenon was apparent, to a less extent in the right leg; each attempt at extension increased the intensity of the tremor.

Hysterical convulsions are divided into partial and general, and those with or without loss of consciousness. The muscles of the limbs are most frequently involved. Strong emotions have an especially injurious effect upon the production of hysterical convulsions.

In one-third of the three hundred and five cases collected by Briquet, the hysteria began with convulsive seizures. The attacks were most numerous in the first year of the disease, and in ten per cent. of the cases consciousness was unaffected during the convulsions.

The *hysterical seizure* is often preceded by certain prodromata, such as languor, malaise, slight pains in the legs, tingling in the limbs, vesical tenesmus, or a feeling of oppression in the epigastrium. In the majority of cases the attack develops rapidly, with symptoms of reflex irritation of the medulla oblongata, palpitation of the heart, feeling of suffocation,. spasms of the pharynx, and hiccough. The reflex acts soon extend to various paths in the cerebro-spinal system ; consciousness may be preserved in great part, or it may rapidly disappear in the vortex of symptoms. In the first case the convulsive movements are less violent and the special senses are less involved, but the patients are unable to speak, to perform any voluntary movement, or to give any sign of intelligence. After the attack they remember distinctly the pains which they experienced in the head, limbs, and epigastrium. According to Briquet, among three hundred patients affected with hysterical convulsions, there were only thirty in whom consciousness remained intact. In severe hysterical paroxysms the patient, after palpitation of the heart and loss of con-sciousness, gives utterance to a piercing cry, and then the face becomes pale and grimacing, tonic and clonic contractions succeeding one another rapidly in the muscles of the face, eyes, and jaw, in the limbs of one or both sides, in the muscles of the back, thorax, and abdomen; then follow spasms of the glottis with symptoms of asphyxia, tumidity, and cyanosis.

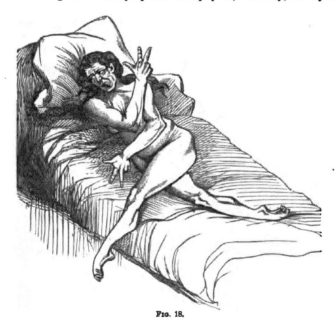

FIG. 18.

of the face, bloody froth at the mouth (from biting of the tongue or lips), convulsive respiration, interrupted by cries, automatic movements or retraction of the head, projection of the pelvis forward, opisthotonos, pleurosthotonos, or other analogous symptoms. These cases constitute the affection known as *hystero-epilepsy*. (Fig. 18.) At the close of the attack, which may last a few minutes to several hours under the most variable aspects, a condition of exhaustion often develops, with a sensation of emptiness in the head, and relaxation of the limbs. This dramatic scene is usually followed by a shower of tears, by an abundant development of gas in the stomach and intestines, and by the emission of a large quantity of pale, inodorous urine. In rarer cases the patients sink into a profound sleep or syncope, or into a condition of catalepsy, delirium, or somnambulism.

Hysterical paralyses.—Hysterical patients, as a rule, suffer from a great diminution of muscular power. Briquet has found paresis, or paralysis, one hundred and twenty times in four hundred and thirty patients; Landouzy, forty times in three hundred and seventy cases. The limbs are most frequently involved, especially on the left side; the lower limbs, the muscles of the trunk, of the larynx and face are affected, with regard to frequency, in the order mentioned; paralysis of the diaphragm is a very rare event.

Facial paralysis in hysteria sometimes coexists with paralyses in the limbs, is almost always upon the same side as the latter, and is usually accompanied by anæsthesia of the skin and special senses. Hysterical ptosis and alternating paresis of the motor muscles of the eye have also been observed.

Paralysis of the pharyngeal and œsophageal constrictors have been noticed by several observers. *Paralyses of the laryngeal muscles* are more frequent and better understood. Double paralysis of the vocal cords may develop spontaneously; it often, however, follows a convulsion, and is accompanied by considerable hyperæsthesia of the isthmus of the fauces (Tuerck). According to this author, disorders of co-ordination, rather than paralysis, constitute the cause of certain cases of hysterical aphonia.

Paralysis of the diaphragm, first described by Duchenne, forms one of the rarest motor disorders in hysteria; Briquet has only observed it in two cases. The affection, which is usually obstinate, is characterized by inversion of the respiratory rhythm and by extinction of the voice. During inspiration, the epigastrium and hypochondria are depressed and the thoracic walls are elevated. During expiration, the abdominal walls are raised and the thorax contracts.

Paralysis of the extremities may be limited to certain portions of the limbs, or may involve an entire member; in very rare cases it affects all the limbs. The most frequent hysterical paralyses are those involving one limb, hemiplegia and paraplegia.

Hemiplegia (observed by Briquet in one-sixth of his cases) usually appears after excitement or after a convulsive seizure. The paralysis is generally less marked in the upper than the lower limb, which, during walking, is dragged along like an inert mass. Anæsthesia and analgesia of the deeper parts frequently coexist, with diminution or abolition of the functions of special sense. Paraplegia (which existed in about one-twelfth of Briquet's observations) may be either partial or complete; it is usually accompanied by anæsthesia of the lower limbs. *Hysterical ataxia* also develops in some cases.

Paralysis of the bladder almost always accompanies hemiplegia and especially hysterical paraplegia. It is very rebellious in such cases, and is sometimes complicated with anæsthesia of the vesical mucous membrane. *Paralysis of the rectum* occurs in very rare cases, and is accompanied by constipation, tympanites, or even anæsthesia of the rectum.

Electrical reactions in hysterical paralyses.—Duchenne first called attention to the following characteristic signs of hysterical paralysis : *integrity of electro-muscular contractility, with marked diminution or complete abolition of electro-muscular and electro-cutaneous sensibility.* In some exceptional cases, however, the electrical contractility of the muscles is also markedly diminished. We have previously called attention to the fact that in certain apoplectic paralyses or those due to compression of the cord, in which the paralysis is accompanied by anæsthesia of the deeper parts, the electro-muscular contractility may be preserved and the electro-cutaneous and electro-muscular sensibility be abolished as in hysterical paralysis. In these doubtful cases we must have recourse to other signs to aid us in the differential diagnosis.

Faradization of the nerve-trunks, and the passage of strong galvanic currents from the vertebral column to the plexuses, nerves and muscles of the affected limbs, produce energetic contractions in hysterical paralysis, although the patients are unconscious of them.

Exploration with the aid of electro-puncture is the best means of ascertaining the depth of the anæsthesia. In severe forms even the mucous membranes are insensible to electrical irritation.

Disorders of vegetative life.—On the part of *respiration* we frequently observe an abnormal frequency of inspirations, with or without a sensation of dyspnœa; in other cases there is a real want of air, with attacks of asthma and asphyxia, although physical examination of the thoracic organs reveals nothing abnormal. The *cardiac functions* are only disturbed in a few instances; in such cases we notice periodical palpitation and systolic cardiac bruits, the latter being due to anæmia.

The *digestive organs* are affected in various ways. Certain patients take very little nourishment, experience profound disgust for certain dishes, and may even abstain entirely from food (usually under the influence of a pathological mental condition). Other patients suffer from bulimia, and can hardly satisfy their inordinate appetite. In this category we may also mention frequent and distressing epigastric pulsation, belching, obstinate vomiting, tympanites, and constipation. *Menstruation* is usually very irregular and scanty, and is very frequently suppressed for a long time. Hæmoptysis is observed in some cases (vicarious menstruation).

Retention of urine (with anæsthesia of the vesical mucous membrane), to which hysterical patients are very subject, requires the prolonged use of the catheter. *Hysterical ischuria* may be complete, and may last twenty-four or thirty-six hours (Laycock), in consequence of excitement or during menstruation, after which it gradually disappears. Very curious examples have been observed of *hysterical oliguria and anuria, with vomiting of matters containing urea.*

The first case, published by Charcot and Gréhaut, occurred in a patient suffering from hysterical contracture, hemianæsthesia, and hemiopia. Retention of urine soon occurred, and the quantity of urine withdrawn by the catheter grew progressively smaller; the patient then began to vomit. She was carefully watched for two months, and the urine obtained during this time did not average more than eighty grammes a month. After being anæsthetized with chloroform, the quantity of urine increased and some drops wet the bed. During the period of anuria, the patient vomited daily. The vomited matters were rich in urea; the blood, which was analyzed once, contained 0.036 grammes of urea per 100.

The *psychical disorders* of hysteria are manifested in the slighter forms, by an abnormal sensitiveness to external impressions, by the sudden passage from gayety to sadness, and by obstinacy or apathy; there is frequently a desire of attracting attention. The more severe psychical changes are either acute or chronic. *Acute attacks* consist of hallucinations, delirium, ecstasy, or even of mania; they generally terminate in recovery, and the patients are then unable to recall their past condition. *Chronic hysterical psychoses* assume the form of melancholia or mania. The mental condition develops, according to Griesinger, by a progressive increase of the previous intellectual disorders; the invasion is sometimes, also, acute, as after emotional excitement, acute diseases, and hysterical convulsions. There is, at first, a slight change in the character, unusual vanity, impatience and violence, absence of volitional power, and excessive uneasiness of the patient with regard to her health. Then follow disturbances of sleep, digestion, and menstruation, and profound melancholia, stupor, and an irresistible desire to remain in bed. Erotic manifestations are often observed in this condition ; it rarely terminates in true dementia. Ecstasy may also develop in this state. *Somnambulism* may be placed in this category of phenomena ; the patients perform a series of extraordinary movements during sleep; they walk around, either with a fixed look or with the eyes closed, returning to bed after a longer or shorter interval. If they are suddenly awakened, they utter a loud cry, become greatly terrified, and are often seized with convulsions. The next day they remember absolutely nothing of the events of the preceding night.

It is evident, from the description just given, that in somnambulism the connection of the mind with the organs of special sense is temporarily abolished, but that the faculty of forming ideas and their influence upon the production of movements persist. Thus, while a centripetal stimulus is not furnished by the organs of special sense, the impulse derived from the cerebral cortex may pursue its centrifugal course and reach the anterior roots through the foot of the cerebral peduncle. The language which the patients utter during their sleep, and the airs they sing, evidently prove that the cells of the cerebral cortex, as the basis of ideas, and their communications with one another, which serve for the association of ideas, functionate actively, and that movements may be produced by the centrifugal action of the cells of the cerebral cortex along the corona radiata.

It is probable, also, that a certain amount of consciousness is present in such cases, but of a character so fleeting that it leaves no impression on the memory.

The psychical phenomena of depression in hysteria consist of an *inclination to sleep*, which may be intensified into true *sopor* or *lethargy*. Lasègue described, under the title of *temporary catalepsy* (Arch. Génér. de Méd., 1866), a condition in which the patients, when the eyes were covered with the hand, became cataleptic, and fell into a more or less profound sleep, from which it was sometimes difficult to rouse them. Somnolence manifests itself with varying intensity and is preceded by various spasmodic phenomena. In the slight forms it consists of a half-sleep into which the patients fall from time to time in order to satisfy a natural need; in the severer forms, a heavy sleep, like that of drunkenness, may be prolonged for several days.

Somnolence is sometimes transformed into complete lethargy. In an observation reported by Pfendler, it continued uninterruptedly for six months. There were eight cases of lethargy (lasting one to eight days) among four hundred and eighty cases reported by Briquet.

Respiration becomes infrequent and barely perceptible, the pulse is very small and intermittent, the skin cold and dry, evacuations from the bowels are suspended for weeks, and the bladder must be emptied with the catheter. We must resort to powerful stimuli in order to awaken the patients for any length of time. This sleep should not be mistaken for the condition of somnolence which often forms the termination of hysterical convulsions, which usually lasts but a short time and is followed by a certain remission in the symptoms of the disease.

Trance in hysteria.—It now remains for us to describe the trance of hysterical patients, which constitutes the severest and, fortunately, the rarest of these conditions of somnolence. Several cases of this kind are reported by Briquet (loc. cit., pp. 417–420).

I have pointed out an unmistakable means of recognizing the persistence of life, based upon personal investigations and observations (Jahrb. d. Ges. d. Wien. Aerzte, IV. Heft, 1872).

I have demonstrated by experiments upon the cadavers of patients, of drowned individuals and upon amputated limbs, that *electrical excitability disappears within an hour and a half to three hours after death.* The faradic contractility and galvanic reaction, in conformity with the law of their responses, diminish from the centre to the periphery, the excitability of the nerves disappearing sooner than that of the muscles. The diagnosis of death may be made with certainty after the abolition of the farado-galvanic excitability, *even when the joints are still flexible and the temperature of the rectum is raised to 38°–37° C., and that of the axilla to 32.5°–33° C.*

The value of these observations is considerably increased by their agreement with investigations made in the human subject, and with experiments upon muscular rigidity in living animals. I have made experiments upon animals which were either curarized or narcotized with morphine ; one of the iliac arteries and the crural artery (below the origin of the epigastric) were then laid bare and ligatured. The electro-muscular contractility of the corresponding limb was found to have disappeared at the end of about two hours. When the circulation was allowed to return freely, the electrical contractility was gradually restored. After artificial respiration was interrupted, the farado-galvanic reaction in the ligatured limb disappeared at the end of two and a half to three hours, while it persisted much longer in the limb which had not been deprived of blood.

My conclusions have also been verified by the investigations of Crimotel (De l'épreuve galvanique ou Bioscopie électrique, 1866).

In hysterical trance, as in profound syncope, the cerebral activity may be lowered to an imperceptible minimum; or, as in a case under my observation, the impressions of the senses (especially of hearing) continue to be transmitted in part to the cerebral cortex, by the centripetal conductors of the corona radiata, while the centrifugal stimuli of the cortical cells to the motor ganglia and to the centre of language are temporarily suspended, and, consequently, no movement can be performed, no word uttered. An analogous condition exists in nightmare, when the most painful impressions attack us in dreams, and we are unable to call for help or to perform any movement in order to escape from these terrors.

In apparent death in hysteria, the lowering of the circulatory and respiratory functions may be reduced to a barely perceptible minimum, showing the slight activity which the nutritive changes undergo in these conditions.

Vaso-motor disorders.—We shall first speak of *fever*, with its phenomena of general vascular spasm starting from the medullary centre (stage of chill), and the subsequent vascular dilatation (stage of warmth) with warmth and perspiration; the latter symptom is sometimes observed irrespective of the febrile attack. *Hysterical fever* usually occurs in con-

sequence of emotional excitement.   It often begins with a chill, followed
by heat and congestion; the patients experience a sensation of heat in
the head and face; they sometimes become delirious as soon as they close
the eyes; they have convulsions and tremor, the tongue is dry, the appetite is lost.   But, as I have observed in several cases, the temperature in
the axilla does not rise above 37.4°–37.6° C., despite a pulse of 100 to 120,
while the temperature of the skin (measured upon the face, neck, and
thorax) may reach 35.20–36.4°C.   This pseudo-febrile condition may continue several days (even several weeks, according to Briquet), and, when it
disappears, characteristic paralyses of sensation and motion remain.
Briquet collected twenty cases of this kind.

The *flashes of heat*, and *the alternations of heat and cold*, so often
observed in hysteria, are almost always accompanied by redness or pallor
of the skin, and form part of the disorders of vaso-motor innervation.

Salivation in hysteria is a vascular secretory neurosis, due to irritation
of a centre in the medulla oblongata, according to the recent experiments
of Gruetzner (Pflüger's Arch., VII. Bd., 1873).   According to this
author, salivation follows irritation of the central origin of ·the chorda
tympani and sympathetic fibres.   It is a rare symptom in hysteria (if we
exclude those cases in which the saliva is expectorated on account of the
impossibility of deglutition).   In one of these cases, according to Mitscher-
lich's analysis, the saliva presented an acid reaction, a light specific
gravity, and a marked diminution of its characteristic elements.

We observe in hysteria (most frequently after convulsions) *an abundant emission of very pale, clear urine, deficient in salts;* this phenomenon
is caused by an irritation transmitted, by reflex means, from the sensory
nerves to the vaso-motor centres of the kidneys in the medulla oblongata
(the stimulus then passing through the cord, the communicating branches, the plexuses of the sympathetic and the renal plexuses).   Finally, the
joint affections described by Brodie (hyperæsthesia with enlargement and
œdema) must also be referred to vaso-motor hyperæmia of the articulations.

Pathological Anatomy.

The opinion, transmitted to us from the ancients, that the genital organs must be considered as the only source of hysteria in the female, has
caused physicians, even until very recent times, to devote all their attention to the examination of the sexual apparatus, in hysteria, and to pro-
fess themselves satisfied if they were able to discover in the cadaver any
change whatever in the uterus or its annexes.

While Scanzoni found 1,328 cases of hysteria among 1,724 women affected with diseases of the genital organs, this proportion falls to an insignificant figure in Briquet's
tables.   According to a recent publication by Bernutz (Gaz. des Hôpit., Fev., 1874),
among 32 cases of hysteria, no abnormality was found in the genital organs in 19
cases.   The genital organs have been found perfectly healthy in a large number of
autopsies upon women who have undeniably been hysterical.   Grisolle (Gaz. des Hôpit.,
18, 1853) and Castiaux (eod. loc.. 1873) have seen *congenital absence of the vagina and*
uterus in two undoubted cases of hysteria.

The *central nervous system* has been scarcely examined in autopsies of
hysterical patients, and when it has been (as in Ollivier's, Brodie's, and
Briquet's cases) the observers have been satisfied with naked-eye examinations; the negative results thus obtained have led them to believe that

there was no material change in the nervous centres. Lancisi observed an interesting fact, which has hitherto escaped the attention of other authors (in Morgagni, Adversaria Anat., I., p. 18): "Pluries animadvertimur in hystericis, quæ post diros convulsivos motus tonica brachii vel cruris convulsione dui venatæ tandem diem suum obierunt, *ganglia partibus affectis respondentia ampliora reddi, hydatidibusque obsessa.*"

A lesion may be found upon careful examination, as is shown by the following case reported by Charcot (Gaz. Hebdom., N° 7, 1865). In a woman, who had suffered since the age of fourteen years from hysterical convulsions, followed by motor disturbances, permanent contracture of all the limbs and of the muscles of the trunk developed during the last two years of life ; intelligence remained intact, and the patient died from an intercurrent affection. The autopsy revealed the presence of *sclerosis of the lateral columns,* extending from the medulla oblongata to the lumbar enlargement, with partial atrophy of the anterior roots.

Etiology.

If we examine the psychical peculiarities of women, in whom the passions and feelings play such a variable part, we will find that the germs of hysteria exist in the majority of females, but that the soil is essentially different in different individuals. These variations depend upon the individual *predisposition.* The predisposition to hysteria is very frequently hereditary (according to Briquet's statistics, hysterical mothers transmit the disease to their daughters in half the cases). Other nervous diseases or insanity in the parents, especially in the mother, may lead to the transmission of analogous conditions to the children and of hysteria in the daughters. *Education* plays a considerable rôle in the development of the disease. The prolonged contact of children with older persons will develop in them a precocious intelligence and a want of simplicity; the intellectual faculties of young girls are artificially stimulated at the expense of their physical powers; their sensibility becomes excessively developed, and their imagination becomes excited by theatrical performances, novels, and balls. Feelings are thus stimulated in women which are often seriously at variance with the stern necessities of life. All these conditions which are so often found united, especially in large cities, and which are frequently accompanied by anæmia and chlorosis, diminish the energy of the nervous system at an early period of life, stimulate the brain to an excessive degree, and exaggerate the reflex excitability of the spinal cord.

A very large proportion of cases of hysteria develop at the age of puberty. The first symptoms, in more than half the cases collected in Briquet's statistics, were manifested between the age of twelve and twenty years; one-third of the cases developed from the fifteenth to the twentieth years. Menstruation itself does not favor the appearance of hysterical phenomena, but rather the disorders of menstruation (suspension, scanty or abundant flux, combination with painful symptoms). Childhood also furnishes, according to Briquet, a large contingent to the number of cases of hysteria. Briquet has observed its occurrence during this period in one-tenth of all his cases. Although this statement appears to me to be exaggerated, since we are rarely justified in considering as hysterical the convulsive seizures occurring during childhood, I can nevertheless state, from personal experience, that well-marked attacks of hysteria may de-

velop in children of both sexes, varying from ten to twelve years of age.
(I shall hereafter report a very clear case of this character, occurring in
a boy ten years of age.)   The disease rarely occurs after the age of
forty, but a few examples have been observed between the ages of fifty
and sixty years.

Hysteria occurs in the extremes of northern and southern climates (according to
the statements of physicians in different countries).   It is very frequent in the Orient,
in which the women begin to menstruate at the age of ten years, and are engaged in
no serious pursuits, their entire aim in life consisting in the gratification of the ca-
prices of their master.   The precocity of the women, especially among the Polish
Jewesses, and the " mariages de convenance " which are so numerous among them,
are powerful causes of hysteria, as is especially well recognized by Vienna physicians.
In large cities, in which worldly excitement and the social conditions produce such
violent impressions upon the psychical life of women, hysteria finds a fertile field,
especially among the well-to-do classes.   It is much less frequent in the country ;
here hard labor, privations, and ill-treatment are the chief factors which predispose
certain constitutions to the development of hysteria.   Women who possess an impressionable and susceptible disposition are most exposed to hysterical affections,
although we are able to recognize no appreciable influence in the temperament,
constitution, or various conditions of nutrition.   The character of the occupation
pursued is an important element ; sedentary pursuits, prolonged labor within doors,
the absence of sufficiently varied and invigorating muscular exercise, deprivation of
fresh air and insufficient nourishment, are the unfavorable factors which may implant
the germs of hysteria, by interfering with hematopoiesis and with the energy of the
nervous system.   Religious exaltation and excessive devotion also favor the development of hysterical phenomena, and we have previously alluded to the fact that the
" convulsionnaires," the " possessed," and the epidemics of chorea, which occurred in
the last century, consisted in a great measure of hysterical paroxysms.

The female sex furnishes by far the larger proportion of cases of
hysteria.   Those who maintained the Hippocratic opinion, that the sole
source of hysteria lies in the uterus and its annexes, have denied the
existence of the disease in the male sex.   Even physicians of the present
day, such as Landouzy, Monneret, Louyer-Villermay, share this incredu-
lity.   But we are unable to accept this narrow view, contradicted as it is
by certain facts which it is unable to explain.   We must admit that
moral causes, which very often lead to hysteria in the female, as we shall
see further on, may also produce the same disease in delicately constituted
members of the male sex.

Although hysteria does not belong exclusively to the female sex,
nevertheless experience teaches us that the proportion of cases occurring
in men is very small when compared with the great frequency of the
disease in women.   Sydenham, with his habitual clearsightedness, did not
fail to remark that one-half of the chronic affections occurring in females
are due to hysteria.   Briquet, after numerous observations, states that
one-quarter of all females are affected with hysteria, and that one-half
present some signs of hysteria, or an excessive impressionability which
differs very little from it.   Among one thousand cases of hysteria, either
personal or taken from other authors, Briquet cites fifty examples which
occurred in males.   The predisposition of males to hysteria is therefore
one-twentieth of that of females.

The symptomatology of hysteria in man presents the same characteristics as ordinary hysteria.   Briquet reports, in addition to the cases
observed by other authors, seven personal observations of hysteria in
males, in which the following characteristic symptoms were noted: hyperæsthesia, anæsthesia, and analgesia, under the forms with which we
have previously been acquainted; various painful phenomena, spasmodic

seizures, convulsive attacks, with partial or complete loss of consciousness; ecstasy, momentary suspension of the functions of special sehse, variable degrees of paralysis of the extremities, with diminution or loss of electro-cutancous and electro-muscular sensibility and preservation of electro-muscular contractility. Why apply the term hypochondria to such cases which are so evidently hysterical in their nature, and why not embrace identical conditions under the same category ?

I had under observation a boy, eighteen years of age, pale and nervous, whose mother had had intermittent hysterical paroxysms, and who suffered, after a violent emotion, from cephalalgia, vomiting, tremor, with temporary muscular contractions and pains in the limbs, and from a rapidly developing feeling of fatigue while walking. Upon examination, I found anæsthesia and analgesia in the anterior portion of the lower limbs, occupying, anteriorly, the abdominal region as far as the border of the ribs, and, posteriorly, the gluteal region as far as the third lumbar vertebræ. The trunk, upper limbs, and face were perfectly sensitive above this limit of the anæsthesia. The affection disappeared in about two weeks, after the employment of cool baths and affusions to the vertebral column. Guibout has lately published a similar case.

Hysteria is also observed in young girls during the first ten years of life, and examples have been reported by the older authors (Willis, Hoffmann, Lepois, etc.). Briquet has observed hysteria in eighty-seven children, from five to twelve years of age, under the form of convulsive attacks, of other well-marked spasmodic seizures, or of disorders of sensation and motion. In almost all the cases there was a history of hysterical antecedents in the mother, of hereditary nervous disease, or of bad treatment, fright or grief ; irritation of the genital apparatus very rarely coexisted. In one family (Obs. 33), in which the father, two brothers, and six sisters suffered from well-marked hysterical paroxysms, the seventh sister, who was nine years of age, had her first attack after having been accidentally present during an hysterical seizure in one of her sisters. Her attacks became even more violent *after marriage*, and had not even disappeared in her forty-sixth year.

Independently of the hysteria of young girls, it also occurs in young boys, though this is a very rare occurrence; Briquet has not observed a single case. I have seen two cases of hysteria in boys. The first occurred in a boy, twelve years of age, a spoiled child, whose mother suffered from nervous headache and gastralgia, and whose sister was affected with nervous deafness. Whenever the child became angry he was seized with spasms throughout the entire body and with hiccough. After having left his home and lived for a long time in Switzerland, he was completely cured at the end of two years. The second observation, which is a more remarkable one, occurred in a boy ten years of age ; the following were the most striking symptoms :

The child was pale, but active ; the mother was nervous. Since the age of seven years the patient had suffered from spasm of the extensors in the lower limbs, which sometimes disappeared spontaneously, and, on one occasion, after an agreeable surprise. He then complained of dorsal pains, attacks of dyspnœa, and, at the age of ten years, after having been severely punished by his tutor, he suffered from aphonia and eructations.

Laryngoscopic examination showed paralysis of the transverse muscle, and abrupt movements of the œsophagus, which was drawn upwards and dilated. Faradization caused the reappearance of the voice, but produced intense reflex movements. Nervine remedies, such as castoreum, quinine, and moist frictions, were useless. Two weeks later, convulsive laughter and general convulsions, with loss of consciousness, supervened. In the intervals during these attacks he was affected, when contradicted, with true ecstasy, during which he played scales and waltzes very correctly upon the piano. If the father began to sing suddenly, the child was seized with convulsions. His responses, at such times, were always correct; but, after these attacks, he remembered nothing which had transpired, and stated that he had been asleep. The skin was hyperæsthetic over a large surface; paraplegia finally developed, which yielded in a few days to quinine (0.5 daily); the voice was restored, but the convulsive attacks only disappeared at the end of three months.

In the chapter upon catalepsy, I shall mention a third case of hysteria in a boy, with the results of the autopsy. After the consideration of the causes which tend indirectly to produce hysteria, we will discuss those pathogenic conditions which lead more directly to the development of hysterical affections. The principal causes included in this category are psychical affections and irritations arising in the genital apparatus.

Among the *psychical influences,* those of a depressing nature have the most marked effect upon the development of hysteria. They include anxiety, fear, disappointed love, regret, care, and jealousy. The effect of these causes upon the naturally impressionable brain of certain females, and the cessation of the menses which often goes hand in hand with them, especially give rise to the convulsive forms of hysteria. Among moral causes we may also mention ill treatment, which may give rise to hysteria in women, young girls, and even in boys (an example of which has been reported above).

Another fruitful source, and one which was, for a long time, considered the only cause of hysteria, consists of irritations starting from the *genital apparatus.* These irritations may be local or general. As we have stated above, *local diseases* of the genital organs (displacements tumors, hypertrophy, ulcerations of the uterus, affections of the ovaries or vagina, leucorrhœa, etc.), may give rise to hysteria.

The cure of the local disorder often causes disappearance of the hysterical manifestations. But in a large number of cases, the origin of the hysteria can be traced to a *perversion of the sexual functions.* Thus, onanism in young boys and girls, excessive continence or sexual indulgence in the female, the prolonged stimulation of sexual desires by lewd plays or books, are very frequently the cause of the development of hysteria. In this regard I have also observed another pathogenic condition, which I have never seen referred to, viz. : *pollutions in females.*

I had under my care a young hysterical female who performed peculiar suction movements during her paroxysms, during sleep and in a condition of semi-consciousness. One day, as her consciousness was returning, I discovered a mucous fluid upon the external genitals, although the genital organs were normal. After having often observed a similar occurrence, I decided to warn the patient that she was concealing secrets from me which would undoubtedly result to her detriment. She then confessed that she secretly read light novels at night, that she then had erotic dreams, and, that upon waking, she felt exhausted and worn out. The hysterical paroxysms developed after this condition of excitement had lasted several months. A trip to the country and hydrotherapeutic measures caused the disappearance of the pollutions, and the hysterical seizures yielded soon afterwards. In another case, a patient, during profound sleep, saw her dead mother appear before her, and begged her pardon for concealing the fact that she had a mucous discharge from the genitals after voluptuous dreams, blaming the obscene books, loaned by a friend, as the cause of the discharge and of the hysterical paroxysms. This flux, caused by erotic excitement of the nervous system is produced by the glands of Bartholin and by the acinous glands surrounding the meatus urinarius.

Nature of Hysteria.

With the exception of Charcot's case, the examination of the nervous system in hysteria (always undertaken without the aid of the microscope) has merely given negative results. From this quarter, therefore, we can receive no aid in forming a conception of the nature of this neurosis. Since pathological anatomy sheds no light upon the question, we are forced, as far as possible, to seek its solution by other means, without resting upon the quicksands of theory. We will endeavor to show that the data at our command are sufficient to enable us to form a correct idea concerning the central modifications which preside over hysteria.

In tracing the clinical history of this malady, we have studied, in detail, hysterical anæsthesia as one of the most characteristic sensory disturbances. More or less marked paralysis of sensation has been observed by Briquet in sixty per cent. of his cases, and by Szokalsky in all his patients. If we also take into consideration the cases of initial hyperæsthesia which afterwards pass into anæsthesia, the proportion will become even greater.

If we differentiate anæsthesia and analgesia, we will find (and, in this respect, I concur entirely in Beau's opinion) that many hysterical patients have lost their sensibility to pain (over a large part of the body), but that tactile sensibility is often preserved. We are thus brought face to face with a condition, which Schiff first produced experimentally, and which we have observed in traumatic lesions of a lateral half of the cord, and in two cases (reported above in detail) of compression myelitis after vertebral caries, a condition which we attributed to changes in the nerve-cells of the gray horns demonstrated by the microscope.

Another important fact which is brought into prominence in hysteria is that the anæsthesia and analgesia conform, in their distribution, to the laws established by Voigt with regard to the distribution of the cutaneous nerves, and we have observed the same phenomenon in the spinal paralyses which we have previously discussed. The sensory nerves form, at the periphery, a sort of mosaic, corresponding to an analogous arrangement in the spinal cord, although the design is much more complicated here on account of the difference in the amount of space. According to the degree of change in this central distribution, and in conformity with the law of excentric sensations, the terminal organ will give rise, on its part, to corresponding functional disorders of varying intensity and extent.

The hypothesis of an alteration in the peripheral nerves (admitted by Valentiner) is contradicted by the fact that a lesion of the nerve-roots, explanatory of the phenomena of local anæsthesia, has never been demonstrated in hysteria.

This hypothesis is still further combated by observations of general anæsthesia of sudden origin, as after fright, since in these cases we cannot admit that the transmission of nerve force has been suddenly interrupted in all the nerve-roots and nerves. Finally, the theory of a peripheral affection will not explain those multiple forms which embrace both motor and sensory disturbances, or those in which motion or sensation is affected separately ; or why, at other times, the sensibility to pain or temperature, or the muscular sense alone, disappears.

It is not alone by way of exclusion that we locate the lesion of hysteria in the centres (and often, indeed, in the spinal centre); the analyses of the cases, which we have reported under the head of symptomatology, will lead us to the same conclusion. In fact, if we regard the cord as the site of origin of hysterical phenomena, we can readily explain how the morbid increase of the reflex sensibility of the gray substance produces the general increase of reflex excitability which is so general in hysteria. We can thus comprehend how temporary obstructions in the conducting functions of the gray substance of the cord will be followed by various sensory disturbances; how a lesion of the central mosaic will be accompanied by disorders which are exactly limited to the projections which these central parts send to the periphery; how the amputation performed by Mayo, in a case of intense hyperæsthesia of the knee, was unsuccessful, since the hyperæsthesia was merely the peripheral expression of a condition of irritability in the cord.

It is evident, from the preceding remarks, that the peripheral disorders in hysteria merely represent, so to speak, an exact reproduction of the central changes, and that the latter are situated, in great part, in the spinal cord.

This rational interpretation of the symptoms is also strengthened by other observations. Electrical exploration teaches us that, in extended anæsthesia of the limbs, strong galvanic or faradic currents, passing from the dorsal spine to the plexuses or nerve-trunks, readily produce muscular contractions, but no sensation; and that, when improvement begins, the transmission of sensibility is restored to the nerves *from the centre to the periphery.* I have shown, by a very characteristic example (*vide* symptomatology), the important part which the vaso-motor centres assume in anæsthesia and hyperæsthesia, in which we can observe alternations of spasm and dilatation of the vessels, evidenced by local modifications of circulation and temperature. The periodical and frequent returns of the vascular spasm render the consequences of this spasmodic anæmia more persistent. We can convince ourselves that there is no profound material alteration in the sensory conductors, if we remember that even anæsthesia of long standing sometimes disappears with surprising rapidity. *We must, therefore, attribute a large part of the symptoms of hysteria to a congenital or acquired want of resistance on the part of the vaso-motor nervous system.*

Motor hysterical disorders are also due, in the beginning, to a simple functional hyperæmia; but, in certain forms, the chronic hyperæmia may lead to an inflammatory process, which may terminate (as in Charcot's case) in secondary changes in the columns of the cord and in the nerve-roots.

The brain is also involved in hysteria. This is chiefly due to•violent psychical stimuli, which, originating in the cerebral hemispheres, are transmitted, according to Budge, to the vaso-motor conductors, excite their centre by reflex action, and produce alternations of flushing and pallor, and unilateral hyperæsthesia or anæsthesia, and stimulate the cardiac, abdominal, and secretory nerves. The pallor, weakness of the pulse, and loss of consciousness which, together with convulsive symptoms, are observed in certain cases of hysteria, must be attributed to *reflex spasm of the cerebral arteries and to the consequent cerebral anæmia.*

It is evident that obstacles are also present *in the peripheral conductors,* since, side by side with the increase of the electrical excitability in the central portion of the nerves, the peripheral ramifications may be found insensible to the current. Another phenomenon appears to point towards the same conclusion. When improvement begins, the passage of a labile galvanic current from the cord to the plexus, or from the latter to the nerves, produces cutaneous sensibility and conscious movements; while currents acting solely upon the peripheral nerves or muscles pass unnoticed, until the peripheral ramifications have finally recovered their conductibility.

Diagnosis.

Hysteria, in all its varied aspects, is usually recognized without any difficulty. A few isolated symptoms of the disease will suffice to reveal its nature to the practised eye. Certain signs are almost always present, even in the intervals between the paroxysms, which disclose the latent forms of hysteria. These consist of an abnormal impressionability, dating from childhood, and the frequent occurrence of a condition of mental excitement; of sensations of compression or tension in the head, larynx, or epigastrium, and restlessness of the limbs after vexation; of vague neuralgias, of pains and a sensation of compression, especially referred, according to Briquet, to the epigastrium, to the false ribs, particularly on the left side (pleuralgia), and to the vertebral column; often of ovaralgia; of various hyperæsthesias, analgesia persisting after emotions or hysterical paroxysms, and its combination with anæsthesia. Intermittent spasms, partial paralyses, and contractures, and the peculiar results of electrical exploration in these cases, furnish more positive results.

It is only in relatively rare instances that hysterical paroxysms will be confounded with other spasmodic affections possessing analogous symptoms. In almost all cases we will be able to obtain sufficient data to form a positive diagnosis, if we take into consideration the pathogenic factors and the *ensemble* of the pathognomonic symptoms. Hystero-epilepsy, beginning with loss of consciousness, may be mistaken for epilepsy proper, eclampsia, tetanus, or trismus. *True epilepsy* is distinguished by the frequency of nocturnal attacks, the symmetrical character of the convulsions, their short duration, the cry which is almost always heard only at the beginning of the attack, and by the absence of secondary disorders of motion and sensation. Hystero-epileptiform seizures occur with the greatest frequency during the day; they begin with spasmodic phenomena, and are accompanied by repeated cries; the attacks are divided into several periods, terminate by hiccough, weeping, and a characteristic excretion of urine, and are often followed by motor and sensory disturbances. In hystero-epilepsy, energetic pressure over the ovary may modify the attack, and sometimes even terminate it, a phenomenon which is never observed in epilepsy (Charcot). Furthermore, *a succession of epileptic fits (status epilepticus) gives rise*, according to Bourneville, *to a considerable elevation of temperature* (as high as 41° C.), accompanied either by delirium or apoplectiform coma, and constituting a grave, if not absolutely unfavorable, prognostic sign. This elevation of temperature, during similar conditions, is also observed in the course of general paralysis of the insane, of disseminated sclerosis, and of cerebral hemorrhages or tumors. *On the other hand, even when the hystero-epileptiform attacks follow one another with unusual frequency, the temperature undergoes no appreciable modification*, and the general condition remains satisfactory. Wunderlich (Arch. der Heilk., 5. Bd.) refers to a patient who had hysterical attacks of this character for eight weeks, with an insignificant rise of temperature, and who, two days before death, fell into a condition of collapse, with a temperature of 43° C. The autopsy revealed hyperæmia of the brain and medulla oblongata and pulmonary œdema. In order to distinguish *puerperal eclampsia* from hysterical paroxysms of pregnant females, we must pay attention to the previous history, to the persistence of attacks attended with complete loss of consciousness, and to the presence of albumen and casts in the urine. It is believed that even the most violent hysterical paroxysms do not compromise the life of the fœtus. *Trismus* and *tetanus* are characterized by the fact that traumatism plays a part in the etiology, by the manner of the extension of the convulsions, and by their relaxation and termination.

Hypochondria is recognized by its much greater frequency in man, its rarity before the thirtieth year, the absence of convulsions, the constant preoccupation of the patient with his own person, the frequency of hallucinations and illusions, and its almost constant termination in insanity.

A condition which very much resembles hysteria, and presents considerable analogies with it, is the abnormal excitability known as "nervosisme," or spinal irritation. The factors in the differential diagnosis have been referred to in the chapter on Neuroses of the Spinal Cord. Hysterical paralyses are sometimes a source of error in diagnosis. *Hysterical hemiplegia*, occurring after intense excitement, and accompanied by loss of consciousness, may be mistaken for cerebral hemiplegia. We have discussed the question of differential diagnosis under Cerebral Apoplexy (Vol. I., p. 53). We have also pointed out the distinction between *hysterical paraplegia* and spinal paraplegia, in discussing the latter affection.

Prognosis.

Despite its chronic course, hysteria very rarely endangers life. Death may occur from suffocation during an attack of spasm of the glottis, from cerebral hemorrhage, from syncope, from exhaustion, or from an intercurrent disease in debilitated patients. The most unfavorable prognosis, as regards recovery, pertains to hereditary hysteria, or to constitutional hysteria acquired during the period of development under the influence of injurious conditions. Nevertheless, puberty or marriage may give a favorable turn to these forms, and may render the treatment more efficacious. Hysteria, induced by anæmia, chlorosis, chronic hemorrhages, or leucorrhœa, may be cured by improving the quality of the blood and increasing the vigor of the nervous system. As a rule, hysteria is more grave, according to Briquet, when it begins during youth than if it appears between the twenty-fifth and thirtieth years of life. Those forms which attack sanguine subjects, who possess a certain embonpoint, and those which begin with convulsive seizures, as is especially observed in the well-to-do classes, are more severe and rebellious than the hysteria which develops slowly in weak patients and under the influence of moral causes. From all points of view, hysteria must be regarded as one of the most distressing diseases of females, since it may continue to the menopause or even beyond; and we should not bear the patients any ill-will if they complain greatly, and if they manifest less resignation than their physicians, who are apt to adopt the theory of affectation or simulation.

The *different symptoms of hysteria* do not, by any means, furnish the same prognosis. As a rule, the disorders of sensation are less obstinate than those of motion.

Cutaneous *hyperæsthesia*, however painful it may be, is never followed by serious consequences ; it disappears spontaneously or under appropriate treatment. At the beginning of the affection it is often the forerunner of anæsthesia. If, on the other hand, well-marked and widespread anæsthesia exists, the appearance of hyperæsthesia heralds the beginning of improvement in the conducting power of the centrifugal paths. The most rebellious and annoying form of hyperæsthesia is that occurring in the articulations. *Anæsthesia* yields so much the more readily, the less complete and widespread it is. Slight anæsthesia, following emotional excitement, disappears spontaneously; but that which results from prolonged moral causes (grief, anxiety) is less amenable to treatment. A more severe form of anæsthesia, viz., that which accompanies hysterical paralysis, disappears when recovery begins, and then (as we have stated above) gives place to hyperæsthesia, which is almost always the forerunner of the restoration of motor power. Anæsthesia of the organs of special sense rarely continues for any length of time. *Hysterical neuralgias*, due to persistent moral causes, are as obstinate as they are painful. They present great changeableness, and are often replaced by other symptoms of sudden origin.

Among the motor disturbances, the *convulsive phenomena* are so much the more grave and rebellious to treatment the more frequently they are accompanied and followed by loss of consciousness. Nevertheless, the prognosis is not unfavorable in young subjects who are placed under favorable conditions. The *contractures* which develop around a hyperæsthetic articulation, or which accompany the paralysis of a limb, may recover even after they have lasted a year or more. But when the contractures appear in several limbs, and even in the trunk, after repeated paroxysms, we can hardly look for a return to the normal condition. According to Tuerck, the *paralysis of the vocal cords* may disappear spontaneously; it is sometimes relieved by a violent emotion, in which the patient is forced to cry out, or during a convulsive seizure. With regard to *paralyses of the limbs*, the prognosis is more favorable in partial paralyses. Hemiplegias are much more grave and persistent; paraplegias are regarded as incurable. I have, nevertheless, seen three cases of recovery in young subjects who were otherwise in good health, and the observations of Althaus and others are in accord with my own. The beginning and progress of improvement are manifested by the transition from anæsthesia to hyperæsthesia of the skin and nerve-trunks to electrical irritation, by the return of cutaneous and electro-muscular sensibility from the centre to the periphery, by the return of the power of perception of passive movements, and by a gradual restoration of motion. *The psychical disorders of hysteria* usually follow the progress of the general improvement. Their transformation into incurable forms of insanity is happily a rare event.

Treatment.

The numerous difficulties which the treatment of hysteria presents, and the frequent annoyance of arriving at incomplete results, have long since induced physicians to adopt certain precautions, in order to prevent the appearance and development of hysteria as much as possible. Prophylaxis affords very excellent results, when the causes are properly proportioned to the effects to be obtained. The necessity of this method is especially marked when the predisposition to hysteria is hereditary and involves a certain amount of danger. Great care must then be bestowed upon the education of the child in its earliest years. It must be provided with a good nurse, and should be habituated to cool baths and lotions; it should be allowed to play in well-ventilated apartments. These constitute the first elements upon which its physical education must rest.

As soon as the child can walk and its mind begins to develop, we should endeavor, by rational means, to increase and stimulate its physical and moral energies. From a physical point of view, we should permit the child to run freely in the open air, should avoid burdening her with a useless amount of clothing, should send her out of doors even though the weather be somewhat unpleasant, and should accustom her to an animal diet and to regular meals. From a moral point of view, spare the child the recital of frightful tales or ghost stories, judiciously strengthen her natural tendencies and her desire to acquire a knowledge of surrounding objects. Accustom the children, from an early period, to a knowledge of the harmlessness of little animals (spiders, chafers, toads, etc.), stimulate their courage, cause them to associate often with strangers, and accustom them to entering dark rooms, etc.

An excellent method of inuring and strengthening children (a method which is too little known and even less applied) consists in *rubbing the entire body* (morning and evening) with a cloth dipped, at first, in tepid, and then gradually in cooler and cooler water. This practice, continued for several years, summer and winter, is very refreshing, and stimulates the appetite; after the rubbing, the child should be compelled to take active exercise. Feeble children may be subjected to this procedure as early as the fifth year. Swimming and gymnastics produce excellent results at a later period, Children must not be permitted, as so frequently happens, to dine or associate with adults, since these generally forget that children are present, while the latter pay attention to everything that transpires around them, and their precocity is thus stimulated.

At the period of puberty, when womanhood is first budding into full growth, the young girl must be the object of careful supervision and continued watchfulness. We must continue the habits of childhood as long as possible, and the sexual desires must not be stimulated in any manner. Bodily exercise; attention to household duties; carefully selected books, which do not excite the imagination, but point out the vicissitudes of life ; simple habits; intercourse with suitable acquaintances; abstinence from extravagance in the toilet; precautions against coquetry and vanity; frequent references to the charms of simplicity : these are the principal elements of the *moral education*, and should be the objects of our constant care during the developmental period. We are thus able to establish a happy equilibrium between the various faculties of the mind. Marriage should not be one of " convenance," but in accordance with the affections of the young woman; it is well known that a happy union often causes the disappearance of hysterical manifestations, while unhappy marriages frequently act as an exciting cause.

The first object of *medical treatment* is the cure of the hysteria, and, in those cases in which we are unable to obtain a mastery over it, we must endeavor to relieve the most annoying symptoms. We must, above all, pay especial attention to the individual modifications existing in each case. Every hysterical female should be subjected to a careful vaginal examination with the aid of the speculum, and appropriate treatment should be employed for the relief of such congestions, displacements, alterations of texture, and ulcerations of the uterus, as may be present. Mild ferruginous preparations are serviceable in the frequent cases of anæmia and chlorosis. Ferruginous mineral waters, slightly charged with carbonic acid, are well tolerated in small doses (from half a glass to a glass), especially when they are followed by moderate exercise in the open air. If gastric disorders (cardialgia, vomiting, anorexia) coexist, the use of iron may be preceded, for some time, by the administration of small doses of quinine, and of the bitter tonics. When the quality of the blood is defective, all attempts to restore the menstrual discharge are unavailing and needlessly irritating. Plethoric hysterical patients react less energetically to emmenagogues, although these sometimes fail, even here, to effect their object. Bleeding, which was formerly practised in these cases, is discarded at the present time. Briquet applied wet cups along the spinal column in robust patients suffering from convulsive seizures. I have derived benefit in similar cases, and in rachialgia, from the prolonged application to the back of an india-rubber bag filled with cold water. Good effects are also obtained in these patients from the whey-cure, and from the methodical employment of the grape-cure.

The so-called anti-hysterical remedies have lost much of their former reputation. They relieve the spasmodic seizures and act as sedatives, but they possess no specific curative action. Castoreum enjoys great favor among physicians; it may be prescribed as it is found in nature, or under the form of powders or pills. On account of its high price, we may also employ the tincture of castoreum, or the ethereal tincture of castoreum added to aqua laurocerasi, or other similar preparations (tinc-· ture of asafœtida or valerian), giving ten to fifteen drops upon a lump of sugar. Valerian is especially employed, in spasmodic attacks, under the form of tincture or extract, and most frequently as the infusion, either internally or in enemata. It is often given in combination with a metal, as valerianate of zinc, in increasing doses. Asafœtida is used in the form of tincture or ethereal solution, associated with other remedies to which we shall refer at a later period. In hysterical spasms and meteorism, it is given in an enema, in the form of a powder mixed with the yolk of an egg; it may be given to fastidious patients in pill form. (℞. Asafœtida, pulv. valerianæ rad., āā 5 grains; extr. anthemidis q. s., ut. f. pil. No. 50. Sig. Pil. 2–4 t. i. d.)

Ergot (under the form of the infusion, in enemata and vaginal injections), galbanum, lupulin, and camphor are rarely employed alone, but are associated with other substances, to relieve the irritative phenomena of hysteria. The same remark holds good with regard to the aromatic spirits of ammonia, aromatic infusions, and ethereal oils (the ethereal oil of chamomile (1–2 drops upon 3–4 grains of sugar, and divided into six parts) is recommended on account of its pleasant odor and taste).

Among the metallic antispasmodics, we may mention arsenic, which Romberg prescribed, under the form of Fowler's solution (3–4 drops t. i.d.),· in hysterical neuralgias and convulsive affections; it is also administered as the Asiatic pills, or as the arseniate of iron (4–5 milligrammes), wher· the patient is, at the same time, anæmic. We may also employ the vari ous compounds of zinc, nitrate of silver, and subnitrate of bismuth (em ployed by Gendrin, especially in gastralgia). The action of these metalli·· preparations is merely palliative and temporary.

Narcotics are well tolerated by the majority of hysterical patients, provided we begin with small and gradually increasing doses. Subcuta neous injections of morphine relieve the spasms, the hiccough, the hy peræsthesia, and the insomnia. Opium (either crude or in tincture, in enemata) is highly praised by Gendrin and Briquet. Gendrin begins with 0.50, and increases the dose to 0.60–0.75 per diem; the hysterical seizures improve as soon as symptoms of narcotism appear, and the dose should then be diminished until somnolence has disappeared. Recovery is said to occur under this plan of treatment in more than half the cases. I have rarely obtained a positive cure from the use of this drug, but rather a considerable improvement in the irritative phenomena. Belladonna, either alone or combined with quinine, is useful in convulsions and in disorders of deglutition; atropine renders good services in convulsive seizures and in obstinate hiccough. It must be given cautiously, especially when administered hypodermically. Inhalation of chloroform (stopping short of complete anæsthesia) is employed in severe and painful paroxysms; a few inhalations, given at intervals, will diminish the number and violence of the attacks. When the inhalations are too frequent and are carried too far, they are sometimes followed by extreme exhaustion.

Finally, we may mention two new substances which have been tried in hysteria, viz., curare and bromide of potassium. In two cases of epileptiform hysteria I obtained no benefit from the prolonged employment of subcutaneous injections of curare (0.05 of curare to 5–10 grains of water, with the addition of 3–4 drops of absolute alcohol; 5–10 milligrammes injected at one dose). In many cases I have seen large doses of bromide of potassium (3–5 grammes daily, in wafers) diminish the reflex excitability and erotic propensities, and relieve the insomnia; on the other hand, its effects were but slight in other patients.

Baths play an important part in the treatment of hysteria. The older physicians used them very largely, and Pomme (vide Traité des Affections vaporeuses, Lyon, 1767) allowed his patients to remain from six to ten hours in a tepid bath. Thermal waters are employed in spasmodic and neuralgic forms and in hysterical contractures. Among the watering-places indicated in such cases, we may mention Pfaeffers, Schlangenbad, Wildbad, Baden-Baden, Gastein, Teplitz, Tueffer, and Neuhaus, whose good effects are due not alone to the temperature of the waters, but also, in great part, to the change produced in the habits of life of the patient. In hysteria of anæmic origin, benefit is derived from the waters of Spa, Pyrmont, Franzensbad, Szilacs, Rohitsch, or from the indifferent cold waters of Voeslau and Tobelbad; in abdominal cramps, neuralgias, articular pains and contractures, slime-baths are indicated, and, in delicate patients, they should precede the use of ferruginous baths, or of small quantities of ferruginous mineral waters taken internally. In certain abdominal disorders (yellowish complexion, tenderness over the liver, digestive disorders) we may prescribe the waters of Kissingen, Marienbad, Carlsbad, Vichy, etc.

Sea-bathing possesses indisputable advantages in the treatment of hysteria; the calm waters of the Baltic are preferable for delicate, nervous constitutions, and the North Sea, with its stronger billows, may be recommended in torpid constitutions. On account of the excessive sensibility of the majority of hysterical patients, hydrotherapeutics should be employed, at the onset, in its mildest forms. The action of cold is as injurious as the exciting effect of warm baths.

We may commence by washing the entire body in a half-bath, at a temperature of 24°–22° C., and gradually adding colder water. At a later period we may employ frictions with a cloth dipped in water at 18°–16° C., and followed by a half-bath at 24°–18° C., with affusions to the vertebral column. In spasmodic and neuralgic attacks, the wet pack (continued until the return of warmth to the body) and the half-bath are useful; in abdominal pains and sexual erethism, we prefer sitz-baths, followed by moist frictions; in addition, we may advise the patient to wear a moist waistband, renewed several times a day, or the caoutchouc bag to which we have previously referred, and may also prescribe small, but frequently repeated, enemata of cold water. Hydrotherapeutic treatment, continued perseveringly for a long time, diminishes the extreme impressionability of hysterical patients, strengthens them, and increases their power of resistance to irritating influences, stimulates the organic functions, combats the anæmia, calms the abnormal excitability of the peripheral nervous system, and, by diminishing the morbid increase of reflex power, relieves the violence of the spasmodic symptoms. Even chronic forms, which are combined with severe paroxysms of convulsions, are susceptible of recovery under this plan of treatment.

With regard to the electrical treatment of various hysterical phenomena, we may derive benefit from faradization in hyperæsthesia by employing strong secondary and progressively increasing currents (Frommhold), one of the previously moistened conductors being applied to the vertebral column, and the other electrode (which is made very broad) being passed up and down over the affected portions. If the hyperæsthesia is very intense, a galvanic current should be passed several times through the nerve plexuses or trunks during chloroform anæsthesia (Benedikt), or after a subcutaneous injection of morphine, as I have done with good results. In neuralgias we may pass the uninterrupted constant current through the vertebral column, and from thence to the affected nerves.

Anæsthesia may be combated in the same manner as the hyperæsthesia, by passing the electrical brush over the anæsthetic parts, or by applying the negative pole of a strong galvanic battery until the appearance of sensibility combined with redness of the skin. If the anæsthesia extends to the deeper parts, it is best to moisten the skin before applying the electrical brush; when the sensibility increases, we may diminish the force of the current. In the treatment of paralysis, we must resort to faradization of the muscles, or alternate this measure with galvanization of the nerve-trunks, starting from the nerve-roots and plexuses.

Contractures are treated, like paralyses, with mixed currents. Aphonia may be cured by faradization through the skin, or by intra-laryngeal faradization, by means of a conductor in the form of a catheter. In spasms of deglutition, benefit is derived from galvanization of the hypoglossal nerves; in hiccough, from galvanization or faradization of the phrenic nerves; in meteorism, from faradization of the epigastric and abdominal regions.

In conclusion, we will make a few remarks upon the moral treatment of hysteria. In certain cases we may obtain good effects by appealing to the volition of the patients; but at other times, in weak and long-suffering individuals, it will be as useless to expect from them the exercise of self-control and of muscular power, before the general condition has improved, as it is to look for the production of harmony in a poorly-constructed instrument.

CLASS V.

SPASMODIC CEREBRAL AND SPINAL NEUROSES.

CHAPTER XXVIII.

CATALEPSY.

WE shall now pass to the study of the spasmodic affections which are due to irritation of the brain or cord, and shall first take up the consideration of catalepsy, one of the most interesting of these neuroses.

Catalepsy is an intermittent neurosis, characterized by a complete or partial abolition of consciousness and sensibility, with abolition of voluntary motion, and persistence of the position in which the limbs are found at the commencement of the attack, or of the attitudes in which they are artificially placed, until they finally yield to the action of the force of gravity. Catalepsy is not, properly speaking, an independent disease, but merely one symptom of various affections of the nervous system. But the peculiar character of its manifestations has induced the majority of authors to treat of it as a distinct morbid entity.

Our knowledge of the anatomical lesions in catalepsy is extremely imperfect, since a fatal termination is exceedingly rare. In two cases inflammatory exudations or alterations were found in certain central organs. We shall refer to them in detail in the discussion upon the nature of catalepsy.

The first case was published by Schwartz (Rigaer Beitr. zur Heilk., 1857, Bd. IV., p. 118), and occurred in a boy, seven years of age, who was seized with persistent gastric pains after the receipt of an injury. These were superseded, upon the eighteenth day of the disease, by choreiform phenomena, attended with disorders of sight and abolition of speech. These symptoms ceased at the end of six weeks, and were followed by gastralgia, constriction of the pharynx, and asthmatic symptoms; this condition had terminated at the end of the seventh week, and a *cataleptic and tetanic condition* (with wax-like mobility) was then observed. Despite the use of narcotics, induced electrical currents, and baths, the alternations of spasm and relaxation continued for more than two years, and the patient finally died of anæmia and cachexia. The autopsy revealed an abundant collection of serum in the cavity of the arachnoid, *softening of the optic thalami and corpora striata*, especially on the left side, and of the optic nerves as far as the chiasm; upon the posterior surface of the cord was found *a reddish brown, gelatinous substance, covering the dura mater, adherent in places, and extending from the cervical to the lumbar region.* The cord appeared normal; unfortunately, no microscopical examination was made.

The second case, published by Meissner (Arch. d. Heilk., 1860, p. 512), occurred in a shoemaker, æt. forty-seven years, who, without known cause, had been affected, for six years, with catalepsy. During the last three years he suffered from epileptiform spasms upon the right half of the body, with paralysis of these parts in the intervals of the attacks; the patient died with symptoms of mania and epilepsy. At the autopsy *an epithelioma was found in the anterior cerebral fossa, above the ethmoid, and starting from the dura mater; the anterior third of the right hemisphere, extending to the cortex, was markedly softened, together with the external portion of the right corpus striatum.*

Symptomatology.

Catalepsy rarely begins suddenly, and usually occurs in the form of paroxysms, after prodromata, consisting of nervous excitement, insomnia, headache, intellectual malaise, illusions of the senses, hiccough, or slight convulsions.   When the attack occurs, the muscular system, usually in its entirety, rarely involving merely certain limbs, is affected with a sudden stiffness.   The patients remain, as if petrified by the head of Medusa, in the position which they last assumed, the features immovable, the eyes having a wild expression and directed forwards and upwards, the eyelids sometimes closed.   In the beginning, the muscles are tense, and resist passive motion; after a certain period this tension and resistance disappear, and give place to the peculiar condition known as *flexibilitas cerea* (*waxen flexibility*).   A slight impulse to the upper limbs, the hands, or fingers then suffices to fix the large or small joint in the most abnormal attitudes for several minutes; on account of the weight of the lower limbs, a greater effort is required to produce this phenomenon in them.

According to my experience, the patients do not fall when placed upright, but preserve the vertical position, and can even, with a little support, remain leaning forwards.   The muscles of organic life are less influenced by catalepsy.   Morsels, introduced far back in the pharynx, are sometimes swallowed without difficulty; but the peristaltic movements, as well as micturition and defecation, are performed slowly; the respiratory and cardiac movements are notably weakened, sometimes scarcely appreciable, and the pupils react little to light.   The *disorders of sensation* present certain interesting peculiarities.   Anæsthesia and analgesia occur in severe cases, and the patients have no consciousness of what has occurred during the attack.   At other times sensibility is not abolished, but there is absence of reflex movement, even upon irritation of the mucous membranes; sometimes the sole response consists in the closure of the eyelids upon touching the conjunctiva or cornea.

In a case, reported by Jones, the patient made an outcry when he received a strong current of electricity, and afterwards retained the memory of this disagreeable sensation.   Exceptionally (as in Puel's case, Arch. Gén., 1857) hyperæsthesia occurs during the paroxysm; the slightest touch or noise will then cause the patients to grind the teeth or give vent to cries.   In an interesting observation, reported by Skoda (Zeitschrift der k. k. Ges. d. Aerzte, 1852. p. 504), general sensibility was abolished, but a lighted taper, rotated rapidly before the eyes, gave rise to tremor of the lids, and strong odors induced slight movements, redness of the cheeks, lachrymation, acceleration of the pulse, and elevation of the temperature.   When the attack of catalepsy ceased, the patient did not immediately recover the power of speech, but was compelled, for some time, to express himself by gestures or by writing.   It is to be remarked, in addition, that the entire surface of the body was often cold, and that this condition of algidity lasted, on one occasion, forty-eight hours.

The anæsthesia and analgesia, as well as the *flexibilitas cerea* (when the position of the limbs is changed without the knowledge of the patient), may even persist irrespective of the attack, although voluntary movements are performed with perfect freedom in these cases.

The *loss of consciousness* may be complete during the paroxysms; in other cases, cerebral activity is not completely suspended, and the patients retain an indistinct idea of what is transpiring around them; some of them have a perfect recollection of surrounding circumstances.

I have examined two patients with regard to the electrical reactions during cataleptic paroxysms ; in one of these cases the reactions to both currents were normal ; in the other there was manifest increase of electro-muscular contractility and of the galvanic excitability of the plexuses and nerve-trunks. The ," waxen flexibility " was very well marked in the latter case, *but the attitude produced by the faradic stimulation of the extensors and flexors of the arms, or by the galvanization of the corresponding nerves, disappeared when the application of electricity ceased, and the hand resumed its previous position.* In the beginning we were able, by means of galvanization of the phrenics, to stop the hiccough which formed the precursor of the attack, and to prevent the paroxysm. At a later period the affection increased in intensity, and electricity lost its influence.

The duration of the periodical attacks of catalepsy is as variable as their frequency and intensity. It sometimes terminates after a few minutes, but in other cases only after several hours or days. In rare instances the disease (as in Skoda's case) is prolonged for months with short interruptions. The paroxysms generally occur without any regularity, and, during the intervals, the patients are either in good health or present various symptoms of hysteria. The intensity of the latter phenomena usually varies according to the gravity of the attacks of catalepsy. The *termination* of the cataleptic paroxysm almost always occurs suddenly, the patients take deep respirations, sigh, wake up as if from a profound sleep, then yawn and stretch their limbs. In two cases, in which the approach of the paroxysm was announced by hiccough, this symptom also appeared at the close of the attack. When the attacks have lasted but a short time, the patients return to their occupation as if nothing had happened; when the attacks are more severe and frequent, the patients suffer, for a certain length of time, from cephalalgia, vertigo, and physical and mental prostration.

In concluding the symptomatology of catalepsy, I shall give, with further details, the history of an interesting case, which I have previously published in the Wien. Med. Presse, 5, 1867 :

A nervous girl, nineteen years of age, after having been badly frightened, was soon seized with severe general spasms, at first occurring several times a day, then regularly every two nights. The prodromata of the attack consisted of cardiac palpitation, a sense of oppression, and hiccough ; without treatment the latter symptom lasted several hours. About half an hour before the beginning of the paroxysm the fingers and toes became congested. Upon examining the patient shortly after the attack, *complete anæsthesia and analgesia of the entire surface of the body and of all the organs* were observed, with loss of hearing and smell. If a hypodermic injection of 0.03 of morphine was given when the hiccough appeared, this symptom could be arrested ; ten or fifteen minutes later, loss of consciousness and epileptiform convulsions supervened, often interrupted by hiccough, and terminating in a *cataleptic condition* (with very marked " *waxen flexibility* "). These attacks terminated, although not invariably, in a very peculiar delirium, during which the patient, with her eyes closed, conversed with her father, who had been dead several months. (She often clasped my hand, mistaking it for her father's.) She related to him (mentioning names, dates, and figures), and often in an ironical tone, the family affairs which had transpired since his death. From time to time these strange dreams were interrupted by painful scenes ; the patient uttered terrible cries, and imagined herself in the midst of a fire or surrounded by enemies. Hiccough and slight spasms occurred towards the close of the attack, and the patient then awoke, and displayed great embarrassment when informed of the remarks she had made.

The anæsthesia persisted for twelve to twenty-four hours after the attack. *When the patient was not permitted to use her eyes, or when the lids were closed on account of the frequent bilateral spasm of the orbicular muscles, she was forced to remain absolutely quiet*, and was only able to perform a voluntary movement when she could see her own limbs. *The " waxen flexibility " persisted in severe paroxysms, even after the return of motor power.* Faradic and galvanic exploration, after the attack, gave the following results : preservation of electro-muscular contractility and of the excitability of the nerves, abolition of electro cutaneous and electro-muscular sensibility ; at times, however, the prolonged application of the wire-brush with a strong current produced a sensation of pricking and burning.

Large doses of morphine, administered subcutaneously, gave good results in the beginning ; but, after a while, they failed to produce any effect, and it became necessary to administer chloroform, followed immediately by a subcutaneous injection of morphine. In order to stimulate the nervous system and the organic functions, I prescribed the arseniate of iron (in doses of 0.0005), mild hydrotherapeutic measures, cool baths, and a trip to the country. After having continued six months, the attacks diminished in frequency and intensity, and disappeared during the winter, but returned again in spring, after emotional excitement. In addition to the measures previously mentioned, subcutaneous injections of curare were made for several weeks, without marked benefit. (.005–.006 of a solution, composed of 0.07 to four grammes of water, with two drops of absolute alcohol, were administered every two days.) The patient recovered, after the lapse of several months, during her residence in the country and under the influence of treatment with baths. The menses, which had been suppressed for a year, were slowly re-established, the catalepsy disappeared, and the patient was restored to excellent health.

Etiology.

The large majority of cases of catalepsy originate in hysterical patients. As Puel has shown, in his prize essay on catalepsy (Mémoires de l'Acad. de Méd., Paris, 1856, T. XX., p. 409–526), and also according to Georget, Favrot, etc., catalepsy almost always occurs in females in whom careful examination will reveal signs of hysteria. This holds good of the three examples which came under my own observation. In the majority of cases we are able to discover the motor and sensory disorders and the electrical reactions characteristic of hysteria. Catalepsy usually supervenes upon hysterical paroxysms of old date ; in rarer instances it precedes the development of such phenomena (Georget). During the period of the epidemics of hysteria (Loudun, Louviers, Cologne) the hysterical convulsions were intimately associated with cases of catalepsy. As we have previously stated, the condition which Lasègue denominates as *temporary catalepsy* may be produced at times in hysterical patients by covering their eyes with the hand or with a cloth. Finally, it has been shown that the chief causes of hysteria (emotional excitement, suppression of the menses, unrequited love) also predispose to the production of catalepsy.

In addition to violent emotions, the appearance of catalepsy is favored by *over-excitement of the intellect and by religious exaltation*, when a morbid psychical susceptibility coexists. This also holds good of the causes which lead to *a condition of exhaustion of the nervous system*, such as masturbation, chlorosis, and certain forms of phthisis. We also observe the development of cataleptic rigidity of the muscles, combined with anæsthesia, analgesia, and abolition of the functions of special sense, *in chorea magna*, and in *psychical affections associated with depression or exaltation* (melancholia attonita, mania, ecstasy). I have observed partial catalepsy in an insane patient suffering from *progressive cerebrospinal paralysis ;* Meissner also reports a similar observation.

The facts which we quoted in the beginning of this article serve to show that the symptoms of catalepsy may be present in *degenerations of the brain ;* partial catalepsy is also observed after *typhoid fever,* with severe cerebral symptoms, and in meningitis (as I have often had occasion to notice). According to Medicus and Eisenmann, certain cases of prolonged intermittent fever may be combined with cataleptic attacks. The administration of *narcotics* and *inhalations of ether and chloroform* are also followed, at times, by symptoms of temporary catalepsy.

Almost all cases of the disease are found in young people. The periods of puberty and early menstruation and pregnancy furnish the most favorable causes for the development of cataleptic seizures in predisposed individuals. Cases are of rare occurrence at a more advanced age, and are then due to intense excitement. The female sex, which furnishes such a large contingent to hysteria, is also more subject to catalepsy. Nevertheless, the male sex does not entirely escape.

In Jones's case, reported above, the patient was a man of sixty, previously healthy, with the exception of a slight neuropathic tendency ; he was affected with the cataleptic symptoms, after suddenly receiving the news of the death of his wife ; the paroxysms disappeared at the end of eleven days. In a case coming under my own observation, the disease also occurred in a man, æt. sixty years. In the Vienna General Hospital I had under my charge a boy, æt. twelve years, who, after having been greatly excited, suffered from headache and convulsions, with incomplete loss of consciousness. During these seizures, which lasted from eight to ten minutes, *the upper limbs were in a condition of "flexibilitas cerea ;"* the attacks occurred several times a week, and almost always presented the same characteristics ; they were never followed by sleep. After the administration of oxide of zinc (1.50 grammes in six doses during the day), the paroxysms soon disappeared, and remained absent for a month, when the patient was removed from the hospital.

The Nature of Catalepsy.

The recent results of experimentation, and the advances in the histological data concerning the relations of the various parts of the nervous system, enable us to understand more fully the peculiarities of this intermittent neurosis of the cerebro-spinal system. As Schiff first demonstrated in rabbits, and Goltz, later, in frogs, animals deprived of their cerebral hemispheres, including the motor ganglia, retain the most abnormal positions in which they are placed, although their joints remain flexible. If a part of the body is mechanically irritated, the rabbit will jump forwards with precipitate movements, and, when it is arrested by some obstacle, it remains immovable in the position which it had last assumed.

Thus, although by removing, in animals, the fibres of origin of the foot of the cerebral peduncle, contained in the corpus striatum and lenticular nucleus, and the radiations which these organs send into the anterior lobes, voluntary motion is abolished, reflex impulses may, nevertheless, be transmitted from the optic thalamus and tubercula quadrigemina to the anterior roots, through the tegmentum of the peduncle (Meynert).

In the same manner, in the cataleptic paroxysms in man, as well as in hysteria, melancholia, insanity, and other affections, there is an abnormal resistance to transmission in the motor ganglia and in the corona radiata, which start from the cortex and transmit impulses to the anterior roots. The stimulation of the muscles is thus reduced to a minimum; the latter, therefore, offer no resistance to the reflex stimuli which may reach them through the tegmentum pedunculi, and it is in this manner that the most marked actions are produced.

The data furnished by pathological anatomy also favor this interpretation. The autopsies performed in man, although leaving much to be desired, have demonstrated the existence of changes in the domain of the corpus striatum and in the cortical zone of the anterior lobes. In the first case which I observed, the retardation of motor impulses, even advancing to complete suspension, could be noted under the eyes of the observer; it was only then that the waxen flexibility occurred. In my second case the latter symptom remained permanent, and the retardation of the motor impulses was very evident from the manifest heaviness and slowness of the movements of the patient; during walking the reflex acts assumed the ascendancy, so that the patient, despite himself, walked more and more rapidly, until some obstruction compelled him to stop. Thus, while the direct action of stimuli upon the skin, or (as in one of my cases) the electrical irritation of the muscles or nerves, produced no reflex, and although the limbs did not retain the positions which were artificially given to them, nevertheless the stimulus communicated by passive movements to the sensory nerves of the bones and articulations could be reflected to certain groups of muscles. According to the progress of the recovery, this abnormal resistance to the nerve current diminishes in the central organs, and, as the motor innervation reassumes its ascendancy, the preponderating action of the reflex movements is abolished.

I had occasion to observe, in my second patient, that the power of the cerebral activity could be temporarily recovered, when stimulated by necessity. I accidentally entered his house as his wife was being threatened by a drunken neighbor. His wife fled, pursued by the drunkard; the patient, seeing her danger, rose from his couch, ran towards the ruffian, and, raising his right hand, called out loudly to him. After I had succeeded in re-establishing quiet, I found the patient stretched upon the bed and evidently exhausted; he had fallen back into the same condition in which he had been previous to the scene. He had succeeded, in the face of this urgent necessity, in surmounting the obstacles to which the actions of his nervous system were subject.

Diagnosis and Prognosis.

When the patients are seized with the cataleptic paroxysm, while engaged in some occupation, they remain like statues in the position which they had assumed at the time, and the diagnosis can be made at the first glance. The invasion of catalepsy is less significant and more insidious when it affects the patients while lying in bed. It then becomes necessary, while relying upon the symptoms of some pre-existing affection (hysteria, chorea magna, psychical disorders) and upon the appearance of tonic spasms, to undertake a more careful examination of the motor and sensory functions, and to look for the characteristic flexibility.

We will find, on looking over medical literature, that many cases have been regarded as catalepsy upon very slight grounds. In many instances which have been regarded as such (catalepsy without flexibility was called *catochus*, and the forms with more continuous symptoms, *lethargus*) it is evident that the phenomena were merely those of hysteria, with predominance of tonic spasms, loss of insensibility, and lethargy. It is clear, from our description of the clinical history, that each of the disorders regarded as characteristic of catalepsy (disorders of the sensorium, perceptions, and reflex actions), as well as the "*waxen flexibility*" may be absent in some cases, while the other symptoms are more or less marked.

In such cases the diagnosis of catalepsy is often very uncertain, and may depend upon the personal bias of the observer.

If we wish to assign to catalepsy a distinct place in the nosology, I think the chief stress must be laid upon the existence of the "*waxen flexibility.*" This is the most characteristic symptom of the affection, and belongs to no other disease. If we do not impose this rigorous criterion, we are brought in contact with various conditions, which will introduce confusion into the pathology of the affection, and embarrass investigation.

Simulation of catalepsy is very rare. It is not easy to remain for some minutes in an abnormal attitude, as can be seen in those taking part in tableaux, in which the actors show by their frequent starts that they can with difficulty sustain their rôles. Energetic electrization of the skin, mucous membranes, and nerves will, however, cut short any attempts at deceit; the behavior of the individuals before and after the attack must also be taken into consideration. The case of cataleptic lethargy, published by Macedo (Il Siglo Medico, June, 1864), and which recovered upon the application of an induced current to the neck, face, temples, and sympathetic nerve, after three seances of five minutes' duration, is, to say the least, suspicious.

From a *prognostic* point of view, simple catalepsy is not a serious affection, and usually disappears spontaneously at the end of a certain time. When it accompanies hysterical or psychical affections, it is generally a severe complication; and, when it appears in the advanced periods of the disease, it testifies to a more marked invasion of the nervous system, and is often combined with symptoms of ecstasy, somnambulism, and hystero-epilepsy. When the neurosis lasts several months, it may either be intermittent or merely present (as in Skoda's case) exacerbations and remissions; it then becomes necessary to keep up the strength of the patient and to resort to artificial nourishment. The improvement in the temperature and pulse and the return of olfactory and gustatory sensibility are the first indications of a return to a condition of health. As we have seen in the observation reported at the beginning of this article, the patients may die from anæmia and inanition.

Judging from the facts which I have observed, we should regard the integrity of motion and sensation during the intervals of the attacks as a favorable prognostic sign. Even when the anæsthesia and analgesia return during the paroxysms, their momentary disappearance nevertheless indicates that improvement is progressing. The return of appetite, the restoration of the menses, and calmness of mind may be interpreted as indications of convalescence. We not infrequently notice, towards the close of the disease, that the cataleptic attacks and the deliriums become more frequent and severe, the other signs of improvement continuing, however, during the intervals.

Treatment.

As the cataleptic paroxysms are usually manifestations of hysteria or of some mental disorder, we should direct all our attention to the primary disease. If the latter improves, the cataleptic symptoms will also gradually disappear. The best results are obtained by an appropriate symptomatic and moral treatment. Tonics, the antispasmodics (to which we have referred in the chapter on hysteria); mild hydrotherapeutic measures, the neutral mineral waters, and a trip to the country or to the mountains, in addition to methodical education of the will, constitute the surest means of producing recovery. In the chronic forms we must pay especial attention to alimentation, and, if necessary, use the œsophageal sound. In certain cases we are able to produce movements of deglutition by placing the food at the base of the tongue.

Calvi succeeded in relieving the cataleptic stiffness, in one case, by an injection of a solution of tartar emetic into the brachial vein. If the symptoms of catalepsy occur after intermittent fever, we may give large doses of quinine. I have twice employed the continuous current (from the head and vertebral column to the nerves) for a certain length of time, but I observed no appreciable effect upon the course of the disease. I have also employed, but without success, hypodermic injections of curare. We may, by accident, administer a new remedy, at a time when the disease is spontaneously improving, and we must, therefore, not exaggerate the value of the drugs to which we have resorted.

CHAPTER XXIX.

EPILEPSY.

Pathological Anatomy and Experimental Investigations.

SCHROEDER VAN DER KOLK first pointed out the changes occurring in the nervous system in epilepsy (Bau und Functionen d. Med. spin. u. oblong., nebst Ursache u. Behandlung d. Epilepsie, 1859). He found *considerable dilatation of the vessels, especially in the posterior half of the medulla oblongata,* extending from the fourth ventricle to the hypoglossal and pneumogastric nerves or olivary bodies, whose roots receive the larger part of the vessels of the medulla. Kroon has observed in epileptics an abnormal and unsymmetrical development of the olivary bodies, with asymmetry of the medulla. Solbrig found, in nine cases of epilepsy, *a constriction of the spinal canal* from hypertrophy of the jugular process of the occipital bone and of the posterior arches of the atlas and axis, with *secondary atrophy of the medulla oblongata,* the latter being regarded as the point of departure of the epileptic attacks.

Lélut and Delasiauve have called attention to *sclerosis of the Ammon's horn,* a lesion which Meynert has more recently investigated. According to the latter author, this lesion is merely secondary, and the epilepsy is due to changes in parts remote from this point. A circumstance which appears to substantiate the theory of the secondary character of this localized affection of the cortical region, is found in the fact that, in Kussmaul's experiments upon animals, removal of the Ammon's horn had no effect either upon the production or upon the intensity of the general convulsions. Nothnagel has recently produced lesions of the cornu Ammonis (by incision or injection of chromic acid), which resulted in no disorders of this nature, although the animals succumbed rapidly, as a rule, to meningitis.

It is evident that pathological anatomy furnishes us with very few data with regard to the nature of epilepsy, and more importance must therefore be attached to the experimental investigations which have been made in this direction. These experiments have been performed under the following different conditions : compression of vessels more or less remote from the brain; arterial anæmia or venous hyperæmia, and, as a consequence, epileptiform convulsions; general convulsions, produced by direct irritation of the surface of the pons and medulla; epileptiform attacks, from lesion of the cord or of certain spinal nerves and from traumatic or electrical irritation of the encephalon; finally, irritation of the cord, by means of toxic substances, rendering the animals epileptic.

The first experiments which opened the way for the study of epilepsy were performed by Astley Cooper ; he demonstrated upon rabbits (Guy's Hosp. Rep., 1836, I., p. 465) *that ligature of both carotids and compression of the vertebrals gave rise to loss of consciousness, suspension of the respiratory movements, and convulsive attacks.* If the compression of the arteries was stopped, the animal recovered in a few minutes ; when

·compression was again made (about six times in forty-eight hours), the
same symptoms were reproduced.

Travers and Marshall-Hall noticed, for the first time, the similarity of
the convulsions which rapidly occurred in man and warm-blooded animals
after excessive hæmorrhage, to the convulsions of epilepsy and eclampsia.
The latter author placed the origin of these phenomena in the cord.

Twenty years later, Kussmaul and Tenner (Moleschott's Untersuch-
ungen, 1857, Bd. II., p. 248) repeated these experiments more cautiously
and rigorously upon rabbits, dogs, and cats.   In vigorous animals, rapid
and abundant hæmorrhages produced epileptiform convulsions, similar to
those due to ligature or compression of the carotids and vertebrals.   The
·convulsions were not produced if one of these four arteries remained permeable.   Other experiments, made by Kussmaul and Tenner, upon compression of both carotids, which were confirmed at a later period by
Wachsmuth (Götting. gel. Anz., 1857, p. 187), and a certain number of
·cases of ligature of the carotid in man, have shown that, under such cir-
·cumstances, all the symptoms of an attack of epilepsy may appear.

By ligaturing both subclavian arteries and the arch of the aorta in
rabbits, and by bleeding the animals after transverse section of the cord,
it has been found that interruption of the supply of blood to the cord
never produces strong convulsions (as Marshall Hall believed), but merely
paralysis or slight tremulous movements.

Kussmaul and Tenner have shown, in a series of experiments, by placing a watch-glass in the opening of a trephined skull, without allowing
the air to enter (Donder's plan), that compression of the carotids causes
capillary anæmia and venous hyperæmia of the brain and meninges ;
when the blood is again permitted to freely transverse the vessels of
the neck, the brain assumes a rosy red hue, and a very marked, momentary cerebral hyperæmia occurs, which is unattended by convulsions.
Raising the vault of the skull, or allowing the escape of the cerebro-spinal
fluid, had no effect upon the convulsions produced in the experiments
which we have mentioned, and consequently they were not due to the
·cessation of the mechanical pressure upon the brain, but to the interruption of the supply of blood and to the sudden arrest of nutrition thus
produced.

Other experiments have been performed in order to locate more exactly in the brain the centre of convulsive movements (various parts of
the brain were carefully removed, after compression of the corresponding vessels).   These experiments showed that this centre is situated in
the motor regions behind the optic thalamus (cerebral peduncles, tubercula quadrigemina, etc.), which were irritated by the sudden interruption
·of their nutrition.   In a case of ligature of both vertebrals and one carotid, epileptiform attacks were produced by electrical irritation of the
sympathetic nerve upon the side of the permeable carotid.

Landois has obtained interesting data (Centralbl. f. d. med. Wiss.,
1867, 10) with regard to the influence of venous hyperæmia of the brain
and cord upon the appearance of epileptiform convulsions.   Upon mo-
mentarily obliterating the superior vena cava in rabbits, he observed a
diminution in the number of pulsations; venous congestion of the parts
situated between the tubercula quadrigemina and the cord caused complete arrest of the heart, as in asphyxia, with epileptiform convulsions.
Herrmann has also produced epileptiform convulsions in rabbits, by simultaneous ligature of the superior and inferior venæ cavæ.   These experiments substantiate those made by Schroeder van der Kolk.

Nothnagel has experimentally demonstrated *the 'role played by the pons varolii and medulla oblongata in general convulsions* (Virch. Arch., XI. Bd., 1. H., 1868), and, by irritating the brain of animals with a needle, he has endeavored to locate the true boundaries of the "*convulsive centre*."

Upon irritating the floor of the fourth ventricle, the lower limit is found to be the upper part of the *alœ cinereœ ;* the upper limit is situated above the *locus cœruleus ;* the inner limit is formed by the upper border of the *eminentia teres ;* the outer boundary is more difficult to determine, and appears to be formed above, by the lateral border of the *locus cœruleus,* and, below, by the acoustic tubercle and the *fascic. gracilis.*

The depth of the puncture is immaterial. We cannot believe that the irritation of a small number of motor fibres is the cause of the convulsions, since this would be insufficient to produce general convulsions; the latter must, therefore, be reflex in their nature. Since, after section of the medulla oblongata, the spasms are not produced except upon irritation of the surface which unites the lower border of the pons with the upper border of the acoustic tubercle, it follows that the convulsive centre, which transmits the stimulation of the sensory to the motor fibres, is not situated in the medulla oblongata, but in the pons varolii. This agrees with the experiments of Schiff and Deiters and with certain pathological observations (hæmorrhages into the pons).

The relations of lesions of the cord or of certain spinal nerves to epilepsy were noticed, for the first time, by Brown-Séquard, who has cleared up this question by numerous investigations (Soc. biol., 1850; Arch. gén., 1856; Lancet, 1861; Bull. de l'Acad. de Méd. de Paris, Jan., 1869). These experiments were most successful in guinea-pigs; after making a transverse incision through one of the lateral halves or through the posterior part of the cord, in the dorsal or lumbar regions, it was found that epileptiform spasms developed during the next three or four weeks, when the skin of the lateral portion of the neck or face (epileptogenic zone) was pinched. At a later period the convulsions also appeared spontaneously. The same results are obtained by incising the cord very near the medulla, or by cutting the sciatic nerve near its origin. But epilepsy will not result if the cord has been cut immediately above the point of emergence of the roots of the sciatic nerve. Convulsions may be experimentally produced in guinea-pigs, even after the removal of the cerebrum, pons, and cerebellum, by keeping up artificial respiration. In one case the young of one of the animals, which had been rendered epileptic, suffered from spontaneous attacks of epilepsy.

Westphal has shown (Ber. Klin. Wschr., 38, 1871) *that, in guinea-pigs, blows upon the head may immediately give rise to the production of epileptiform attacks,* and that, in these cases, the convulsions will result, even after several weeks, from pinching the skin of the epileptogenic zone. Transverse sections of the cervical cord and of the medulla oblongata showed, as constant lesions, small hæmorrhages, attaining the size of a pin's head, in the white and gray substances. The lesions often extended downwards into the dorsal region, and there was usually a hæmorrhagic effusion into the cavity of the spinal dura mater. In rare cases a slight hæmorrhage was observed at the base of the brain. According to Ferrier's recent researches, epileptiform convulsions may be produced upon the opposite side of the body, *by passing strong induced currents through one of the cerebral hemispheres.* An analogous observation has been made by Bartholow; in a woman, whose left cerebral hemisphere was exposed by a carcinoma of the skull, the application of an induced current to the brain gave rise to epileptiform convulsions upon the opposite side of the body.

According to Magnan (Études expérimentales sur l'Alcoolisme, Paris, 1871), *injections of absinthe in dogs give rise to epilepsy, followed by stupor.* Autopsies upon these animals showed intense hyperæmia of the medulla oblongata and a diffuse rose color and strong vascular injection in thin sections of the brain and cord.

In conclusion, we may add that Brown-Séquard has observed *contraction of the vessels of the cerebral pia mater* in epileptic animals. The investigations of Loven, Nothnagel, and others have shown that irritation of the peripheral nerves acts in the same manner upon the cerebral vessels. This explains the appearance of epileptic seizures under the influence of peripheral irritations.

Symptomatology.

Typical epilepsy is characterized by three categories of phenomena, viz., disorders of intelligence, of sensation, and of motion, which, in the severe cases, appear suddenly and simultaneously, and, in less severe forms, follow each other in a certain order, while the lightest attacks (petit mal) only include one order of symptoms. The disorders of these various functions are usually preceded by slight symptoms of peripheral irritation; these constitute the aura, or first peripheral manifestation of the vascular spasm which is beginning in the central parts, and the nature of which we shall discuss further on. According to the variations in this vascular spasm, the aura may alternately affect the sensorial functions, sensation or motion (vertigo, feeling of anguish, illusions of the senses, painful sensations, spasms, etc.). The aura often presents an ascending course, which may be explained by the dissemination of the central irritation from below upwards; the possibility of sometimes interrupting the attack by the ligature of a limb may be interpreted as the effect of counter-irritation.

When the attack proper begins, the patient falls unconscious, giving utterance to a sharp cry (reflex spasm of the muscles of phonation and respiration), and the face is almost always pallid; then follows a tonic spasm of the abdominal walls and inspiratory muscles, which lasts from ten seconds to one minute, and is replaced by clonic convulsions involving the limbs and trunk. The head is drawn backwards, the muscles of the haggard and livid face are in a condition of spasmodic contraction, the gaze is fixed, froth appears at the mouth, the teeth are ground together, the tongue is bitten, the carotids are distended, and the respirations cease; from time to time rapid muscular contractions occur; the thumb is flexed strongly upon the palm, the pulse is small, consciousness and reflex action are lost. These are the usual features of the attack; partial sweats, vomiting, meteorism, involuntary emission of urine and fæces, and erections are observed more or less frequently.

After the convulsive stage has lasted from two to five minutes, these tumultuous symptoms gradually subside. The spasmodic movements disappear, relaxation of all the limbs occurs, the respirations become less labored, the cyanosis passes away, the pulse becomes stronger, and consciousness returns, or the patient falls into a profound sleep, interrupted by delirium and frequent starts. The paroxysms are usually followed, for a certain length of time, by exhaustion, disordered ideas, weakness of memory, and malaise, more rarely by dimness of vision, paresis, or hemiparesis.

The *cadaverous pallor* of the onset of the attack, which forms so important a sign in the diagnosis of epilepsy, is regarded as a very frequent symptom by Trousseau, Brown-Séquard, Sieveking, and Radcliffe, while Russel-Reynolds (Epilepsy : its Symptoms, Treatment, and Relations, etc., London, 1861) has observed it in only one-fourth of his cases. In the majority of my patients the pallor hardly lasted a few seconds; under these conditions it may readily pass unnoticed. Not infrequently patients suffering from chronic epilepsy habitually possess a pale color, and this pallor may become very much increased without being noticed.

Epilepsy, the most marked form of which (haut or grand mal) we have described above, embraces certain varieties, which are distinguished by the intensity, duration, and number of the paroxysms. In a somewhat lighter form, there is more or less complete loss of consciousness, but without the utterance of a cry or foaming at the mouth; there is no spasm of the laryngeal muscles, and cyanosis, strong pulsation of the carotids, and the projection of the eyeballs are wanting. The lightest form of· the disease is that known as epileptic vertigo or petit mal. In this form the patients suddenly stop in their work or occupation, remain immovable for a few seconds, and then return to their previous occupation. At other times the patients are suddenly seized with vertigo, are forced to sit down, lose consciousness for a very short period or even incompletely, and merely present fugitive contractions of the eyelids, the arms, or hands. At the termination of such attacks, the patient comes to, looks around with astonishment, and all the symptoms have disappeared within five to eight minutes.

The existence of an epileptogenic zone in man has not been hitherto observed except in a few cases of traumatic epilepsy. In Schnee's case, a wound in the head, which had given rise to epilepsy, had left a very painful cicatrix, by touching which a convulsion could be produced. The cicatrix, in which evidences of neuritis were found, was excised, and the epilepsy then disappeared. In a very recent case, reported by Neftel (Arch. f. Psych., VII. Bd., 1877), the epilepsy developed in a young man, after a blow upon the head. A hyperæsthetic epileptogenic zone was found above the right eye, with anæsthesia of the corresponding part of the healthy side, and paralysis of the frontal nerve. Internal treatment was at first employed without success, and recourse was then had to electricity (the negative pole to the neck, the positive pole with the stabile current in the auriculo-mastoid fossa), which furthered the disappearance of the spontaneous pains and of the other symptoms of the disease.

The use of the ophthalmoscope in epilepsy has produced peculiarly interesting results, and enables us to judge of the condition of the cerebral circulation from that of the retina.

Koestl and Niemetschek have observed (Prag. Vjschr., Bd. I. and III., 1870) retinal anæmia with pallor of the papilla and pulsation of the central veins, especially upon the left side (on account of the incomplete filling of the internal carotid, with increase of pressure in the venous system). Tebaldi (Riv. Clin., IX., 1870) has also recognized pallor of the papilla, increase in the venous circulation, and (upon examining the eye immediately after the attack) marked congestion of the veins, with relative emptiness of the arteries — phenomena which are secondary to arterial anæmia and venous hyperæmia occurring in the cerebral vessels during an attack of epilepsy.

In the very large majority of cases, epileptics present more or less-marked psychical disorders. Previous to the attack, as we have stated above, intellectual malaise and prostration and sensorial illusions of various kinds may be present; mental excitement is observed at times. During the paroxysm we sometimes notice delirium, but only in attacks of petit mal. After the seizure, various grades of the so-called " folie épileptique " (Falvet) are noticeable. In the slight forms the patients have attacks of melancholia, they are morose, dispirited, associate ideas with difficulty, wander around without any definite aim, and manifest a tendency to self-destruction or even to robbery, incendiarism, and murder; after they have recovered their calmness and consciousness, they remember nothing of past events. In the more severe forms they suffer from great excitement with mania, from frightful visions, hallucinations, and complete delirium. In the same patients we may observe intermediate degrees or alternations between the two extreme forms. Epileptic insanity may last from several hours to two days.

In chronic forms the psychical disorders may become permanent. According to Esquirol (Des Maladies mentales, I, p. 274, Paris, 1838), among three hundred and eighty-five epileptic women, forty-six suffered from hysteria, one hundred and forty-five from imbecility, fifty from exaltation or weakness of memory, forty-eight from mania, and eight from idiocy. Hoffman found seventeen cases of imbecility, twelve of mania, two of furious delirium, and two with entirely normal intellects, among thirty-three epileptic patients. According to Schroeder van der Kolk, the light forms of epilepsy often give rise to more profound psychical disorders than the severe convulsive varieties.

Epileptic attacks usually occur without regularity; it is only rarely, and for a short time, that they follow a determinate type. The attacks present a much greater frequency in children and young subjects than at a more advanced age. The convulsions are almost always isolated, but, in rare cases, they occur in groups composed of paroxysms occurring in rapid succession, continuing several hours or even days, and endangering the life of the patient.

Another severe form of epilepsy has been carefully investigated and described by Calmeil, Trousseau, Delasiauve, Charcot, and, more recently, by Bourneville, under the name of *status epilepticus*. It presents the following characteristics: rapid succession of attacks, presenting very slight remissions and without return of consciousness (convulsive stage); a comatose condition secondary to these attacks, with abolition of reflex power, except during short periods of temporary increase (meningeal stage); more or less complete and permanent hemiplegia; acceleration of the pulse and respiration; and, especially, a marked elevation of temperature (40°–43° C.), which even persists in the intervals of the paroxysms, and may increase after their disappearance (Bourneville). The duration of these severe attacks may vary from three to nine days; more than one-half the cases terminate in death. In some observations, made at the Salpêtrière, unilateral cerebral atrophy and a hæmorrhagic extravasation into the pia mater were found upon autopsy, thus explaining the paralysis present upon the opposite side of the body.

Etiology.

Epilepsy is attributable either to an individual predisposition or to certain exciting causes. Heredity is one of the chief predisposing agencies. This factor, in the strictest ·sense, refers merely to epilepsy properly speaking (Esquirol found one hundred and five cases of heredity among three hundred and twenty-one epileptics), or, in a larger sense, to the tendency to nervous diseases which exists in certain families. From the latter point of view, Herpin (Du Pronostie et du Traitement curatif de l'Épilepsie, Paris, 1852), in examining the condition of the parents of two hundred and forty-three epileptics, found heredity as regards nervous diseases in almost one-fourth the cases (epilepsy, seven times, insanity, eighteen; apoplexy and hemiplegia, eleven; meningitis and hydrocephalus, seven). Nevertheless, Petit (Gaz. de Paris, 18, 1860) cites examples of married couples with healthy children and grand-children, although the parents were epileptics at the time that their offspring were born.

Epilepsy may occur at all ages. The most marked predisposition is found in childhood and up to the age of thirty years; the largest number of cases between the ages of twenty and thirty years. Epilepsy may exist in children from birth; in cases of congenital syphilis it may appear in the course of the first ten years, or, at a later period, in children who have suffered from eclampsia during early childhood. (I am acquainted with a family in which two children, born of a nervous mother, died of eclampsia; the third recovered from eclampsia, and remained well until the age of twelve years, when, during the first menstrual period, and without any known cause, she had an epileptic attack (petit mal); she has been subject to severe and light attacks for the last fifteen years.) The female sex is more exposed to epilepsy than the male, on account of the greater impressionability of women and the clearly demonstrated influence of menstruation. We also know that certain disorders of nutrition produce an abnormal irritability of the nervous system, and give rise to epilepsy under the influence of very slight exciting causes. These nutritive disorders include anæmia, chlorosis, scrofula, and rickets. But in certain cases the blood is only affected secondarily after the epilepsy has persisted for a long time. According to Westphal, chronic alcoholism is a cause of epilepsy in drunkards; one-third of the patients suffering from delirium tremens were previously affected with epilepsy. Observations of this kind, collected by Magnan, only refer to individuals who have indulged to excess in absinthe.

Among the exciting causes, the most important are psychical impressions, either those which are manifested suddenly, as fright, anger, surprise, or those which slowly undermine the resistance of the nervous system, as anxiety, care, misery, and privation. The diseases of the brain and its membranes, which may give rise to epilepsy, consist of cranial exostoses, hypertrophy of certain apophyses, neoplasms of the dura mater, and cerebral tumors. Among the latter, the tumors of the convexity, of the anterior, middle, and posterior lobes, and of the motor ganglia, are most frequently accompanied by epileptic seizures. Epileptiform symptoms are also observed in hydrocephalus, cerebral hypertrophy, cerebral syphilis, parasites of the brain (cysticerci), and in insanity. We possess some observations with regard to the spinal origin of epilepsy in man, to which we have previously referred in the chapter on vertebral caries and other lesions of the vertebræ. Some cases of epilepsy due to a lesion of the sciatic nerve have been published by Billroth (Langen. Arch., Bd. XIII., 1871—disappearance of the attacks after exposure of the adherent sciatic nerve) and Schaffer (Aerztl. Intelligenzbl., 1871). Examples of epilepsy caused by a wound in the head are mentioned by Kelp, Leyden, Meschede, and others, but a feeling of terror was often produced, simultaneously with the wound, and it is very difficult to determine the part played by each of these factors.

Irritation proceeding from the genital organs may give rise to epilepsy by its reaction upon the nerve-centres. We have discussed this question at sufficient length in the chapter on hysteria and hystero-epilepsy (uterine epilepsy of the ancients). In a case reported by C. Mayer, the epileptic convulsions ceased after the restoration of a uterine anteversion. In young subjects, onanism frequently develops epilepsy and causes its continuance. I have seen two cases in which the disease developed after the first acts of sexual intercourse, but there was an undoubted hereditary influence acting upon these patients.

The reflex origin of epilepsy is as rare as it is interesting. I have had the opportunity of observing one example of this character. A young woman, twenty-four years of age, who had been previously healthy, suffered, at the end of the fourth month of marriage, after the performance of the sexual act, from acute pains in the abdomen, which were soon attended by convulsions combined with loss of consciousness. During the following weeks the patient abstained from coitus, and enjoyed perfect health. When she again indulged in sexual intercourse, the epileptic seizures returned and soon began to occur spontaneously, at first only at the menstrual epochs, and, at a later period, irrespective of the menses. The patient did not place herself under medical care until after separation from her husband. Upon examination, a very sensitive point was found at the anterior and inferior portion of the vestibule of the vagina, at the level of the remains of the hymen and of the adjacent mucous membrane. An attack of epilepsy could be invariably produced by pressing upon this point, and even by touching it lightly with nitrate of silver; if the examination were prolonged, the attack lasted much longer. The uterus was normal and insensible to pressure; there were no symptoms of hysteria. Ferruginous mineral waters and local treatment proved ineffectual, but the attacks of epilepsy disappeared after the excision of the sensitive parts, and have remained absent for the past two years.

Finally, *peripheral irritation* (cicatricial retractions, foreign bodies, worms, neuromata) may implicate the brain, by direct irradiation or by reflex means, and may give rise to symptoms of epilepsy. Levinstein has published (Deutsche Klinik, Oct., 1867) two cases in which the patients, after having borne heavy burdens, became affected with convulsive movements in the arms; shortly afterwards these movements also affected the face, and terminated in loss of consciousness. The discovery of these etiological factors determined the nature of the treatment to be employed in these cases. (Recovery was obtained by the employment of the continuous current.)

The Nature of Epilepsy.

For a few years past, experimenters have been busily investigating the pathogeny of epileptic affections. Although they have been unable to discover the intimate changes which lie at their foundation, experimentation has, nevertheless, revealed to us various factors which are capable of giving rise to epileptic seizures. We shall attempt, in the following remarks, to throw into relief the essential features of the present theories on this question. Solly's theory of arterial congestion appears insufficient to explain the phenomena of epilepsy. This hypothesis is contradicted by the appearance of convulsions in animals who have been deprived of blood, and by the experiments of Kussmaul and Tenner. By artificially producing intense cerebral hyperæmia (by section of the cervical sympathetic, and ligature of the internal and external jugular veins), these authors noticed the development of dizziness, weakness of the legs, exophthalmia, and slowness of the respiration, but no epileptiform convulsions. It must also be remembered that in epilepsy the loss of consciousness occurs at a period when the face is pale, and that in those cases in which there is a considerable flow of blood to the brain (as in hypertrophy of the left ventricle), vertigo, apoplexy, and paralysis occur, while epilepsy never does (Romberg). The appearance of epileptiform attacks under the influence of venous stases has been rendered doubtful by Kussmaul; nevertheless the experiments of Landois and Herrmann, which we have quoted above, have directly demonstrated their occurrence.

According to Schroeder van der Kolk, the pathogenic condition in epilepsy is an exaggerated excitability of the medulla oblongata, which is always associated with dilatation of the vessels in this organ and in the neighboring parts. This dilatation, which increases with the continuance of the paroxysms, gives rise, on the one hand, to reflex movements from congestive irritation of the ganglion-cells, and, on the other hand, to exudations, thickening, and, finally, to fatty degeneration of the vascular walls. The dilatation of the vessels also extends to the cerebral cortex, causing psychical disorders attended by excitement from irritation of the ganglion-cells, and, later, produces imbecility and idiocy from destruction of these cells. The disorders of speech, which are sometimes observed in epilepsy, may be explained by changes in the olivary bodies and in the nuclei of the hypoglossal and facial nerves. While admitting that Schroeder's deductions are not invulnerable at all points, they nevertheless possess the merit of calling attention to the part played by the medulla oblongata in epilepsy, a view which is still further confirmed by later experiments.

Marshall Hall has attributed the principal part in the production of epilepsy to the tonic spasm of the muscles of the neck (trachelismus) and of the muscles of the larynx. Some of the symptoms (loss of consciousness) are due to obstruction to the return circulation, and others (clonic spasms) to the asphyxia. This theory is refuted by the fact that the paroxysm does not always begin, as Marshall Hall supposed, with spasm of the glottis, but, in the large majority of cases, with loss of consciousness; at other times the clonic convulsions are well marked, before laryngismus has developed. But to M. Hall belongs the credit of having first pointed out the analogies between spasm of the glottis and strangulation, and epilepsy.

Finally, the previously mentioned experiments of Kussmaul and Tenner demonstrated that the loss of consciousness and the convulsive movements are due to a sudden and considerable cerebral anæmia, caused by a spasm of the cerebral arteries. According to these researches, the point of departure of the vascular spasm is found in the medulla oblongata; in the attacks of epilepsy, caused by spasm of the glottis, it is found in the nuclei of origin of the pneumogastric and spinal accessory nerves. The loss of consciousness and the insensibility have their origin in the cerebral hemispheres, the convulsions in the excitable region situated behind the optic thalami.

We will now examine with greater attention the characteristic symptoms which are manifested on the part of the vascular system. As the majority of authors admit, almost all epileptics become pale a short time previous to, and at the beginning of, the attack.

In some cases reported by Rosenstein (Berl. Klin. Wschr., 21, 1868), the sensory disorders constituting the aura were situated in nerves, whose relations with the vascular nerves of the brain are well known (pains radiating into one of the supraorbital nerves, into the occiput, cheeks, and nose, redness of one-half of the nose, swelling of the eyelids, followed by pallor of the face, loss of consciousness, and convulsions); in other patients the aura consisted chiefly of disorders on the part of the vaso-motor nerves. In epileptic guinea-pigs, Brown-Séquard has seen narrow-ing of the arteries of the pia-mater at the beginning of a convulsion. As Voisin has observed in epileptics by means of the sphygmograph (Ann. Méd. Psychol., July, 1867), the initial contraction and subsequent relaxa-tion of the arteries are recognized by the following signs: the line of as-cent of the pulse, which is at first lower, becomes markedly higher, its convexity becomes more pointed, and the line of descent is markedly di-crotic. The pulse gave the same trace in patients who suffered from epi-leptic vertigo, although similar phenomena were not observed in healthy subjects. The occurrence of vascular spasm is further confirmed by an arterial anomaly observed by Pereira in an individual in whom the carotid originated from the vertebral through the medium of the basilar; this patient was epileptic, and absence of the radial pulse (from spasm of the carotid and vertebral) was observed during the epileptic fits. I have also published (Vol. I., p. 100) a case of cerebral tumor which supports this theory; in this case the epileptiform attacks were accompanied by sud-den pallor, and the pulse became small and feeble. Finally, the anæmic origin of epilepsy is still further substantiated by observations of embo-lism of the carotid (as in a case of aneurism of the aorta, in Oppol-zer's Clinic), accompanied, during life, by severe eclamptic attacks, and, by the analogous phenomena which occur in certain puerperal metrorrha-gias, and after certain operations of ligature of the carotid.

In fact, the hypothesis of a vaso-motor neurosis of the brain offers the most satisfactory and simple solution of the phenomena which occur dur-ing an attack of epilepsy. A vascular spasm, starting from the vaso-mo-tor centre, rapidly becomes general, and causes cerebral anæmia, thus causing an obstruction to the reciprocal reactions which transpire between the blood and the brain. This circulatory disturbance in the cerebral hemispheres gives rise to loss of consciousness, and acts, on the other hand, as a powerful stimulus of the centre of convulsive movements which is situated in the pons varolii and medulla oblongata. The nuclei and the root fibres of the sensory cranial nerves, which occupy this region, and the fibres of the tegmentum, which are interspersed with ganglion-cells, readily transmit the stimulus to the motor fibres.

The cerebral anæmia also acts as a strong irritant to the respiratory centre bordering upon the regions which we have mentioned. The irri-tation is gradually propagated to the centres of innervation of the various respiratory muscles, and produces severe dyspnœa and spasm of the re-spiratory muscles, thus tending to increase the venous repletion of the brain. The irritation of the trigeminus in epilepsy, which Brown-Séquard has observed in his experiments, is explained by the part which the large root of this nerve takes in the formation of the tegmentum pedunculi.

When this abnormal excitability of the nerve-centres, which is pecu-liar to epileptics, is present, it is very probable that the irritation of the cerebral and spinal centres, which we have mentioned, is produced simul-taneously. This appears to be especially so in severe and old forms. In the milder forms, in which either the loss of consciousness or the convul-sions predominate at first, it appears that the stimulation of one of these centres prevails over that of the other. This depends probably upon the primary degree of intensity and extension of the vaso-motor irritation. A rapidly subsiding vaso-motor irritation, with unequal distribution of the blood in the cerebral lobes, will give rise to epileptic vertigo, or petit mal. A circumscribed vascular spasm produces partial epilepsy; severe attacks depend upon a central vascular spasm, recurring periodically and developing rapidly; the status epilepticus is produced by a continuous central irritation, preventing, in the beginning, the return of consciousness, and then terminating in inflammatory exudations, and perhaps even in paralysis of the vaso-motor centres.

Diagnosis.

As a rule, no difficulty is experienced in recognizing an attack of true epilepsy; but certain forms may lead to error, especially those which are characterized by incomplete paroxysms. The comatose condition following an attack may be mistaken for apoplectic coma (Sauvages, Trousseau), especially when the onset of the attack has not been seen, or when the slight spasms have been overlooked. When the coma is prolonged (this occurs in certain cases, especially in old age), the diagnosis is rendered certain after it becomes evident that no paralysis exists during and immediately after the coma.

The signs which distinguish an epileptic fit from an hysterical paroxysm have been referred to under the head of Diagnosis of Hysteria. In eclampsia all the characteristic signs are similar to those occurring in epilepsy. In order to exclude epilepsy, we should pay attention to the existence of pregnancy or the puerperal condition, to disorders of the urinary secretion, to the presence of an abundance of albumen and of casts in the urine, to the existence of dropsy and the discovery of carbonate of ammonia in the blood drawn by venesection. It is much more difficult to discover positive signs which will enable us to differentiate the eclampsia of children from epilepsy. On account of the delicate organization and peculiar excitability of the brain of the child, an increased flow of blood to the head, the exhaustion following diarrhœa, or an irritation originating in the digestive canal, may give rise to epileptiform convulsions. In order to make a correct diagnosis, the physician must take into consideration all the surrounding circumstances, and all symptoms which may indicate an affection of the cranial meninges or of the brain; the development of tuberculous cerebral tumors, which are accompanied by disorders of motion, sensation, and the special senses, must also be considered.

Many authors have complicated the discussion of epilepsy in adults by establishing artificial categories which are hardly justifiable. This classification, moreover, possesses no interest, either from a theoretical or a practical point of view. The simplest and, at the same time, the best plan is that of determining in each case whether the disease is central or peripheral, idiopathic or symptomatic.

Idiopathic central epilepsy is recognized without difficulty, in the majority of cases, by devoting some attention to the etiological factors. *The symptomatic forms* of central epilepsy are distinguished by the previous history and by other characteristic signs belonging to the primary disease. The epileptiform attacks which occur as intercurrent phenomena in cerebral tumors (tumors of the convexity, anterior and posterior lobes, motor ganglia, and cerebellum) are almost always sufficiently explained by the coexisting motor and sensory disorders. We have previously mentioned (Vol. I., p. 139) the probable signs of epilepsy caused by cysticerci of the brain. The epileptiform symptoms of cerebral syphilis and of congenital cerebral syphilis have also been discussed (Vol. I., p. 152). Epileptiform seizures which are caused by cerebral hypertrophy and embolism of the internal carotid (three times in thirty-nine cases, according to Lancereaux) are accompanied by other grave symptoms, to which we have previously referred. In paralytic dementia, epileptiform attacks occur in the beginning, or, more frequently, at a more advanced period; but the parts affected by the convulsions almost always remain paralyzed for a certain length of time, and contractures are observed during and after the attack ; not infrequently some embarrassment of speech, or other characteristic phenomena of paresis or paralysis in the muscular system, is noticeable after the epileptic seizure.

In *peripheral epilepsy* the disorders of motion or sensation precede the loss of consciousness; the secondary participation of the brain, leading to the attack, occurs from irradiation or reflex action. In order to diagnosticate this variety of epilepsy, we must be able to find, by examining or questioning the patient, a peripheral irritation or a nervous lesion, which will account for the starting-point of the disease. Epilepsy, which is thus produced by irritation from worms, cicatrices, or traumatism (Levinstein), is readily susceptible of recovery. The simulation of epilepsy is frequently attempted, and is sometimes difficult to detect; but careful observation will usually enable us to recognize the deceit. The satisfaction with which the individuals refer to their disease, and the time and place which they choose for the attacks in order to accomplish their end, contrast markedly with the disposition of true epileptics, who confess to the existence of their complaint with timidity and sorrow. The exaggeration of the symptoms of the fit, the imperfect copy of the asphyxia, the fatigue which rapidly develops, the signs of irritability produced by the sudden application of strong electrical currents, the action of light upon the pupils (according to Romberg they do not react in true epilepsy) are other features which enable us to unmask the imposition. Voisin has recently employed for the same purpose the examination of the pulse with the sphygmograph; we have seen that this instrument gives a peculiar trace in epileptics, on account of the existence of vascular spasm.

Prognosis.

Hippocrates, Galen, Morgagni, Boerhaave, Tissot, and Odhelius admit the curability of epilepsy; Esquirol, Georget, Valleix, Monneret, Delasiauve, Beau, etc., took a pessimistic view of the question, and abandoned the patients to their unhappy fate, without any attempt at treatment. In later times, Trousseau, Herpin, and Portal have endeavored to free epilepsy from this long proscription, and Trousseau has stated (Gaz. des Hôpit., April, 1855) that in twelve years he obtained twenty recoveries among one hundred and fifty cases of epilepsy. We can readily understand why a recovery from this disease should be much more strongly doubted by hospital physicians than by those in private practice, the former coming in contact with chronic forms, complicated with mental diseases, and the latter seeing cases in the early stages. Spontaneous recoveries are exceedingly rare (about four per cent., according to Beau and Maisonneuve). The elements of the prognosis are: the etiological conditions of the disease, the age at which it develops, its duration, and the frequency of the attacks. The idiopathic variety presents a favorable prognosis when it is treated early and is not complicated by any hereditary influence. We must not neglect to treat petit mal, and must take into consideration all the individual circumstances of the case. Symptomatic epilepsy has slight chances of recovery. The most severe form is that due to the presence of cerebral tumors; there is much more chance of recovery when the disease is secondary to cerebral syphilis or lead-poisoning. Those forms which are complicated with insanity present few chances of recovery. Schroeder van der Kolk has, nevertheless, seen patients, who had become insane from the influence of epilepsy, recover from the mental disorder after a cure of the epilepsy had been effected. The prognosis is more favorable in reflex epilepsy; if we can succeed in removing the causes of irritation, which are acting from the periphery, the epilepsy will disappear at the same time. It is stated that the disease is curable when it develops during the period of dentition ; it is regarded as incurable when it begins in the early years of childhood and is prolonged beyond the age of puberty. Cases which develop during youth, especially those which are due to disorders of the genital organs (with the exception of those caused by an inveterate habit of onanism), have a more favorable prognosis than those appearing in adult life. Nocturnal epilepsy is more dangerous than the diurnal form, because it affects the patient during sleep and often when he is not under surveillance. The varieties attributed to chlorosis, anæmia, or other unfavorable conditions, may recover if these causes are removed in time. The duration of the disease is of the greatest importance with regard to prognosis, and recovery is so much the more difficult the longer the disease has lasted. The prognosis improves if, during the course of the disease, the fits appear more infrequently and are shorter and lighter. When the patients have long remissions, during which they merely present epileptic vertigo, we may always hope for recovery, according to Herpin, if the disease has not lasted more than ten years. The prognosis is not unfavorable if the number of attacks does not exceed one hundred ; if the attacks number from one hundred to five hundred the situation is grave, and becomes still more serious if they exceed the latter figure.

We should be very reserved in giving a prognosis, and very skeptical with regard to cases of recovery, since relapses are frequent, and may occur even after the attacks have disappeared for several years. The fits may become more infrequent under the influence of strict habits of life and diet, and the patients may enjoy satisfactory health for years, but, as a rule, they do not live to an advanced age. Death may occur during a convulsion from a fall, from asphyxia, pulmonary œdema, cerebral hæmorrhage, or rupture of the heart (Short and Voisin). Irrespective of the convulsions, death is caused by marasmus, tuberculosis, cerebral softening, and various intercurrent diseases.

Treatment.

At the onset of the affection the chief aim consists in relieving the morbid impressionability of the nerve-centres, and the extreme excitability of reflex action, before the functional disorders have become established in a chronic form and have produced tissue changes in the nerve-cells.

Recovery is impossible unless we are able to moderate, by a sufficiently complete and prolonged rest, the peculiar erethism of the nerve-centres. Before we can state with certainty that recovery from epilepsy has occurred, the nervous system must have presented no derangement for a number of years, and its integrity must have been proven by its resistance to numerous and varied irritations. If this is done, the number of so-called recoveries will be found to diminish very considerably.

During the attack we should endeavor to protect the patient from injuring himself, from falling out of bed, and from biting the tongue (by placing a cork, or a small piece of wood covered with a cloth, between the teeth), and should remove the mucus which accumulates in the mouth and which may give rise to symptoms of asphyxia. Parry has employed compression of the carotids or the inhalation of chloroform in order to shorten asphyxial attacks of long duration ; these measures are only indicated in extremely rare cases.

The treatment of epilepsy should be begun by endeavoring to remove the cause although this is usually more easily said than done. It is, above all, necessary to examine the various internal viscera as carefully as possible. Retracting cicatrices, tumors, osseous sequestra, foreign bodies, worms, and concretions sometimes give rise to attacks of epilepsy, which do not disappear until the offending substance is removed. In Rosenstein's cases, in which the attacks were preceded by vaso-motor irritation, and in Levinstein's two patients, who, after having carried heavy burdens, suffered from spasms in the upper limbs, terminating in true epileptic convulsions, recovery followed tonic treatment and the application of the constant current to the diseased nerves.

In young, delicate subjects, especially those near the age of puberty, we can evidently produce the most favorable conditions for recovery, by methodically increasing the vigor of the nervous system, by calming its abnormal excitability, and by developing its power of resistance against all forms of irritation. A prolonged trip to the country, the removal of everything which tends to stimulate the intellect and sexual appetite, and well-regulated hydrotherapeutic treatment (frictions, half-baths, dorsal affusions) may cause the attacks to disappear. I know that this result can be achieved in many cases. In a young man under my care attacks of epilepsy which were due to onanism, disappeared after moderate indulgence in sexual intercourse.

With regard to medicinal treatment, we shall only discuss those old remedies which are still in use, and the new remedies with whose action we are somewhat better acquainted.

The salts of zinc (oxide, valerianate, and lactate) have been highly praised by Herpin, who obtained good results therefrom (in more than one-half of his cases), especially in children and old people. The preparations of zinc should be administered to children, in increasing doses, from 0.05–0.50 p. d., and continued for several months. In adults 0.50–3. grammes are given daily, and treatment should not be discontinued unless fifty to one hundred grammes of the remedy have been taken without any good effects. Other observers are much more guarded in their praises of this drug.

The preparations of copper, bismuth, and antimony are very little used at the present time, with the exception of the ammoniated sulphate of copper, which is sometimes employed (0.03–0.07 p.d., Herpin). Nitrate of silver is one of the most highly recommended of the metallic preparations. It is prescribed in pill form, 0.006–0.02 being given twice a day in the beginning, and the dose being then increased until 0.20 is administered in the twenty-four hours. I have never seen argyrism produced before the patient had taken five grammes of the drug. In all cases, it is well to suspend treatment temporarily after it has been continued for a certain length of time, especially if the patients complain of pains in the stomach. Cases of complete recovery under this plan have been reported, but, in very many cases, the only results obtained were the production of symptoms referable to the argyrism. Trousseau has seen one patient who experienced no benefit despite the existence of argyrism, and despite castration and tracheotomy, which were performed upon the patient, at a later period, in England.

Fowler's solution is given in doses of five to ten drops p. d. (upon a lump of sugar), and has a favorable effect upon the form of the disease. The ferruginous preparations, especially the carbonate and cyanide of iron, often produce good effects in anæmic patients. Belladonna, which was first employed by Greding, has been extolled more recently by Michéa and Trousseau. On account of the ready decomposition of the leaves and of the extract of belladonna, and the unequal proportions of atropine which they contain, even in the fresh condition, it is better to prescribe atropine in the form of the sulphate (according to Michéa in the form of acid valerianate). According to Skoda (Allg. med. Zeit., 14, 1860), atropine is relatively the best remedy against epilepsy in our possession. 0.03–0.05 of sulphate of atropia are dissolved in five grains of water, and one to two drops of this solution are given daily. The dose is increased each week by a drop daily; the patient is held at the dose which has produced manifest improvement, and the dose is then gradually diminished in an inverse ratio. From time to time it is necessary to suspend treatment, especially if considerable dilatation of the pupils occurs, with marked dryness of the throat, muscular weakness, and disorders of the special senses.

Bromide of potassium was first administered in epilepsy by Locock and M'Donnel, and the latter author called attention to the efficacy of the drug in large doses. For some time past the remedy is also used largely in France and England.

According to the experiments made by Eulenburg and Guttmann, both upon cold-blooded and warm-blooded animals (Virch. Arch., 1. H., 1867), bromide of potassium acts chiefly upon the central nervous system, and gradually diminishes motor power, as well as sensory perceptions and reflex excitability, until they entirely disappear. In order to obtain results in man which are at all comparable to the effects just described, large doses must be administered. We begin with four grammes daily (which the patient dissolves in a glass of sugar-water, or encloses in a wafer), and increase this dose, in ordinary cases, until six to nine grammes are taken daily. In severe forms we may begin with the latter dose and increase it up to twelve grammes (rarely much higher). I have become convinced that this drug is more useful in recent than in old cases, but, even in the latter, it almost always diminishes the number and violence of the attacks. Radcliffe, Brown-Séquard, Russell-Reynolds, Voisin, Legrand du Saulle, Pletzer, and Eulenburg have reported cases of permanent recovery from the employment of bromide of potassium. In epileptic hysteria, in which the attacks occur with the menses, benefit is derived from the use of the drug for a short time before each menstrual period.

According to the observations of Guttmann and Sander, the effect upon the nervous system is due to the alkaline base, but the same results have not been obtained from chloride of potassium. The use of bromide of potassium may be attended with some annoying symptoms, such as the appearance of acne pustules, and, much more rarely, of angina or gastric disturbances, which disappear after a short suspension of the treatment. This remedy may be given for several months in succession, with short intermissions, and the gravity of the disease demands that this method of treatment should receive the necessary care and attention. In sensitive patients we may employ the bromide of sodium, which, in my experience, acts as a milder remedy than the corresponding salt of potassium. Curare was first recommended in epilepsy by Thiercelin (Acad. des Sciences, Nov., 1860), and then by Benedikt. In a certain number of cases, I have employed a solution of 0.05 of curare in five grammes of water, with the addition of three or four drops of absolute alcohol. For a period of two or three months I gave a subcutaneous injection every two days, increasing the dose gradually from 0.004–0.009. In seven patients whom I treated in this manner (of which four cases were without hereditary antecedents, and two suffered from epileptiform hysteria), and in five other patients treated similarly at the Vienna Lunatic Asylum, the drug produced no permanent good effects. Beigel, Voisin, and Liouville have since arrived at a similar conclusion. In one of my cases (Wien. Med. Presse, 6, 1867), after an injection of 0.01, symptoms of poisoning appeared, consisting of nausea, vertigo, redness of the face, painful throbbing in the temples, general exhaustion, acceleration of the pulse, and great thirst; chemical analysis of the urine showed the presence of sugar. These symptoms disappeared after rest and simple treatment.

Narcotics must be cautiously administered in this affection. I have seen one patient (loc. cit.) who, after great excitement, had fifteen to twenty attacks in one day; his excitement and cries induced me to give him, for three days, a hypodermic injection of 0.01 of morphine; the patient then became more quiet, and remained free from the epileptic seizures for six months. Quinine is sometimes useful in intermittent epilepsy.

We may finally mention Chapman's plan of treatment, in which a caoutchouc tube filled with ice-water is applied to the back of the patient (for two to eighteen hours, according to the circumstances of the case), the limbs are rubbed while plunged in warm water, and are then placed in dry cloths. These operations should be followed by exercise, deep inspirations, etc. Treatment is ineffectual in the status epilepticus; Browne has lately observed good effects from the cautious employment of nitrite of amyl in inhalations.

CHAPTER XXX.

ECLAMPSIA (ACUTE EPILEPSY).

UNDER the generic term eclampsia are included those various conditions which have also been called acute epilepsy, on account of their great analogy with that affection, and which present, as a common characteristic, alternations of tonic and clonic spasms, with loss of consciousness. In the absence of any other guide, we must rely upon the etiological conditions for the differentiation of the various kinds of eclampsia. We shall therefore study, in succession, the eclampsia of pregnant and puerperal women, the eclampsia of children, toxic eclampsia, and the eclampsia due to contagious and miasmatic influences.

A.—ECLAMPSIA OF PREGNANT AND PUERPERAL WOMEN.

This, on the whole, infrequent affection (one case in five hundred pregnancies) may occur in the last two or three months of pregnancy, but much more frequently during delivery, and especially in the periods of dilatation and expulsion. Primipara are most exposed to the disease (about eighty in one hundred cases, C. Braun); robust, sanguine, young, or nervous females are, as a rule, more liable to the affection than feeble and older women. Multipara, who have previously had eclampsia, sometimes manifest a certain predisposition to its development (Litzmann).

Eclampsia may develop suddenly or may be preceded by certain prodromata. The latter consist of an unusual agitation, cephalalgia, pains in the epigastrium or uterus, a feeling of heaviness in the limbs, illusions of the senses, etc. If, in addition to these symptoms, œdema develops, especially in the labia majora and around the malleoli, if the urine contains albumen, or if an analysis of the blood shows the presence of carbonate of ammonia, there is every reason to fear an attack of eclampsia. (In one case Oppolzer and Braun predicted its appearance two days in advance, from the results of the analysis of the blood.) An attack of eclampsia presents the same symptomatology as epilepsy, and we may therefore omit its description.

The seizure may last from a few minutes to a quarter of an hour, and is followed by a condition of coma. The disease often terminates after a single convulsion; in those cases in which the seizures are separated by long intervals, each attack is preceded by the prodromata to which we have previously called attention. In severe cases the patients only rally from the coma to fall into another attack, and death occurs without a restoration of consciousness. When the attacks cease, the stage of coma often continues several days until consciousness and the functions of special sense are gradually restored. Memory is very much affected in these cases; the patients do not know that they have been confined, and refuse to recognize their offspring.

The labor pains and the act of delivery undergo various modifications in different cases. If the paroxysm occurs during the first period of labor, the uterus is contracted and firm to the feel (although this circumstance does not influence the dilatation of the cervix), and the progress of labor is retarded. When the eclamptic attack occurs at the moment of spontaneous expulsion, the delivery of the child occurs very rapidly.

There is often no trace of pains when the paroxysm begins, but the eclampsia provokes pains, and the delivery of the child therefore is almost always produced prematurely. Nevertheless, the eclamptic attack and the labor pains may be separated by an interval of several weeks, and, even when the pains appear, the woman is almost always delivered of a dead child. The death of the fœtus is not attributable, as Kiwisch thinks, to circulatory disturbances developing in the placental vessels, but rather to uræmic poisoning affecting the child through the blood of the mother. Upon several occasions considerable quantities of urea have been found in the blood of the umbilical cord of children who were born alive and whose mothers had suffered from uræmic convulsions.

The termination of the disease is extremely variable. Certain women make a perfect recovery; but others have hardly escaped the danger connected with the convulsions when another presents itself, in the shape of puerperal fever, for which the exudative processes of eclampsia appear to create a predisposition, and which almost always proves fatal to the patients. Very many patients succumb to the eclamptic attacks; according to C. Braun, among forty-four women, nine died during the convulsions and five from the sequences of puerperal fever. Death may occur from asphyxia, hæmorrhage, serous infiltration of the brain, secondary cerebral inflammation, or pulmonary œdema. A much more important and striking fact, which is often observed upon autopsy, is the alteration in the kidneys, characterized by the lesions of the stage of hyperæmia or exudation in Bright's disease. On account of the short duration of the affection, the stage of fatty degeneration and renal atrophy is rarely observed.

Authors are still divided in opinion with regard to the nature of eclampsia. As Frerichs first showed in his classical treatise (Die Bright'sche Krankheit, Braunschweig, 1851), puerperal eclampsia is only observed in those women who have suffered, during pregnancy, from Bright's degeneration of the kidney. In consequence of the disorders in the urinary secretion, the albumen of the blood passes into the urine, while, inversely, the urea of the blood is eliminated by the urine in insufficient quantity; hence results an accumulation of urea in the blood. The urea is then transformed in the blood into carbonate of ammonia by the action of an unknown ferment, and the poisonous action of this substance upon the nerve-centres gives rise to eclamptic attacks. The presence of urea in the blood does not suffice, in itself, to give rise to the symptoms in question, for, according to the experimental researches of Frerichs, the injection of urea into the vessels does not produce eclampsia. Urea is often found also in the blood of patients who have died from Bright's disease without having presented any symptoms of uræmia during life.

According to Treitz, the saturation of the blood with urea in Bright's disease is followed by its elimination throughout the intestinal canal; the substances with which it here comes in contact cause its transformation into carbonate of ammonia, which passes into the blood and produces eclampsia from ammonæmia.

Spiegelberg and Gscheidlin have recently succeeded in demonstrating the presence of carbonate of ammonia in the blood of an eclamptic patient (Arch. f. Gynaek., I. Bd.). Stockvis, Spiegelberg, and Heidenhain have produced eclamptiform attacks in animals by the injection of carbonate of ammonia into the crural vein or artery. Rosenstein's experiments (Virch. Arch., Bd. 56, 1872) were attended with similar positive results and the attacks did not cease until the spinal cord was separated from the brain. But carbonate of ammonia merely gives rise to eclamptiform attacks, while uræmic poisoning produces convulsions, delirium, and coma.

The theory just advanced has been strongly combated, at different times, by Kiwisch, Scanzoni, and Krause, who regarded the coexisting Bright's disease as merely of secondary importance, and considered it as an accidental complication. They regarded the eclampsia as due rather to the mechanical action produced upon the nerves by pregnancy and parturition (rigidity of the lower segment of the uterus, abundance of the amniotic fluid, transverse presentations, manual interference, abundant hæmorrhages). Puerperal eclampsia should therefore be regarded as a reflex process, like the reflex epilepsy produced by peripheral irritation.

According to the observations collected by Braun at the Vienna Maternity Hospital, there were forty-four cases of eclampsia in twenty-four thousand confinements; eight other cases were merely accidental complications of pregnancy, two being due to hysteria, four to habitual epilepsy, one to capillary cerebral hæmorrhage, and one to poisoning with carbonic oxide gas. Albuminuria was present in all the other cases. According to the observations referred to, eclampsia was immediately due to Bright's disease in the very large majority of the cases in question. Degeneration of the kidneys was observed in a considerable number of autopsies, and we must remark, in addition, that the symptoms of uræmia, which are observed in animals after extirpation of both kidneys, present the same characteristics as the acute albuminuria of pregnant females. Even before the eclampsia develops, albumen and casts are found in the urine of pregnant women. The appearance of casts in the urine is especially important, since albumen may be found in a normal pregnancy. Blot gives the average proportion of albumen in the urine of those patients who suffer from albuminuria, but are not eclamptic, as thirty-three per hundred, and in eclamptics as about seventy-four per hundred.

Nevertheless, the renal affection does not appear to be sufficient to fully explain the morbid process in all cases of the affection. In certain instances we must also take into consideration the cerebral anæmia following profuse hæmorrhages, the changes in the blood which predispose to puerperal fever, and, in a very large proportion of cases, we must admit the existence, as in epilepsy, of an abnormal excitability of the nervous system. The latter, under the influence of pregnancy and especially of the labor pains, or in consequence of the compression exercised by the uterus upon the sacral plexus, will give rise to convulsions.

From a diagnostic point of view, we readily comprehend how serious are the consequences of mistaking eclamptic attacks for other paroxysms presenting analogous symptoms, since the prognosis and treatment are equally affected by such an error. A careful physician will not readily mistake uræmic eclampsia for cholæmic convulsions, the symptoms of poisoning, chorea gravidarum, and the syncopal attacks or spasms which are sometimes observed during pregnancy. According to Bourneville's recent investigations, the temperature in uræmia becomes progressively lower until death, while in puerperal eclampsia it follows an ascending course (42°–43° C). A sinking of the temperature curve is a favorable prognostic sign. Hysterical and epileptic convulsions furnish the most frequent source of error. In the chapters on Hysteria and Epilepsy we have given, in detail, the characteristic signs of these affections. If the patients have suffered from convulsive attacks previous to pregnancy, and if, after having become pregnant, they present similar symptoms, we can readily determine their true character; the negative results of the urinary examination (absence of albumen and casts) are of great importance. The convulsive affections, which we have previously discussed, do not present such a grave prognosis as do the attacks of eclampsia. The former do not interrupt pregnancy, have very little influence upon the life of the fœtus, and do not present greater dangers to the mother than in the non-pregnant condition, while an attack of eclampsia seriously threatens the life of the mother as well as that of the child.

The physician may be greatly embarrassed in making a diagnosis, in the case of a pregnant woman who is seized, for the first time, with a convulsion, and whose previous history furnishes no clue. If no œdema is found in any part of the body, or no abnormal constituents in the urine, we will be forced to suspend the diagnosis until the case is cleared up by the appearance of new attacks. A second or third seizure may furnish decisive results on the part of the urine, and relieve the physician from annoying uncertainty. If no albumen is found in the urine, even after several attacks, and if the relatives of the patient positively assert that she has never suffered from previous epileptic or hysterical attacks, we must take into consideration the possible existence of a disease of the brain or its meninges, of typhoid fever, cholæmia, etc., and we must look for new explanations in the later evolution of symptoms.

The *prognosis* is unfavorable in the majority of eclamptiĉ affections. It becomes much more so when the convulsions follow one another in rapid succession, when the patients do not recover consciousness during the intervals, and when the quantity of albumen in the urine increases after each attack. The mortality varies from thirty to eighty per cent.

The *prognosis*, with regard to mortality, is much more unfavorable than in epilepsy, though much more favorable with regard to curability. In the eclampsia of pregnant women, abortion or premature delivery often occurs (about twenty-five per cent., Braun). It is rare that the convulsions cease and delivery occurs normally without the supervention of eclamptic phenomena. In a general way the danger is greater the earlier the period of pregnancy in which the attacks begin, and a repetition of the convulsions may cause the death of mother and child long before confinement.

During the period of dilatation, especially when this is slowly consummated in consequence of deformity of the pelvis or of a vicious position of the child, a stasis of venous blood occurs in the veins, and the prognosis is unfavorable. The prognosis is better when the eclampsia begins during the expulsive period, as the delivery may then terminate promptly and the convulsions cease immediately or shortly after. In the majority of cases the convulsions cease after delivery is accomplished. During the expulsive period, the atony of the uterus may give rise to hæmorrhage, and, in certain cases, instrumental delivery must be resorted to. Sometimes the attacks continue after confinement, and in certain very severe forms they only develop during the puerperal condition (from the first few days to the sixth week). At times the patients manifest for a long time, and perhaps even during their whole lives, certain psychical disorders (melancholia, mania, imbecility), which vary according to the situation and intensity of the secondary modifications of the puerperal period. The disease may also be followed by amaurosis, hemeralopia, hemiplegia, and contractures. If the symptoms of the renal affection and the œdema persist for several weeks after confinement, they will pass into a chronic condition, which may continue a long time. Nevertheless, recovery occurs more readily in these cases than in Bright's disease due to other causes.

The effects of eclampsia upon the child are very disastrous; nearly half of the children die, and the mortality is larger the earlier the period of pregnancy at which the affection has developed. Viable infants, at full term, are not endangered by the uræmia which existed in the mother, since the disease is never hereditary. In one of Simpson's cases, however, albuminuria was detected in the child of an eclamptic mother.

In the treatment of uræmic eclampsia especial importance must be attached to prophylactic measures, with a view to moderating the symptoms of Bright's disease. Beginning hydræmia should be combated by nourishing diet, tonics, and warm baths. In order to neutralize the carbonate of ammonia in the blood, we may administer benzoic acid (0.30–0.60 at a dose, according to Frerichs), lemon-juice, and tartaric acid mixed with ice-water. In order to favor the elimination of urea in the urine, we would recommend the plentiful ingestion of fluids; laxative enemata are useful in cerebral congestions.

The most energetic measures have been resorted to in order to suppress the terrible phenomena of eclampsia. Venesection, so often performed in former times, is much less frequently employed at the present time, since it appears to increase the hydræmia and exhaustion of the patients and to favor the development of puerperal thromboses and pyæmia. With the exception of cases of intense cyanosis and vigorous pulsation of the carotids, or in patients with a vigorous constitution, in whom venesection, performed at the proper time, may prevent the occurrence of a cerebral hæmorrhage, we must entirely reject the practice of repeated bleedings at short intervals.

The opiate treatment gives good results, especially after delivery, when the attacks occur during the puerperal period, and when other anæsthetics do not act with sufficient promptness. Opium may be given in doses of 0.03–0.08, and morphine in doses of 0.01–0.02. When the drug cannot be swallowed, we prescribe hourly injections per rectum of fifteen to twenty drops of laudanum, until the convulsions have ceased. The best effects are obtained by means of subcutaneous injections of morphine (0.01–0.02). If the patient is comatose, opiates should not be administered, as we are unable to sufficiently control their toxic effects. According to the experience of obstetricians, the inhalation of chloroform is one of the most useful measures at our command. It may be given, according to Braun, as soon as the increased agitation of the patient, the increasing rigidity of the muscles of the arm, and the jactitation, indicate the beginning of a convulsion; the inhalations may be continued until quiet and sleep are produced (one to two minutes). During the attack, as well as during the stage of coma, the anæsthesia must be suspended and fresh air be permitted to enter the lungs. The administration of chloroform may even be employed in cases of persistent trismus, and, by hastening the progress of delivery, it contributes strongly towards saving the life of the infant. Braun reports sixteen cases of eclampsia, treated with chloroform and acids, which were followed by complete recovery. When delivery is retarded in women suffering from Bright's disease, Chailly advises (Union Médic., 1855) the inhalation of a small amount of chloroform as a prophylactic measure. For some time also hydrate of chloral has been largely employed in cases of eclampsia.

Cold applications may be made in the form of compresses of ice-water which completely cover the head). This is more useful in excited patients than the application of leeches to the mastoid processes. During the paroxysms, and especially during the stage of coma, benefit is obtained from cold affusions to the head, the patient being placed at the edge of the bed.

The active revulsive measure recommended by some authors (hæmospasia (Junod's boot), tartar emetic, ammonia, etc.) are not followed by any marked benefit. We have previously referred to the precautionary measures to be adopted during the convulsions, in the article on Epilepsy. In a case of puerperal eclampsia, published by Lange (Prag. Vjschr., IV. Bd., 1868), the convulsions began before delivery, and continued into the puerperal period, despite local bleeding, applications of ice, inhalations of chloroform, and injections of morphine. Two hundred and forty-five grains of defibrinated blood were then injected into one arm, while four hundred and ninety grains of blood were being drawn from the other. The respirations soon became easier, the cyanosis disappeared, and, although another slight attack occurred, consciousness was soon restored, and the patient made an excellent recovery.

B.—ECLAMPSIA OF CHILDREN.

The eclampsia of children and of the new-born presents an importance equal to that of eclampsia parturentium, but its nature is less understood and less exactly defined. Under this term are included the varied convulsive conditions observed in children, which are characterized by the occurrence of phenomena dangerous to life, and attended with complete or partial loss of consciousness.

The symptoms of the disease are often preceded by certain significant prodromata. Among these we may mention the perverseness of the children, a marked tendency to stumble, sleep disturbed and broken by frightful dreams, grinding of the teeth, cries, spasms of the muscles of the face and eyes, and subsultus tendinum. The eclamptic attacks develop after a longer or shorter duration of these prodromata (though sometimes suddenly), are similar to those occurring in adults, and are manifested under the form of tonic and clonic spasms, attended with loss of consciousness. At first the convulsions are almost always limited to certain portions of the body, and consciousness is partially preserved ; at a later stage it disappears completely, and the convulsions at the same time increase in extent and intensity. In the majority of instances the trunk is affected by tonic and the limbs by clonic spasms. The intense cyanosis of the face, the swelling of the jugular veins, the stertorous and sometimes intermittent breathing, and the frequent and small pulse, testify to the serious disturbances occurring in the organs of circulation and respiration.

The duration of the attacks is extremely variable. Sometimes they terminate quickly, sometimes they continue, with interruptions, for hours and even days, consciousness remaining disordered, and the little patients being excited and extremely irritable. The eclampsia, whether partial or general, terminates after one or two paroxysms, or it may be divided into a series of attacks, which recur more or less frequently.

In the cases which terminate fatally we may find the following anatomical lesions: hæmorrhages into the mucous membranes, œdema and hæmorrhages into the brain or other organs, rupture of muscles, luxations, and even fractures (in consequence of the violence of the convulsive movements).

From an *etiological* point of view, the majority of authors regard the existence of nervous diseases in the parents and hereditary influence as creating, in very many children, a predisposition to eclamptic affections. As the convulsions are most frequently observed during the period of first dentition, the development of the teeth has been looked upon as a cause of the disease, but this hypothesis has very little foundation in fact. The eclamptic attacks occur during that period in which the child's brain possesses extreme delicacy of structure and marked excitability. Local causes (hyperæmia or cerebral anæmia following diarrhœa), as well as peripheral irritations, readily give rise, therefore, to convulsive symptoms.

Another source of the convulsive seizures in children is found in the acute exanthemata (scarlatina, variola, rubeola), which develop most commonly after the age of two or three years. The stomachal affections of childhood (milk of poor quality, undigested food), intestinal affections (worms, for example, which are not found, however, in infants), and diseases of the kidneys (Bright's degeneration following scarlet fever, the passage of calculi through the kidneys or bladder), may also act as causes of eclamptic attacks. They are produced in nurslings, though less frequently, by mental excitement occurring in the mother or nurse, and in older children they may be due to emotional causes. Diseases of the brain (meningitis, acute cerebral tuberculosis, cerebral tumors) may also be the source of eclamptiform phenomena; finally, the latter may follow irritation of the peripheral nerves (wounds, pricks).

With regard to *diagnosis*, we must endeavor to determine whether the affection is central or peripheral, idiopathic or symptomatic, a distinction which it is, however, impossible to make in many cases. How often may not anatomical changes be present in the central nervous system, which we do not even suspect, much less detect? If we are able to find none of the diseases mentioned above, in any remote part of the body, which may act as the source of irritation to the nervous centres, we may be enabled, after prolonged and careful observation, to determine to which category the case in question belongs.

We have several times referred, in the preceding chapters, to the characteristic signs of the various cerebral diseases which are accompanied by eclamptic symptoms. In acute hydrocephalus the convulsions are usually preceded by cerebral phenomena (cephalalgia, pupillary anomalies, contracture of the neck, retardation of the pulse, retraction of the abdomen, etc.), the symptoms of the primary disease persisting in the intervals of the attacks, while the true eclampsia of childhood is not, as a rule, accompanied by the above-mentioned cerebral symptoms, and presents no characteristic phenomena apart from the convulsions. In the affection which was described in detail by Elsaesser, under the name of craniotabes (Der weiche Hinterkopf, etc., Stuttgart, 1843), and which is often accompanied by eclampsia, we are able to detect, in the neighborhood of the lambdoid suture, certain points in which the cranium is reduced to the thickness of a sheet of paper, or in which there are complete losses of substance in the bones, with adhesion of the dura mater to the pericranium. The other symptoms of this affection are the sensibility of the head to contact and during the recumbent posture, insomnia, sparseness of the hairs, irritability, and convulsions accompanied by spasms of the glottis. One-half of these cases prove fatal. At the autopsy, hyperæmia and inflammation of the spinal meninges are found to be present. Craniotabes is a form of rachitis which usually develops towards the second quarter of the first year, while the eclamptic convulsions do not appear before the third quarter (during the period of dentition, which is delayed in rachitic patients).

The *prognosis*, in accordance with the statements previously made, is almost always very grave. It is most unfavorable in central, symptomatic eclampsia, and the disease usually proves fatal in these cases. In idiopathic eclampsia a large number of the patients survive and recover completely, but various sequences of the disease often remain permanent, such as contracture of the limbs, strabismus, disorders of speech, hemiplegia, and imbecility. Frequency of the attacks or repeated relapses are very unfavorable prognostic elements. Sometimes, also, the disease may terminate in habitual epilepsy. In reflex eclampsia the attacks may subside if the cause be removed or if it disappear spontaneously.

The *treatment* of infantile eclampsia is concerned chiefly with prophylaxis. Children who manifest a certain tendency to the development of convulsive movements, or whose mothers have suffered from convulsions, should be placed upon a generous and chiefly animal diet; they should sleep in well-ventilated apartments, and be restrained from precocious intellectual exertions; they should live in the country, and be subjected daily to moist frictions of the entire body.

In light attacks we may employ, as sedative measures, enemata of cold water, to which some vinegar has been added, and warm baths. In severe cases, and when the children are more advanced in years, advantage is derived from the administration of chloral, in increasing doses, or of inhalations of chloroform; but the latter should only be employed until the muscles are relaxed, and must not be pushed to the production of complete anæsthesia. When manifest symptoms of stasis and respiratory disorders are present, we may prescribe frictions of the body with warm cloths, cutaneous revulsives, irritating enemata, and the internal administration of a little wine or some of the aromatic infusions with a few drops of tincture of musk. When there is danger of collapse, the majority of authors recommend cold affusions to the head while the patient is in a warm bath. In teething children, the English physicians often practise incision of the gums. This operation will hardly facilitate the protrusion of the tooth, but its effects are rather due to the hæmorrhage produced from the swollen and congested gums and to the diminution of the pressure to which they are subjected.

C.—Toxic Eclampsia.

Experience teaches us that a very large number of poisons of every description may give rise to the most dangerous attacks of convulsions. Certain metallic poisons, irrespirable gases, and poisons of organic origin are included under this category. Lead occupies the most prominent place among the metallic poisons, but lead eclampsia is nevertheless a rare disease. It is almost always associated with other symptoms of chronic lead-poisoning (colic, arthralgia, lead paralysis, delirium, disorders of the special senses, and maniacal attacks), and, as a rule, does not last more than a few days. According to Tanquerel des Planches, one-fifth of the patients affected with this disease recover; Grisolle lost almost all his patients. The former author denied the existence of any relation between this form of eclampsia and uræmia or albuminuria, as he was unable to discover in his patients the presence of albumen in the urine or any lesions in the kidneys. More recently Rosenstein (Schuchardt's Zeitschr. f. prak. Heilk., 4. H., 1867) demonstrated, by a series of experiments on dogs (the animals died from lead amaurosis and eclampsia, after the prolonged administration of acetate of lead), that chronic lead-poisoning produced neither albuminuria nor anatomical changes in the kidneys; that, despite less abundant diuresis, no carbonate of ammonia, and only a very small proportion of urea, was found in the blood; that, after the death of the animals, chemical analysis demonstrated the presence of lead in the brain; and that cerebral anæmia must be regarded as the anatomical cause of the eclampsia. In lead eclampsia, in the human subject, the brain has been found of a dusky color, the parenchyma anæmic and sometimes indurated, and the ventricles dilated; upon chemical analysis the sulphate or albuminate of lead has been found in the cerebral tissues.

Antiphlogistic measures and venesection formerly played an important part in the treatment of this disease. In these cases Stoll prescribed opium, especially when the patient suffered from delirium and attacks of mania. Tanquerel resorted to the administration of croton oil, but its employment produced no more permanent effects than the purgative treatment of the Charité. At the present time the treatment is chiefly symptomatic, consisting of local bleedings, cold compresses to the head, cold affusions, and the administration of opium when the patient suffers from pain and delirium.

In poisoning with irrespirable gases, such as carbonic oxide and carburetted hydrogen, eclamptic phenomena also make their appearance. In these cases we must immediately remove the patient from the action of the deleterious gases. If there is intense congestion of the brain, we may practise venesection; when the respiration is suspended, we must begin artificial respiration. If a faradic battery is readily accessible, we should, according to Ziemssen, faradize the phrenic nerve in the neck. In conditions of sopor and cyanosis, benefit is sometimes derived from cold affusions to the head, frictions of the entire body, and enemata of vinegar.

The vegetable poisons (prussic acid, coniine, nicotine, picrotoxin (the extract of menispermum cocculus), cicuta aquatica, œnanthe crocata) may also give rise to eclamptiform convulsions combined with symptoms of tetanus and trismus. The symptomatology and treatment of these various conditions are still very defective, and we refer for further information concerning the poisons to the special treatises on the subject.

In conclusion, we may say a few words concerning eclampsia arising from contagious and miasmatic influences. Eclampsia sometimes precedes the development of the acute exanthemata, but it quickly ceases. The eclampsia is much more severe when it appears at the height of the affection, when it is accompanied by high fever or by Bright's disease, as in the advanced stages of variola and scarlatina, or by pyæmia and meningitis, as in variola. Eclamptic symptoms may also appear in the first stage of typhoid fever, in acute articular rheumatism, and in facial erysipelas, although these affections are uncomplicated with meningitis or encephalitis. In some cases metastatic foyers are found in the brain, or there is merely a slight serous infiltration of the parenchyma, a fluid condition of the blood, or relaxation of the muscular tissue of the heart. Often, however, none of these changes are observed, and we are left in complete ignorance of the cause of the convulsions. Eclampsia also occurs in pseudo-membranous angina, in œdema glottidis, and in spasm of the glottis in children (thymic asthma). In these cases the convulsions may be attributed to the obstruction to the flow of arterial blood to the brain.

Certain abdominal diseases, acute atrophy of the liver, and the passage of renal or biliary calculi may also be accompanied by eclampsia. Finally, the severe intermittent fevers of certain districts are accompanied by eclamptic attacks, which yield to large doses of quinine.

CHAPTER XXXI.

TETANUS.

TETANUS is a motor spinal neurosis, characterized by an exaggerated. excitability of the motor functions and of reflex action, with alternations. of muscular contractions of a convulsive or tonic character, and running a rapid and very frequently fatal course.

Owing to our complete ignorance of the anatomical lesions of tetanus, an exaggerated importance has been attached to the etiological conditions. in classifying the disease into its various forms. Tetanus has been divided into traumatic, rheumatic, hysterical, inflammatory, toxic, intermittent, endemic, and tetanus neonatorum. This classification groups together entirely dissimilar types, and embraces hysterical tetanus, which is. merely a tonic muscular spasm, of a rapid and benign course, and intermittent tetanus (tetany), which is a partial reflex spasm, due to various. affections, and possessing no gravity.

In the following remarks we shall consider tetanus and trismus conjointly, since they are nearly always combined.

Pathological Anatomy.

Rokitansky first showed, in his important investigations upon the structure of the connective tissue of the nervous centres (1856), that in tetanus the alterations in the connective tissue chiefly consisted of a deposit of a semi-fluid, grayish colloid substance, which abundantly infiltrated the tissues of the cord, separated them from one another, and appeared, upon cut section, like white bands upon an opaque, grayish background. In less advanced forms the microscope reveals the presence of a. delicate, semi-liquid substance, strewn with small granular nuclei, a varicose and disintegrated condition of the nerve-fibres, fatty granules, and colloid and amyloid corpuscles. A few years later Demme's observations. (Beitr. zur path. Anat. des Tetanus, 1859) confirmed these statements, and. showed that the usual sites of this proliferation of connective tissue are, in addition to the cord, the medulla oblongata with the fourth ventricle, the crura medullæ ad cerebellum et ad corpora quadrigemina.

According to the researches of Lockhart Clarke (Med.–Chir. Trans., 48, 1865) upon nine cases of tetanus, inflammatory changes with softening (granular disintegration) occur in the gray substance of the cord, especially around the central canal; the gray horns had often lost their symmetry, and their dilated vessels were surrounded by an abundant exudation, containing nuclei and the débris of nerve-fibres.

Dickinson has described similar changes (eod. loc., 51, 1868) in a case of traumatic tetanus terminating in death at the end of eight days. Michaud (Arch. de Physiol., 1, 1872) has found, in one-quarter of the cases of traumatic tetanus, the following lesions of a subacute central myelitis:

a reddish color of the parenchyma of the cord; small spots of a semi-liquid consistence, with abundant nuclear proliferation into a finely granular substance, in the white matter as high up as the pons, and especially in the central portions of the gray columns. These lesions appeared to result from an exudation which was furnished by the enormously dilated vessels, and were especially observed in the neighborhood of the latter. The nuclear proliferations were abundant in the central canal (which may be entirely obliterated) and in the posterior commissure. The lumbar region was most seriously involved; in one case a subacute spinal meningitis was also present. With regard to the peripheral nerves, extravasations into the neurilemma were found in two sciatic nerves; in two cases there was diminution of the myeline with abundant proliferation of the nuclei in the sheath of Schwann. Hayem has recently studied two cases of tetanus (Arch. de Physiol., 1874) in which he found a colloid exudation into the white and gray substance of the cord, and, in one case, swelling of the nerve-fibres and also of the nerve-cells.

Symptomatology.

Tetanus rarely attacks all parts of the muscular system simultaneously. As a rule, the paroxysm is preceded by certain symptoms, such as chills, a feeling of oppression, painful twinges in the neck, stiffness of certain muscles, lancinating pains starting from the wound, yawning, difficulty in deglutition and in speech. These prodromata may last a few days or hours; the muscles of the jaw are then seized with a tonic spasm, which afterwards extends to the neck, thorax, abdomen, and extremities. At this time the muscles are almost always as rigid as wood, but in some cases this rigidity is less pronounced. It does not always affect all the muscles to the same extent, and it often passes from one to the other. The limbs are more often extended than flexed. The facial muscles are not free from these symptoms. During the periodical exacerbation of the spasms, the features assume an expression of pain or sardonic laughter, the brow and eyebrows frown, the gaze is fixed, and the lips are drawn apart and expose the teeth, the tongue being often caught between them.

At a more advanced stage of the disease the body may be arched with the convexity forwards (opisthotonos). The reverse direction (emprosthotonos) is very rare, having occurred, according to Friedreich, only three times in five hundred and twenty-two cases, and the lateral curvature (pleurosthotonos) only once. Sometimes the rigid body forms a perfectly straight line (orthotonos). Opisthotonos, which is the most frequent form, is often accompanied by lancinating, constricting pains in the back or hypogastrium, which are indicated by the cries of the patient. The contractions may be so violent in certain places that they produce rupture of the muscles, especially of their primitive fibrillæ (Bowman, Todd). The muscular fibres then present transverse ruptures, without lesion of the sarcolemma. In one case of tetanus (strychnine poisoning in a suicide, nineteen years of age) the cardiac muscle was apparently healthy; but I found, in various places, numerous transverse ruptures of the muscular fibres, with hæmorrhagic extravasations, some of which were punctate, while others presented a beautiful appearance, like branching coral.

In the majority of cases the muscular spasms are not alone manifested during the day, but sometimes increase in intensity during the night. During the paroxysms the voluntary movements are entirely abolished, but they reappear in the intervals of the attacks. The remissions may be complete, or slight spasms may occur during the intervals. The mere intention to execute a movement often suffices to produce a spasm. They are also excited by the slightest irritation, such as a touch, a shock communicated to the bed, or a gentle current of air. Consciousness and the special senses undergo no modification during the paroxysms. This distressing situation plunges the patients into a condition of anguish and oppression. They are usually deprived of sleep, the convulsive seizures preventing repose. In the more favorable cases, in which the muscles grow quiet under the influence of a calm sleep, the muscular rigidity resumes its original violence when the patients awake.

Sensibility presents various disorders in tetanus. At the onset, pains occur in the neck, back, epigastrium, or in the muscles which are the seat of the convulsions; sometimes they appear in distant parts, and radiate along the trunks of the nerves or nerve-roots. In two cases observed by Demme, diminution of sensibility to contact and pain occurred, with abolition of sensibility to temperature.

Profound modifications of respiration and circulation are also noticeable. The respiratory muscles are affected, in great part, by the tonic spasms, and the automatism of the respiratory movements is maintained by the diaphragm. Respiration is usually short, labored, and interrupted; during the paroxysms it is difficult and intermittent, followed by symptoms of dyspnœa, oppression, lividity of the skin, perspiration, and miliary eruptions. When the paroxysm has passed, the respiration becomes deeper and slower, and resumes its normal rhythm during the remissions. As a rule, the cardiac movements are also affected. The pulse is frequent and full, and often intermittent; when severe paroxysms follow one another in rapid succession, it becomes small and fluttering. In a case observed by Howship, the heart was found strongly contracted and firm at the autopsy (performed eleven hours after death).

The voice becomes more or less harsh and hoarse; the speech loses its timbre, and in some cases it is unintelligible. Deglutition is almost always embarrassed from the beginning, and is sometimes accompanied by a sensation of ulceration in the pharynx. The mouth is dry, the tongue coated, the saliva viscid, thirst increased, and the appetite diminished.

Constipation is a frequent symptom in tetanus, and is often accompanied by flatulence and tenesmus.

But in certain cases some of the symptoms referred to may be due to the remedies which are employed. The urinary secretion may be normal; if dysuria and anuria are present, the perspiration will be more abundant. The urine is usually alkaline, and sometimes contains sugar (Demme); the earthy phosphates are increased in quantity, the urea diminished; albumen is merely present in minute traces. As Wunderlich first showed, and as the researches of Billroth, Fick, Ebmeier, Erb, Ferber, and Leyden have since confirmed, a considerable elevation of temperature sometimes occurs in tetanus (especially in the last stage), and at times to such a height as is rarely seen in febrile diseases ($43°$–$44°$ C., in one case even as high as $44.7°$); according to Wunderlich, this may be followed, after death, by a further rise of several tenths of a degree. The miliary eruptions occur without rise of temperature. Nevertheless, even in severe cases of tetanus, we usually observe only subfebrile temperature, and, whenever it exceeds the lower grades of febrile movement, we must regard it as indicative of the existence of some complication. The excessive temperatures to which we have referred, as well as those observed in acute lesions of the brain and cervical cord (Brodie), indicate, according to Wunderlich, that the brain is the seat of moderating centres, a paralysis of which will cause a morbid increase of the processes of calorification.

The different varieties of tetanus present, with some slight modifications, the same symptomatology. In trismus and tetanus of the newborn, certain characteristics are found peculiar to the conditions of the first periods of life. The tetanus of the new-born appears within five to six days after the separation of the funis. It is preceded by certain prodromata (fretful sleep, isolated convulsions, relaxation of the features, refusal of the breast on account of the inability to nurse). The paroxysms usually begin with trismus, contortions of the face, and disorders of deglutition. The tonic spasms then extend to the neck, back, the respiratory muscles, and the limbs. Reflex excitability is so much increased that simple contact, or a movement of deglutition, produces convulsions of several minutes' duration, which recur spontaneously with increasing violence and progressively shorter remissions. The disease almost always terminates fatally in two to three days, with symptoms of collapse.

In conclusion, we may say a few words with regard to the affection known as *tetany*. This disease appears under the form of circumscribed tonic spasms, attacking paroxysmally the different muscles of the limbs. It is characterized by its intermittence, the symmetrical affection of the muscles, and the cessation of the spasm when the arteries are compressed (Trousseau). In two cases Erb has succeeded (Arch. f. Psych., IV. Bd., 1873), by acting upon the spinal nerves, in producing tetanus upon closure of the cathode with comparatively weak currents, as well as at the opening of the anode. (This is the first time in which these facts were observed in the human subject.) This morbid excitability of the spinal centre generally disappears under treatment.

Etiology.

ι Tetanus occurs not only in man, but also in the lower animals. Thus, in the tropics, in which the disease is more frequent, cattle and horses are subject to a very fatal form of this affection. If we disregard these endemic foyers of the torrid zone, and those occurring in certain wars, we will find that, under ordinary conditions, tetanus is a comparatively rare disease.

Among 239,911 patients in the Vienna General Hospital, there were 50 cases of tetanus, or .208 per 1,000. In Guy's Hospital there were 72 cases of tetanus among 113,020 patients, or .63 per 1,000. In Bombay, however, Peat found 195 cases of tetanus among 26,719 patients, or 7.3 per 1,000.

With regard to age, experience teaches us that the disease is most frequent from the tenth to the thirtieth years (39.2 per cent., according to Thamhayn). Men are much more predisposed to this affection than women. Among the 50 cases of tetanus occurring in the Vienna Hospital, there were 37 men and 13 women. (Thamhayn found 329 men and 68 women among 397 cases.) The frequency of the disease is also influenced by race ; in Peat's statistics, 11,929 natives furnished 161 cases of tetanus, 115 of which proved fatal ; among 2,733 Europeans there were 21 cases and 15 deaths. The natives are, therefore, not only more subject to tetanus than Europeans, but the disease also proves much more fatal to the former.

The constitution and habits of life do not appear to play an important part in the etiology of this affection. The influence of climatic and atmospheric conditions also seem to have been exaggerated. Certain military surgeons have observed a large number of cases of tetanus, while, during other wars, despite considerable changes in temperature and numerous wounds and operations, very few cases have been seen. In tropical regions, in which the changes of temperature are so marked, tetanus is usually as rare as in temperate zones; but, under the influence of unknown conditions, it suddenly attacks human beings as well as the lower animals, whether living upon the mountains or in the valleys and plains, in moist, dry, hot, or temperate localities. The epidemics are variable, sometimes benign, sometimes virulent in character. Apart from exposure, there are other etiological conditions which may give rise to this disease. It may be classified as rheumatic, traumatic, toxic, and tetanus neonatorum. The large proportion of cases are caused by injuries of the peripheral nerves, due to compression, wounds of various kinds, complicated fractures, opening of abscesses, amputations of limbs, or operations upon various portions of the body.

Tetanus may also occur after central lesions (falls upon the head or back, without appreciable external injury). The reflex stimulation of the spinal system may be produced and maintained by an irritation of the sensory fibres, proceeding from the periphery or from the internal organs. Those forms which have received the name of idiopathic tetanus will usually be found, upon careful examination, to have developed from some internal traumatic origin. Tetanus is thus produced by parturition, uterine affections, intestinal irritation, and inflammatory exudations which have irritated the pneumogastric or phrenic nerves. I will here mention an interesting case of tetanus, developing during the resolution of a pneumonia, which I observed in the Vienna General Hospital.

A patient, suffering from pneumonia of the right lung, took a simple enema (about the eleventh day of the disease) in order to relieve constipation of the bowels, which had lasted several days. After the enema, he complained of a pain in the anus, which became more intense at the end of the second day. When pressure was made upon the coccygeal region, which was spontaneously painful, reflex contractions of the gluteal muscles were produced; the pulse was one hundred. Despite the immediate administration of the extract of cannabis indica and then of large doses of opium, tetanic spasms occurred during the night, followed, upon the next day, by trismus and opisthotonos, with a pulse of one hundred and fifty-two, but without loss of consciousness. The patient died upon the following day. The lesions found, upon autopsy, were serous imbibition of the brain, reddish-brown coloration of the cerebral cortex, the lower lobe of the right lung hepatized and friable, the heart contracted. The veins of the anus were greatly dilated; about two centimetres above the anal orifice was an ulceration as large as a three-cent piece, with poorly defined borders. The spinal meninges were injected, the cord projected above the cut section, and was strewn with a grayish, transparent substance, which increased in quantity from below upwards. The tetanus was probably a complication of the rectal ulceration.

Tetanus occurs most commonly during the period of the cicatrization of wounds. According to Watson, it is more frequent in complicated wounds and in losses of substance, attended with arrest of suppuration, than in recent and simple wounds. As a rule, the violence of the symptoms bears no relation to the severity of the local affection. The time which elapses between the receipt of the injury and the development of tetanus is also extremely variable. Among seven hundred cases collected by Thamhayn, six hundred and three were traumatic and ninety-seven idiopathic. Toxic tetanus is produced by the administration of strychnine and brucine, and the poison is either carried by the blood to the central nervous system or is applied directly to the cord, as in experiments upon animals. After the destruction of the cord, strychnine produces neither spasms in the limbs nor violent contractions of the intestines. If the lesion of the cord is only partial, the tonic spasms will occur in those muscles which are connected with the intact portions. A transverse incision through the posterior columns will prevent the manifestation of the tetanic spasms. If the posterior roots of all the spinal nerves are cut before the animal is poisoned with strychnine, no spasms will follow irritation of the skin. Decapitation of the animals before poisoning, or the extirpation of the medulla oblongata, does not prevent the occurrence of reflex spasms. The application of the poison to the peripheral nerves alone produces no effect.

The tetanizing action of strychnine varies with equal doses, and evidently depends upon the force of resistance of the spinal system. Taylor mentions the case of a physician who died after having taken 0.03 of strychnine. Christison regards this dose as fatal when it is introduced into the blood through the surface of a wound. 0.2 has been known to cause opisthotonos, though not followed by death. Watson refers to two patients, each of whom took 0.07 of strychnine by mistake; one of them suffered from well-marked tetanus, while the other merely complained of vertigo, tremor, disturbances of speech and deglutition, and spasms in the neck. According to Christison, we must regard the absence of tetanic symptoms, during the first two hours after the ingestion of a preparation of nux vomica, as a favorable sign. Van Hasselt, after an exhaustive review of medical literature, found only one case of tetanus which did not occur within three hours after the administration of the strychnine. This patient, however, was an opium eater, in whom the influence of the narcotic perhaps favored recovery. According to Andral and Magendie, the action of brucine is from twelve to thirty-two times weaker than that of strychnine.

Patients who were poisoned with strychnine have been known to recover, even after repeated convulsions and attacks of asphyxia. In these cases the convulsions diminish in frequency and intensity, and finally disappear completely, being followed, for a long time, by exhaustion, paresis of the limbs, and intellectual torpor. In more severe cases the spasms of the jaw, back, and limbs increase rapidly in intensity, the eyes protrude, the pupils are markedly dilated and do not contract under the influence of light, the action of the heart becomes weak and irregular, the respiration becomes labored, finally terminating in cyanosis, and the sense-perceptions and consciousness become less clear. There are usually several paroxysms, and death occurs at the end of a few minutes to a half hour, with symptoms of asphyxia and general collapse.

Tetanus neonatorum is often of a traumatic character, and is due to an inflammation of the umbilicus after the detachment of the funis. The frequency of tetanic spasms in these conditions is important from an etiological point of view. But it would be going too far to attribute all cases of trismus and tetanus neonatorum to affections of the umbilicus. Robust infants tolerate disorders of this character without the slightest inconvenience. Sudden exposure and wounds (circumcision, according to Loewenstein) may also give rise to tetanic spasms in infants. Numerous cases have been reported of hyperæmia, of serous infiltration of the brain or cerebral meninges, of meningeal apoplexy, stasis in the venous sinuses, hyperæmia of the spinal meninges, pulmonary congestion, etc., in which tetanus (probably secondary) was observed during life. Microscopical examination of the nerve-centres has rarely been made in these cases. The disease occurs most frequently from the fifth to the twelfth day after birth; it then becomes rarer up to the age of five years.

Nature of Tetanus.

The clinical symptoms and the data afforded by pathological anatomy concur in demonstrating that the spinal cord is involved in the affection under consideration. The opinion has been entertained that trismus and tetanus are merely functional disorders, due to exaggerated reflex action without any anatomical lesions. The existence of the lesions in wounded nerves, which may sometimes be traced to the cord, gave rise more recently to the reflex theory, while, on the other hand, the theory which attributed to the blood the initial pathogenic rôle also found distinguished advocates.

Upon examining these various opinions, it becomes evident that the theory of reflex irritation furnishes us with the most satisfactory explanations of this affection. The action of cold or of a wound of the peripheral nerves causes, by reflex means, a condition of vascular erethism in the spinal system, and this condition will be produced more readily when the nerves are very sensitive or over-stimulated. This vascular erethism especially involves the gray substance, which is richer in capillaries than the white matter; for the same reason, also, the gray matter receives, in cases of poisoning, a comparatively much larger amount of the toxic principle. The intense irritation of the delicate network of nerve-cells will produce hyperæmia, and the latter, on account of the excessive sensibility of these elements, may itself give rise to reflex spasms. The prompt disappearance of these congestions, before they have produced more marked tissue changes, will also explain the fact that so many cases terminate favorably. If the congestive processes are repeated and prolonged, they give rise to nuclear proliferations and to the formation of new-formed connective tissue. In a certain number of cases a neuritis ascendens develops at the site of the wound, and is propagated along the posterior roots to the white and especially to the gray substance of the cord, where it terminates in a subacute central myelitis.

The greater sensibility and more complex action of the nerve-cells of the medulla oblongata explain the fact that the functions of the latter are affected earlier than those of the cord itself. A lesion of the nucleus of the facial nerve and of the motor nucleus of the trigeminus, situated in the upper half of the medulla oblongata, causes the tonic spasms of the jaw and face with which the disease begins. The lesions then extend to the lower portion of the medulla, which contains the nuclei of the hypoglossal, pneumogastric, glosso-pharyngeal and spinal accessory nerves, and cause disorders of speech, respiration, deglutition, and phonation. The morbid process may also involve the point of decussation of the motor fibres of the limbs, and a large number of the vascular nerves, whose centres are contained in the medulla, as well as the different masses of gray substance, with the prolongations and communications which they send into the cord. The participation of the gray substance of the cord explains the fact that both halves of the body are almost always affected simultaneously with tetanic spasms, and that unilateral tetanus (pleurosthotonos) is so rarely observed. When this condition of exaggerated excitability of the motor functions of the spinal system is prolonged and aggravated, it will result in a paralysis which involves the medulla oblongata and is most frequently the cause of death.

Numerous observations controvert the opinion that local irritation of the nerves is the only cause of tetanus. Thus, after considerable lesions of the nerves of the upper or lower limbs, I have seen anæsthesia develop, with atrophy and paralysis, but without the slightest manifestation of tetanic symptoms. Remak has observed quite a number of cases of traumatic neuritis nodosa without the appearance of reflex spasms, much less of trismus or tetanus. Froriep mentions a case of inflammation and swelling of the sciatic nerve which could be traced to the spinal cord, but was unattended by any tetanic symptoms.

Velpeau, Betoli, Thompson, Spencer Wells, Roser, and Herberg have advanced the opinion that tetanus is a zymotic disease, due to a virus or miasm *sui generis*. These authors refer to the great analogy between tetanus and hydrophobia, and to the fact that tetanus frequently appears epidemically and endemically. They believe that the surface of the wound, whose secretion is perverted, produces a toxic substance, the absorption of which gives rise to a disease of the blood. To these arguments we may reply that, in the first place, the advocates of the "ferment" theory have failed to substantiate their opinions by analysis of the blood or by practising inoculation with the fluids secreted by the wound, or with the muscular fluid or urine of patients suffering from tetanus. On the other hand, this theory does not explain those cases in which section of a diseased nerve, the removal of a foreign body or of a ligature, or the reduction of fractures attended with considerable displacement (Langenbeck) have caused the prompt subsidence of the symptoms of tetanus. In such cases we cannot regard the blood as the pathogenic factor of the disease; it is more natural to consider the local lesions of the nerves as the primary cause of the affection. According to the investigations of Funke and Ranke, the normal alkaline reaction of the nervous tissues becomes acid in tetanus. Heidenhain has also observed this acidity of the central nervous system, but it has not hitherto been demonstrated with regard to the peripheral nerves

Diagnosis and Prognosis.

Upon examining the medical literature of the subject, it will become evident that many cases have been reported as tetanus which were merely varieties of tonic spasms affecting the trunk and limbs. In all these cases the characteristic sign of morbid increase of reflex action has been entirely lost sight of. The diseases which are most frequently mistaken for tetanus are spinal meningitis, catalepsy, hysteria, hydrophobia, and spasm of the muscles of mastication.

In spinal meningitis, tonic spasms occur in the neck, back, and limbs, and are attended with febrile symptoms. But they are distinguished from true tetanic spasms by the absence of the enormous increase of reflex excitability, and of the periodical remissions, and by the contractures, the muscular atrophy, and the paralyses which persist after the acute stage of the disease has subsided. (For further details, *vide* Vol. I., p. 188.) The tonic spasms sometimes observed in hysteria are characterized by their short duration, their admixture with various other hysterical phenomena, and by the absence of abnormal reflex excitability. In cataleptic rigidity (especially in the catochus of the ancients) loss of consciousness is observed, with suppression of reflex motion, abolition of the functions of the special senses and of the sensibility to pain; finally, we almost always discover, in the previous history, some indications of hysteria, of chorea magna, or of insanity. In epilepsy and eclampsia the tetanic stiffness is temporary; the nature of the convulsions, their sudden appearance, the characteristic cry, which precedes them, the loss of consciousness, the abolition of the functions of special sense, the prompt termination of the attack, and the condition of the urine in the eclampsia of pregnant women, afford us sufficient data for forming a diagnosis.

Hydrophobia is also characterized by an exaggeration of the reflex acts, by tetanic symptoms, and by spasms of respiration and deglutition. But there are numerous other signs which enable us to exclude tetanus, such as the much slower development of hydrophobia after the receipt of the wound, the excessive sensibility of the patients to the slightest current of air, their dislike of water or shining objects, the sight or contact of which also produces terrible spasms, the unusual precipitation which they evince in their movements, and often, also, in their conversation, and the attacks of loss of consciousness with furious delirium which they sometimes present.

The tonic spasm in the distribution of the motor portion of the trigeminus (facial spasm of the masticators, Romberg) is observed in cerebral softening, inflammation of the brain and its meninges, or in consequence of irritation of the sensory nerves. In the first case its real nature can be determined by the remaining symptoms; when it is of peripheral origin, by the integrity of the function of deglutition, the freedom of the other parts of the muscular system from spasm and the absence of convulsive paroxysms. Finally, the tetanic symptoms which sometimes develop in the course of typhoid fever, the acute exanthemata, pyæmia, and intermittent fever (in tropical regions) are readily recognized by their irregular development and termination, and especially by the ensemble of symptoms peculiar to each of these diseases.

We possess no definite signs which will permit us to form a positive conclusion with regard to the termination of each individual case. Experience has shown that recovery is possible, even after an exceptional violence of the symptoms. On the other hand, treacherous remissions occur, which may be followed by fresh attacks, or during which the patients may die of exhaustion. We may state, in general terms, that a favorable termination may be looked for when the patient has previously enjoyed good health; when he is younger than ten years or older than thirty years of age; when the wound is simple and recent; when the disturbances of circulation, respiration, and nutrition are not very severe or do not appear very early; when the skin, which is at first dry and cold, recovers its warmth and moisture; and, finally, when the temperature of the body returns to the normal.

Treatment.

If we consider the large number of successful results obtained by the most varied remedies, and, on the other hand, the equally large number of fatal cases, despite all the measures which may have been employed, we will become convinced that we possess no specific remedy for tetanus, and that, in each case, the object of medical intervention is to diminish the consequences of the local lesion, to relieve, at least in part, the disorders of the nervous system, and to maintain the strength of the patient until the disease has run its course.

Let us discuss, in the first place, the various measures which constitute the external treatment. The neurotomies, which have been practised by some authors, often prove ineffectual, because we cannot positively determine the location of the primarily injured nerve, and because the nerve-centres are always affected unless the section has been performed at an early period. Amputation is inadvisable, unless the operation has been rendered necessary for other reasons.

Venesection has few adherents, but, when cautiously employed, it may be useful in certain cases which are accompanied by dangerous hyperæmia. We may also derive benefit, at times, from leeching, wet-cups, and moxæ along the vertebral column. Applications of ice to the spine have been recommended by Todd, and especially by Carpenter (the latter cured sixteen cases out of seventeen by this plan of treatment). Warm baths of several hours' duration have a beneficial effect. Moist packs, followed by cool half-baths, are extremely useful, according to Ebert and Stein, in combating the reflex excitability and the tetanic paroxysms. Finally, we may resort to the use of irritating enemata (turpentine); narcotic salves and chloroform liniment are used to relieve local pains.

Among the anæsthetic agents, chloroform and ether are most frequently employed. Chloroform diminishes the severity of the spasms, but only during the continuance of the anæsthesia, and the tetanic symptoms reappear soon after the termination of the latter. According to Hobart, no permanent benefit is obtained, even though the anæsthesia is continued for several days. In one case this plan of treatment resulted in severe congestion of the bronchi, which were found to contain a large accumulation of mucus. Dick, Ord, and others have administered chloroform internally in combination with other sedative agents. Lately good results have been obtained from increasing doses of hydrate of chloral.

The narcotics have been highly esteemed from the earliest periods. Aconite, recommended by Paget and Campbell, and, more recently, by Wunderlich (tincture of aconite, five to ten drops, three or four times a day, in increasing doses), lessens the frequency of the pulse and retards the convulsions.

Belladonna, according to Dupuy and Fournier, diminishes the rigidity of the muscles, but is more efficacious when given in the form of hypodermic injections of atropine than when administered internally. Extract of cannabis indica is given in doses of 0.20–0.30 every hour. According to experiments made upon frogs, nicotine has the power of neutralizing the tetanizing action of strychnine. Harrison and Haughton have given it in doses of two to four milligrammes (dissolved in water and alcohol) every two or three hours; it diminishes the action of the heart and the muscular spasms, and stimulates the functions of the skin. This substance is an active cardiac poison, and its administration is sometimes attended with danger ; in the majority of cases it is preferable to administer strong enemata of tobacco in its stead. Opium is one of the most frequently employed and most useful remedies in this affection. It is given in large doses, from 0.05–0.10 hourly, until the appearance of symptoms of relaxation. In periodical tetanus it is combined with quinine, and the patients sometimes tolerate enormous doses. Subcutaneous injections of morphine have also been employed, especially in trismus. The good results which certain authors attribute to this plan of medication have not been obtained in many of the cases observed in the Vienna General Hospital.

Other remedies have been recently employed, such as bromide of potassium, curare, extract of calabar-bean, and electricity. Bromide of potassium, to the depressing action of which upon reflex action we have so frequently alluded, has been particularly recommended by Thompson. It must be given in large doses (sixteen to eighteen grammes daily). The experiments of Cl. Bernard have proved that curare abolishes the irritability of the cord and of the motor nerve-trunks, but has no effect upon the excitability of the muscles. The first experiments upon man were made in 1859, by Vella, who employed it in trismus in the form of compresses soaked with curare and applied to the wound. Shortly afterwards, Demme and Gherini published cases of tetanus cured by subcutaneous or intra-muscular injections of curare. The dose to be used as injection is 0.01–0.07; at the end of a few minutes the spasms diminish and the pulse becomes less rapid; the injection may be renewed at the end of three or four hours, after the effect of the former one has passed away. Among ten cases of tetanus from gunshot wounds, which were treated with curare by Busch, five cases recovered. The extract of calabar-bean is also preferably employed in the form of hypodermic injections, 0.02–0.07 every two or three hours; it is advisable to add some carbonate of potash to the solution, in order to diminish the pain which the injection causes and to prevent the formation of abscesses. Up to the year 1868 six cases of recovery under this plan of treatment were reported.

In 1838 Matteucci published a case of traumatic tetanus, in which he had succeeded in diminishing for some time the violence of the paroxysms by means of the constant galvanic current (Volta's pile of forty elements). In a case published by M'Dowall (Lancet, 1861), the dyspnœa was diminished and the spasms suspended for two hours by a single application of an electro-magnetic apparatus. The physician having left, the electrization was suspended, and the patient died. Nobili, and, more recently, Ranke, having stated that the muscles of tetanized frogs relax under the influence of the constant current, E. Mendel employed the galvanic treatment with good results in several cases of tetanus in man (Ber. Klin. Wschr., 38, 1868). He placed the negative pole upon the cervical vertebræ, the positive pole upon one of the lower or upper limbs, and allowed the current to pass from ten to fifteen minutes. The relaxation which was thus obtained remained persistent after several seances, and the patient made an excellent recovery.

CHAPTER XXXII.

HYDROPHOBIA.

At the commencement of this century the specific nature of hydrophobia was often called in question, and the disease was either regarded as an epidemic catarrh of the pharynx, with secondary affection of the brain, as traumatic tetanus, or as a psychical neurosis. At the present day all these theories are abandoned, and hydrophobia is now considered to be a cerebro-spinal neurosis of a contagious nature.

When individuals are bitten by animals, such as dogs, cats, wolves, and foxes which are mad or suspected of madness, and the necessary measures are not immediately adopted, the patients usually become affected with that peculiar and terrible toxic neurosis known as hydrophobia. The period of incubation varies considerably in duration. According to Hamilton's and Thamhayn's statistics, it generally occupies from eighteen to fifty-nine days. The earliest outbreak of the disease occurs during the first week; sometimes the period of incubation may last several months, and there are a few examples on record (though they must be looked upon with suspicion) in which it lasted several years.

The following prodromata of the disease are often observed: chills, malaise, distaste for fluids, embarrassment of deglutition and respiration, painful sensations in the neighborhood of the bite, or pains radiating from this locality along the nerve-trunks; finally, muscular contractions in the limbs and psychical disorders. The duration of this stage varies from one to four days.

The onset of the disease may develop from the increase of the prodromata mentioned above, or it may begin suddenly. The primary difficulty in deglutition may be followed by an intense spasm of the pharynx, and respiration, which was previously labored, is rendered still more so by spasm of the respiratory muscles; or perhaps the patient is suddenly seized, while about to drink, with a terrible spasmodic paroxysm. In less severe cases the patients are able to drink, but they carry the glass very rapidly to the mouth, and swallow precipitately. Upon closing the eyes, or upon handing them the liquids in opaque vessels, the disturbances of deglutition are sometimes overcome more readily.

This feeling of abhorrence of water may increase to such a degree that a paroxysm will develop from the mere sight of water, from contact with it, from hearing the noise made by pouring it from one vessel to another, or, perhaps, from merely hearing compresses wrung out. In severe cases there is an absolute impossibility of swallowing liquids (deglutition of solid substances is almost always difficult, but is preserved). If the patient attempts to drink, or if the skin is moistened with water, spasms develop, which are attended with asphyxia, convulsions of the pharynx, face, and entire body, and a condition of intense excitement. A piece of ice placed upon the tongue will produce a paroxysm; this will also be provoked by swallowing saliva, and the patients therefore expectorate

considerably. It is a remarkable fact (according to Thamhayn and Voltolini) that the patients generally tolerate warm baths quite well at this stage of the disease.

The irritability of the senses is manifested by the extreme sensibility to the slightest currents of air, to light and to shining objects. Under the influence of these causes, the patients make active movements of inspiration, carry the head backwards, or are even affected with general convulsions. They manifest extreme precipitation in all their movements, and sometimes display an astonishing loquacity. In children, hydrophobia usually assumes the characteristics of some form of insanity, the hyperæsthetic symptoms predominating, but without any especial tetanic phenomena.

The face is pale or very livid, and bears an expression of restlessness or sadness. The eyes are usually fixed and glassy, more rarely they roll in the orbits; the pupils are dilated, but sometimes contract temporarily under the influence of light.

During the course of the disease convulsive movements are observed in the muscles of the face, jaw, neck, and trunk, and tetanic spasms may even occur in the limbs. The patients complain of painful sensations in the head, neck, back, epigastrium, or in the limb which has been bitten.

Consciousness is often preserved until death; in certain cases it is lost from the third or fifth day, and the patient presents illusions of the senses, delirium, exaltation, or even attacks of mania and insanity, with or without attempts at biting the attendants. Insomnia occurs in most cases, but we may also observe the various phases of half-sleep.

The respiration often presents no peculiarity in the interval of the attacks; during the paroxysms it is more or less labored, panting, and irregular, and at times the dyspnœa becomes excessive.

The respiratory disorders may be isochronous with the pharyngeal and laryngeal spasms, or may precede them. As a rule, the patients avoid deep inspirations, because they are apt to produce convulsions. The pulse is frequent and small from the beginning, and these qualities increase in intensity towards the termination of the disease.

The digestive apparatus is usually but slightly affected. Despite the great increase of general sensibility, the nerves of the stomach react very feebly to the action of tartar emetic, and, according to Schuh, it may often be given in large doses without producing any effect. The appetite is usually lost. The patient almost always suffers from excessive thirst, together with a sensation of burning in the throat; and the saliva, which is expectorated with frequency, is frothy, mucous, and adherent. The pustules, described by Marochetti under the term "lysses," are found, in the first few days of the period of incubation, upon the sides of the frænum linguæ. In a case published recently by Créquy, the urine contained an abundance of sugar.

Towards the termination of the disease, which almost always proves fatal, the symptoms become more severe. The patients are extremely agitated, and are continually expectorating in all directions ; bluish spots appear upon the sweat-covered skin. Vomiting very frequently occurs, and the vomited matters are frothy, sanguinolent, and look like coffee-grounds; the pulse is extremely weak. The patients die suddenly in convulsions, or in the midst of symptoms of jactitation, attended with loss of consciousness. A few hours before death a deceptive calm is sometimes observed, during which the patients may even recover the power of drinking.

Pathological Anatomy and Histology.

Among the autopsies collected by Thamhayn, we find the following lesions mentioned on several occasions: abundance of blood in the brain, dark coloration of the cortical substance, foyers of softening in the optic thalamus or corpus striatum, extreme vascularization of the medulla oblongata, congestion of the spinal meninges, congestion of the cord with partial softening; at times the sympathetic and phrenic nerves and the cerebral branches of the pneumogastric nerve have been found injected. In some cases the peripheral nerves of the arm which had been bitten presented a reddish coloration. The respiratory apparatus was almost always extremely hyperæmic. The papillæ of the tongue and pharynx sometimes projected to an extreme degree, and now and then small bullæ were found upon the lower surface of the tongue.

In 1869 Meynert made some extremely interesting histological investigations upon the brain and spinal cord of two patients (a boy and a girl) who had died of hydrophobia in Oppolzer's service. In these patients the hydrophobia had manifested itself as a form of psychosis, with predominance of symptoms of hyperæsthesia, temporary spasms of the respiratory muscles, especially when about to drink, but without any tetanic symptoms.

In the first case the cord presented the following appearances: the reticulum had preserved its delicacy; the vessels were filled with blood (the latter was coagulated, and looked like small colloid masses), and their walls partially affected by amyloid degeneration; in some of them the tunica adventitia presented nuclear proliferations. Some of the nerve-fibres were surrounded by a considerably swollen medullary substance, which resisted mechanical action (traction); others presented all the stages intermediate between this and colloid degeneration and destruction of the fibres; in certain places the axis cylinders had disappeared. These lesions were somewhat more marked in the lumbar than in the cervical region.

In the second case the reticulum of the posterior spinal columns was hypertrophied from excessive enlargement of the stellate neuroglia-cells; in the antero-lateral column the reticulum was transformed into small, finely granular fibrillæ, the vessels were filled with blood, and their walls were partially affected with amyloid degeneration. The cortex and medullary substance of the brain presented a large number of irregular vacuoles, which did not always contain anatomical elements, and which pressed the bundles of white fibres aside in a curved form. Traces of colloid substance were found in the perivascular spaces and in some of the vacuoles scattered through the nervous tissue. A large number of the ganglion-cells of the cerebral cortex presented the appearances of molecular destruction, while others were very much swollen and sclerosed. According to Meynert, these appearances were due to an œdematous process, caused by an exudation from the markedly congested vessels. He thinks that the exudation was beginning to diffuse itself into the nerve-tissues (because no obliteration of the perivascular spaces was noticeable). On the other hand, the exudation presents the appearances of a very thin colloid matter which has assumed, from an exchange with the protein compounds scattered throughout the tissues, their optical characteristics.

In a more recent case, reported by Hammond, microscopical examination of the cerebral cortex showed enlargement and thickening of the vessels; the outer, and, to a less degree, the second layer of nerve-cells were infiltrated with fatty granulations and amyloid corpuscles; the cerebral ganglia were normal. In the nuclei of the pneumogastric and hypoglossal nerves the vessels were also enlarged, and the ganglion-cells were granular and markedly diminished in number and size; the roots of the pneumogastric, spinal accessory, and hypoglossal nerves were involved in the same degeneration. Analogous changes were present in the gray substance of the cord; the neuroglia-cells in the white substance were undergoing nuclear proliferation. Clifford Albutt made a similar series of observations in two cases of hydrophobia.

We may, finally, mention the results obtained by Prof. Ragsky (Oester. Jahrb., Aug., 1843) from a chemical analysis of the blood. He found that the blood acquired a neutral reaction, whereas in the normal condition it was feebly alkaline; it contained 73.59 parts per 100 of water, instead of the normal amount (80 per 100); and 2.9 parts of solid matters, instead of 4.42. 1,000 parts contained 4.8 of fibrin, 133 of hemato-globuline, 80.2 of albumen, 12.4 of extractive matters and salts, and 796.6 of water. It is very desirable that new analyses of a similar character should be undertaken.

Nature of Hydrophobia.

The pathognomonic symptoms, as well as the anatomical lesions found in the brain and cord, prove that hydrophobia in man is due to a toxic change in the nerve-centres. The rabietic poison which is inoculated by the bite acts, to all appearances, like a fixed ferment. The part played by the blood, as the agent for the transportation of the morbid principle, was demonstrated by the experiments of Hertwig (Hufeland's Journ., 1828, p. 168), who found that the virulent action was transmitted by the fluid extracted from the salivary canals and by the venous and arterial blood. Magendie and Breschet successfully inoculated two dogs with the saliva of a man who had died of hydrophobia. The lesions indicative of œdema, observed by Meynert, lead us to suspect a vascular transudation into the adjacent tissue, and this process is rendered easy by the changes found in the walls of the vessels.

We may apply to rabietic poisoning the remark which we made in the preceding chapter, viz., that the medulla oblongata undergoes more profound changes than the cord, and that the centres of respiration and deglutition are the first to react to these lesions. The phenomena which appear soon afterwards, such as hyperæsthesia, painful sensations, convulsive and tetanic symptoms, denote the invasion of the spinal cord by the toxic action, and the psychical disorders correspond to the implication of the cerebral cortex. These symptoms are due to the tissue changes which were first discovered by Meynert in the nerve-centres. The prodromata, which precede (for one to four days) the invasion of the disease, are evidently the first manifestations of the toxic irritation. The duration of the period of incubation depends upon the activity of the poison and upon the greater or less length of time in which the textural changes develop.

The receptivity of the organism is very variable, as Hertwig has experimentally demonstrated upon animals. Of fifty-nine animals which were inoculated, only fourteen were infected; in some a single inoculation sufficed to produce infection, in others three or four inoculations became necessary. It has been shown in man that certain accidental causes (emotions, excesses, exposure), which diminish the force of resistance of the nervous system, may also favor the onset of the disease.

Diagnosis and Prognosis.

The *diagnosis* of hydrophobia lyssodes is rendered positive by the fact that the patient has been previously bitten by a rabid animal, and by the progressive aggravation of the spasms of respiration and deglutition. The hydrophobic symptoms, which are sometimes observed under the influence of other diseases, are readily distinguished with a little attention. Imaginary hydrophobia is merely the result of excessive fear; it is unattended by any exaggeration of reflex action, and moral treatment is alone required. The development of spontaneous hydrophobia has not been hitherto demonstrated in man.

In hysterical hydrophobia, spasms of the pharynx and glottis also occur, but these attacks are usually of short duration, and they are accompanied by other hysterical symptoms and by characteristic disorders of sensation and motion. Finally, symptomatic hydrophobia, which is observed as a rare complication of diseases of the pharynx and larynx, of cerebral affections, of typhoid fever, and of pernicious fevers, is recognized without difficulty by the other symptoms of the disease.

The *prognosis* is generally extremely unfavorable. Of two hundred and sixteen cases collected by Thamhayn, there were only six observations by Smith (four of which occurred after bites of dogs which were undoubtedly rabid) which terminated in recovery, or a proportion of one to thirty-six. The majority of the patients die upon the fourth or fifth day from the appearance of the first paroxysm. According to the medical laws of Austria, every individual, suspected of hydrophobia, must remain forty-two days under medical surveillance. At the expiration of this period, if no general symptoms have appeared, it is very probable that the disease will not develop.

The prognosis is more favorable if the virus has been destroyed by immediate cauterization of the wound, or within twenty-four to forty-eight hours. According to the recent observations of Renault, the absorption of the virus from the wound occurs with such rapidity that very little is to be hoped for even from immediate cauterization. Nevertheless, in a large number of cases energetic cauterization, performed within twenty-four or forty-eight hours, has prevented the development of the disease. Some cases have been reported in which the affection developed with a slower course than usual, despite cauterization performed upon the day after the bite; other cases have escaped, in which the cauterization was only performed several days after the receipt of the wound. We must, therefore, conclude that the individual receptivity, as well as the energy of the virus, is liable to variation.

Treatment.

The chief importance should be attached to the prophylactic treatment. The best measure consists in cleansing the wound and cauterizing it with the hot iron or with caustic potash; nitrate of silver is ineffectual. The wound should be kept open for five or six weeks by means of ung.

basilic., since experience has proved that if the disease does develop, the symptoms will be less severe if the wound suppurates. When the wound changes its appearance, or when it becomes the seat of unusual sensibility, the cicatrix must be opened without delay and suppuration induced. In a case reported by Hooper, which terminated in recovery (Med. Times, May, 1847), the cicatrix had reopened and suppurated spontaneously. In addition, care must be taken that the patient is kept perfectly quiet. When the patient has been wounded in several places, Fuchs has obtained good results by immediately placing the patients in mercurial baths (which cauterize all the affected parts).

The efforts which have been made for centuries, to discover an anti-dote to the rabietic poison, have proved fruitless. Nevertheless, re-newed experiments upon dogs may not prove useless with regard to treat-ment. Injections of warm water into the veins, performed by Magendie upon dogs, have also produced in man a marked improvement in the most threatening symptoms, though only for a certain length of time. To judge from the happy effects of transfusion in eclampsia, this meas-ure should also be employed in hydrophobia. Venesection and amputa-tion of the bitten part must be avoided on account of their debilitating and exciting action.

Opium, belladonna, cantharidis (internally and externally), and mer-curials (either alone or combined with musk), have proved as useless as the innumerable other extraordinary measures which have been em-ployed. Warm baths produce a certain degree of calm ; Buisson has obtained good effects from vapor-baths, and Gosselin by producing copi-ous perspiration. We may finally add that Schivardi caused a cessation of the hydrophobic symptoms by employing the continuous current for several days (from the soles of the feet to the forehead); his patient died, however, from exhaustion. The results obtained by several authors in tetanus, by early injections of curare, should encourage us to employ the same remedy in hydrophobia. Offenberg (Diss. Inaug., Berlin, 1875) has recently published a case in which injections of 0.02 of curare (seven doses within five and a half hours) caused the complete disappearance of the spasms and of the hydrophobic and photophobic symptoms. These symptoms were replaced by paralysis of the limbs, which was only re-lieved after a period of two months, the patient still manifesting great slowness in his gait at the end of that time.

CLASS VI.

NEUROSES ASSOCIATED WITH TREMOR AND DISORDERS OF CO-ORDINATION.

CHAPTER XXXIII.

TREMOR AND PARALYSIS AGITANS.

a. Tremor.

TREMOR consists of a series of intermittent clonic muscular spasms, or short excursion, which may be called into action by central action or by peripheral irritation. It may be experimentally produced in decapitated animals, by subjecting the cord to a weak current furnished by an induction apparatus with slow interruptions (Volkmann). Upon repeating the same experiment upon frogs which have been poisoned by nicotine, tremor will be produced throughout the entire body. It will not develop if curare has been previously injected or if the nervous centres have been destroyed; tremor will occur, however, if the pons and medulla oblongata have been preserved (Vulpian). According to Schiff, by detaching a motor nerve from its centre (the facial or hypoglossal, for example) movements of oscillation will occur in the muscles which have been paralyzed by the nerve section. These movements continue, as a rule, for two days, and may even persist for weeks or months.

In man, tremor indicates an abnormal condition of irritation of the nervous centres. This exaggeration of excitability may have its seat in the brain, as in psychical excitement (sorrow, fright, anguish), when the whole body is affected with tremor; or it may be observed, as the first symptom of motor irritation, in tumors, sclerosis, or softening which involve the cerebral ganglia or adjacent parts (Duchek, Leyden, Charcot). It is evident that the morbid excitability which accompanies tremor is frequently situated in the spinal cord. Intermittent muscular spasms may be produced in the various degenerations of the cord (after traumatism or in progressive muscular atrophy) under the form of limited contractions, or of more extended clonic spasms occupying the limbs or trunk. These spasms are reflex and are caused by irritation of the cord, especially of the gray substance. Tremor is not infrequently due to shortening of the antagonistic muscles, causing trembling and jerking movements. In cases of intense irritability of the nerve-centres (as in cerebro-spinal sclerosis and certain forms of myelitis and ataxia), the influence of volition will suffice to irritate the motor nerves and produce very marked tremor of the limbs.

In the affections to which we have referred above, the tremor only occurs after voluntary motion, psychical irritation, or peripheral impulses (as in passive movements). In another series of cases, however, it persists during repose, and only disappears under the influence of sleep. In these instances voluntary impulse may nevertheless serve to increase the intensity of the tremor. The momentary expenditures of force usually preserve their normal vigor, though often accompanied by extreme exhaustion. The various forms included in this category result from the action of toxic substances (alcohol, opium, metallic poisons), or of severe diseases (typhoid and intermittent fever, pneumonia of drunkards). In these conditions of morbid excitability of the nervous centres the oscillations of the current of blood will suffice to produce muscular spasms. In recent forms the motor and sensory action of the galvanic current upon the nerves may be considerably increased, but it is diminished, on the other hand, in the older forms. In sclerosis of the nerve-centres, and in the tremor caused by disturbances in the spinal axis, intense tremor may often be produced by means of strong induction currents.

The tremor may only involve individual limbs (more frequently the upper than the lower) or merely the muscles of the neck or head. But in other cases almost all the muscles are affected, including those of the face, lower jaw, and tongue; speech is then markedly embarrassed. The tremulous movements are sometimes limited to the ocular muscles (under the form of nystagmus). Tremor may also, as we have indicated above, appear temporarily under the influence of certain sensorial impressions, or in the course of certain diseases; it sometimes constitutes a symptom which continues during life. The modifications with regard to intensity generally depend upon causes to which we have referred above.

From an *etiological* point of view, we may state, in the first place, that tremor preferably attacks nervous and easily excited individuals. Delicate children, born of a nervous mother, very frequently manifest the affection during the first years of life. This is noticeable by the manner in which they hold their spoon, or in their first attempts at writing; it disappears as the children grow stronger. The female sex, more sensitive and more readily excited, generally presents a greater predisposition to tremor than the male sex. In the latter, irritation of the genital functions, and especially onanism, are the causes of the early and obstinate forms of the affection.

At a more advanced age it may be produced by chronic alcoholism, the opium habit, the abuse of strong tobacco, the action of mercurial vapors, or of lead preparations to which the system is subjected in certain trades, and the prolonged use of cosmetics or paint containing mercury or lead. Severe diseases are not infrequently followed by tremor of the limbs. This is also true of copious hæmorrhages, hysteria, continued or repeated depressing moral agencies, and physical or intellectual efforts. Finally, the weakness of old age also favors the appearance of tremor.

In the *treatment* of tremor, we must endeavor to remove the primary cause, to diminish the morbid excitability of the nerve-centres, and to suppress certain injurious influences. The nervous tremor of childhood and puberty may be combated by washing the entire body with cold water or vinegar, and by means of cold affusions to the back while the patient is in a lukewarm half-bath. In the anæmia or general weakness following severe diseases, we may employ, in addition to the preceding measures, ferruginous mineral waters, quinine, light wines, and a trip to the mountains.

In the tremor resulting from extreme excitability of the spinal system, Eulenburg (Ber. klin. Wschr., 46, 1872) obtained good effects from the administration of arsenic.

Starting from the experiments of Sklarck (Reichert and Du Bois' Archiv., 1866), who found that preparations of arsenious acid produced paralysis of the sensory portions of the cord with preservation of the motor functions, Eulenburg at first gave Fowler's solution internally, but without success. The tremor only disappeared after the employment of subcutaneous injections (one part of Fowler's solution to two of water; a third or half of a syringeful, representing 0.11–0.17 of the mixture, was at first given daily, and then every two days).

Excellent effects are often obtained from the use of hydrotherapeutic measures; they diminish the morbid excitability of the centres and the excess of reflex action. We may begin with cool dorsal irrigations in a half-bath whose temperature is gradually lowered. As the nervous system recovers its tone, these measures may be replaced by douches and full baths. Sea-baths are also useful in these cases.

Electrical treatment appears advantageous in certain forms of tremor. Ascending or descending stabile galvanic currents may be passed through the vertebral column, and from this situation to the nerves of the affected limbs. This plan is more advantageous than faradization, because currents whose tension is too great increase the excitability of the centres and may aggravate the tremor. In tremor limited to the hands, such as occurs in convalescents from typhoid fever, and in lead and mercurial poisoning, the movements may be made to disappear by moderate stimulation of the muscles of the hand by means of induced currents. Good effects have also been obtained, in certain cases, by well-regulated gymnastic exercises.

Alcoholic tremor is favorably influenced in the majority of instances by the use of morphine or of extract of opium administered either internally or subcutaneously. Chloral is indicated (three to five grammes at a dose) when the opium or large doses of digitalis prove insufficient. It is necessary, in such cases, to resort to even much larger doses, when the patient is accustomed to strong spirituous liquors. Oulmont has obtained good results from the administration of hyoscyamine (0.003–0.012 daily) in several cases of mercurial and senile tremor.

b. Paralysis Agitans.

Paralysis agitans represents the most severe form of tremor. It was observed and carefully described for the first time by Parkinson (Essay on the Shaking Palsy, London, 1817). The gravity of this affection results from its peculiar intensity, from its continuous progress and extension, and from its termination in general paralysis. The tremor is a characteristic sign of the decay of the motor power, and it is also the precursor of the paralysis.

The *anatomical lesions* peculiar to paralysis agitans are unknown. In some cases, reported by Parkinson, Marshall Hall, Oppolzer, Lebert, etc., indurations and hyperplasiæ were found in the pons varolii, tubercula quadrigemina, and medulla oblongata, but microscopical examinations were not made. But if we may judge from the clinical histories, these cases belong under the category of disseminated sclerosis, the symptoms of which were unknown at that period.   Foyers of softening in the brain and cord, and encephalitis and sclerosis of the Ammon's horn (Chvostek) have been observed in this disease; but these lesions must be regarded as accidental complications.

Greater importance is attached to the changes recently observed in three cases by Charcot and Joffroy (Soć. de Biol., 1871).

In all these cases there was obliteration of the central canal from proliferation of the epithelial elements, a development of nuclei around the canal and marked pigmentation of the nerve-cells, especially in the columns of Clarke; in two cases the pons varolii contained masses of amyloid corpuscles, and in one it was partially sclerotic.   Further investigations must decide upon the pathological significance of these inflammatory changes in the cord and other regions.

The onset of paralysis agitans is often preceded by prodromata, such as cerebral congestion, chronic insomnia, marked irritability, muscular contractions, or temporary feeling of weakness in the limbs.   The disease proper begins with a slight trembling, usually in the upper limbs.   It appears at first in small groups of muscles, often under the form of slight movements of pronation and supination of the forearm, which follow one another in rapid succession.   In the beginning these involuntary movements may be completely controlled by the patient, or at least diminished by supporting the limb in which they occur; they also cease during sleep. At a later period the trembling movement increases in intensity, becomes exaggerated under the influence of emotional excitement, cold, and effort, and extends to one-half of the body (often beginning on the right side).   It then extends to the arm and leg of the opposite side and to the muscles of the lower jaw, lips, and tongue.   Paraplegic and alternate forms of tremor are very rare.   If the patient is placed in a position of extension, and the trunk is supported upon each side, the tremor will be arrested for a certain length of time.   The patients usually have very immobile features, and the movements of the eyes are very circumscribed; the mouth is often filled with saliva, which is swallowed with difficulty; speech is difficult and sometimes jerking, and the writing is pointed and oblique.

If we carefully examine the motor functions, we will sooner or later find characteristic disturbances.   The muscles of the limbs, trunk, and, most frequently, of the neck are rigid, and the patients experience in them a sensation of cramp; the voluntary movements are stiff and slow (Charcot).   If the tonic tension predominates in the flexors, the neck and trunk are inclined forwards in the vertical position; the upper limbs and, later, the lower limbs, assume a semi-flexed position (vide Fig. 19).   The thumb is usually adducted and directed towards the palm of the hand, the movements of the phalangeal and carpal articulations are markedly interfered with, and the patients are unable to carry the hand backwards to the shoulder.   In walking, the body inclines towards the hemiparetic side.   When the disease is prolonged, a characteristic position of the limbs develops, as Charcot has pointed out—flexion of the first phalanges, forcible flexion of the second phalanges, and slight flexion of the third.   The gait is precipitate and uncertain.   Sauvage and Sagar have mentioned, as a pathognomonic sign, a tendency to run and to fall forwards or backwards.   This is not always noticeable, is only a complication of the later periods, and is caused by the effort which the patient makes to maintain his centre of gravity within the base of support.   We can sometimes produce a movement of recoil in the patients, by exercising a scarcely perceptible traction upon their clothes (Charcot). The nearer the disease approaches its fatal termination, the more the paresis changes to paralysis. The tremor then persists during sleep, and the latter may be interrupted on account of the shocks communicated by the patient to the bed.

Towards the close, the embarrassment in speech, mastication, and deglutition terminates in complete abolition of these functions.

The following disorders of sensation are observed: a feeling of numbness in the fingers, neuralgic pains in the limbs affected with tremor, pains in the neck or back (observed by Blasius and Topinard), sensitiveness of certain parts of the vertebral column or of the nerve-trunks to pressure, a sensation of cold in the affected limbs, or an abnormal sensation of heat without elevation of temperature (Charcot).

Electrical exploration discloses, at the onset, normal reactions. At an advanced period of the disease, diminution of electrical contractility occurs in the muscles of the forearm and hand.

Fig. 19. — Attitude of patient suffering from paralysis agitans.

The galvanic excitability of the nerves is at first normal, but, at a later period, it is often diminished; the reaction is sometimes increased when the symptoms of irritation become general. Topinard published the case of a physician (Gaz. des Hôpit., 21, 1866) who had illusions of sight, increase of sexual desire, and diabetes mellitus. Psychical disorders occur as terminal symptoms, and are accompanied by loss of appetite, relaxation of the sphincters, and gangrenous ulcers of the integument. The patients die of pulmonary hypostasis or œdema, in a condition of marasmus, sopor, or delirium.

Among the *causes* of paralysis agitans, we may mention debilitating diseases and the prolonged action of cold. Mental shocks (such as fright) which, during the first ten years of life, may give rise to chorea, epilepsy, or hysteria in predisposed individuals, often cause paralysis agitans at a more advanced age. I have seen a man, sixty years of age, in whom a carbuncle of the neck was opened ; he was soon after seized with tremor of the right arm, which began when the wound was dressed, and then extended to the other limbs. When the nerve-centres are endowed with abnormal excitability, either hereditary or acquired under the influence of strong irritation, each period of life presents peculiar reactions, affecting chiefly the motor functions. Double morbid forms are sometimes produced, as is shown by the case reported on page 34, in which hysteria was combined with symptoms of paralysis agitans. Among the predisposing causes, old age holds the first rank. In one case I observed the development of paralysis agitans in limbs which were paralyzed in consequence of cerebral apoplexy.

Paralysis agitans is very often mistaken for tremor of various kinds. Careful observation will enable us to arrive at an exact diagnosis. The points of differentiation from sclerosis of the nervous centres have been referred to in the chapter devoted to that affection. The distinctions between chorea and paralysis agitans will be discussed hereafter. In senile trembling, not alone the limbs, but especially the head, are agitated by continual trembling movements ; furthermore, the former is not accompanied by neuralgic pains, hemiparesis, the characteristic muscular stiffness, the deformity of the hands, or the tendency to movements of propulsion or recoil. Alcoholic tremor is characterized by the excited condition of the patients, by the delirium in which they are pursued by all kinds of imaginary visions (especially by small animals) and by the diminution of the tremor under the influence of stimulants and of large doses of opium. Mercurial tremor is almost always preceded by salivation, ulcerations in the throat, swelling of the gums, fœtid breath, diarrhœa, loss of appetite, and exhaustion. Lead tremor is recognized by the previous occurrence of lead colic, arthralgias, the condition of the mouth, muscular paresis, and the partial abolition of electro-muscular contractility in the extensors of the arm. The tremor of opium-eaters is accompanied by the following symptoms : livid color of the face, dull expression, dull eyes, markedly contracted pupils, considerable emaciation, obstinate constipation, loss of appetite, tendency to vertigo, gloomy forebodings, and uncertain gait. The *prognosis* of paralysis agitans is absolutely unfavorable in the chronic or rapidly developing forms. When the disease is more recent and less extended, it is susceptible of a certain amount of improvement. Recoveries are exceedingly rare, and relapses are very frequent.

In the majority of cases the *treatment* must be confined to limiting or moderating some of the symptoms. Treatment with strychnine, ergotine, opium, curare, and extract of calabar-bean have given no encouraging results. Some authors have prescribed sulphurous mineral waters with a certain degree of benefit. Elliotson reports a case of recovery from the prolonged use of carbonate of iron. In recent cases the galvanic treatment (stabile currents through the vertebral column and from this region to the tremulous limbs) may improve the tremor and the pains, but will not increase the strength; in the chronic forms electricity is useless. Mild hydrotherapeutic measures (frictions, packs of short duration, cool half-baths with dorsal affusions) have a tonic action, and improve the appetite and sleep. According to Charcot, hyoscyamine will moderate the symptoms. Eulenburg has derived benefit from hypodermic injections of Fowler's solution, but the experiments undertaken at the Salpêtrière have not given similar good results. Ordenstein has found nitrate of silver useful.

CHAPTER XXXIV.

CHOREA AND ITS DIFFERENT FORMS.

AFTER having discussed, in the preceding chapters, the affections which are characterized by spasms of cerebral and spinal origin, we shall now investigate another variety of central motor disorders, viz.: the affections of co-ordination. As we have shown in the consideration of the theory of ataxia, we find, in a series of pathological conditions, serious disturbances affecting the centres of co-ordination in the cerebellum and mesocephalon and in the sensory conductors which these organs send into the posterior columns of the cord. Disorders of co-ordination will result from solutions of continuity in the relations of these centres with the spinal system of ganglion-cells and from serious obstacles to the transmission of motor impulses starting from the cerebral ganglia.

In accordance with the principles previously laid down, we shall describe as disorders of co-ordination, those motor disturbances in which the harmonious action of certain muscles, or of certain groups of muscles, in performing definite movements, is interfered with, while the isolated action of each muscle remains intact. In the diseases which we shall study from this point of view, the conductors of co-ordination may undergo, in their long course, disorders of great extent (as in chorea), or merely circumscribed lesions (as in writer's spasm, and stammering).

A.—CHOREA MAGNA.

Chorea magna results from a condition of irritation of certain centres of co-ordination and of the centrifugal conductors which connect the cells of the cerebral cortex with the motor apparatus. Future histological investigations, when carefully performed, will undoubtedly discover, in chorea magna and minor, exudations around the vessels in the cortical and medullary substance of the brain and in the conductors of the cord, and this will explain the combination of psychical disorders with disturbances of co-ordination.

Chorea magna (chorea Germanorum) consists of spasmodic movements, occurring paroxysmally in certain groups of muscles, and presenting the appearances of voluntary motor direction. The movements are sometimes simple, sometimes complex. In this affection the patients execute, against their will, extraordinary combinations of movements which it is extremely difficult to perform in the normal condition, and which are repeated under the influence of peculiar psychical stimuli.

Symptomatology.

The symptoms of chorea may present a great variety of aspects. In the majority of cases the paroxysm is preceded by prodromata, consisting of irritative symptoms of motion, sensation, or of the psychical functions. Isolated muscular contractions, tremors, nausea, cephalalgia or rachialgia, palpitation of the heart, difficulty of respiration, painful sensations, agitation, illusions and visions are the most frequent prodromata of the attack. But in some cases the latter develops suddenly.

The paroxysm, properly speaking, consists of a series of movements which vary greatly in character and intensity, according to the groups of muscles which are the seat of the involuntary actions. The patients run, jump, hop, dance, climb, whirl around, stamp with the feet, cry like animals, exercise like acrobats, declaim like actors, sing, recite poetry (even in a foreign language), etc. They expend in all these actions an extraordinary amount of force, and manifest an address and dexterity which they are incapable of when performing similar acts in their normal condition. The paroxysm may present the same characteristics during its entire duration, or it may appear in various phases.

In severe conditions, accompanied by ecstasy, the patients suffer from anæsthesia and analgesia, tremors, contractures, pareses or paralyses, and cataleptic or tetanic symptoms, attended with loss of reflex excitability. Consciousness and the functions of the special senses are clouded in a great measure. In less severe cases the senses and psychical faculties are less involved; the patients are conscious of their acts and, now and then, may even perform voluntary movements. In some patients intensified acuteness of the sensorial perceptions and an increase in the intellectual activity are observed, but this is always proportionate to the general education of the individual. In certain conditions of exaltation the patients hold discourses and compose poetry with surprising facility; their sad ideas and presentiments are converted into images of clairvoyance. Blinded by these unaccustomed phenomena, and encouraged by those around them, these patients give free rein to the imagination, and increase, by their recitals, the mystical character of the disease.

The paroxysm may terminate suddenly or may slowly disappear. The phenomena of exaltation and the spasmodic symptoms then cease, and the patients, tired in mind and body, sleep for a longer or shorter period. In light forms the return to the normal condition occurs after the spasmodic symptoms have lasted for a short time. At other times the patients are greatly fatigued, ill at ease, and in bad humor, and only recover after the lapse of a few days. The attacks may develop at any hour of the day or night, without adhering to a definite type, but, on the other hand, they sometimes present the most remarkable regularity. One of my patients could tell in the morning whether the attack, which occurred the same night, would be strong or weak; she was able to foretell this, as she stated, by a sensation of tension in the nerves.

The duration of the paroxysms varies from a few minutes to several hours. In very rare instances it may continue for several days, but remissions always occur in these cases. Franque has published (Journ. f. Kinderheilk., 1867, p. 226) the history of a case of chorea lasting two and a half years, in a boy affected with movements of rotation, skipping, and jumping; after the attacks the urine contained sugar, but was normal during the intervals. In another case, sugar was also found in the urine of a woman suffering from chorea magna, but only after the cessation of the paroxysms. In most cases the disease terminates after a certain lapse of time. But, as a rule, an abnormal irritability of the nervous system, which predisposes the patients to various affections, usually persists for a long time and often even for life. Some patients suffer from hysteria, and, in exceptional instances, from epilepsy or insanity. The disease very rarely terminates in death, and this event is almost always due to complications or to exhaustion.

The gross anatomical lesions which have been found in chorea magna are : venous hyperæmia of the brain and cord, meningeal hæmorrhages, inflammatory thickenings of the spinal nerves (Day), softening of the cord (Vecchietti). These data throw no light, however, upon the nature of the disease.

Etiology.

Chorea magna occurs especially in those individuals who have inherited a peculiar morbid susceptibility, or in whom this condition has developed during the period of puberty. According to Wicke's statistics (Monogr. des gr. Veitstanzes, etc., Leipzig, 1864), among one hundred and seven patients, chorea developed eighty-four times from the tenth to the twentieth years, and sixty-two times from the tenth to the sixteenth years. Two-thirds of the patients were females. The etiological factors of chorea include the following: psychical excitement, liaisons, sexual irritation, onanism, menstrual disorders, and chlorosis. From the etiology and the undeniable resemblance in the principal symptoms of the disease, we are justified in regarding chorea magna as very closely allied to hysteria.

Religious exaltation may also give rise to chorea magna. Many authors attribute to this cause the epidemics of Saint Guy's dance, which were observed during the Middle Ages. But, as Hecker has shown (Maladies populaires du Moyen Âge), this disease was a form of insanity, accompanied by severe convulsive and ecstatic manifestations. Within our own times Davidson (Edinb. Med. Journ., 1867, t. XIII., p. 124) has described an epidemic of choreomania appearing in Madagascar. Paroxysms of dancing, combined with rotatory movements of the head and raising and lowering of the arms, which lasted even for hours, occurred among the lower and superstitious classes, who were excited by social and political changes, and especially among young females. This was rather a form of mania than of chorea. Cantani states (Il Morgagni, 1872) that chorea magna is frequently observed in southern Italy.

Diagnosis and Prognosis.

If we glance over the cases described by various authors, we will find that they have confounded, under the term chorea magna, examples of convulsions attended with exaltation, insanity, saltatory spasms, and even certain forms of chorea minor of a slow course, which were attended by intermittent exacerbations.

Chorea magna is distinguished from insanity properly speaking, by the paroxysmal appearance of irresistible motor impulses, by the frequent coexistence of partial tonic and clonic convulsions, by its appearance at the period of puberty, usually after mental excitement, and by the frequency of hysterical manifestations, intermingled with the other symptoms. Saltatory spasms (of which Bamberger described two cases in 1859, and Guttmann another more recently) have the following characteristics: as soon as the patient, while in the vertical position, touches the ground with his feet, his body is rapidly tossed into the air. These spasms are of a reflex nature and probably due to spinal irritation. In chorea minor, there are no periodical attacks, the tonic muscular spasms and associated movements are made without the appearance of any voluntary impulse, the psychical functions are affected more rarely and to a slighter degree, and the co-ordination of movements presents more marked disturbances. In somnambulism, which we have described as a variety of hysteria, alienation of the psychical functions, and phenomena of inco-ordination also occur. But, in this affection, the attacks only occur during sleep, and the movements do not assume the spasmodic character which they present in chorea.

The *prognosis* of chorea magna depends upon the intensity and duration of the affection. If it has not assumed a very chronic character, and if the nutrition has suffered but little, the termination of the period of puberty, marriage, or improved habits of life, may cause the spontaneous disappearance of the disease. The severe forms, which run a chronic course, compromise nutrition, and lead to anæmia and cachexia. Although life itself is only endangered in very rare cases, nevertheless, in inveterate forms, the prognosis is grave, and is rendered so much the more so, because the disease may run its obstinate course for years, relapses occur upon slight provocation, and the physical and mental condition of the patients is seriously affected. The transition from chorea to insanity, properly speaking, or to epilepsy, is a rare event; the disease is much more frequently followed by hysterical phenomena.

Treatment.

The anæmia and neuropathic condition which are found in the majority of the patients demand, above all, tonic remedies. We may recommend mild preparations of iron, ferruginous baths and mineral waters, a prolonged stay in the exhilarating air of the country, and moderate exercise in the open air. Narcotics are usually but poorly tolerated by the patients; we should reserve them as adjuvants in violent and painful paroxysms. The salts of zinc, in large doses, have been recently recommended, especially by Stunde. The antispasmodics are sometimes capable of moderating the attacks.

In severe forms, we may, at times, suspend the paroxysms by the use of quinine administered for a long time in large doses (two to three grammes daily.) It is worthy of remark that symptoms of poisoning are never observed in these cases. I have employed the nitrate of silver in one case ("hammering," chorea of several months' duration, in a young man who also suffered from infiltration into the apices of both lungs). At the end of the eighth day of this plan of treatment (0.01–0.02 daily), the paroxysms had disappeared and, the use of the drug having been continued, had not returned at the end of several months. I had employed atropine in this patient, as well as in another case, without any favorable results. We may add, in conclusion, that judicious moral treatment, the removal of all sources of worry, an appeal to the will of the patient, and mild hydro-therapeutic measures, very frequently render good services. We must avoid the exciting applications of cold water, and should give the preference to partial frictions of the limbs, cool halfbaths, dorsal affusions, and later to moist frictions.

B.—Chorea Minor.

This disease has been recognized for centuries, but it is only within recent times that its central origin has been discovered by a resort to experimentation and pathological anatomy.

Chorea minor (chorea Anglorum) consists of more or less continuous muscular contractions and associated movements, which occur without disturbances of consciousness, especially under the influence of voluntary motor impulses, and without any apparent aim in view, that is to say, with inco-ordination. This definition comprises the most characteristic signs of chorea, leaving out of consideration the accessory symptoms. It applies equally to the various forms of chorea minor, whether of an idiopathic, or of a secondary, symptomatic or reflex nature.

Pathological Anatomy and Experimental Investigations.

In the old observations of Cruveilhier, Romberg, etc., foyers of softening were found in various parts of the brain. Among more modern authors, Broadbent (Brit. Med. Jour., April, 1869), followed by Tuckwell, Ogle, Russell and Hughlings Jackson, have observed in chorea the presence of capillary emboli in the corpus striatum and optic thalamus, and the production of granular cells around the vessels. Aitken found the specific gravity of the corpus striatum and optic thalamus very much diminished in proportion to the specific gravity of other parts of the brain. In the spinal cord, the new-formed connective tissue, which has been found in other acute diseases attended with spasms, was observed for the first time in chorea by Rokitansky. Brown-Séquard and Gendron have noticed softening of the cord. Tuckwell (Brit. Med.-Chir. Rev., 1867) found in a choreic patient who suffered from vegetations of the heart-valves, foyers of embolic softening in the cerebral hemispheres and cortical substance, and in the posterior columns of the cord (cervical and dorsal regions). L. Clarke (eod. loc., 1868) found softening of the cord, in addition to granular exudation into the corpus striatum.

In a case of chorea reported by Meynert (Ztschr. der Wien. Ges. d. Aerzte, Feb., 1868), microscopical examination showed that a large number of the cells of the cerebral cortex were in a condition of dropsical enlargement, with molecular degeneration of the protoplasm; there was partial sclerosis of the cells in the cortex of the insula and in the cerebral ganglia, with considerable proliferation of the nuclei of the nerve-cells; proliferation of the nuclei of the connective tissue in the medullary substance situated between the ganglia; the cells of the reticulum of the cord were enlarged. Elischer (Virch. Arch., Bd. 61, 1874) has recently observed the following lesions in a pregnant woman who had suffered from chorea: in the corpus striatum, nuclear proliferation, hyperplasia of the connective tissue, thickening of the tunica adventitia of the small vessels; the same changes in the tunica interna of the vessels of the lenticular nucleus; division of the nuclei of the nerve-cells in the claustrum. The spinal cord presented thickening and nuclear proliferation in the walls of the vessels, inflammatory changes in the epithelium of the central canal, and nuclear proliferation in the connective tissue around the nerve-cells of the gray matter; the latter presented a dull appearance, were destitute of nuclei, and filled with pigment; the white substance was hyperæmic;

the lateral and posterior columns contained a fibrillary tissue strewn with nuclei. In the peripheral nerves, the fibres were diminished in number, and a large amount of connective tissue was interposed between them; there were small hæmorrhages in the interstices of this tissue.

Chauveau performed some very interesting experiments (Arch. génér., Mars, 1865) several years ago, with regard to the localization of the lesions which give rise to choreic movements. In an animal which suffered from general chorea, the cord was divided near its junction with the brain, and the movements persisted for several hours until death, without being lessened in intensity or otherwise modified. The choreic movements were, therefore, not dependent upon the brain or cerebellum. In two other choreic dogs who were also affected with partial paralysis and atrophy of the upper limbs, section of the cord, performed as in the preceding experiment, also produced no effect upon the movements. But, after section of the dorsal cord, the convulsive movements of the tail and lower limbs diminished, the muscles remaining sensitive to mechanical irritations.

At the autopsy, the muscles were found atrophied but not degenerated, and the nerve-fibres were intact. The cessation of the movements coincidently with the arrest of the cardiac pulsations and with the incision of the dorsal cord, prove, according to Chauveau, that the morbid process in chorea is located in the spinal cord. The experiments performed by Longet, Bert, and Clarville, lead to the same conclusion.

Legros and Onimus, at a later period, began another series of experiments upon choreic dogs (Compt. Rend., t. LXX., 1870). Upon exposing the spinal cord and irritating the posterior columns with a scalpel, the choreic movements were found to become enormously intensified. They disappeared if the cord was chilled by means of a current of air, but soon returned after an application of warm water. The movements were not diminished by excision of the posterior roots, but only after partial excision of the posterior columns and horns; if a deeper incision was made, the movements ceased completely. The application of a constant current to the cord increased the chorea, while electrical irritation of the periphery diminished the intensity and frequency of the movements. The induced current gave rise to tetanic muscular contractions. From these experiments Legros and Onimus concluded that the site of chorea is either in the nerve-cells of the posterior horns, or in the fibres which connect them with the motor cells. The influence of the brain upon choreic movements (chorea following apoplexy or softening), which has been demonstrated by pathological observations, has been still further confirmed by the following experiment, performed in the Vienna Institute of Experimental Pathology. With a view of producing cerebral embolism an injection of pollen was made into the left internal carotid of a dog who had suffered for some time from choreiform movements, especially in the right anterior limb. After the experiment was made, the animal was unable to rise or change his position. Despite the abolition of voluntary movements, however, violent choreic covulsions occurred in the anterior limbs, in the eyes and tail, and continued for two days until the death of the animal. Autopsy : encephalitis of the left anterior lobe, softening of the left corpus striatum, embolism of the left middle cerebral artery. Microscopical examination of the cerebral substance showed the existence in several places of depots of connective tissue proliferation.

The disorders experimentally produced in the cerebral circulation were therefore followed, on account of the suspension of the functions of the motor ganglia, by an increase in the choreic movements, probably from irritation of the centres of co-ordination situated in the mesocephalon and cerebellum.

Symptomatology.

The prodromata are not constant, and consist of intellectual malaise, abnormal excitability, palpitation of the heart, temporary vertigo, and exhaustion. The first muscular contractions usually occur in the muscles of the face, shoulders, and hands (the children are often accused of being naughty); they then involve the upper and lower halves of the body. Both sides of the body are often affected, though one is more severely involved than the other; sometimes hemichorea alone develops. According to Sée (Mém. de l'Acad. de Méd., 1850, t. XV., p. 373), among one hundred and fifty-four cases the chorea occurred ninety-seven times upon the left side, either exclusively or predominantly.

The choreic movements may involve all the muscles of organic life with the exception of the inferior sphincters. They are manifested by contortions of the head and trunk, grimaces of the face, rotation of the eyes, strabismus, incessant movements of the tongue, and shoulders; the arms and hands are moved and twisted hither and thither, and are flexed and extended.

While walking the legs trip and bend under. This peculiar condition of muscular agitation has been called "folie musculaire" by Bouillaud, and "insanity of muscles" by Bellingham.

In light forms these muscular symptoms are very moderate, but, in cases of considerable intensity, the performance of combined movements becomes almost impossible. The patients are unable to maintain the erect posture and the body is thrown in all directions; when lying down they are in danger of falling out of bed, and involuntarily disarrange the bedclothes. The skin, which is subject to continual friction, becomes irritated, especially over bony projections; the tongue and lips are sometimes severely bitten. These irregular convulsions of the muscles may continue uninterruptedly during the day. As a rule, the patients obtain very little rest and sleep at night; they are disturbed by dreams, toss in bed, and start up out of sleep.

Voluntary acts are performed with difficulty, as the active movements are disturbed by the contractions of the antagonistic or adjacent muscles. These additional movements cause the patients to experience great difficulty in their ordinary occupations. It is only with great exertion that they are able to eat, write, sew, or perform upon musical instruments. The respiratory movements are irregular, speech is embarrassed, and the pulse is often accelerated. These phenomena are due to the spasmodic action of the muscles of respiration, of the larynx, pharynx, and perhaps also of the heart. It is true that the patients are voluntarily able to suppress the spasmodic movements for a certain length of time, but this effort of the will reacts as a cause of irritation, and produces a subsequent increase in the intensity of the muscular disorder. A similar result is produced when the violence of the muscular action is passively restrained. In one case of chorea I observed, at the height of the paroxysms, a very marked dilatation of both pupils. This was not modified by exposure to light or by the introduction of a thin electrode between the sclerotic and conjunctiva. The symptom disappeared spontaneously after the termination of the attack (spasm of the dilator of the pupils from irritation of the cilio-spinal centre).

Sensibility is remarkably increased, especially at the onset of severe attacks. The skin is hyperæsthetic, and pricking, pinching or electrical irritation produce acute sensibility and reflex movements. The vertebral column is extremely sensitive to pressure, especially in the cervical and upper dorsal regions. Constriction of the head, and a feeling of exhaustion, are often experienced, when the muscular contortions are prolonged.

The psychical faculties are also more or less affected, and this fact is explained by the changes found by Meynert in the cerebral cortex. J. Frank, Romberg, Hasse, Skoda, have observed mental disturbances in the course of chorea minor. Marcé, in his Mémoire to the Academy, refers to cases of this character, and Leidesdorf has recently called attention to the feelings of dread, the hallucinations of the senses, and especially of sight, which occur in certain choreics. If febrile complications co-exist, the intellectual disorders must not be attributed to chorea alone. I have observed several cases of simple chorea attended with weakness of memory, marked diminution of the intellectual powers, and inability to carry on a logical train of thought. One woman who suffered from chorea, which had developed after a previous confinement, presented unusual jactitation and loquacity, and often gave utterance to savage cries, though entirely conscious. This condition was moderated by inhalations of chloroform (administered until complete narcosis was produced), and, at a later period, the patient recovered from the chorea, after having safely passed through an attack of variola.

I have resorted to electrical exploration in three cases of unilateral chorea, observed soon after the onset, and have found a marked increase of the electro-muscular contractility (with a weak current, and compared with the healthy side or with other patients of the same age). I have also observed very marked galvanic excitability, manifesting itself by contractions upon making the current at the negative pole, by galvano-tonic contractions with weak currents, and by contractions upon breaking the current of the cathode. The increase in the irritability of the sensory nerves is shown by the exaggerated sensibility of the skin to the action of the current, and by the fact that, when the poles of a constant or induced current are placed upon the cervical or lower dorsal region of the vertebral column, excentric sensations are produced, either in the fingers or in the knees or toes; on one occasion, indeed, these sensations were crossed.

Chorea generally runs a chronic course, and often lasts from six to eight weeks ; severe cases may continue four or five months. The cases observed by certain authors, in which the chorea has lasted for several years or even for a great part of the patient's life, were probably caused by organic lesions in the brain. This is probably also true of those patients to whom Trousseau has called attention, and in whom hemiplegia followed an attack of chorea occurring in early life. In several cases of chorea I have observed temporary pareses of the limbs.

Etiology.

In enumerating the predisposing causes of chorea, I must call especial attention to the hereditary irritability of the co-ordinating apparatus. This disposition is not always shown by the direct transmission of choreic affections, but by the existence of other nervous diseases in the parents or other members of the family. The abnormal irritability of the centres of co-ordination is only an exaggeration of the general excitability of the nervous system, which always exists in such cases in the young people, and which is manifested by extraordinary vivacity, precocious intellectual development, brusquesness and impatience.

Age also constitutes one of the predisposing causes of chorea. According to the statistics collected by Sée and others, a large proportion of cases (about one-third) belongs to the period comprised between second dentition and puberty. Only isolated cases occur at a more advanced age. According to Levick, chorea is observed more frequently among the lower than among the better classes of the population. Sex exercises a great influence upon the development of chorea, since, according to Sée, three-fourths of the cases observed in the Children's Hospital of Paris occurred in girls. Anæmia, chlorosis, menstrual disorders, psychical affections and pregnancy, which give rise to hysteria in predisposed individuals, may also favor the development of choreic symptoms.

The relations of chorea to rheumatism have been recognized since the beginning of this century. The appearance of cardiac bruits during this disease was noticed by Addison, and at a later period by Todd. Romberg and Grisolle considered rheumatism and cardiac affections as mere accidental complications of chorea, but Watson demonstrated, from an analysis of three hundred and nine cases observed by Hughes, and thirty-six by Kirkes, that in twelve fatal cases the heart was found diseased ten times, and that among one hundred and four carefully observed cases, only fifteen were free from cardiac bruits or rheumatism.

Among one hundred and twenty-eight children affected with chorea, Sée (loc. cit.) found sixty-four cases of acute articular rheumatism, a fact which is so much the more important because rheumatism, as we well know, is very infrequent among children.

Senhouse, Heslop and Roger, have endeavored clinically to establish the relations existing between chorea and rheumatism, pericarditis and endocarditis, holding that both affections are the common expression of one and the same pathological condition. According to Roger, chorea almost always makes its appearance in children during the period of decline of the articular rheumatism. As a rule, the rheumatism is neither violent nor obstinate. The more acute, severe, and extensive the articular affection, and the more it is complicated, either in the beginning or at a later period, with cardiac affections, the slighter will be the choreic manifestations.

According to the observations made at Prague by Steiner (Prag. Vjschr., Bd. III., 1868), this pathological relation does not possess an absolute value, since among two hundred and fifty-two cases of chorea, only four appeared during the course of acute articular rheumatism. It is therefore probable that, under the influence of local causes, the coincidence of the two diseases is observed more frequently in certain countries, and that certain conditions render the action of the rheumatic inflammation upon the serous membranes, the articulations, spinal meninges and centres of co-ordination, more frequent and intense.

According to Hughes and Trousseau, chorea occurs frequently after scarlatina. This fact is probably accounted for by the relations existing between rheumatism and scarlatina, for, according to Trousseau, one-third of the cases of scarlatina are also subject to articular affections (light forms) and sometimes even to endocarditis and pericarditis. In conclusion we may state that certain English physicians (Todd, Smith, Beale), in order to prove the rheumatic origin of chorea, refer to the fact that the urine presents the characteristics of the rheumatic diathesis, viz.: high specific gravity and a considerable quantity of urea, urates and oxalate of lime.

Nature of Chorea.

It is evident from the clinical history that the inco-ordination of movements is the predominant factor in the symptomatology of chorea. Chorea is merely the expression of certain irritative disorders, acting more or less profoundly upon the co-ordinating apparatus.

The participation of the cerebrum in this disease is demonstrated by the symptoms of irritation, which are observed on the part of various motor cranial nerves, by the disturbance of ideas and of speech, and by the development of psychical affections. It is also shown by the appearance of chorea in apoplexy, softening and tumors of the brain, and by its aggravation after mental excitement (anger, fear, etc.) We have referred above to an experiment, in which disorders of circulation produced in the brain caused a greater violence of the choreic movements. In patients, an exaggerated effort of the will suffices to bring into play the morbid excitability of the nerve-centres. The anatomical basis of these facts is found in the exudations observed by Meynert, around the vessels of the brain and cord, and in the gray matter. The theory of a condition of irritation of the centres of co-ordination contained in the mesocephalon and cerebellum, and of its propagation to the motor conductors, is thus found to be justified by the positive intervention of the brain in chorea.

The part played by the cord in the production of chorea is readily understood, if we take into consideration the important changes in the sensory conductibility of the posterior columns, as shown by pathological anatomy, and confirmed by experimentation. The exaggerated excitability of the spinal system is also manifested by the cutaneous hyperæsthesia, which is sometimes observed in chorea, and by the abnormal reactions to the galvanic current. Finally, the irritation of the ciliospinal centre is expressed by the spasmodic dilatation of the pupils in severe attacks of chorea (as in the observation reported above).

We are justified in concluding, from the preceding clinical and anatomical facts, that in chorea minor the co-ordinating apparatus is affected both in its cerebral and spinal portions. The form of the disease is sensibly modified, according as the affection predominates in the one or other of these parts. In cases which recover, the symptoms of irritation disappear with the cessation of the functional hyperæmia, which accompanies the motor irritation and its irradiations to neighboring cells (associated movements), or with the absorption of the slight exudations which have formed. It is only in very rare cases that the changes in the vascular walls, and in the nerve-fibres and cells, terminate in secondary lesions and persistent disorders of some segment of the apparatus of co-ordination.

The chorea which is manifested in articular rheumatism, in inflammations of the pericardium or endocardium, in affections of the female sexual organs, in intestinal irritations, etc., is of reflex origin. It is due to a congenital exaggeration of the excitability of the apparatus of co-ordination, the latter being disturbed in its functions by the period of puberty, by psychical excitement, and by constitutional debility. According to Bright, irritation originating in the pericardium may be propagated to the cord along the phrenic nerve.

Diagnosis and Prognosis.

In a large number of cases, as in children, and during the period of puberty, pregnancy or the puerperal state, the symptomatology is so expressive that no confusion with other morbid affections is possible. In adults, certain conditions are accompanied by clonic spasms which present more or less resemblance to chorea, but may be readily distinguished by well determined symptoms. Paralysis agitans is recognized by its preference for advanced age, by the peculiar gait of the patients, the muscular rigidity, and the deformity of the hands; voluntary acts are not disturbed, as in chorea, by associated movements, the limbs which are subject to tremor become more quiet when they are supported, and finally the disease not infrequently terminates in true paralysis. In the facial spasms occurring in adults (convulsive tic), the spasms are symmetrical, paroxysmal, and limited to certain muscles of the face and neck. The disease which Dubini has termed electrical chorea (muscular twitchings and shocks affecting the entire body, occurring after pains in the head and back), and tetanic chorea, are probably due to acute diseases of the brain and cord or their meninges, and cannot be regarded as primary forms. The choreic movements which sometimes occur in certain cerebral tumors, are accompanied by other tumor symptoms.

We should, therefore, always endeavor to determine whether choreic movements are due to a primary, idiopathic affection (it is more exact to regard it as a sympathetic affection, from irritation of the centres of co-ordination, due to chlorosis or anæmia), whether they are symptomatic of a cerebral or spinal affection, or whether they are reflex phenomena occurring in the conditions to which we have previously referred. We will be enabled to make this distinction in the majority of cases, by an attentive observation of the symptoms.

The *prognosis* of chorea is usually favorable, and the large proportion of cases recover completely. A fatal termination from exhaustion, marasmus, decubitus, or inflammatory complications, occurs in exceptional instances. Obstinate insomnia, which debilitates the patients, offers, according to Trousseau, an unfavorable prognosis when delirium and fever are superadded. When the chorea is symptomatic, the prognosis depends upon the primary affection. In ordinary chorea, the symptoms mend in a progressive and continuous manner, until recovery is complete.

The morbid disposition, which gives rise to the disorders of co-ordination, may disappear spontaneously, as the organism of the young patients becomes more vigorous, or it may yield to the remedies employed to restore the energy of the nervous system. If neither of these events takes place, experience teaches that relapses not infrequently occur, and almost always terminate in severe and rebellious forms. As a rule, relapses develop much more frequently in the female sex. Recent forms of chorea may be arrested by the development of intercurrent diseases (acute exanthemata).

Treatment.

Starting from the doctrine that the disease was due to an inflammatory irritation of the spinal cord, chorea has been treated by antiphlogistics (venesection or scarification along the vertebral column) and derivatives (Rasori and Laennec recommended tartar emetic). At the present time, venesection or scarification along the vertebral column are only employed in full-blooded, vigorous subjects.

Among the nervines, iron, zinc (valerianate or oxide in doses ranging as high as a scruple daily), bismuth, and nitrate of silver, are employed when the patients are anæmic. Arsenic (under the form of Fowler's solution) is especially recommended by Romberg; it is prescribed in doses of three to five drops, three times a day. In two cases, I gave increasing doses of Fowler's solution up to eight drops at a dose, and obtained rapid diminution of the choreic symptoms, without the appearance of any phenomena of poisoning. According to J. Lewis Smith (Med. Rec., 1872), subcutaneous injections of Fowler's solution, employed in the manner to which we have previously referred, are useful in rebellious forms of the disease.

Narcotics should only be employed in very marked conditions of excitement. In obstinate insomnia, we may prescribe, in addition to warm baths, hypodermic injections of morphine, or doses of opium repeated hourly until sleep is produced. In certain severe cases, Trousseau has seen the patients tolerate enormous doses of this drug. Inhalations of chloroform have been successfully employed by Marsh, Prevost, Fuster, Géry, etc., especially when the disease was attended with violent convulsive movements. I have also seen good results from chloroform narcosis, in cases of violent excitability and jactitation. When the necessary precautions are adopted (empty stomach, strict watch over pulse and respiration, frequent inspiration of air during the inhalation), the anæsthesia may be repeated twice a day for several days in succession, and quiet is almost always obtained in this manner.

According to Trousseau and Lubelsky, irrigation of the vertebral column with sulphuric ether is useful in obstinate cases which are subject to relapses. The use of strychnine, which is recommended by Trousseau and Forget, has not been attended with good results in Sée's hands. At all events, this remedy must be given with caution, on account of the general excitability of the patients.

According to Dumont, bromide of potassium (in increasing doses) produces rapid improvement in the symptoms. Ogle extols the action of the tincture of Calabar bean (five grammes of Calabar bean to thirty-five grammes of alcohol; ten to twenty drops are given three times a day in a little water). Turnbull has obtained excellent effects in six cases from the sulphate of aniline (0.05–0.08 three times a day); Steiner has not obtained similar results from the employment of this drug. We must mention, as a disagreeable effect of this remedy that, after its prolonged use, the lips, tongue, nails and even the hands are colored blue, and the skin assumes a sombre hue. After the administration of the drug is suspended the coloration disappears in twenty-four hours. Hydrate of chloral also gives good results.

Finally, reference must be made to electricity and hydrotherapeutics in the treatment of chorea.

Many English physicians apply strong sparks of static electricity to the vertebral column in cases of chorea. Muscular faradization is employed by Duchenne, and cutaneous faradization by Becquerel and Briquet; the latter author administered chloroform previously, on account of the cutaneous hyperæsthesia. From my experience in a large number of observations, I give the preference to the continuous current, a stabile current of moderate intensity being passed from the vertebral column to the nerves of the affected parts (for three to five minutes). I have not been able to observe, as Onimus asserts, that the direction of the current exerts any influence upon the final result. In many cases, the muscular spasms improve very rapidly; at other times, on the contrary, several weeks elapse before any good effects are produced.

Hydrotherapeutic measures have been long employed in the following manner: the patients are placed in a warm half-bath, and the vertebral column is douched with cool water falling in a small jet from a moderate height. A much more soothing and invigorating effect is produced (as I have shown in a large number of cases) by moist packs of the entire body, employed until the body is moderately warm, and followed by a half-bath of 22° C., which is gradually cooled to 18° C., the body being frequently douched and rubbed during the entire procedure. In severe cases, this plan may be practised morning and evening, and the patient may then take moderate exercise in the open air.

CHAPTER XXXV.

WRITER'S CRAMP (SPASM OF THE HAND WITH INCO-ORDINATION).

NOT alone those spasms of the hand which render writing impossible, but the more or less analogous phenomena which present obstacles to sewing, knitting, drawing, and performing upon the violin or piano, have all been collected under the improper term, writer's cramp. We shall therefore discuss those spasms which evidently result from disorders of co-ordination, and involve delicate and complex motor acts, under the term "*spasm of the hand with inco-ordination,*" or "*artisan's neurosis.*"

Symptomatology.

The spasms of the hand with inco-ordination, which are manifested in writing, appear most frequently within the territory of the median nerve (spasm of the flexors), of the radial nerve (sudden extension of the fingers), or, finally, of the ulnar nerve (deviation of the hand to the right and outwards). The spasm in the direction of the median nerve may be tonic, in which case the thumb and index-finger are curved inwards and seize the pen convulsively; at other times the spasm is clonic, and then these two fingers are forced to perform a movement of propulsion, which often causes the pen to twirl around its own axis.

In the beginning of the affection, a disagreeable sensation of tension in the hand is only felt after the patient has been writing for a long time, and hardly attracts attention at first, until the hand becomes more and more fatigued, and, together with the fingers, soon becomes affected with tremor, which forces the patient to rest frequently while writing. As this difficulty in writing becomes more marked, the formation of thick and fine strokes becomes interfered with, and the letters become small, poorly formed, and indistinct. When the attempt is made to correct this imperfection by increasing the attention and the efforts to handle the pen, an increase in the spasms and weakness of the hand is the result. This is soon followed by complete spasm of the flexors and extensors, or by clonic spasms in certain muscles of the fingers, producing a painful tension, more marked in the extensor muscles of the forearm, but involving even the muscles of the shoulder and thorax.

If we analyze in detail the physiological series of acts concerned in writing, as has been done by Duchenne, and especially by Zuradelli (Del crampo degli scrittori, Gaz. Med. Ital., Lombard, 36–42, 1857), it will be found that this act results from the combination of delicate and complex movements, demanding an harmonious and precise co-ordination, and an alternating action of certain muscles of the fingers. The formation of the thick and fine strokes, which is carried on by the thumb and first two fingers, is performed, in its first half, by the synergic extension of the last, and flexion of the first phalanges (by means of the interossei, lumbricales, flexor, opponens and extensor pollicis); in the second half, an inverse action is produced by a simultaneous contraction of the deep flexor and common extensor of the fingers. The propulsion of the hand from left to right along the lines, and the movements of immersion and drawing back of the pen, are effected by contractions of the teres minor, infraspinatus and deltoid (with the aid of the flexors).

It is evident, therefore, that in this complex series of movements we especially call into requisition the small muscles which, in certain conditions of individual excitability, are readily affected with spasm. The repetition of the latter will result in progressive weakness of combined movements, and may finally jeopardize the power of writing. According as the movements which we have enumerated are embarrassed in different degrees or perhaps even abolished, various forms of writer's cramp will be manifested. Sometimes the formation of the fine lines is markedly interfered with, the first and second phalanges forming, during flexion, a more obtuse angle than usual.

The muscles which are most frequently affected with spasm are the small muscles of the phalanges and those of the thumb. The cramp may manifest itself under the form of clonic contractions (spasm with tremor), or of tonic spasm of the flexors, affecting chiefly the thumb, which then forces the pen firmly against the paper. Spasm of the extensors may be temporarily produced, and the pen will then be suddenly removed from the paper; this is, on the whole, a very rare symptom, and may be due to spasm of the muscles which carry the hand across the paper. In the beginning of the disease isolated spasms are observed from time to time, and cause an obstacle to one or the other movement in writing. In general, the spasms and functional disturbances involve the different muscles of the fingers and thumb, and, if the work is nevertheless persisted in, they will also affect the muscles of the forearm and arm.

Artisan's cramp is not produced merely by writing. In predisposed subjects it may manifest itself in the following occupations : sewing, knitting, drawing, playing piano, violin, or harp; in engravers, printers, etc., whose work demands continuous activity in the movements of the fingers and hand. Coarser movements, which involve the muscles of the fingers and arms to a less extent, do not give rise to similar disturbances.

Some patients suffer from neuralgic pains, painful points along the nerves of the arm, and sensibility to pressure and to electrical stimulation of certain portions of the vertebral column. Electrical exploration reveals perversions of the normal mode of contractions in some forms of writer's spasm. The contraction upon closure at the anode is produced in certain nerves more quickly and strongly than the contraction upon closure at the cathode, or the opening contractions at the negative pole appear earlier than at the positive pole. We may also be able to detect anomalies in the primary excitability, and an increase of irritation from the action of the poles. Eulenburg (loc. cit.) has also made similar observations.

Etiology.

The most frequent cause of this disease is the excessive labor to which the small muscles of the fingers are subjected in the different pursuits to which we have above referred. The use of steel pens, on account of their rigidity and slight elasticity, perhaps favors the development of writer's cramp. But this is not the sole cause, since the disease sometimes appears in patients who have always made use of quills. In some cases of clonic writer's spasm, Remak has observed a chronic inflammation of the median nerve. This author also states that inflammatory irritation of purely sensory nerve-fibres, such as the superficial branch of the radial nerve, may give rise to writer's cramp, and he has obtained recovery in some of these patients by the local application of the constant current.

With regard to the etiology of the disease, great importance must be attached to predisposition. In the patients whom I have observed, abnormal conditions of sensibility of an hereditary nature were almost always present. They were of a very excitable or timid disposition, suffered more or less from nervous palpitation, from spasms in various parts of the body, or from hysterical symptoms. Among twenty-five cases of writer's cramp collected by Fritz, seven suffered from strabismus, choreic movements, spasm of deglutition, etc. The dynamic and traumatic influences, which have been regarded as exciting causes, constitute the exceptions.

Writer's cramp is chiefly due to the morbid susceptibility of certain individuals. The irritation produced by manual effort proceeds from the sensory muscular fibres (Fritz), and, in addition, from the nerves which are distributed to the articulations of the fingers and hand, and causes, by reflex action, a disturbance in the co-ordinated action of the muscles. Then follows a more and more marked disorder in the regular and associated play of the muscular actions, a spasmodic perturbation of their function, and marked exhaustion of the co-ordinating apparatus, which only lapses into this condition of weakness from the over-excitement following frequent spasms. Writer's cramp may be artificially produced, as I have shown by experiments upon myself and upon various patients, by means of stimulation with the faradic current. If a strong current is applied to the first two interossei and to the thenar eminence simultaneously, while the hand is occupied in writing, a tonic spasm will be produced in the extensors of the thumb and index-finger, especially during the formation of the fine lines. The letters become distorted, the pen rotates upon its own axis, and finally leaves the paper. If the current is brought to bear upon the dorsal surface of the forearm, over the motor points of the extensor indicis and of the long extensor of the thumb, the pen will be drawn away, and if the current is continued for a certain length of time, the fingers are seized with tremor and persistent spasm. If we employ two induction coils of different intensities we can produce spasms of unequal force in the hand.

The central situation of these disorders of co-ordination only extends over a small space, as a rule, for we have previously shown that the inco-ordination rarely affects other groups of movements. In this respect writer's spasm is analogous to the disorders in the co-ordination of speech which constitute stuttering, and we may term the former affection, stuttering of the hand or of writing. Nevertheless, in writer's cramp, the symmetrical portion of the nerve-centres, on the opposite side, shows a tendency to become involved, for, if the patient learns to write with the other hand, the latter soon becomes affected with the spasm.

Diagnosis and Prognosis.

Writer's cramp may be mistaken for analogous conditions which have been produced by lesions of the brain and spinal cord. In unilateral ataxia, similar phenomena may appear (I have seen two examples) among the first symptoms of the disease. But these phenomena are almost always combined with sensory disturbances (numbness, anæsthesia, neuralgia) in the fingers and arm, sometimes also in other parts of the body, and even in the lower limbs. In addition, temporary muscular spasms, sexual excitement, and a marked increase in the galvanic reactions, are also observed. Zuradelli has noted cases of writer's cramp, attended with hyperæsthesia or anæsthesia, loss of sensibility to contact or pain, or of muscular sensibility. These symptoms must be referred to a central cause, as they are not noticed in ordinary cases.

In cerebral diseases the associated movements of the fingers or hands may be disturbed by spasms and paresis, simulating writer's cramp. But we will then find uncertainty and weakness, even in performing coarse movements, combined with sensory disturbances and paresis in the lower extremity on the same side, and later in the territory of the cranial nerves.

In hysteria, progressive muscular atrophy, and lead paralysis, a symptomatic writer's cramp may occur after exertion, but the other characteristic signs will clear up the nature of the disease.

The trembling movements which characterize certain forms of writer's cramp are distinguished from other forms of tremor by the fact that the latter are also manifested in movements which do not require co-ordinated action, and that they pursue a much more continuous course.

The *prognosis* in spasm of the hand with inco-ordination is so much the more unfavorable, the more severe and extensive the disease has become. The light forms, which sometimes occur with symptoms of anæmia, dyspepsia, and after prolonged exertion, may be arrested by methodical tonic treatment and by abstinence from all manual occupations which demand considerable effort. If the necessary measures are adopted, even more advanced forms may remain stationary for several years, or may, perhaps, present an appreciable degree of improvement, although this is soon lost if these precautions are dispensed with. Some of these cases are, perhaps, susceptible of recovery under appropriate treatment and continuous care.

Severe and extensive forms may improve somewhat, but offer no hope of recovery.

Treatment.

Writer's cramp was formerly treated with narcotics, tonics, stimulants, nervines, and blisters, but the complete inefficacy of these measures has long been recognized. Strychnine, which has been recently employed by some physicians, is too dangerous, even in small doses, to be employed as a mere adjuvant. Surgical treatment (subcutaneous muscular section) was successful in a case reported by Stromeyer, in which the spasm was limited to the long flexor of the thumb. In other cases, however, which were operated upon by Dieffenbach and Langenbeck, it produced no benefit or only temporary relief. The mechanical contrivances invented by Gerdy, Cazenave, and others do not produce any permanent advantage. Massage is followed by better results.

Methodical hydrotherapeutics (frictions, packs of short duration, followed by half baths, dorsal affusions, gentle douches to the lumbar region and neck), a prolonged trip to the country, and sea-baths, have a favorable influence in counteracting the nervous excitability of the patients and in moderating the spasms.

Electricity also gives good results in this affection; but the number of recoveries always remains very small, compared with those cases which are merely improved. Duchenne and M. Meyer have seen good effects from galvanization of the affected muscles. The constant current is preferably employed, on account of its slighter tension. A stabile current of moderate intensity is passed through the upper part of the vertebral column or from the spine to the brachial plexus, and then to the affected nerves and muscles, each sitting lasting from three to five minutes. In some cases I have obtained great benefit by combining galvanization with a few sittings of localized faradization to the paretic muscles, or with mild hydrotherapeutic measures.

But whatever the plan of treatment adopted, it is absolutely necessary that the patient abstain completely, for at least six months or a year, from the work in which he had been previously engaged, and it can only be resumed slowly and gradually. It is well to premise the return to work by carefully graduated gymnastics of the articulations of the fingers and hands, and by rhythmical exercises of the brachial muscles.

CHAPTER XXXVI.

STUTTERING.

THE consideration of this affection naturally follows that of writer's spasm, while, on the other hand, certain undeniable characteristics point very clearly to its affinities with chorea.

Symptomatology.

Stuttering develops between the ages of five to ten years, or a little later, and first becomes evident by the difficulty experienced in pronouncing certain syllables, and by the repeated efforts and interruptions which accompany the pronunciation of linguals, labials, and gutturals. If stuttering manifests itself in the first years of childhood, it becomes an obstacle to intellectual development, inasmuch as the child is supposed to be weak, and all mental exertion is carefully avoided. We therefore find that the stuttering, which was expected to disappear as the child developed, increases with years and becomes more obstinate.

At a later period, when the stuttering is more marked, the face becomes affected, while speaking, with spasms and contortions, corresponding to the efforts of will which the patient makes; the tongue is moved upwards and downwards in a convulsive manner, or is forced between the teeth; the head is turned to one side; the eyes roll in their orbits with an expression of anguish; the saliva is expectorated in jets by the convulsive contractions of the labial commissures; the muscles of the jaw and lip become rigid at times, during which the expiration remains suspended; the face is turgid and has an anxious expression. After numerous expiratory efforts and repeated movements of the tongue, the lips finally open, and the pseudo-suffocatory paroxysm is terminated by the utterance of a sound. In severe cases this scene is soon renewed; whenever the patient wishes to express an idea, the same insubordination of the organs of speech makes its appearance. In this miserable situation he is isolated from the society of his fellows, and the exercise of his profession or even life itself becomes embittered thereby. Singing and declamation are performed perfectly by the majority of these patients; it is only in very advanced cases that the infirmity becomes apparent even when they recite poetry. In whispering, or even in speaking in a low tone of voice, stutterers can pronounce words with surprising facility. Under the influence of embarrassment or depressing moral conditions, speech is produced in the form of fragments of words; anger, quarrels, or an animated conversation with friends, facilitates the flow of speech.

The pronunciation of vowels, which is effected by intonation, *i. e.*, by the intervention of the larynx and glottis, does not present any especial difficulty to the majority of stutterers.

Vocal stuttering (stuttering of the initial vowels) constitutes a severe form of the disease. The pronunciation of consonants plays a much greater part among the pathological phenomena of stuttering. In the pronunciation of consonants in the normal condition there is no change, or merely a slight modification in the relations of the larynx and hyoid bone; but the expired air, which is forced through the glottis and escapes through the buccal cavity, must overcome certain obstructions or constrictions in its passage, thus giving rise to the various consonants. According to the point between the larynx and buccal orifice at which this occlusion or narrowing occurs, Bruecke (in his classical work upon phonation) divides the consonants into three classes, each corresponding to a certain region of articulation, and these again are subdivided into two series. Those isolated sounds, whose pronunciation is accompanied by manifest vibrations of the walls of the thorax and of the larynx, are called "resonant," and those which are unaccompanied by such vibrations are called "non-resonant."

In order to obtain a practical survey of the defects of speech, it is advisable to recognize three centres for the production of sounds, viz., the anterior, middle, and posterior. The anterior centre, or space in which Bruecke's first group of consonants is formed, is narrowed or closed by the rapid opening and closure of the upper and lower lips, or of the lower lip and incisor teeth; the consonants p, b, f, v, m, are produced in this manner.

In the middle space, corresponding to the formation of Bruecke's second group, the occlusion or narrowing is produced by means of the anterior part of the tongue and upper incisors, or the anterior part of the vault of the palate; t, d, l, n, s, are thus formed. The posterior space in which the consonants of the third group originate is closed by means of the posterior halves of the tongue and palatine vault; k, g, ch, j, are here formed. The letter r belongs to all three groups, being either a labial, lingual, or guttural (more properly, a uvular). Certain languages, such as the Chinese, do not possess an r, and it is then usually replaced by l.

This sketch of the physiology of speech furnishes us with the basis of several divisions in stuttering. Thus the condition in which the sounds produced in the anterior space are combined with convulsive, involuntary movements of the lips and anterior parts of the tongue, has been called by Colombat labio-choreic stuttering (on account of its analogies with chorea). The variety in which the emission of sounds, produced in the posterior, and partly in the middle space, is attended with a certain degree of rigidity in the pharynx and larynx, was called gutturo-tetanic stuttering. As a rule, both these forms are combined, to the great distress of the patient as well as of his physician.

Etiology.

The real pathogenic cause of this affection consists of an hereditary morbid excitability, which affects by preference the organs of language. Children suffering from this disorder are usually of a delicate, lively, and very excitable nature, in whom a temporary and sudden cause of irritation (fright, anger, traumatic causes) will suffice to produce stuttering. In very rare cases the affection is hereditary. Thus, I had under observation, at one time, a girl, ten years of age, affected with stuttering, whose father was similarly affected, and whose grandfather had stuttered until the age of forty, at which time the infirmity disappeared. The largest number of cases occur in the male sex within the first twenty years of life.

According to Chervin, from the years 1852 to 1862, six thousand seven hundred and seventy-three conscripts in France were declared unfit for service on account of stuttering.

Anæmia, chlorosis, and the weakness due to masturbation, favor the development of stuttering in predisposed subjects. It may also appear as a concomitant symptom in other disorders of co-ordination. I was acquainted with an officer who was obliged to retire from service because he became affected with stuttering, during the course of locomotor ataxia, and was rendered incapable of giving commands (spinal stuttering).

Among the cases of writer's camp collected by Fritz, stuttering co-existed in several instances.

Our views concerning the nature of stuttering are clearer to-day than in the time of Colombat, who attributed it to a perversion of cerebral irradiation and to overstimulation of the muscles of language. As we have shown above, in the remarks on the formation of speech, the pronunciation of consonants depends chiefly upon the point at which the expired air meets with an occlusion or narrowing of the passages, before escaping through the buccal orifice. The more the different sounds, which must be uttered, belong to distinct groups, the more rapidly must the action of the corresponding organs succeed one another, the greater must be the certainty and precision in the modification of the relations between the various parts of the apparatus, and the greater also is the difficulty experienced by the stutterers in producing regular and harmonious combinations of sounds.

Stuttering is therefore a disorder of co-ordination concerned in the emission of sounds, and, as in writer's cramp, is similarly circumscribed. The cause of stuttering is a congenital weakness of the apparatus of respiration and phonation, situated in the medulla oblongata. This apparatus, which has been affected since childhood by some psychical shock, does not recover its proper tone, and responds, therefore, to the mere impulse of the will by inco-ordinated movements. The stimulation is irradiated to the adjacent nerve nuclei, and thus gives rise to concomitant spasmodic movements of the muscles of the face, eyes, tongue, and even of the neck. Colombat had also called attention to the irregular, interrupted, and rapid breathing occurring in stutterers.

In consequence of the habitually short, irregular respirations, and under the influence of mental excitement, a large portion of the air contained in the thorax is lost before it can be employed in the formation of words. With increase of the anxiety and embarrassment, the disorders of co-ordination become intensified. The stutterers endeavor to control the disturbances in expiration by contracting their abdominal muscles. If the patients hold their breath and, at the same time, contract the abdominal muscles, an occlusion of the larynx will result (as Czermak has shown by means of the laryngoscope) from juxtaposition of the arytenoid cartilages and of the processus vocales, until the vocal cords are brought into contact with one another, and the epiglottis, forming a convexity internally, is applied to the glottis and completes the occlusion.

The stimulation is also propagated along the pneumogastric nerves, and is manifested in the constrictors of the pharynx which it innervates, in the palato-glossus, and partly in the thyro-hyoid muscles. The contraction of these muscles causes the tongue to be applied to the roof of the mouth, the pharynx is narrowed and fixed, the communication of the mouth with the nasal fossæ is partly interfered with, and the expired air is therefore unable to escape. The expired air only escapes after repeated efforts and after elevating the epiglottis ; or, under the influence of the want of air, the glottis enlarges, and the fauces, which were previously narrowed, relax. The dyspnœic phenomena then cease; the frequent repetition of such scenes increases the disorders of co-ordination to such an extent that even rational therapeutic measures are unable to re-establish harmony between respiration and the other muscular movements, and to direct co-ordination, by the aid of the will, into proper paths.

Diagnosis and Prognosis.

Stuttering is most frequently mistaken for stammering. The latter consists of a difficulty in performing the movements requisite for the articulation of certain consonants, phonation remaining intact. It is never accompanied by spasmodic or congestive phenomena, nor by difficulty in respiration. The stuttering which occurs in cerebral diseases may be due to motor disturbances within the territory of the hypoglossus, or it may be of an aphasic nature. The stuttering observed in cerebral tumors and facial paralysis (especially double) consists of a difficulty in the pronunciation of labials, due to motor paralysis of the lips or tongue.

All these disturbances are wrongly classified, by certain authors, under the term stuttering. They should be termed *alalia*, as they have nothing in common with the disorders of co-ordination. Among the latter we must also place the special form of stuttering which sometimes develops in ataxia. All the other so-called varieties of stuttering (constitutional, nervous, psychical, etc.) are caused, as we have stated above, by a congenital weakness of the apparatus presiding over the co-ordination of speech, and are consequently not entitled to be regarded as distinct varieties.

The *prognosis* is not unfavorable in young subjects who enjoy good health, apart from their nervous excitability. The slight forms often disappear spontaneously at a more advanced age. Severe and chronic types are so much the more rebellious according as vocal stuttering is more pronounced, and as the choreic movements and dyspnœic phenomena are manifested to a greater extent. All other things being equal, young people, who have already attained a certain age, present better chances of recovery than undeveloped children. Heredity renders the prognosis much more unfavorable. Relapses not infrequently occur after recovery has apparently taken place.

Treatment.

The labial gymnastics first employed by Mrs. Leigh, and perfected by Malbouche, and the constant application of the tip of the tongue to the roof of the mouth, are insufficient as a means of treatment. Neither have I observed any better effects from the long-continued application of constant and induced currents (to the larynx, hypoglossal nerve, or passed through the head).

The rhythmical method was first instituted by Colombat, and then perfected by Klenke and others. I have employed this plan successfully in a large number of cases. The chief end in view is to regulate the precipitate, irregular form of respiration, which occurs in the majority of stutterers. In order to become habituated to a certain rhythm, the patient should for a long time keep the eyes fixed upon the baton with which the time is kept, and should endeavor to regulate, in this manner, the movements of inspiration and expiration. The interval between these two periods should be made longer and shorter at different times, the teacher alternately beating time more rapidly or more slowly, sometimes accelerating, sometimes retarding the respirations. In patients who are able to sing, it is well to combine the respiratory gymnastics with " crescendo " and " de-crescendo " exercises on the scales, the notes being sustained as long as possible.

With regard to the correction of speech itself, it is better, in my opinion, to direct the patient for a long time to speak in syllables, in four-quarters time, and in a not too loud tone of voice. The physician should always beat the time himself. The latter act is merely a regulator which prevents the precipitation of speech, and forces the patient to carefully watch the succession of words.

Before the patient begins to speak he should take a few deep inspirations, and then pronounce the words according to a regular rhythm, accompanying himself with movements of the hand. Each phrase should be scanned like a word of several syllables, slowly and with a distinct intonation, and each syllable should have an equal duration. At each punctuation in the course of a phrase, the patient takes a fresh inspiration, but without interrupting the rhythm of the pronunciation. In addition, it is necessary to carefully watch any vicious intonations made by the patient, and when the tongue is protruded too forcibly, or when it is kept too long upon the floor of the mouth, the patient's attention must be called to the fact, and he should endeavor to correct it.

In order to prevent a relapse it is necessary to continue the gymnastics (for six months, a year, or even more) until the patient habitually speaks correctly. The education of stutterers is best accomplished in special institutions; but we can often succeed in private practice, by teaching the principles of the method to the relatives of the patient.

CLASS VII.

———◆———

TOXIC NEUROSES.—POST-FEBRILE NERVOUS DISORDERS.—ANÆ-MIC AND REFLEX PARALYSIS.

———

CHAPTER XXXVII.

TOXIC NEUROSES.

a. *Saturnine Nervous Affections.*

AMONG the metallic preparations, lead and its combinations deserve especial attention on account of the frequency and severity of its effects upon the nervous and muscular systems. Lead may enter the organism through different channels, most frequently through the intestinal tract, and less often through the other mucous membranes (cases reported by M. Meyer, Erdmann, Moeller, Geenen, etc., of lead-poisoning from the use of snuff containing lead; Sabatier's observation, in which lead colic and arthralgia were due to the prolonged application of the acetate of lead to the eyes, in a case of blepharophthalmia). Carbonate of lead may also be introduced through the lungs, as I have observed in rabbits, and in work-ingmen pursuing various trades (Beobachtungen ueber Bleieinwirkung auf den Thier-Koerper, Zeitschr. f. prak. Heilk., 48–51, 1865).

In one factory, in which powdered glass, containing lead, was used in the construction of telegraphic apparatus, Archambault found sixteen females and three males suffering from lead affections. Finally, lead may be introduced into the system through the intact skin, as has been proven by the observations of Schottin (poisoning from the use of plates of lead in order to dye the hair; at the autopsy a gelatinous foyer of softening, containing lead, was found at the base of the left middle lobe), and by the cases reported by Eulenburg, Spoerer, etc. I have also seen manifest symptoms of lead-poisoning (arthralgias, tremor, muscular weakness, confusion of ideas and of speech) caused by the prolonged use of rouge containing lead.

The susceptibility to the toxic action of lead varies greatly according to the individuals. I have noticed the development of well-marked paralyses of the limbs without the previous existence of colic, neuralgia, or tremor. At other times we may note repeated attacks of colic, men-strual disorders in female type-setters, profound anæmia with cardiac bruit, frequent abortions, or delivery of still-born children, although these phenomena are not followed by symptoms of paralysis. Individuals who have passed through several attacks of colic, experience weakness in the limbs, and their muscular power often diminishes to such an extent that they are unable to do heavy work, although they do not present real paralysis. In two cases of this kind, attended with polyuria, I found the urine markedly albuminous. Some authors have seen these symptoms terminate in nephritis. When arthralgia occurs after violent colic, and is accompanied by delirium, even though it is merely temporary, the patient is threatened with an eclamptic attack. When there is an hereditary morbid disposition to central affections, the absorption of lead may have a still more disastrous effect upon the nervous system. Duchenne (Gaz. Méd. de Paris, 1863) has published the case of a grinder of lenses, working in lead, whose father and brother had died of epilepsy, and who, after suffering from constipation, cephalalgia, and a blue line upon the gums, was attacked with lead eclampsia followed by meningitis. This diagnosis was confirmed upon autopsy. Orfila, Meurer, and Devergie have determined the presence of lead in the brain in patients who had died of saturnine affections. According to the experimental investigations recently undertaken by Heubel upon dogs (Pathogen. u. Sympt. d. chron. Bleivergiftung, Berlin, 1871), the lead is found in much larger quantities in the brain and spinal cord than in the liver and kidneys. According to Heubel's experiments, and contrary to the results previously obtained by Gusserow (Virch. Arch., XXI. Bd.), the muscles contain less lead than the central nervous system.

Gueneau de Mussy and Lemaire have reported (Gaz. des. Hôp., juillet, 1863) the case of a painter, æt. thirty years, who died in convulsions after having had several attacks of colic and delirium. At the autopsy a large hæmorrhage, communicating with the fourth ventricle, was found in the brain; the heart and lungs presented a normal appearance. When cerebral symptoms, associated with paralysis, occur in a worker in lead, we are frequently justified in attributing the cerebral phenomena to lead-poisoning. Duchenne mentions the history of a painter who was seized, after several attacks of colic, with a hemiplegia which was regarded as saturnine, until its central origin was discovered, by noticing that the electro-muscular contractility and sensibility were normal. At the autopsy an abundant hæmorrhage was found in the cerebral lobes. I have also published the case of a painter (Electrotherapie, 2d Edit., Observ., 32) who presented, in addition to coloration of the gums and anæmia, a right hemiplegia, which was looked upon as saturnine until electrical exploration revealed the cerebral character of the disease. At the autopsy a hæmorrhage was found in the external portion of the left corpus striatum and lenticular nucleus; the arteries at the base were thickened.

Saturnine eclampsia was attributed by Traube (Med. Centralzeit., 1861) and Rosenstein (Schuchardt's Zeitschr., 1867) to capillary cerebral anæmia, caused by cerebral œdema. Heubel has succeeded in demonstrating the anæmia and increased proportion of water in the cerebral substance. The lead albuminuria and granular atrophy of the kidneys, observed by Ollivier and Lancereaux (Union Méd., 1864), were not noticed by Rosenstein and Heubel. I have seen a case of lead encephalopathy in the Vienna General Hospital, which was interesting on account of its favorable termination. The patient was a painter, twenty-four years of age, who was suddenly seized, after six attacks of lead colic, with convulsions in the face and limbs, vomiting, loss of consciousness, and retardation of the pulse. All the threatening symptoms disappeared in a few days after the application of leeches to the temples, cold compresses to the head, and the administration of intestinal derivatives. We may finally refer to saturnine amaurosis, occurring in man, and also observed by Rosenstein in dogs that have been poisoned with lead. Meyer has published (Union Méd., 1868) the case of a bleacher of laces, who suffered from headache, convulsions, and amblyopia, and in whom the ophthalmoscope revealed the existence of neuro-retinitis. Treatment with derivatives improved the power of sight, but produced no noteworthy changes in the condition of the fundus of the eye.

Medication was also unsuccessful in five cases of saturnine neuro-retinitis reported by Hutchinson (Ophthalm. Hosp. Rep., VII.). A case of saturnine bilateral neuro-retinitis (numerous white spots around the optic papilla), with complete recovery from the ocular affection, has been recently published by Stricker (Ber. Charité-Annal., I., 1874).

The motor and sensory disturbances, occurring in the course of saturnine affections, often assume the characteristics of medullary symptoms. The exaggeration of sensibility may manifest itself by hyperæsthesia of the superficial parts, or by neuralgias of the deeper parts. The cutaneous hyperæsthesia, as I have observed in several cases, often accompanies the paroxysms of pain, and after the disappearance of the latter is only present to a slight degree. This hyperæsthesia, which is barely alluded to by authors, alternates very frequently with anæsthesia, and is therefore somewhat similar to hysterical sensory disorders, with their variable manifestations.

The symptoms which are described by authors under the term arthralgia, are, in my opinion, of a neuralgic character, and should be regarded as vague neuralgias. This is proven by their periodicity, their frequent relapses, the presence of points in the neighborhood of the vertebral column, which are painful upon pressure, the partial muscular spasms, and the sensations of pricking or numbness which are experienced at the close of an attack. These neuralgias may occur in the upper or lower limbs, in the lumbar region, the intercostal spaces, and even in the branches of the trigeminus. The boring or tearing pains chiefly involve the flexor muscles, the extensors being more subject to paralysis. According to Tanquerel's observations, there were thirty-two cases of arthralgia among fifty-two of lead colic. Sieveking (Lancet, I., 1861) found seven cases of lead neuralgia in men, and only one (of doubtful character) in a woman.

Lead anæsthesia is a more frequent symptom, and considerable attention has been devoted to it. Beau (Arch. Gén., 1848) observed anæsthesia upon the upper or inner surfaces of the limbs, and more rarely upon the trunk and head, among thirty workers in lead. Touching or tickling the mucous membranes did not produce any painful sensations in these patients. In other parts, tactile sensibility was preserved, but analgesia was present.

Falk distinguishes, in chronic saturnine affections (Virch. Handb. der Path. u. Ther., p. 210) a superficial and deep anæsthesia. When improvement begins, the latter disappears sooner than the former. Smoler found more or less marked cutaneous analgesia in fifteen cases of lead-poisoning; anæsthesia was not present, but cutaneous impressions were poorly localized.

Archambault has recently published some analogous observations. In lead paralysia, attended by abolition of the excitability of the nerve-trunks, I have found a large portion of the paralyzed parts analgesic, but the sensibility to contact was usually preserved. In much rarer instances, and irrespective of the paralysis, the sensation of burning, which is produced by stroking the skin with the cathode of a galvanic battery, is lost, although the mere contact of the electrode with the skin is felt with perfect distinctness. There is no doubt that the analgesia occurring in lead poisoning is of spinal origin. In two cases of lead poisoning, with abolition of sensation and loss of consciousness, Tanquerel observed catalepsy with "waxen flexibility."

Saturnine motor disturbances are much more severe than the disorders of sensation. They may involve almost all the muscles of the body. Trousseau has observed paralysis of the muscles of the glottis in horses employed in red-lead factories. The respiration of these animals is normal during repose, but when in motion it becomes hurried and noisy, the entire body is tremulous and bathed in perspiration, and, finally, they fall down exhausted. If the disease continues, the life of the animals can only be saved by performing tracheotomy and keeping the fistula open for several years. Guenther, Gurlt, and Hedwig have observed, upon autopsy, in cases of this character, atrophy and discoloration of the recurrent nerves, with atrophy and fatty degeneration of the dilators of the glottis.

According to Romberg, the left half of the larynx would be usually more affected in the analogous condition in man, and would be pressed inwards more rapidly than on the healthy side. Upon exercising energetic and prolonged pressure upon the arytenoid cartilage of the affected side, the healthy half of the larynx being fixed, we would observe acceleration of the respiration and increased violence of the respiratory movements. Independently of these signs, laryngoscopic examination in man would furnish important data concerning the shape of the glottis, and would reveal difficulty in or abolition of, the movements of the vocal cord upon the affected side. Tanquerel has observed sixteen cases of aphonia, and fifteen cases of stammering and stuttering (psellismus saturninus) from partial paralyses in the laryngeal region. Baglivi and De Haen refer to analogous cases. These paralyses of the muscles of the larynx and of speech are often combined with partial paralyses of the muscles of the trunk, and almost always pursue a chronic course.

Lead paralysis develops after a condition of exhaustion of the vital energies has become manifest. It may involve isolated groups of muscles or the entire muscular tissue of the upper or lower limbs; it more rarely involves the muscles of the thorax and back, those of phonation and speech, the intercostal muscles and the diaphragm (Duchenne). Among ninety-eight cases of paralysis of the upper limbs, Tanquerel has only seen this condition general in five, and only once among fifteen cases of paralysis in the lower limbs; in all the others, the paralysis was partial. Lead paralysis usually affects the muscles in a regular order. Paralysis of the common extensor of the fingers is followed by paralysis of the extensors of the index and little finger. Then the long extensor of the thumb, the extensors of the wrist, the short extensor and the long abductor of the thumb, become affected.

The long supinator usually preserves its electrical excitability; in extensive paralysis, the deltoid and triceps are affected earlier than the biceps. I have, however, observed and published a case in which the paralysis was propagated from above downwards. Paralysis of the lower limbs is much more infrequent and chiefly involves the extensors of the thigh and leg. Lead hemiplegia, described by Stoll, Tanquerel, and Andral, is exceedingly rare. In the paraplegic form, the sphincters are always unaffected.

Among the *anatomical lesions*, the older observers found atrophy, fatty degeneration and discoloration of the paralyzed muscles, contraction of the blood-vessels, and diminution of the hemato-globuline in the

blood. Lanceraux (Gaz. Méd., Nov., 1862) found granular or fatty degeneration of the myeline. Gombault (Arch. de physiol., IV., 1875) has recently published a case of lead paralysis of the upper and lower limbs in
a florist; the spinal cord and nerve-roots were intact; in the muscles, the
transverse striæ were only preserved in places, and here and there the
volume of the muscular fibrillæ was increased, with formation of fissures
and proliferation of nuclei. In the peripheral nerves, side by side with
intact fibres of the radial nerve, were others whose myeline presented a
granular appearance, and certain sheaths were almost entirely empty,
although the axis cylinders were well preserved. Upon transverse section, nuclear proliferation was found in the intra-fascicular connective tissue. In a case of lead paralysis reported by Westphal (Arch. f. Psychiat.,
IV. Bd., 1874), the affected muscles were emaciated, with partial disappearance of the transverse striæ and multiplication of the muscular nuclei.
Upon transverse section of the radial nerve after hardening, the myeline
of the fibres was found to have been markedly diminished in quantity;
the intermediate spaces, which were streaked with red and feebly colored,
were grouped under the form of small circles and represented transverse sections of the nerve-fibres, such as are observed in regenerated nerves. These
fibres were more numerous in the nerve-trunk than in its branches (primary
affection of the radial nerve); the cord, the anterior horns, and the nerve-
roots were intact.

In one case of chronic lead poisoning (with dyspepsia, colic, vomiting,
diarrhœa, and fatal collapse), Kussmaul and Mayer observed (Deutsch.
Arch. f. klin. Med., IX. Bd., H. II.) sclerosis of the cœliac and upper
cervical ganglia, with proliferation of the connective tissue and deformity
of the cells; the brain and cord presented a slight grade of periarteritis
(an inflammatory change in the cerebral capillaries may give rise, in lead
poisoning, to rupture of the vessels and extravasations of blood). In addition, the mucous and muscular coats of the stomach were found atrophied. Peyer's patches and the solitary follicles were diminished in number and extremely atrophied, and the submucous coat of the intestines
was thickened from an abundant proliferation of the connective tissue.
The dyspepsia must therefore be attributed to chronic gastro-intestinal
catarrh, with atrophy of the lymphatic glands. During the attacks of
colic, there is irritation of the sensory fibres of the abdominal ganglia
and of the connective tissue which surrounds and traverses these organs.
Ségond has also found the cœliac ganglion indurated in patients who had
died from the endemic colic of Cayenne. According to Tanquerel, this
disease, as well as the colic of Poitou, of Devonshire, and of Madrid, is the
result of lead poisoning.

Electrical exploration in lead paralysis furnishes many points of interest, both from a scientific and a practical point of view. Electricity was
first successfully employed by Gardane (Conject. sur l'électricité méd.,
etc., Paris, 1768), and soon after by De Haen (Ratio medendi, t. III., 1771).
In the beginning of this century, electro-puncture was in vogue. The
English physicians employed statical electricity, by allowing the sparks
of an electrical machine to pass to the dorsal spine.

At a later period, the researches of Duchenne showed that electrical
contractility and sensibility are diminished in the paralyzed muscles, and
that the contractility becomes affected in them in the order which we
have previously pointed out. Atrophied muscles, which do not contract
under the stimulus of electricity, are not susceptible of spontaneous recovery; if a strong current is applied, it will pass through the atrophied

extensors to the flexors. In many cases which have come under my observation, the electro-muscular contractility was affected before voluntary motion; during the progress of recovery, the latter may be re-established, while the electro-muscular contractility is still decidedly below the normal. In some cases of lead paralysis, Eulenburg and Erb have observed abolition of farado-muscular with preservation of galvano-muscular contractility.

In severe and extensive forms of paralysis we are able to follow (as I have shown in my treatise on electrotherapeutics) the diminution or abolition of galvanic excitability from the nerve-roots to the plexuses and nerve-trunks; in less extensive paralysis, the nerve-roots preserve their excitability to galvanism. The excitability may therefore persist in the parts adjacent to the spinal centres, although it has disappeared in the peripheral regions; it may also be preserved in the plexuses, after it has been abolished in the nerve-trunks. If recovery takes place, the return of excitability occurs from the centre to the periphery, and gradually advances from the nerve-roots and plexuses to the trunks of the nerves.

The *treatment* of saturnine affections has for its object the elimination of the poison from the system and the palliation of the distressing symptoms of the disease. Great advantage is obtained in lead colic from the employment of large doses of opium. In very painful attacks, the drug should be administered in such a manner that it may be readily absorbed. In the course of my experiments upon resorption and absorption of preparations of iodine (Sitz. d. Kais. Akad. d. Wiss., XLVI. Bd., 1872, and Med. Wschr., 1863), I incidentally demonstrated the practical advantages of enemata containing opium, and of intestinal absorption in lead colic. Hypodermic injections of preparations of opium or belladonna act even more rapidly. The injection should be repeated as soon as the first signs of another attack become manifest; in rebellious cases, we may also administer the opium during the remissions. According to Didierjean (Gaz. hebdom., VII., 1870), workers in lead factories who are in the habit of drinking milk several times a day, are not subject to colic or to other saturnine affections.

The treatment with iodide of potassium, first recommended by Melsens, is usually employed in the various forms of lead poisoning. It is held that the iodide of potassium forms a soluble combination with the lead which has accumulated in the organism, and thus favors its elimination from the body. According to the careful experiments of Overbeck, Waller, and Schneider in Vienna, the administration of iodide of potassium does not favor the elimination of mercury to any marked extent. This fact being demonstrated with regard to mercury, there is no good reason for admitting a more active elimination of lead under the influence of this drug. The deficiency in experimental investigations upon this question, is not supplied by the results of clinical observations. In chronic lead poisoning, the combinations of lead are only eliminated through the natural emunctories (liver, digestive canal, kidneys) after a long time. So long as the organism has not recovered its normal functions under the influence of a vital reinvigoration, iodide of potassium will not aid in the restoration of the diseased economy, and in the regulation of its disordered functions.

I have obtained no better results, in lead cachexia, from the immediate employment of electrical treatment, than from the use of iodide of potassium. Electricity has proved useful in my hands, only after the general condition has improved under the influence of warm baths, pure air, nutritious diet, and wines. In view of the facts to which we have called attention above, it is necessary, in severe cases of lead paralysis, to expose, as far as possible, the central portions of the nerve-paths to the action of the current, and to pass the labile descending galvanic current (eight to ten minutes daily) from the nerve-roots to the plexuses and nerve-trunks. The galvanic current can act in this manner upon the nerves at a period in which the intra-muscular nerve-fibres will not permit the current to pass through them, and in which the local application of faradism possesses, therefore, very little utility. It is preferable, in the majority of cases, to resort to a mixed treatment, by alternating, every other day, galvanization of the nerve-trunks with faradization of the paralyzed muscles. In severe cases, recovery does not occur until the expiration of several months.

Experience has shown that repeated warm baths, and after a time, vapor baths of short duration, followed by douches to the paralyzed limbs, produce good results in lead cachexia, while, as a rule, the patients tolerate cold baths very poorly. The good effects of sulphur baths, which are praised so highly by Tanquerel, are due less to the sulphur than to the temperature of the bath. Preparations of strychnine and brucine which were recommended by Fouquier, have been also highly praised by Tanquerel. Among forty cases treated in this manner, the larger number recovered completely and the remainder were considerably improved. In one case of lead paralysis, I obtained good effects from the employment of hypodermic injections of strychnine (one to five milligrammes on alternate days). Finally, hydrotherapeutic measures are very efficient in lead dyscrasia and its sequences. At first, moist frictions should be employed daily, followed by half-baths at 18°–16° C.; we may then resort to moist packs (until the body becomes warm), to affusions in a half-bath, and finally to local douches or to whole baths of short duration. I have been able to convince myself that this method furnishes excellent results.

The consideration of *mercurial nervous affections* will next engage our attention.

They are due to the absorption of mercury through the skin or mucous membranes, or to the inhalation of vapor of mercury floating in the atmosphere, and may cause more or less profound disturbances in the peripheral and central organs. In the latter event, mercurial arthralgia occurs, combined with tremor of the upper and lower limbs, general paralysis of the arms and legs and affections of the organs of special sense. When the brain becomes affected by the toxic agent, vertigo, insomnia, hypochondria, epileptiform attacks, and sometimes, though rarely, mania and idiocy, make their appearance.

From a therapeutic point of view, after having removed the patient from the influence of the poison, we may hasten elimination by stimulating the intestinal and renal functions by means of baths and a trip to the country. I have obtained good results in several cases of mercurial tremor and paresis from galvanization of the nerves or faradic treatment of the paretic muscles.

In *chronic arsenical poisoning*, tremor of the limbs, atrophy, and paralysis of the extensors of the upper limbs, and paraplegia may develop in the midst of cephalic symptoms, vague neuralgias, and sensations of numbness and anæsthesia. In one case which I have published, and in a second observation by Smoler (Zeitschr. f. prak. Heilk., 19, 20, 1863), the electro-muscular contractility and sensibility were considerably diminished. In the latter patient, whose limbs remained paretic for a long time, im-

provement of electrical contractility and a return of motor power rapidly
occurred after daily faradization of the muscles.

The paralyses and disorders of speech produced by *carbonic oxide* are
attributed (but only in severe cases) to the development of foci of cerebral softening (Th. Simon).   Atrophy and paralysis of the limbs from inhalations of *sulphide of carbon* (workers in caoutchouc factories, Del-
pech) occur very rarely.   This is also true of the paralysis of the fingers
from *aniline* poisoning (as in Clemens' case of wound of the skin), of the
phosphorus paralyses of the forearm (Gallavardin), and of the paralyses
due to acute poisoning (from hydrocyanic acid, nicotine, etc.).

CHAPTER XXXVIII.

NERVOUS AFFECTIONS DUE TO FEBRILE DISEASES.

NERVOUS disturbances and multiple paralyses may be observed, both during the course and after the termination of febrile affections. These disorders are the expression of phenomena of irritation or of depression in the cerebro-spinal system, or of peripheral changes occurring in the nerves and muscles. The anatomical character of these lesions is not sufficiently understood from all points of view. In the present chapter we shall discuss those nervous disorders which occur during febrile affections (febrile) and those which follow them (post-febrile).

Nervous disorders occurring in infectious diseases.—An entire series of nervous disorders, from slighter to more severe manifestations, may occur during the course of *typhoid fever.* Hyperæsthesia is the earliest disturbance of sensation, and has been especially investigated by Fritz (Gaz. Méd., 5–7, 1864). It is one of the first symptoms of the disease, and may last a few days or continue into the second week. This hyperæsthesia is chiefly observed in women and children, and may be so marked that pinching up a fold of skin, slight pressure of the nails, and even, in the most severe cases, the weight of the clothes, give rise to intense pains.

The cutaneous hyperæsthesia usually involves a considerable portion of the limbs or trunk, and it generally pursues an ascending direction. Muscular hyperæsthesia, often combined with spontaneous muscular pains and cutaneous hyperæsthesia, is the cause of intolerable suffering to the patients. It renders all movement impossible, condemns them to absolute rest, and may terminate in distressing contractures. Muscular hyperæsthesia may involve almost all the muscles of the limbs, neck, thorax, and abdomen, and usually occurs simultaneously with the cutaneous hyperæsthesia. More or less extensive anæsthesia is often a very rebellious symptom, and almost always occurs during convalescence. I have observed anæsthesia of the superficial layers and hyperæsthesia of the deeper parts (as Tuerck has noticed in neuralgia) in the calves of the legs after typhoid fever.

In a convalescent from typhoid fever, æt. twenty years, anæsthesia of the left median nerve was observed, and also of the anterior and external surfaces of the lower limb upon the same side, with right mydriasis and feebleness of accommodation, and loss of hearing on the right side (the ticking of a watch was only audible when applied directly to the concha ; the membrana tympana was found normal by Politzer). Upon passing strong galvanic currents from the dorsal spine to the brachial plexus, or from the plexus to the median nerve, peripheral sensibility was found to be absent, in the first three fingers ; motor power was preserved. Galvanization produced rapid improvement.

Among the nervous disorders of typhoid fever we may also mention the neuralgic pains which occur during the first week in certain nerves (frequently the occipital or supraorbital), or may develop after the termination of the disease in the vertebral column, the loins, in the nerves of the arms or feet, and may even be accompanied by temporary hyperæsthesia.

We have previously spoken of contractures as among the motor disturbances occurring in the train of typhoid fever. It may also be followed by various paralyses. Thus paralysis of the vocal cords has been observed by Tuerck in adults, and by Bierbaum and Friedreich in children. Hervieux and Griesinger have published cases of ptosis and external strabismus.

In one case of this kind, which terminated in death, no changes were found in the brain or nerves. Wunderlich, Griesinger, and Seitz mention examples of complete or incomplete paralysis of the lower limbs. In an observation made by Leudet (Gaz. des Hôp., 58, 1861), ascending paralysis developed during convalescence from a mild attack of typhoid fever, and extended from the lower to the upper limbs, then to the muscles of respiration, and terminated in death after a duration of six days. No changes were found in the nerve-centres or in the larynx. M. Meyer reported the case of a boy, æt. sixteen years, who suffered from anæsthesia of the right half of the body, atrophy of the right arm, and complete paralysis of the muscles supplied by the right ulnar nerve, during convalescence from typhoid fever. From the observations which I made in the Vienna General Hospital during two epidemics of typhoid fever, it appears that the paralyses vary in extent and intensity. In slight cases there is merely paresis of certain groups of muscles, the patients cannot "make a fist," the grip is very feeble, writing is accomplished with difficulty, and the electro-muscular and electro-cutaneous sensibility are markedly diminished. In severe and, fortunately, rarer cases the paralysis may involve one side of the body or both lower limbs.

I observed left hemiplegia in a young man, æt. twenty-six years, five months after a severe attack of typhoid fever. The movements at the shoulder and elbow were seriously interfered with, and those at the ankle-joint were only accomplished with great effort. The electro-muscular contractility was diminished in the leg (compared to the healthy side).

In two cases (boys of fourteen and sixteen years of age) marked paralysis of the lower limbs, which had been mistaken by several physicians for spinal paralysis, developed six and nine months respectively after typhoid fever. The electro-muscular contractility and the galvanic excitability of the nerves were extremely feeble or abolished in the lower limbs. Sensibility and, finally, motion were gradually restored under the influence of warm baths and nutritious diet. The galvanic excitability of the nerves then reappeared, while the electro-muscular contractility returned more slowly, especially in the legs, and was not entirely restored even after the patient was able to walk.

The nervous disorders which develop during or after typhoid fever may be of central or peripheral origin. As proof of their cerebral nature, we often observe symptoms of irritation or depression (unilateral contractures, tremors, aphasia, partial or maniacal delirium, acute insanity, hemiplegia with preservation of electro-muscular contractility). The spinal origin of many of the nervous disorders in question is demonstrated by certain coexisting symptoms (extensive hyperæsthesia or anæsthesia on both sides of the body, paralysis of the bladder and rectum); by the acute ascending paralysis, observed by Leudet, affecting the lower limbs and then the arms, and rapidly terminating in death; by the occurrence of progressive muscular atrophy, ataxia, and sclerosis of the cord, after typhoid fever; finally, by the atrophy of the sympathetic observed by Astegiano in a patient suffering from ulcerations extending over one-half of the body. Beau reports four cases in which, in addition to spinal hyperæmia, foyers of softening occurred in the gray matter. Certain monoplegias occurring after typhoid fever are of peripheral origin. These include the paralysis of distinct groups of muscles, with partial anæsthesia and abolition of electrical excitability, due to nutritive disorders in the corresponding nerves. In some cases these symptoms may be attributed to neuritis. Zenker has demonstrated the peripheral character of a large number of paralyses following typhoid fever, by pointing out the anatomical lesions of the muscular tissue (Veränderungen der willkürl. Muskeln im Typhus abdom., 1864). This writer distinguishes a granular degeneration (deposit of fine molecular granules in the contractile substance of the muscular fibres) and a waxy degeneration (transformation of the contractile substance into a homogeneous, colorless, glistening mass, with disappearance of the transverse striæ). These degenerations occur most frequently in the adductors of the thigh, the transversalis abdominis, the psoas, obturators, triceps, and pectoralis minor. They sometimes develop symmetrically upon both sides of the body. They appear to attain their greatest development during the second or in the beginning of the third week, remain stationary during the third and fourth weeks, and disappear during the fifth or six weeks.

At this period, the perimysium is found to contain cells which are either small, round, or angular, or are large, fusiform, or stellate; elongated fibres are also scattered throughout groups of nuclei, and the transformation of these into muscular fibres is demonstrated by the appearance of transverse striæ in them. They present a great analogy with the appearances presented during the embryonic development of striated muscles. According to Waldeyer, the regeneration of the fibres occurs from rows of "muscle-cells," and, according to E. Neumann, from longitudinal fission of the old fibres.

The alterations in the muscular tissue, which were afterwards described by Hayem (Arch. de Physiol., T. III., 1870) in typhoid fever and other febrile affections, are of an inflammatory nature. Popoff (Virch. Arch., 61. Bd., 1874) has observed granular transformation of the muscular tissue (parenchymatous muscular inflammation, Virchow) in a large number of infectious diseases (typhoid and typhus fevers, cholera, recurrent fever, puerperal affections, pyæmia). Side by side with the waxy degeneration and increase in the nuclei of the muscular fibres, inflammatory changes occur in the internal and middle coats of the vessels in the affected muscles. This produces a diminished power of resistance in the walls of the vessels, and thus explains the vascular ruptures and hæmorrhages observed in the muscular tissues. The arteries of other organs present no abnormal changes.

The *prognosis* of the nervous disorders under consideration is favorable. In the majority of cases they terminate in recovery, though this may occupy from three to seven months in the paraplegic forms (Kennedy, Rilliet). If convalescence is very prolonged, we may prescribe with advantage a trip to the country and light ferruginous waters. In persistent anæsthesia and paresis of the limbs good effects are obtained from electro-therapeutics (galvanization of the nerve-trunks, faradization of the skin and muscles) and from hydrotherapeutics (frictions, packs of short duration, cool half-baths; local douches in anæsthesia). If the psychical disturbances are prolonged, we may resort to mild hydrotherapeutic measures. In conditions of excitement, Delasiauve recommends enemata containing quinine and camphor. In severe forms, associated with torpor, acetate of ammonia (thirty to forty drops daily) may be employed, with exercise in the open air, travel, and moral treatment.

Nervous disorders following acute febrile diseases and the exanthemata.—Motor and sensory disturbances are also observed as sequences of acute articular rheumatism, pneumonia, pleurisy (Durozier), bronchitis and tuberculosis. The motor disorders have been described by Gubler (Arch. gén., 1860) under the term "amyotrophic paralysis," but they do not always result, as he believes, from neuritis with nutritive disturbances in the muscular tissues. I have published a case of paraplegia following pneumonia, in which the paralysis of the right leg was accompanied by anæsthesia of the anterior part of the thigh, with diminution of the electro-muscular contractility and sensibility. Recovery occurred after four weeks' treatment with faradization and warm baths. We have previously mentioned, upon page 18, Vol. I., the abolition of electro-muscular contractility and sensibility observed in a case of cerebral rheumatism complicated with profound melancholia.

Numerous motor and sensory disorders, either of a central or peripheral nature, may occur after the acute exanthemata. Thus rubeola is sometimes followed by hemiplegia (Barthez and Rilliet) and general (Liégeard) or circumscribed paralysis. Hemiplegia (Kennedy), paraplegia (Revillout, Shepherd), and apoplectiform paralysis with persistent aphasia (Eulenburg) have been observed after scarlatina. Variola is sometimes followed by severe and rebellious sequences, under the form of aphasia (in a patient under my care it was accompanied by cephalic symptoms), initial hyperæsthesia followed by anæsthesia, and coexisting paralysis. The paralysis is sometimes circumscribed and limited to the upper limbs, but more frequently assumes the paraplegic type and involves the lower limbs. In two cases of this character, Westphal recently found (Arch. f. Psych., IV. Bd.) disseminated myelitis (softening with production of granular cells), involving the white substance, especially the lateral columns, but also the gray matter. Similar lesions were found in a case of pulmonary phthisis, with motor and sensory disturbances in the lower limbs. We may finally add that paralysis of cranial nerves and paraplegia, usually with a favorable termination, have been observed after erysipelas.

Diphtheritic nervous disorders.—Diphtheritic paralysis has been carefully studied by Trousseau (Gaz. des Hôp., 1855), Bretonneau (Arch. gén., 1855), Maingault (De la Paralysie diphthérique, 1860), Jenner (Diphtheria, etc., 1861), Weber (Virch. Arch., 1862), etc. After the termination of the local disease, which usually involves the pharynx, much less frequently the skin, nasal fossæ, conjunctivæ, vulva, or the external auditory canal, an interval of several days or weeks may elapse before the first symptoms of the nervous affection become manifest. They consist, in many cases, of violent vomiting and retardation of the pulse.

Paralysis of the pharynx and velum palati (difficulty of deglutition, nasal voice, inability to suck, gargle, or blow, anæsthesia of the uvula and velum palati, abolition of faradic excitability) is one of the earliest and most frequent symptoms. The diphtheritic paralysis may then affect various other muscles, the epiglottis, vocal cords, the tongue, the ocular muscles, the sphincter of the pupils and the tensor of the choroid (with mydriasis and loss of accommodation).

I have observed in the St. Joseph's Children's Hospital, in Vienna, an example of diphtheritic facial paralysis, which is, I believe, a unique case (Med. Presse, 26, 1868). The middle paralyzed muscles of the face had lost their faradic contractility, but preserved their irritability to the continuous current. Even after the disappearance of the paralysis, the same difference existed with regard to the action of the two currents. The patient, aet. two and a half years, died two weeks later of chronic intestinal catarrh, and no abnormal appearances were discovered upon microscopical examination. Negative results were also obtained by Ziemssen (Die Elektricität in der Medizin, 1866) in a case of diphtheritic paralysis of the velum palati and pharynx.

In addition to the small muscles mentioned above, the paralysis may also extend to the trunk and extremities. Paralysis of all possible grades may occur, from a slight uncertainty in the gait to ataxia (Eisenmann and Brenner), but rarely complete paralysis. Electro-muscular contractility and sensibility, and the galvanic irritability of the nerves, are usually diminished. The latter is sometimes increased, but only in very marked disorders of co-ordination. The sensory disorders include, at the onset, hyperæsthesia, then anæsthesia, and a slight sensation of numbness. The visual disturbances (asthenopia, dilatation of the pupils, hypermetropia, more rarely myopia, without any changes appreciable with the ophthalmoscope) often appear simultaneously with the difficulty in deglutition. The other special senses are also more or less affected. During the period of paralysis the bladder and rectum may become paralyzed. Trousseau, Maingault, etc., have observed impotence in young men, lasting several weeks and sometimes even months. The character of the primary disease bears no relation to the intensity of the secondary nervous affections, as some light forms of diphtheria are followed by paralysis, while severe cases may terminate without any nervous complications. Among one hundred and ninety observations by Weber and other authors, motor disturbances occurred sixteen times (about 8.5 per hundred). In the Children's Hospital of Paris, Roger found thirty-six cases of paralysis among two hundred and ten of diphtheria, or more than sixteen per cent. The diphtheritic poison may be transmitted directly through solutions of continuity in the external integument.

In Patterson's case (Med. Times, p. 858, 1868) a man became affected with paralysis of all the limbs, in consequence of a phagedenic ulceration of the right index-finger. This man, having a slight scratch upon the finger, had introduced it into the mouth of his child, who was suffering from ordinary diphtheria. The father's throat remained unaffected. When diphtheria is epidemic, surgical wounds, even in isolated patients, are predisposed to the development of diphtheritic affections, as has been recently proved by the sad death of the illustrious Griesinger. After incision of a large perityphlitic abscess from which he was suffering, the wound became diphtheritic, but this soon yielded to simple measures. After it had completely cicatrized, widespread symptoms of paralysis developed (muscles of speech, deglutition, of the limbs, and finally of respiration), and death ensued at the end of the seventieth day.

In the cases of sudden death, which Thompson has observed in convalescents who presented retardation of the pulse, syncope, vomiting, and often epileptiform attacks, the right ventricle was found to contain firm, laminated clots, adherent to the columnæ carneæ and chordæ tendinæ. In other cases the patients died of fatty degeneration of the heart, of an intercurrent pneumonia, of Bright's disease, or of paralysis of the diaphragm.

Very few observations have been made with regard to the anatomical changes in the nervous and muscular systems. According to Buhl (Zeitschr. f. Biol., III. Bd., 1867), the diphtheritic exudation, which consists of a nuclear infiltration into the connective and mucous tissues, is also found in the sheaths of the paralyzed nerves. Charcot and Vulpian have found a degeneration of the motor nerves of the velum palati in diphtheritic paralysis of the pharynx. According to Oertel's experimental investigations (Arch. f. klin. Med., VIII. Bd., 1871), diphtheria in man may be transmitted to animals, and is characterized by an abundant proliferation of micrococcus spores. In a case of diphtheritic ataxia, abundant nuclear proliferations were found in the mucous membranes, in the muscular substance (with atrophy and fatty degeneration), in the meninges and vessels of the brain and cord, in the anterior horns of the cord and around the central canal (a croupous exudation rich in cells), and in the sheaths of the nerves. In addition, capillary hæmorrhages occurred in the white and gray substance of the nerve-centres and in the sheaths of the nerve-roots and peripheral nerves. Further observations are necessary in order to confirm these results.

All observers concur in the opinion that the *prognosis* is usually favorable. Recovery may occupy several weeks or, in severe cases, six months and upwards, according to the intensity and extent of the nervous disorder. Persistent slowness of the pulse (less than forty per minute) is a serious symptom.

A certain number of cases recover under the use of ferruginous preparations, fresh air, nutritious diet, and baths.

When the paralysis continues for a long time, good effects may be obtained from subcutaneous injections of strychnine (five milligrammes to one centigramme daily), from local faradization, and from galvanic stimulation of the nerves. But we should not wait too long before beginning the use of electricity. Good results are also obtained by methodical hydrotherapeutics and sea-baths.

CHAPTER XXXIX.

ANÆMIC AND REFLEX PARALYSIS.

WE shall now devote our attention to the consideration of those paralyses in which the motor action of the nerve-centres is interfered with by a general weakness of the organism and a morbid insufficiency of the afflux of blood (essential anæmic paralysis). We shall then discuss those cases in which a circumscribed arrest of the circulation produces local disturbances of motion (local anæmic or ischæmic paralysis); finally, we shall refer to the so-called reflex paralyses.

A.—ANÆMIC AND ISCHÆMIC PARALYSIS.

The qualitative changes in the blood which are left over by severe general diseases often exercise a disastrous influence upon the motor functions of the nerve-centres. Important modifications of the blood, consisting in a diminution of the red globules and an increase in the amount of water, may give rise to those forms of anæmic paralysis which are observed after many chronic diseases, such as profuse diarrhœa, dysentery, scorbutus, metrorrhagia, intestinal hæmorrhages, hematuria, diabetes, intense chlorosis, severe intermittent fevers, and various cachexiæ. In these cases walking is rendered difficult, and becomes altogether impossible towards the end. The temperature of the limbs, the paralysis of which is almost always incomplete, is lowered and the electro-muscular contractility is diminished. Nevertheless, movements can be partially performed while the patient is lying in bed, and the bladder and rectum preserve their functions.

In ischæmic paralysis the motor and sensory disorders are caused by a partial or complete suspension of the afflux of arterial blood. The first experiments in this direction were performed by Stenson (Elem. Myolog. Specimen, Flor., 1667). By compressing or ligaturing the abdominal aorta in rabbits below the renal arteries, he produced complete paraplegia of the posterior limbs, which disappeared after a certain period if the compression was not maintained for too long a time. According to Longet, Stannius, Schiff, Kuehne, Vulpian, and especially according to the experiments of Schiffer (Centralbl., 37 and 38, 1869), the paraplegia and anæsthesia obtained in Stenson's experiments were due to spinal anæmia from obliteration of the spinal branches of the lumbar arteries. The irritability of the nerves diminishes from the centre to the periphery, as does the electro-muscular contractility, though the latter is retained for a much longer period.

Barth has reported a case of ischæmic paraplegia in a woman fifty years of age (Arch. gén., 1835). At the autopsy the aorta, below the origin of the renal arteries, was found to be obliterated by a solid clot. In Gull's patient (Dublin Quarterly Journ., 1856), who suffered from paraplegia and anæsthesia of sudden origin, together with paralysis of the sphincters, no pulsation could be detected in the abdominal aorta and in the arteries of the lower limbs, but the mammary arteries were found to be dilated. During the following months, collateral circulation became established through the thoracic and abdominal vessels and the motor power improved, though the pulsations were still absent in the abdominal aorta and its branches. Paralysis, confined to certain limbs from obliteration or compression of their arterial trunks, is much more frequently observed. The intermittent character of these paralyses is due to the insufficiency in the supply of blood and to the fact that the nerves are readily exhausted. Thus, Charcot's patient (Gaz. Méd., 1859) had an attack of paralysis of the right leg after having walked a short distance, and the paralysis always disappeared during repose. At the autopsy an aneurism was found in the right primary iliac, with fibrous transformation of the lower third of the vessel, and considerable narrowing of the corresponding branches. Frerichs also published an analogous case (without autopsy).

In the experiments on rabbits, to which I have previously referred (compression of the iliac and crural arteries of one side, in curarized or merely narcotized animals), muscular rigidity occurred, and I also observed, after resorting to electro-puncture, a gradual diminution of farado-galvanic muscular excitability, advancing to complete abolition (at the end of about two hours). When the compression of the arteries was interrupted, the excitability of the muscles to both currents was gradually re-established. If we cease to perform artificial respiration in the curarized animal, the electro-muscular contractility will disappear more rapidly in the limb which is deprived of blood than in its fellow, the nutrition of which is maintained for a much longer period by the current of blood. As a sequel to these experiments, I will here give the principal symptoms of a case of ischæmic paralysis of the left leg with rapid disappearance of the galvanic excitability, due to an aneurism of the left crural artery.

A man, æt. fifty years, stated that on October 31, 1869, he was suddenly seized, while walking, with a violent pain in the left leg, rendering motion impossible, and necessitating the removal of the patient, on the following day, to the Vienna General Hospital. Upon examination, a solid tumor was found in the region of the left obturator foramen, a little larger than a chestnut, pulsating isochronously with the crural artery, and presenting no bruit on auscultation.

Two days afterwards I found the left thigh much colder than the right, the movements of extension scarcely appreciable, and the electro-muscular contractility and sensibility considerably diminished in the extensors of the thigh (upon comparison with the corresponding muscles on the healthy side). Upon November 3d (four days after the beginning of the disease) the electro-muscular contractility to faradism was found to be abolished on the anterior surface of the thigh. Gangrene of the limb then set in, followed by chills, and the patient died on November 24th.

Upon autopsy, a sacculated aneurism, as large as a walnut, was found in the neighborhood of the obturator foramen. It originated from the posterior surface of the left crural artery, pushed the vessel upwards, and opened into its lumen by an elliptical opening as large as a coffee-bean. The wall of the artery was thickened around this opening, and, on account of the strong tension existing above the neck of the aneurism, the calibre of the artery was narrowed to such an extent that it only permitted the passage of a small-sized sound. The deep femoral artery and the point of emergence of the popliteal artery were obliterated by solid, adherent thrombi.

B.—REFLEX PARALYSIS.

The reflex paralyses which are observed in diseases of the digestive canal, uterus, and urinary passages (Leroy d'Étiolles) are, according to Romberg, Stanley, and Graves, motor spinal paralyses, due to a suspension of the sensory influence of the fibres of the sympathetic system. According to Brown-Séquard, they result from chronic irritation of the genito-urinary organs with secondary contraction of the vessels of the cord and atrophy of the corresponding parts. In support of his opinion, Romberg refers to the experiments of Comhaire, who has observed, after extirpation of a kidney in dogs, a paresis of the corresponding posterior limb. Gull calls attention to the importance of the nervous lesions which are always present in these experiments; he has also observed that the paraplegia almost always occurs in chronic cases, after the innervation of the mucous membranes has been lowered. In his opinion the paralyses in question result from the propagation of the inflammation of the urinary passages to the spinal cord. Remak regards these affections as sacro-lumbar neuritides. Finally, Jaccoud has expressed the opinion that the irritation of the inflamed bladder produces exhaustion of the spinal centres, but he presents no physiological or pathological considerations in support of this opinion.

Levisson has been more fortunate in his experimental demonstrations; (Reichert and Dubois-Reymond's Arch., 1869). He found that compression of the uterus, kidneys, intestines, or bladder produced, in addition to abolition of reflex excitability, a paralysis of the posterior limbs which persisted during the continuance of the traumatism, and disappeared after the latter had ceased to act. This paralysis was due to an arrest of the functions of the motor nerve-centres, in consequence of excessive irritation of the sensory fibres.

While these experiments demonstrate that peripheral irritation of the nerves may temporarily suspend the functions of the cord (conduction and reflex action), Tiesler's and Feinberg's investigations have shown that violent peripheral irritation may be propagated to the cord and involve the latter in the morbid process. By cauterizing the sciatic nerve in rabbits, Tiesler (Ueber Neuritis, Diss., Koenigsberg, 1869) was able to produce paraplegia, terminating in death after a few days. At the autopsy a foyer of inflammation was found at the cauterized spot and a second one in the cord, corresponding to the point of entrance of the roots of the sciatic nerve.

In animals that have received a coating of varnish and who suffer, in consequence, from tremor, hyperæsthesia, partial anæsthesia, increased reflex action, spasms, and paralysis, Feinberg has observed (Centralbl., 35, 1873), in addition to dilatation of the cutaneous vessels, of the capillaries of the lung and the ramifications of the vena porta, hyperæmia of the meninges, and a dusky redness of the cervical cord (capillary apoplexies). If the animals survive for a certain length of time, proliferation of the neuroglia occurs with atrophy of the nerve-tubes from compression. Thus the irritation of the cutaneous nerves produces a reflex paralysis of the centres of vascular innervation in the cord.

If we carefully examine the medical literature of the subject we will find that a large number of cases of reflex paralysis were associated with material lesions in the cord.

In several cases (Fournier, Mannkopf, Feinberg) tumors were found between the vertebræ and spinal meninges; Gull's cases (paraplegia following cystitis or nephritis) were associated with spinal meningitis, softening, and atrophy or fatty degeneration of a portion of the anterior columns. In Kussmaul's case of paraplegia, following chronic inflammation of the urinary passages (Wuerzb. Zeitschr., IV. Bd., 1863), there was fatty degeneration of the nerve-fibres in both sciatic nerves, with atheromatous degeneration of the arteries of the pelvis. In another case, reported by Kussmaul and Mayer (Arch. f. klin. Med., 5. H., 1866), the paralysis began with fever and nephritis, and rapidly extended to all the limbs, with acute muscular pains and insensibility to electrical irritation. The disease was due to a periarteritis nodosa (thickening and nodosities in a very large number of arteries, nuclear and abundant cellular proliferation in the walls of the vessels, granular or fatty degeneration of the muscles, with accumulation of fat in the nerve-filaments situated around the arterial nodosities). Leyden (Diss. Inaug.) reported three cases of paraplegia following affections of the bladder, which were characterized in the beginning by symptoms of motor and sensory irritation, and later by paralysis. Diffuse softening of the cord was found, upon autopsy, in two of these cases.

We must also take into consideration another circumstance, which usually passes unnoticed, viz.: that an affection of the bladder sometimes constitutes, even for years, the sole symptom of a spinal disease which is pursuing a latent course.

In several cases which were referred to me by Prof. Dittel, exploration of the bladder had given negative results, while a careful examination of motion and sensation showed a diminution or abolition of the various forms of sensibility in the legs; in the trunk there was abnormal excitability of the nerve-trunks or of the genital organs, etc. Often, in cases of this nature, the spinal symptoms are only manifested after the lapse of a long period. It is very probable that many cases of central myelitis, running a slow course, have been regarded as reflex paralyses, especially when no characteristic changes were found upon microscopical examination of the cord.

Levisson's hypothesis of reflex paralysis is only applicable in rare instances. Thus, Echeverria reports the history of a patient (Amer. Med. Times, 1863), suffering from anteversion and ulceration of the cervix uteri, in whom he applied a weak galvanic current, one electrode being placed upon the symphysis pubis and the other upon the cervix uteri. This procedure gave rise to violent pains and tremors in the legs, which were completely paralyzed for four hours; the paralysis disappeared entirely after the lapse of fourteen hours.

In a case published by Nonat, loss of consciousness and paraplegia were caused by cauterization of the cervix uteri.

In Landry's patient, the paralysis disappeared after restoration of the deflected uterus. I have published the case of a girl, æt. twenty-three years, who suffered, for three weeks, from paresis of the legs, coming on after pains and cramps in the abdomen. Upon examination I found a needle deeply imbedded in the vagina, and the paresis rapidly disappeared after the removal of the foreign body.

From the preceding remarks it is very evident that the class of reflex paralyses will diminish more and more, in proportion as the doubtful cases are more carefully examined. Functional reflex paralyses constitute very rare exceptions.

We need merely state with regard to the treatment of reflex paralysis, that especial attention must be paid to the primary disease. We may resort, according to circumstances, to iodine treatment, baths, hydrotherapeutics, or to galvanism (the current being directed from the vertebral column to the nerves of the affected limbs). After having relieved the pains, we should endeavor to improve the power of motion. The constant current is recommended in the treatment of the existing neuritis (in affections of the bladder, Leyden thinks that a sacro-lumbar neuritis may be propagated to the cord).

CLASS VIII.

NEUROSES OF THE SEXUAL APPARATUS.

CHAPTER XL.

A.—SEMINAL LOSSES.

THE term spermatorrhœa usually includes all involuntary discharges of semen, occurring generally in the day-time and without previous erection. But more careful observation has shown that true spermatic fluxes (the excreted fluid containing spermatozoids) are exceedingly rare. In the majority of cases the so-called seminal losses are composed of prostatic, mucous fluid, the emission of which may be accompanied by voluptuous sensations. In patients affected in this manner, a moderate action of the bulbo-cavernosus muscle will suffice to produce an intermittent discharge of mucus and prostatic fluid. In the majority of patients this spermatorrhœa is merely a consequence of pollutions, and its occurrence is attended with an incomplete erection.

As a rule, involuntary seminal losses occur at night, during a state of more or less complete erection, and are then known as pollutions. The most frequent *etiological factors* are: masturbation during childhood and youth (especially in patients who are naturally very excitable), erotic thoughts (obscene books or pictures), and over-excitement of the genital system from excessive venery. In many cases the affection is due to anatomical lesions and functional disorders. In habitual constipation the evacuation of hard fecal matter is often accompanied by a loss of semen (recognizable with the microscope), leaving after it a disagreeable sensation in the urethra, which often lasts more than an hour.

Diseases of the rectum (hæmorrhoids, abundant oxyuri, as I have observed in two cases), diseases of the bladder (calculus, catarrh), of the seminal vesicles, of the prostate, of the urethra (blenorrhagia), and of the glans (herpes, phimosis, accumulation of sebum) may also give rise to pollutions.

Finally, certain irritative conditions of the cord are accompanied by frequent pollutions. Although we do not agree with Tissot, who regards all patients suffering from pollutions as threatened by insanity, amaurosis, impotence, and ataxia, we nevertheless recognize the fact that frequent seminal losses, continued for several years, are not without danger, as denoting a diminution in the energy of the spinal nervous system. We have entered into this question more in detail in the remarks on the etiology of ataxia (p. 245).

Infrequent pollutions, which have no effect upon the vital energies and upon nutrition, may disappear spontaneously upon regulating coitus and the habits of life. But seminal losses which, by their frequency, rapidly debilitate the organism during youth and continue for years, may finally exhaust the nervous system, affect its power of resistance to external influences, lead to hypochondria and to marked intellectual weakness, and very frequently act as the cause of spinal affections. The pollutions of the stage of irritation in ataxia are usually accompanied by other characteristic signs, such as frequent neuralgia (especially sciatic), temporary diplopia, weakness of the efforts at coitus, and increased electrical excitability.

In the *treatment* of pollutions we must especially endeavor to remove their cause. When due to hæmorrhoids, habitual constipation, and oxyuri in the rectum, we should prescribe injections of cold water or vinegar, or a weak solution of corrosive sublimate. No less importance must be attached to the regulation of the habits of life of the patients. Physical exercise and a moderate amount of mental labor are indicated in order to maintain the vigor of the body, and to prevent erotic dreams. The diet should be nutritious, to the exclusion of fatty, spiced food, and of stimulating drinks. At night the patient should merely take a little milk or an ice, and should drink very sparingly, since fulness of the bladder is apt to produce erections. The patient should sleep upon a hard mattress and pillow, be lightly covered, and not assume the dorsal decubitus; he should not sleep too long, and must avoid taking a siesta during the day.

Among the internal remedies, quinine and iron are useful in anæmic subjects. Camphor, lupulin (two to four decigrammes morning and evening), and bromide of potassium (two to three grammes daily) have a sedative effect upon the erections; daturine is a costly and uncertain preparation. Good effects are also obtained from belladonna (administered in the form of extract, internally or in suppositories) and atropine (the dose being cautiously increased). Fowler's solution is an excellent sedative of the genital functions. It may be given for a long time, in doses of five to ten drops upon a lump of sugar, before going to bed. I have also obtained good results from this remedy in priapism.

Lallemand recommended cauterization of the prostatic portion of the urethra by means of a stick of nitrate of silver, concealed in a catheter. Two or three cauterizations, repeated after an interval of two or three weeks, are said to cause the disappearance of the disease in the majority of cases. Dittel (of Vienna) recommends a less painful and more certain remedy, consisting of the introduction with the caustic holder (as far as the prostatic region) of a urethral suppository of butter of cacao and nitrate of silver (eight to twelve milligrammes), its position being determined by the rectal touch. We may also resort to the intermittent introduction of elastic or wax bougies, coated with belladonna ointment, or of steel sounds. The urethral canal is almost always hyperæsthetic.

Hydrotherapeutic treatment furnishes the most prompt and efficient means of arresting pollutions at the beginning of the affection. The beneficial effects of cold sponging of the entire body (with the exception of the genital organs) have been recognized for a long time. Even more permanent effects are obtained from sitz-baths of short duration, taken in the morning, and followed by moist frictions. These are afterwards combined with cool half-baths, dorsal affusions, and slight douches to the perineum or lumbar region. In employing electrical treatment, the anode of a battery of moderate strength is placed upon the lumbar region, and the cathode is applied for three or four minutes along the spermatic cord, the perineum, and penis. Too prolonged or frequent sittings are injurious.

B.—IMPOTENCE.

The inability to perform coitus with sufficient frequency or energy is commonly termed impotence. The physiological capacity for indulging in sexual intercourse varies greatly according to the individual, in the same manner that hunger, thirst, sleep, and muscular power vary. It depends upon the condition of the physical powers, the manner of life, and the force of habit.

I have recently had occasion to observe the influence of habit upon sexual innervation. A man, who was married to a young and pretty woman, was compelled to abstain from sexual intercourse for a period of eight months, on account of the illness of his wife. After her recovery, he was unable to accomplish the sexual act with his wife, though his love for her had not changed, and he experienced no difficulty in having intercourse with other women, who were older and less attractive. In her presence he could only obtain an erection by imagining himself in company with another woman; he could then begin intercourse, but ejaculation never followed, although the act could be performed completely with others.

Impotence, especially in large cities, is very often due to long-continued onanism or to excesses in *venere et baccho*. In much rarer instances it is symptomatic of a central affection. When masturbation has not been practised too long and too often, sexual impotence may be usually attributed to the absence of desire for natural coitus. Young men, who are warned in time of the danger of their evil habits, may recover their natural desire by frequenting female society, and may be completely restored by an early marriage. We may also hope for a favorable recovery when, after practising masturbation to a moderate extent, the young men, who are otherwise healthy, only have incomplete erections when they attempt intercourse, and are therefore discouraged from any further attempts. In these cases we may restore the physical and mental tone of the patient by appropriate hydrotherapeutic and electrical treatment. The most serious cases are those in which the patients have practised masturbation from childhood or puberty, in whom the physical and moral tone is very low, and who only have infrequent and incomplete erections. The prognosis is then grave as regards the restoration of the genital functions, but is not absolutely unfavorable in young patients.

In the impotence which follows sexual excesses and obstinate pollutions, the sexual desire is often more intense than in the normal condition, but the erections are incomplete, and the ejaculation of semen is almost always precipitate. In old cases the skin of the glans and scrotum is pale, flabby, often traversed by varicose dilatations, cold, and not sensitive to touch; the penis is flaccid and retracted, and the testicles are soft and do not present their normal sensibility to pressure. After these patients have attained a certain age, they are rarely susceptible of improvement.

Finally, impotence may be symptomatic of diseases of the spinal cord. In some cases weakness of the genital functions is the first indication of incipient ataxia. Rapid diminution of the virile power in a patient in the prime of life should awaken serious apprehensions in the mind of the physician. The medical attendant should not regard this symptom as unimportant, but should place his patient under prolonged hydrotherapeutic and electrical treatment, and should advise him to husband his powers, especially if he presents an hereditary neuropathic tendency.

In many cases long-continued pollutions, which were at first accompanied by increase of sexual desire, finally terminate in impotence and in the developmont of spinal symptoms. The irritative symptoms which frequently appear after exposure or extreme fatigue (vague neuralgia, sciatica, temporary diplopia, frequent erections or pollutions during the night) are often accompanied by an early abolition of the virile power. The latter is manifested by premature ejaculation, incomplete erections, or by temporary, intermittent impotence, and often terminates in suppression of voluptuous sensations and complete extinction of the sexual functions.

From the preceding remarks it is evidently of the highest importance that we determine whether the impotence is due to sexual excesses, to moral depression, or whether it constitutes the initial symptom of an affection of the spinal cord. The physician is often consulted by this class of patients with regard to the advisability of marriage.

In patients belonging to the first category, marriage with a person of calm temperament may be permitted, after the impotence has undergone marked improvement. Matrimony should be strenuously opposed, however, in those patients who present spinal symptoms.

In the *treatment* of impotence, electricity and hydrotherapeutics furnish the most efficient remedies. In the electrical treatment a constant current is at first passed through the vertebral column (five minutes). The cathode is then placed over the perineum, spermatic cord, testicles, and dorsum penis (six to eight minutes), the anode being applied to the lumbar region. The sittings should at first be held every other day, and then daily (six to eight weeks). If a sensation of cold and numbness is experienced in the penis, the electrical brush may be applied to the glans and dorsum penis, and the corpora cavernosa may be stimulated by means of a moist electrode. Duchenne resorts to the introduction of an electrode into the urethra as far as the veru montanum, the other moist electrode resting on the perineum. The employment of this measure, as well as faradic stimulation of the testicles, demand great care, as their excessive use may lead to neuralgias. Hydrotherapeutic treatment must be regulated according to the condition of the patient. In the impotence which is due to excesses and moral causes, we may employ long-continued moist packs (continued until the return of sufficient warmth to the body), followed by half-baths, full-baths, and by daily douches to the sacrum and perineum. In some cases I have obtained considerable benefit by combining hydrotherapeutics and electricity. In weak, timid patients, and in those who present symptoms of irritation of the cord, we may prescribe moist frictions (with a cloth dipped in water at 18°–20° C.), followed by cool half-baths and dorsal affusions. Cold water, douches, and full-baths must not be employed on account of their stimulating action.

C.—ASPERMATISM.

The term aspermatism refers to that morbid condition in which erection and even voluptuous sensations are produced without the ejaculation of semen. This affection, which presents very remarkable peculiarities, may be produced by various pathological changes.

The absence of ejaculation during coitus may be due to prolonged masturbation, as in Cosmano-Dumenez's case (Gaz. méd. de Paris, 17–19, 1863). When the seminal passages are in a condition of atony, they respond with more difficulty to cerebral influences than to the spinal reflexes produced by onanism. The differences which may occur in cerebral innervation are evident from Hieguet's observations (Bullet. de l'Acad. roy. de Belgique, II., 1861), in which the emission of semen did not occur during coitus, but only during erotic dreams. In Schmitt's case (Wuerzb. Zeitschr., III. Bd., p. 361–366), emission of semen occurred neither during coitus nor in pollutions; nevertheless the patient experienced, as in the normal condition, voluptuous sensations and a feeling of exhaustion after the performance of coitus. In this patient both duct. ejaculat. were supposed to open in common into the obliterated vesicula prostatica.

Gosselin was one of the first who carefully investigated the pathological conditions present in obliteration of the seminal passages (Arch. gén., Sept., 1853). According to this author the obliteration may occur in the efferent canals or in the tail of the epididymis, thus causing an obstruction to the passage of semen into the seminal vesicles (obstructions in the head of the epididymis have no effect upon the course of the semen); finally, there may be partial or total obliterations in the seminiferous tubes of the testicles. Unfortunately, Gosselin has not mentioned whether all the patients who were affected with these anomalies also suffered from aspermatism.

Atrophy of both testes, tubercular and cheesy degeneration of the epididymis, bilateral cryptorchism, congenital absence of the efferent canals (observations by Gosselin and J. Hunter), considerable hypertrophy of the prostate, especially inflammations and abscesses in the neighborhood of the prostate, and narrow urethral strictures (Petit) may also act as causes of aspermatism. In one case, reported by Lapeyronie (aspermatism after recovery from blenorrhagia), the emission of semen only occurred after the erection had subsided. At the autopsy, which was performed several years afterwards, a cicatrix was found in the veru montanum, which was directed towards the bladder. The cicatricial tissue had changed the direction of the ejaculatory ducts in such a manner that they opened towards the neck of the bladder, as was clearly demonstrated by an injection of the efferent canals and seminal vesicles.

Demarquay's patient, who had received a gunshot wound of the bladder and rectum, suffered from inflammation and atrophy of the right testicle; upon the left side the efferent canal and seminal vesicle had been involved in the wound, and thus gave rise to aspermatism. In C. Dumenez's case (large abscess from contusion of the perineum), after opening of the abscess and recovery, the penis remained dry during coitus, although the patient experienced the sensation produced by emission of semen. Microscopical examination of the urine revealed the presence of spermatozoids, and the semen must, therefore, have been discharged into the bladder. Aspermatism may also follow bilateral lithotomy, when the ejaculatory ducts have been cut, or when their direction has been changed by the cicatrization of the wound of the bladder and the semen is discharged into the latter organ.

Aspermatism is not *per se* a serious affection, but it may become so in time from its influence on the mind. The patients fall into a profound melancholy, shun the society of their fellows, and may finally become insane. In Dumenez's case, which was referred to above, the patient thought that his sex had been changed, and wrote long letters to an imaginary lover.

The treatment of aspermatism is very rarely successful. Electricity (especially the introduction of an electrode as far as the veru montanum) and hydrotherapeutics may prove useful, as shown by Vicquet's observation, in atony of the seminal excretory passages.

CLASS IX.

DISEASES OF THE PERIPHERAL NERVOUS SYSTEM.

GENERAL CHARACTERISTICS OF PERIPHERAL PARALYSIS.

THE scope of peripheral nervous affections comprises the various morbid conditions of the cerebral and spinal nerves, from the roots and plexuses to the prolongations which form the nerve-trunks and branches. In various parts of their course the nerves may be subjected to traumatic and rheumatic influences, and to mechanical violence (compression, rupture, concussion). Complete or incomplete paralysis will develop, according to the intensity of the exciting cause. The inflammatory changes in the muscles, which we have described in the preceding chapters as sequences of acute diseases, may also give rise to peripheral paralysis.

Lesions of the anterior nerve-roots within the spinal canal (inflammatory affections, atrophy from neoplasms) produce motor paralysis from interference with conduction. In affections of the nerve-roots beyond the spinal ganglia, the paralysis usually extends to the domain of several nerves, and is accompanied by corresponding anæsthesia. If the plexuses are involved, the paralysis occupies a greater or less extent, but is generally limited to one side of the body. It appears, for example, within the territory of the lumbar plexus, when circumscribed exudations or foci of suppuration are present in the pelvis. Paraplegia occurs in very rare cases, when there are large or multiple morbid products compressing the lumbar plexuses or the nerves of the cauda equina upon both sides. A rapid diminution of nutrition and electro-muscular contractility occurs along the course of the affected nerves.

Paralysis due to neuritis may result from a compression exercised by the meninges upon the roots composing the nerve-trunks, from inflammatory thickening of the sheaths of the nerves, or from degeneration of the myeline. The paralyses are accompanied by intense neuralgic pains, and are attended, when the neuritis occurs in mixed nerves, by disorders of sensation, muscular atrophy, diminution of electro-muscular contractility, and trophic disturbances. When a single nerve-trunk is involved, the paralysis is usually limited to the regions dependent on this nerve and to the corresponding groups of muscles. In peripheral paralysis the electrical reactions present certain characteristic signs, the discovery of which has shed further light upon the interpretation of its pathological phenomena. The manifestations on the part of the nerves and muscles, under the influence of electrical stimulation, vary on account of the degenerative processes which are present in the beginning, and of the regeneration which occurs at a later period. Reserving a more detailed discussion of the electrical phenomena for the chapter on traumatic paralysis, we will here remark that the irritability of the nerves to both currents diminishes, and finally disappears completely, in proportion as the degeneration progresses from the centre to the periphery in the ramifications of the nerves. When recovery occurs, voluntary motion is often restored before the farado-galvanic excitability of the nerves. On the part of the muscles the faradic contractility diminishes early, and then disappears completely, while the galvanic excitability is preserved and often even increased. At a later period the latter reaction progressively diminishes in proportion as the faradic irritability and power of voluntary motion reappear in the paralyzed muscles.

Finally, we may refer to the frequent complication of peripheral paralysis with vaso-motor and trophic disorders. The initial vascular dilatation and elevation of temperature are followed, in the later stages, by retardation of the circulation, livid discoloration of the skin and lowering of the temperature. The trophic disturbances are not only manifested by considerable atrophy of the muscles, but they also appear as general nutritive disorders, atrophy of the skin, anomalies of secretion, exanthemata, changes in the epithelial elements and in the joints. Severe disturbances of nutrition, such as gangrenous ulcerations, may also occur. In the chapter on traumatic paralysis we shall discuss, in detail, the nature of these nutritive disorders and their relations with the trophic centres of the cord.

CHAPTER XLI.

RHEUMATIC LESIONS OF THE NERVES.

AMONG external influences, cold and cold moisture exercise the most deleterious action upon the nervous system. Eckhard, J. Rosenthal, and Afanasieff have experimented upon the action of various grades of temperature on the nerves of frogs. E. H. Weber (Wagner's Handwoerterb. d. Phys., III. Bd.) studied the properties of the cutaneous nerves in man, in his excellent work on the sense of touch and general sensibility. In his experiments with temperatures ranging below zero, the painful sensations were found to present great differences, even in portions of the skin which were situated very close to one another, according to the irregularities in the distribution of the sensory nerves which had been subjected to the action of the cold.

I have made analogous experiments upon the action of cold on the motor and sensory nerves (Wien. Med. Halle, 1864, No. 1–4), in order to determine with more exactness the action of cold upon the nerve-trunks. My observations referred to the condition of sensation and motion, to the oscillations in the temperature, and to the electrical reactions of certain peripheral regions which had been subjected to the action of cold. I have made, upon my own person, applications of ice (two to four minutes) upon the nerves of the arm and foot, and have found that the most marked effects were produced upon the ulnar nerve. The thermometric measurements were made in the second and fourth interdigital spaces, which presented the same temperature before the experiment. In order to give a concise review of the phenomena observed after chilling of the nerve-trunks, we may divide them into three categories, according as they affect sensation, motion, and temperature.

The first effect of the application of ice is a painful exaggeration of the functions of the sensory nerve-fibres. If the action of the ice is prolonged, this phenomenon gradually disappears, and is followed by a diminution in the excitability of the nerve-fibres.

The motor functions of the muscles at first manifest an increased excitability, but if the experiment is prolonged, the reaction of the muscles becomes weaker and weaker, and is, finally, almost completely suppressed (from suspension of nervous conduction). At the beginning of the experiment an electrical stimulus, which is scarcely perceived under normal conditions, will produce muscular contractions, while, in the second period, the excitability and motility of the muscles almost entirely disappear.

The influence of applications of ice upon the temperature are usually manifested, in the beginning of the experiment, by a fall of temperature varying from 0.5°–1° C. In rare cases this fall is preceded by a slight rise of temperature. When the nervous condition is more seriously disturbed, an elevation of temperature occurs secondarily. In addition to motor paralysis, the inner fingers (when the ulnar nerve is experimented upon) present evidences of hyperæmia (redness, heat). After the application of cold has ceased, quite a long time (forty to fifty minutes) elapses before the temperature returns to the normal.

When the ulnar nerve is paralyzed, an elevation of temperature occurs in the inner fingers (from 34.4°–35.6° C.), while that of the other fingers is considerably reduced (from 34.4°–27.7° C.). The elevation of temperature is due to a reflex action upon the vaso-motor nerves and to the increase of the current of blood in the dilated vessels. This reflex paralysis of the sympathetic nerves from the action of cold appears to me to present a great analogy to the symptoms observed by Cl. Bernard and Budge after section of the cervical sympathetic. In their experiments the temperature of the ear upon the side of the section was increased, while it was diminished in the ear upon the healthy side. These experimental results, which were afterwards confirmed by Waller, Eulenburg, and Szymanowski, are also applicable, in great part, to pathological phenomena.

With regard to etiology, experience teaches that the vast mesh-work of peripheral nerves is most threatened with danger when the body, overheated and covered with an abundant perspiration, is suddenly exposed to the action of cold, or quickly passes through various strata of air at different temperatures. The affections which are caused by moisture or cold are limited, in the majority of cases, to small spaces. One of the upper or lower limbs, or merely a portion of a limb, is affected by the paralysis which I have called paralysis from the action of cold, in order to distinguish it from the paralytic form which is commonly termed rheumatic and which does not present the symptoms to which we have referred. In certain cases, paralysis from cold may cause abolition of sensation throughout a large part, if not the whole of the integument of the body. Binz has described, under the term generalized peripheral anæsthesia, a case of this kind in a young woman who had fallen asleep before an open window. In addition to cutaneous anæsthesia, all the mucous membranes (even that of the vagina) were insensible to the prick of a pin; taste and smell were likewise abolished. Recovery occurred, after the lapse of a week, from the application of frictions to the entire body. In Worms' case, a soldier, who was overheated from running, was exposed to a draught of air; one of the legs at first became numb, the next day the other, the third day the trunk became insensible, and, on the fifth day, speech was embarrassed. This was afterwards followed by anæsthesia of the entire surface of the body, analgesia of the feet and mucous membranes, and anaphrodisia. This condition continued for five days, and disappeared completely after the employment of vapor-baths and electricity. Romberg, Mayer, Kaulich, Griffith, and Christophers have also observed sensory disorders due to the action of cold, extending over larger or small areas, and involving motion to a greater or lesser extent. Paralysis from cold may occupy both lower extremities or one-half of the body. Hoppe, Romberg, and E. H. Weber have published examples of the hemiplegic type.

With regard to the nature of the motor and sensory disorders under discussion, we may state, in accordance with the experiments and pathological data previously referred to, that, when the action of the cold is merely superficial, they are due to the direct action of the chilling of the vascular nerves of certain regions. When the action of the cold extends deeper, the phenomena are caused by a reflex irritation of the vaso-motor and spinal systems. In substantiation of the local character of the phenomena, we may call attention to the paralysis of the trigeminus and facial nerves, to the facial neuralgias produced by the action of cold, the local anæsthesia obtained by Richardson's method (spray of ether or similar liquids), and the anæsthesia of the hands, observed in washerwomen. We may, finally, refer to Nothnagel's observations (Arch. f. klin. Med., II. Bd., 2. H.) of local anæmia and sensory disturbances (from spasm of the arterioles of the hands and forearms), especially in women engaged in washing in cold water. I also observed a man, æt. fifty years, of a neuropathic consti- - tution, who, whenever he was exposed to cold during the autumn, became affected with a similar vascular spasm in both hands, especially in the first three fingers. These digits became numb, pale, and flaccid, but were promptly restored to the normal condition under the influence of warmth.

The reflex influence of cold upon the vaso-motor and spinal systems is demonstrated by a large number of observations. The experiments mentioned above with regard to the application of ice, especially to the ulnar nerve, have shown that the increase of temperature observed in the course of this nerve is due to reflex paralysis of the sympathetic nerves. The elevation of temperature in the limbs, which Chapman noticed after the application of ice to the vertebral column; the cases referred to above of analgesia or even of motor disturbances in the limbs after extreme cold; finally, the vascular irritation of the spinal system with secondary proliferation of connective tissue caused by chilling of the feet or back,—are further proofs of the profound reflex action of cold upon the sympathetic and spinal systems.

The *diagnosis* of these paralyses depends upon a history of the action of cold while the body was overheated, and followed by motor and sensory disturbances. The *prognosis* is usually favorable in this affection. In slight forms and in young subjects, who have been previously healthy, the disease may retrogress spontaneously and may disappear in one or two weeks. In more severe forms it may persist for several weeks.

The *treatment* consists, in light cases, of vapor-baths followed by the douche. When the disease is prolonged, we must resort to the use of iodide of potassium internally and externally, and then to electricity. In paralysis of sensation, the employment of the dry electric brush is useful; when the anæsthesia involves the deeper parts, the skin should be previously moistened.

We may diminish the force of the electrical current as the sensibility gradually returns. In paralysis complicated with sensory disorders, good results are obtained from faradization of the muscles, and especially from galvanization of the spinal and muscular nerves. Hydrotherapeutic measures are also extremely useful (frictions, moist packs continued until the warmth of the body has returned, followed by half-baths and douches). Some authors also recommend sea-baths.

Those forms which are usually termed rheumatic paralyses consist of circumscribed disorders of motion, resulting from the action of cold, and appearing in the forearm, shoulder, neck, or lower limb. The paralysis occurs most frequently in the forearm, in which the muscles of the external region, which are innervated by the radial and are more exposed to cold than the others, are usually affected. By mere inspection this affection is differentiated with difficulty from traumatic, lead, and hysterical paralyses. But, in wounds of the radial nerve, all the muscles which it innervates are paralyzed and have lost their electrical contractility. Lead paralysis affects, by preference, certain muscles in a definite order, and almost always appears in both arms at the same time (but not to the same extent).

In hysterical paralysis the electro-muscular contractility is preserved, but electro-muscular and electro-cutaneous sensibility are diminished or abolished.

In recent cases of rheumatic paralysis of the forearm, the electro-muscular contractility is preserved, and the electro-muscular sensibility is almost always increased. In old cases, whether accompanied by muscular atrophy or not, a moderate diminution of electrical contractility and sensibility becomes noticeable. In these cases the motor power becomes re-established after the employment of faradization of the muscles or of constant labile currents (from the dorsal spine to the radial nerve or to the extensors). The use of vapor-baths or mineral waters, combined with electricity, also furnishes good results.

Muscular rheumatism is not infrequently found as a precursor of rheumatic paralysis, but the latter only appears after the cessation of the pains and during the first attempts at motion performed by the patient. As Froriep first showed (Ueber Heilwirkungen der Elektricität, 1. H., Die rheumat. Schwiele, 1843), exudations occur in rheumatic affections which he described, according to their situation, as thickening of the connective tissue, skin, muscles, or periosteum.

True rheumatic myositis originates in the aponeurotic cellular tissue or in the interstitial connective tissue of the muscles. The great vascularity of the muscles, which favors the development of inflammation, also promotes its resolution, though it may, at the same time, lead to other sequences, such as abscess, induration, calcareous degeneration of the exudation, and fatty degeneration. The period of irritative symptoms may be followed by emaciation, fall of temperature, and motor disorders (paralysis, contractures).

In many instances, muscular rheumatism appears to be a neuralgia of the cutaneous and muscular branches of the nerves, which have been subjected to the action of cold. Beau has shown (Arch. Gén., Dec., 1862) that the superficial muscles (occipito-frontalis, deltoid, trapezius, sacrolumbalis) are most sensitive to cold. In order to preserve the affected muscles from further injury, a reflex contraction occurs in the adjacent muscles. Thus, in rheumatism of the deltoid, the arm is pressed against the trunk by the action of the muscles of the anterior and posterior walls of the axilla; in rheumatism of the trapezius, the diseased muscle is relaxed by the contraction of the sterno-cleido-mastoid on the opposite side; in lumbago, the vertebral column is deflected to the opposite side by the contraction of the quadratus lumborum (perhaps also of the intercostals). The treatment must be regulated in accordance with the pathogeny of the case.

Although muscular rheumatism is a mild affection, it may nevertheless terminate in contracture and paralysis.

Acute muscular rheumatism often terminates spontaneously after rest and simple treatment. Chronic forms, which are complicated with atrophy, paresis, or symptoms on the part of the articulations, require local faradization with the secondary current, or local applications of galvanism. Benefit is also derived from daily and long-continued employment of moist packs applied until the body has become warm, and followed by half-baths and douches. Recent rheumatic contractures are often rapidly relieved by the passage of an ascending galvanic current; in chronic cases we may resort to faradization of the antagonists, or to local galvanization with currents of continually increasing intensity. Rheumatic paralysis yields to the prolonged application of the induced or of the constant labile current.

Those conditions, in which the propagation of rheumatic articular inflammations produces myopathic processes, are usually included under the category of muscular rheumatic paralysis. Thus, rheumatic arthritis of the shoulder may involve the deltoid or adjacent muscles, and inflammation of the cervical vertebræ may lead to torticollis. Periostitis in various regions may cause paralysis of the overlying muscles.

We may remark, in conclusion, that muscular rheumatism often forms a mask under which serious affections may remain concealed for a long time.

Progressive muscular atrophy, vertebral caries, and other spinal affections are often mistaken, in the beginning, for muscular rheumatism, although more careful examination would reveal certain motor and sensory disturbances and certain electrical reactions, which would demonstrate the danger of the situation.

CHAPTER XLII.

TRAUMATIC LESIONS OF THE NERVES.

IN his experiments upon section of the pneumogastric nerve in dogs, Waller found (Mueller's Archiv, 1852, p. 392) the peripheral portion of the nerve disorganized twelve days after the operation, the myeline becoming granular, and the nerve-sheath having atrophied in great part. At the end of four weeks the nerve-fibres were found to be regenerated. The experiments of Schiff (Arch. f. gem. Arbeit, 1853), Valentin (Zeitschr. f. rat. Med., XI. Bd., 1861), and others have confirmed the occurrence of atrophy and disorganization of the peripheral ends of the nerves and of the final absorption of the medullary substance which has been transformed into fat. These changes are propagated into the terminal peripheral ramifications of the nerves, the process occupying two months in young animals and six or seven months in older ones.

The reunion of the cut ends of the nerves occurs, in favorable cases, by first intention (Bruch), and the conductibility and normal reactions are often re-established at the end of a month (Lacrousille, Union Méd., 1864). When a considerable portion of the nerve has been resected, the reunion occurs by means of a bridge which projects from the central and peripheral ends ; according to Hjelt, this bridge consists of an enlargement formed by a nuclear proliferation in the interstitial connective tissue. According to the observations of Philipeaux and Vulpian (Gaz. Méd. de Paris, 27 et seq., 1860), and of Schuh (Med. Wschr., 1863), regeneration and re-establishment of conductibility may take place, even if the excised portion of the nerve measures thirty millimetres in length.

After the excision of considerable portions of the sciatic or crural nerves in animals, Mantegazza (Gaz. Lombard, 1865–1867) has observed a multiplication of the muscular nuclei, cloudiness, partial fatty degeneration, or simple atrophy of the primitive fibres; finally, atrophy of the muscles with hyperplasia of the interstitial connective tissue.

In addition, periostitis, abscesses, osseous affections with caries and necrosis, osteophytes, and hypertrophy of the spongy substance of the bones, may develop in the paralyzed limbs.

Erb (Arch. f. klin. Med., V. Bd., 1868), in the course of his experiments on peripheral paralysis, observed the persistence of the axis cylinders, in addition to the previously mentioned degeneration of the myeline; during the period of recovery, a regeneration of the myeline occurred in a centrifugal direction; the neurilemma was the seat of an abundant cellular infiltration, and its connective tissue was considerably thickened.

The changes observed in the muscles consisted of marked atrophy of the fibres (reduced in four or five weeks to less than half their normal dimensions), cloudiness, though not complete disappearance of the transverse striæ, and considerable multiplication of the muscular nuclei; the final change in the contractile substance consisted of waxy degeneration and rupture of the fibres. An early and considerable accumulation of round cells is noticeable in the interstitial connective tissue, and is followed by very marked increase of this tissue.

In the reproduction of divided nerves, the external sheath of the nerve-tubes is formed, according to Robin (Journ. de l'Anat. et de la Physiol., VIII., 1868), from the adjacent nuclei; a liquid, refractile myeline then appears in the centre of the new-formed fibres, and, at the end of six to nine weeks, it becomes more abundant in certain portions of the sheath, imparting to the latter a varicose appearance. The axis cylinder only becomes visible after the lapse of three or four months.

According to the investigations of Hertz (Virch. Arch., 46. Bd., 3. H., 1869), the intermediate substance takes an active part in the regenerative process, by a proliferation of cells (at the expense of the white blood globules) and their transformation into nerve-fibres. The cells of the neurilemma also play an important part, by the transformation of their nuclei into ribbon-shaped masses which become united to the old and new nerve-fibres. We may finally refer to the observations of Bizzozero and Golgi (Wien. Med. Jahrb., 1. H., 1873). After excision of the sciatic and crural nerves in rabbits, these authors have observed enlargement of the joints and ulcers upon the extremities; in the deep muscles, which were pale and waxy, the fibrillary tissue was replaced by a considerable development of fatty cells.

Vulpian (Arch. de Physiol., 1869) has examined the muscles in a case of resection of the hip-joint (six months previously, in removing a tumor, a portion of the sciatic nerve had been excised). He found the histological changes referred to by Mantegazza and Erb. ·

We shall now pass in review the anatomical and experimental investigations concerning *the clinical symptoms* of traumatic lesions of the nerves. The nerve-trunks are exposed to various kinds of traumata, such as section, crushing, tearing, violent concussion, luxation, persistent compression, cauterization, and suppuration. The inconsiderable lesion of the sensory fibres in wounded nerve-trunks has been confirmed by recent observations. According to Schiff's experiments upon the cord, this circumstance must be explained by the greater vulnerability of the motor compared to that of the sensory fibres.

Among the sensory disorders, traumatic hyperæsthesia must be mentioned in the first rank. It may be situated in the skin or muscles. An extremely remarkable but very rare phenomenon is the general hyperæsthesia, which has been observed by American military surgeons, in two cases by Smoler, and in one by myself. The hyperæsthesia may, after cicatrization of the wound, extend to the trunk and to the entire body, and may attain such an insupportable intensity that the patient cannot endure the lightest contact or the slightest current of air, and cannot obtain any repose or execute any movements, except by covering the limbs with frequently renewed compresses of cold water. The irritation caused by the wound appears to extend to the posterior roots and gray columns of the cord, and to produce an exaggerated excitability. The treatment consists of cold compresses, prolonged baths, and subcutaneous injections of morphine.

The anæsthesia of the skin and muscles, which often accompanies motor paralysis of the mixed nerves, may be complete or incomplete, and, in the latter event, it is evidence of the complete isolation of the nerve from the spinal centres. If it accompanies motor disorders which are secondary to acute pains along the distribution of the nerves, we are justified in diagnosing a traumatic neuritis. Before sensibility is restored, the anæsthesia becomes transformed into hyperæsthesia. The treatment consists in the employment of the faradic brush (with the secondary current), or in the passage of strong labile currents through the dorsal spine and the peripheral nerves.

Traumatic neuralgias usually occupy a more or less limited portion of the nerve-trunks and are accompanied by certain painful points. The neuralgia following venesection is due to a wound of the musculo-cutaneous nerve, and not of the median nerve, as was formerly believed. The pains often assume a paroxysmal character, attended with more or less complete remissions. The treatment consists, in slight cases, of the employment of cold compresses, of moist packs continued until the return of warmth to the body, followed by cool half-baths, and of blisters or subcutaneous injections of morphine. In severe or chronic cases we are sometimes compelled to resort to the actual or potential cautery, to subcutaneous section of the nerves (neurotomy), or even to excision (neurectomy).

In a case reported in the work on "Gunshot Wounds and other Injuries of Nerves: Weir Mitchell, Morehouse, and Keen," a portion of the median nerve, two centimetres in length, was excised with temporary success.

Contracture and paralysis constitute the most rebellious and distressing motor disorders of traumatic origin. In many cases the contracture is due to a tonic spasm of the antagonists, caused by paralysis of certain muscles. The stiffness of the joints, which occurs after fractures or other accidents, is due in great part to the forced immobility of the limbs in immovable apparatus. In such cases we may often prevent bad after-effects by passive movements, performed frequently and carefully. In other cases the contractures following traumatism are of reflex origin, such as occurs when acute hyperæsthesia is present in wounds of very sensitive organs, like the joints, and which may cause, by reflex means, a spasmodic contraction of those parts which tend to relieve the pain. In these cases the reflex phenomena are sometimes due to irritation of certain portions of distant nerves.

Treatment.—When the spasmodic contraction of the muscles has only lasted a short time, when there is no atrophy, and when the spasm varies from day to day, relaxation of the muscles may be produced, according to American physicians, by injections of atropine or by etherization. In contractures of reflex origin, benefit is derived from the application of galvanism to the wounded nerves, and from faradization of the paralyzed muscles.

Our clinical knowledge of traumatic paralysis dates back to the excellent investigations made by Duchenne. The discoveries made by experimental pathologists agree, in great part, with the results of clinical observation.

Among the experimental investigations undertaken in recent times, we must especially refer to those of Erb (Deutsch. Arch. f. klin. Med., IV. und V. Bd., 1868), and Ziemssen and Weiss (eod. loc., IV. Bd., p. 599–594). Erb has shown that the nerves and muscles acquire entirely different electrical reactions. In the nerves the irritability to both currents diminishes gradually from the beginning of the paralysis and disappears completely at the end of one or two weeks. After the lapse of a variable time, it becomes very slowly re-established (proceeding from the central end), the galvanic excitability being usually restored more rapidly than the faradic. As a rule, the electrical excitability is not recovered until long after the return of voluntary motion. The peripheral end of the nerve may therefore be permeable to voluntary impulse before it has re-covered its receptivity for external stimuli.

In the muscles the irritability to both currents also gradually diminishes during the first few weeks. The faradic excitability then progressively diminishes, but the galvanic irritability becomes markedly increased from the close of the second week (it is relatively stronger at the closure of the anode than of the cathode). Finally, after the lapse of a variable period the galvanic irritability again sinks below the normal, while the faradic excitability is slowly restored. Simultaneously and almost parallel with the increase of galvanic excitability, the muscles also present exaggerated mechanical excitability.

According to Erb, the anatomical processes which are present in these modifications of electrical excitability, present the greatest analogies with inflammation, especially with those chronic forms which, in certain organs, terminate in cirrhosis. The origin of these lesions must be attributed to the vaso-motor and trophic fibres passing through the nerve-trunks which have been affected by the injury. Erb also believes that the conductibility and mechanical excitability occur through the regenerated axis cylinders, and that the electrical excitability is due to the presence of the myeline sheath. This view is opposed to Eulenburg's theory that the excitability of the nerves is due to the existence of a specific force.

Ziemssen and Weiss have produced paralysis of varying intensity and duration by applying silk ligatures with variable force to the nerves. The slight paralyses were characterized by abolition of motor power, loss of farado-muscular contractility, in-crease of galvano-muscular excitability, and diminution of the electrical excitability of the nerves. In the paralyses of moderate intensity there is loss of motor power, and, at the end of one or two days, the nerves are entirely inexcitable to both currents; the galvano-muscular excitability increases, and the farado-muscular excitability diminishes until it is completely abolished. The duration of these paralyses varies from three to six months, after which the normal condition is slowly re-established. The most severe paralysis (from excision of the nerve) presents almost the same modi-fications as the moderate forms, with the exception that the galvano-muscular ex-citability does not increase, but diminishes *pari passu* with the faradic excitability until it is entirely suppressed; it becomes re-established after six to eight months at the same time with the conductibility. Atrophy of the muscles with induration and contracture is always noticeable, but this condition disappears after the return of con-ductibility.

The results obtained in animals are also applicable in great part to the phenomena observed in man. The excitability of the nerves to the in-duced and constant currents undergoes, from the onset of the paralysis, a diminution which extends towards the periphery. At the end of the second or third week the nerves have manifestly lost their excitability to both currents. The electrical irritability of the nerves returns when the motor power is restored; contractions upon closure at the cathode are temporarily observed at an early period. Experience has confirmed the appearance of all these characteristic symptoms in man. The electrical irritability of the nerves is independent of their excitability to the stimu-lus of the will.

In the muscles the electrical excitability in general is lost in the be-ginning, and this is followed by increase of galvanic excitability with per-sistent abolition of faradic reaction (as is shown by the cases of traumatic paralysis of the nerves of the brachial plexus, reported by Ziemssen, Gruenwald, Erb, and Eulenburg, or by Brenner's cases of traumatic neuritis). This peculiar fact is due, according to Neumann's investigations, to the following circumstances : the muscular tissue, destitute of nerves, is insensible to the momentary action of the induced current, or to the galvanic current when it is also applied interruptedly; it will respond, however, to a current whose duration is not merely instantaneous, although these contractions are always very slow and tardy. An increase of the mechanical irritability of the muscles (Erb) is almost always noted in addition to the increase in the galvanic excitability. At a later period the galvanic excitability diminishes, and the direct faradic irritability gradually returns. The modifications of the muscular irritability are very different from the phenomena presented by the nerves. In certain instances, in which faradization through the skin produced no contraction, I have seen the muscles react to electro-puncture. This is probably due to a quantitative difference in the current, which tráverses the muscles through a very circumscribed space.

According to Duchenne, the electro-muscular and electro-cutaneous sensibility are less altered, as a rule, in traumatic paralysis than the contractility. The former is only abolished in those cases in which the nerve is completely separated from the spinal centre. The muscles whose electrical contractility and sensibility are only slightly affected, recover rapidly under the influence of faradization, while those which are deprived of faradic contractility and sensibility soon atrophy. Nevertheless, a muscle may preserve the power of voluntary motion, although the electrical contractility has been, in great part, lost. Sometimes, on the other hand, a muscle is paralyzed, although its faradic irritability persists.

The paralysis caused by crushing the nerve plexuses sometimes presents the characteristics of progressive muscular atrophy, as I had occasion to notice in a woodsman, who received a blow upon the left shoulder from a falling oak (representing, according to his statement, four cords of wood). He immediately lost consciousness, and the upper limb began to swell; at the end of six months the arm and forearm had atrophied, the movements of the shoulder and neck were abolished, and electrical contractility was lost in the majority of the muscles of the arm (except the common extensor of the fingers, the long abductor of the thumb, and the muscles of the wrist, which still presented a very feeble reaction). In a second case (occurring during the Bohemian war), a ball had penetrated above the axilla, and had produced a partial lesion of the brachial plexus (paralysis and loss of electrical contractility in the majority of the extensor muscles). The latter patient was considerably, and the former very little, improved by galvanization.

During the battle of Sadowa, a private received a gun-shot wound in the lower half of the popliteal space upon the left side ; five days later he was examined in the hospital of Voeslau (near Vienna). Voluntary motion, the galvanic and faradic excitability in the peroneal and tibial nerves, and the electrical contractility of the muscles of the anterior and posterior regions of the leg were abolished. The toes and sole of the foot were anæsthetic in great part, certain muscles reacted slowly to a strong continuous current; the sciatic nerve had been implicated by the bullet at its point of division. After the employment of warm baths and intermittent faradization for a period of twenty days, sensibility first returned, and then, little by little, the patient was able to perform movements while lying in bed. At the end of the sixth week the patient could walk, but he was soon transferred, and I was unable to detect any considerable improvement in the excitability of the nerves to both currents, or in the farado-muscular contractility, at the time of his departure.

Recurrent sensibility (preservation of peripheral sensibility after complete section of the nerves) has been observed by Laugier, Nélaton, Duchenne, Revillout, and Richet, and most frequently in the median nerve. This symptom is explained by the hypothesis that anastomoses exist between the nerves of the arm, which, after section of one of these nerves, permits centripetal conduction in the others. Laveran (Thèse de Strasb., 1868), and Arloing and Tripier (Arch. de Phys., II., 1869) have shown that the peripheral nerve-trunks which remain sensitive contain, at the end of a certain length of time, some nerve-fibres which have escaped degeneration. We may also admit that recurrent fibres of the ulnar and radial, or anastomoses between the median and ulnar (Gruber) give rise to the sensibility in the fibres of the median situated below the point of section. According to Letiévant (Traité des sect. Nerv., 1873), the supplementary sensibility may be indirectly established by irritation of the cutaneous sensory papillæ in the immediate neighborhood. In " supplementary " motor power (preservation of the motor functions without regeneration of the nerves) the adjacent muscles which are supplied by other nerves assume the functions of the paralyzed muscles.

The vaso-motor disturbances which occur in the course of traumatic nerve lesions are explained by the abundance of vaso-motor fibres contained in the large nerve-trunks of the limbs. According to the experiments of Cl. Bernard and Schiff, section of the brachial plexus or sciatic nerve is followed by redness of the limb and considerable elevation of temperature. In section of the large nerve-trunks, in man, an acute stage of vaso-motor paralysis is observed, that is to say, an elevation of temperature from the sudden increase in the afflux of arterial blood. This is followed by a chronic stage, in which the retardation of the current of blood and the passive hyperæmia produce lowering of the temperature. In addition to these phenomena, which authors have not differentiated sufficiently, there are various kinds of trophic disorders. Thus in two cases, reported by Hutchinson (Med. Times and Gazette, 659, 1863), section of the nerves of the arm was accompanied by lividity of the skin, incurvation of the nails, and lesions of the extremities of the fingers (paronychia). American physicians, and Rouget, Fisher, etc., have also observed changes in the skin (glossy skin, eczematous eruptions, disorders of secretion), and arthropathies. Gangrenous ulcerations of the superficial parts, from wounds of the nerve-trunks, have been observed experimentally and clinically. In a case of ulnar paralysis, which I shall report at a later period, the hairs grew very abundantly upon the back of the hand on the wounded side. Schiff and Rettberg have noticed the same fact in animals after section of the nerves of the concha of the ear and of the limbs.

According to Brown-Séquard and Charcot, these trophic disorders are only produced in man when the nerves are irritated, while in animals the inflammatory symptoms do not appear after neurotomy, and are only manifested after contusion of the nerves. The muscular atrophy, which is so pronounced and rapid in traumatic paralysis, is poorly explained by the simple abolition of the muscular functions, since in cerebral paralysis, even when complete and persisting for several years, the nutrition and reaction of the muscles are not essentially changed. The disorders in the nutrition of the muscles, like those in other parts, must be regarded as traumatic disturbances of trophic innervation. We are led to adopt this view so much the more readily because the anatomical and clinical facts, previously discussed in a large number of diseases, have led us to admit the existence of trophic centres in the cells of the anterior gray horns, which are connected with the peripheral parts by means of trophic fibres.

In a case which occurred during the late war (communicated by Dr. Herzog), paralysis of the peroneal nerve occurred, with elevation of temperature at the onset in the corresponding parts of the leg. After the wound had healed by second intention, a considerable reduction of temperature occurred, attended with cyanosis and superficial ulceration of the soft parts of the ungual phalanges.

In a paralysis of the right ulnar nerve (from a sabre wound), I found, at the end of the fourth month, motor and sensory paralysis of the corresponding fingers, a depression in the fourth intercostal space, atrophy of the hypothenar eminence, bluish coloration of the little finger, and a strong growth of hair upon the corresponding dorsal aspect of the right hand. According to the statement of the patient, this had not been present before the receipt of the injury; it contrasted very markedly with the smooth condition of the left hand. Thermometric measurements were made (in a room with a temperature of 16' C.), and showed, upon the right side, between the little and ring fingers, 27.2°, upon the left side 84.8° C.; between the index and middle fingers, on the right side, 34.2' C., on the left 34.5°; upon the dorsal surface of the little finger, on the right side, 26 2°, on the left 32.2° C. After faradic or galvanic stimulation of the nerve or muscles, the temperature rose, upon the right side, between the little and ring fingers, to 30.6° C. The paralyzed muscles did not respond to the induced current; upon galvanization (thirty small Siemens' elements) slow contractions were obtained in the hypothenar eminence and fourth interosseous space; motor and sensory reactions were evinced upon passing galvanic currents from the dorsal spine to the nerves; or faradic currents from the nerves to the muscles. Under the influence of a mixed treatment, continued for six weeks, some of the muscles of the little finger became sensitive to the faradic current, the functions of the right hand were partially restored, and improvement with regard to temperature also occurred.

Different nerves are unequally exposed, on account of their position, to traumatic lesions. Thus, according to Londe's statistics, among fifty-seven cases the median nerve was implicated six times, the radial five times, the internal saphenous three times, the infraorbital three times, the patheticus, facial, ulnar, sciatic, and digital nerves each twice, and ten other nerves each once.

We may also refer to reflex traumatic paralysis, which has been more carefully studied in recent times, especially by American physicians (loc. cit.). After a gun-shot wound or contusion, paralysis, either of motion or sensation or of both combined, develops in a limb which is removed from the seat of injury, although those parts of the body which have been directly affected, remain free from any morbid phenomena. As we have previously discussed the nature of reflex paralysis in general (page 152), we shall merely remark, with regard to the traumatic forms, that the irritation created by the wound may give rise to changes throughout a large part of the nervous centres, if the latter are in a condition of abnormal irritability, such as occurs, among general neuroses, in tetanus. If, on the other hand, the irritation is conveyed to more circumscribed portions of the nerve-centres, it will give rise to isolated paralyses. In the latter event, certain nerves usually present an increased sensibility to pressure and an exaggeration of their reflex and galvanic excitability.

The *prognosis*, in traumatic paralysis, varies according to the intensity of the nerve lesions. If the nerve is completely divided and nutrition markedly affected, the chronicity of the affection will only increase the dangers. The less the electro-muscular contractility and sensibility have been affected, the sooner will electricity produce good results, according to Duchenne. The prognosis is favorable if contractility is abolished but sensation has suffered little or not at all. When all phenomena of contraction and sensation are abolished, the paralyzed muscles will atrophy, even though they respond to the faradic current. A serious grade of paralysis is indicated by loss of farado-muscular and preservation of galvano-muscular contractility. Even in severe lesions of the nerves, persistent treatment may preserve, at least in part, the functions of the limbs. According to Duchenne, the return of sensibility and the transformation of anæsthesia into hyperæsthesia constitute favorable signs which are indicative of beginning recovery; the temperature, muscular tonicity, and power of voluntary motion will then gradually return to the normal. According to the gravity of the case, two, four, six months, and perhaps a longer interval, will elapse before even moderately satisfactory results are obtained. From Baerwinkel's recent observations (Arch. d. Heilk., XII. Bd., 1871), it appears that if compression of mixed nerve-trunks, below the point of injury, produces peripheral sensations, we may conclude that the sensory nerves have preserved their connections with the centres, and this will also apply in part to the motor fibres. In the absence of these effects of compression, we are not justified in admitting a solution of continuity if we can, at the same time, discover symptoms of irritation in the nerves.

With regard to *treatment*, Duchenne favors the faradization of the paralyzed muscles. This is at first employed with strong, rapidly interrupted currents, and then with weaker currents (daily sittings of ten to fifteen minutes). Duchenne states that faradic treatment is more serviceable and more indicated in old than in recent cases. I believe that, without interfering with the process of reproduction, we may resort to electricity at an early period in order to stimulate the muscular nutrition and activity and to prevent tissue changes. It has not been demonstrated that the constant current has a more positive action upon the course of severe paralyses. The treatment which has afforded the best results in my hands has been the employment, upon alternate days, of galvanization of the nerves by means of descending currents (from the dorsal spine and plexuses), and the application of the induced current to the muscles. Further surgical investigations must decide upon the value of sutures of the nerves.

CHAPTER XLIII.

DISEASES OF THE CRANIAL AND SPINAL NERVES.

DISEASES OF THE PERIPHERAL NERVES IN GENERAL.

IN the treatment of diseases of the peripheral nerves (nerve-roots, nerve-trunks, and peripheral ramifications), we are frequently arrested by the insurmountable difficulty of accurately determining the etiological conditions of these affections, which are still involved in so much obscurity. We shall restrict ourselves to the symptomatic part of the question, and, in order to meet the requirements of practice, we shall describe these various nervous diseases according to their clinical signs, referring also to what is known concerning their anatomical changes, and aiding diagnosis and treatment by a minute analysis of the symptoms. Before entering upon the special diseases of the cranial and spinal nerves, we will take a general survey of the most important morbid forms, viz.: atrophy, hypertrophy, and neuroma, neuritis and neuralgia.

a. *Atrophy of the Nerves.*

Atrophy of the nerves is a process which accompanies the most varied central and peripheral affections. In the first chapters of this work the atrophy occurring in cerebral diseases has been discussed in detail. We refer to the corresponding chapters for information concerning the atrophy of the roots of the cranial nerves in bulbar paralysis, that which involves entire nerve-trunks in spinal affections, and the atrophy of the anterior columns and roots in progressive muscular atrophy. The atrophy of the nerves of the organs of special sense has been referred to under the head of cerebral tumors.

In the central parts, as well as in the peripheral nerves, the atrophy may be *primary*, and due to spontaneous amyloid degeneration; or it may be *secondary*, in which event its causes may be traced more accurately. The atrophy of the nerves is sometimes caused by an obstruction to the flow of blood. Solutions of continuity in the nerves, their separation from the central nutritive foci, and the obstacles to the reproduction of the cut ends, constitute some of the causes which lead to atrophy. In many cases, inflammation, by causing a persistent exudation or connective-tissue proliferation, may cause atrophy of the nerves, which are almost always adherent to the surrounding parts. Finally, long-continued compression is often a cause of this process. The compression may follow an injury; or tumors, caries, periostitis of bony canals through which the nerves pass, exostoses, aneurisms, and glandular degenerations may give rise to the atrophy.

The affected nerve is usually thin, and presents a grayish or yellowish appearance. The microscope reveals a considerable number of large nerve-fibres; in others, the myeline and, afterwards, the axis-cylinder become transformed into fat, and the neurilemma is sclerosed; according to Bibra, the atrophied nerves contain a much smaller proportion of water than normally.

When the atrophy is due to inflammation or compression, it is often preceded by symptoms of irritation, such as paræsthesia, neuralgia, isolated contractions ; when the conductibility is abolished, anæsthesia, motor paralysis, loss of reflex excitability and electro-muscular contractility are observed. This succession of symptoms is noticeable in compression of the trigeminus by certain cerebral tumors, and in paralysis of the facial from caries of the temporal bone. The destructive ophthalmia due to atrophy of the trigeminus has been studied upon page 117.

With regard to treatment, it will suffice to state that it must be chiefly directed against the affection to which the atrophy is due. This should be subjected, as far as possible, to appropriate treatment before it has terminated in atrophy. If the nerve is already in such condition, there is little hope of improvement.

b. Neoplasms of the Nerves and Neuromata.

After a solution of continuity in the nerves, a regeneration of the nervous tissue has been observed, both experimentally and clinically, and has been referred to in the preceding chapter on traumatic nerve lesions. A swelling en masse sometimes forms in the nerve-trunks of amputation stumps, during the stage of cicatrization, and becomes excessively sensitive to contact, the pains being referred to the amputated part (sensation of the integrity of amputated limbs). Wedl has observed a rolling in of new-formed nerve-fibres, which has been called cicatricial neuroma by Lebert. Virchow has noticed the development of nerve-fibres in pleural exudations; Rokitansky and Virchow have seen multiplication of the nervous ganglia in ovarian tumors. In the so-called proliferation of the connective tissue of the nerves, a transparent, colloid matter, which is at first gelatinous and then becomes horny, is deposited in the nervous substance. This change is called colloid degeneration; it chiefly affects the nerves in their intracranial course, more rarely those which start from the spinal system, and extends from the periphery towards the centre or vicè-versa.

Pseudo-neuromata must also be mentioned among the neoplasms developing in nerves. They form more or less circumscribed tumors, varying from the size of a millet-seed to that of an egg, hard, elastic, usually movable with the nerve, and very sensitive to pressure. They appear to represent, in general, a connective-tissue formation, starting from the normal interstitial tissue or from the sheaths of the nerve-bundles, and, at times, contain cysts filled with colloid matter. In the majority of cases the neuroma is situated upon the side of the nerves, or it springs from the inner portion of the nerve and separates the nerve-fibres from one another in the form of a rosette. The tumors which develop at the expense of the neurilemma may be either myxomata, lipomata, fibromata, or diathetic tumors. True neuromata are much rarer; according to Virchow, they contain, in addition to a network of connective tissue, bundles of nerve-fibres running in the same direction.

The spinal nerves are the most frequent site of neuromata; they are much rarer upon the cranial and sympathetic nerves. These nerve tumors are usually isolated, though several small ones are sometimes found upon one nerve. In a fresh preparation, taken from an old woman and presented before the Vienna Medical Society by Klob, the majority of the nerve-trunks were covered by neuromata arranged like a wreath of roses, and varying from the size of a hazel-nut to that of a hen's egg, although no noteworthy symptoms were produced during life. Analogous examples of chains of neuromata have been observed and described by Smith, Maher, Payen, Kupferberg, and very recently by Heller (Virch. Arch., 44. Bd.).

We still know very little concerning the *etiology* of neuromata. Compression, traumatism, or rheumatic influences have usually been regarded as the causes of the inflammatory irritation and neoplasm. Solitary neuromata are much more frequent in women. Age appears to play only a secondary part in their production.

Among the *symptoms* of neuromata we must especially refer to the acute neuralgic pain which is present while the neuroma is still in a latent condition. In the nerve tumors, to the characteristic signs of which we have previously alluded, the pain appears in the form of paroxysms, which become more and more frequent and are readily produced by compression or simple contact. Compression causes the pain to irradiate along the peripheral course of the nerve, and is accompanied by a sensation of numbness and formication, rarely by symptoms of motor irritation (contractions, tremor, contracture) or by phenomena of depression (anæsthesia and paresis). Extensive neuralgias and partial or general convulsions sometimes develop as reflex phenomena.

When the neuromata occupy the superficial parts, they are accessible to exploration when the nerve-trunks are examined, and are distinguished from cancer of the nerves by their mobility, the possibility of displacing them, and their gradual development without general symptoms.

Various forms of cancer develop at the periphery of the nerves, either primarily or secondarily, and are accompanied by pain. The tumors adhere to the surrounding parts, proliferate rapidly, ulcerate, and are accompanied by infiltration of the lymphatic glands, cachexia, and complete paralysis of sensation or motion.

Neuromata almost always run a chronic course. They do not threaten life directly, but react unfavorably upon the general condition by the violence of the pains, the insomnia, and the digestive disorders to which they give rise. *Treatment* is chiefly of a surgical nature. Resorbents and nervines are useless, and narcotics only produce momentary relief. Extirpation constitutes the most efficient means of treatment, and, in removing the tumor, the nerve-fibres should be injured as little as possible. If we are forced to include a portion of the nerve in the operation, a corresponding functional disorder will be produced at the periphery. Relapses sometimes occur. When multiple neuromata are present, we can only remove one or the other of the painful tumors with the bistoury.

c. *Inflammation of the Nerves (Neuritis).*

The simple hyperæmias and slight ecchymoses, which are found in the sheaths of the nerves in various acute and diathetic affections (at times mere cadaveric hyperæmia), are not sufficiently intense to be regarded as evidences of inflammation. Apart from the redness, the loss of substance, relaxation, and infiltration of the neurilemma, the inflamed nerve appears injected and swollen, and a serous, gelatinous, or fibrinous exudation is situated between the different bundles of fibres. The nerve-fibres are only affected with fatty degeneration after the inflammation has lasted for a certain length of time. We also know, from the recent experiments of Hjelt (loc. cit.) upon artificial neuritis, that the inflammatory irritation is accompanied by nuclear proliferation and by coagulation and fatty degeneration of the nerve-fibres.

The inflammation of the nerves usually starts from the connective-tissue layer of the neurilemma, and the myeline is only secondarily affected. The inflammatory process constitutes a perineuritis or an interstitial neuritis, according to the degree of hyperplasia and the abundance of the nuclei in the external or internal nerve-sheaths, and according to the nuclear proliferation and fibrillary thickening which may develop in the sheath of Schwann.

The exudation produced by the inflammation may be absorbed, in slight cases, before the nerve-fibres have undergone any permanent changes. When the inflammation follows a chronic course, the sheath of the nerves becomes thickened, fibrous, and resisting, and is frequently adherent to the adjacent tissues. The nervous substance remains intact in slight forms, but in severe cases it undergoes atrophy from the compression exercised by the exudation. If the exudation becomes organized, it will result in the formation of connective tissue, with thickening and sclerosis of the nerves and disappearance of the nerve elements. In traumatic inflammations, and in the suppurations which are propagated to the nerves *per contiguitatem*, purulent infiltration and necrosis of the nervous tissue may develop.

Pain constitutes one of the most important symptoms of neuritis. It is usually continuous, rarely remittent or even intermittent; it is increased by pressure and motion (as Virchow has shown), though this symptom is not sufficient evidence of neuritis. The pain is not only present in the inflamed part, but it also radiates towards the periphery, and is accompanied by formication and numbness. Fever is only present in extensive neuritis. If the exudation increases or compresses the nerves for a long time, the initial symptoms of irritation (hyperæsthesia, painful irradiations, subsultus) are followed by anæsthesia and paralysis. The paralyses of motion and sensation are complicated by trophic disturbances in the muscles, and sometimes in the skin (herpetic eruptions) and articulations; these are also the sequences of inflammatory irritation of the nerves. Anæsthetic lepra (elephantiasis Græcorum) also results, according to Virchow (Die krankh. Geschw., II. Bd., 1864–'65), from a perineuritis with cellular proliferation between the nerve-tubes. According to Boeck and Danielssen (Traité de la Spedalsked., 1848), and to the more recent observations of Steudener (Beitr. z. Path. der Lepra, 1867), the inflammatory process may extend from the peripheral nerves to the nerve-roots and even to the cord (formation of canaliculi in the gray substance, Steudener). We have also seen that reflex paralysis may be caused by the extension of ascending neuritis to the cord, as has been rendered probable by the previously mentioned experiments of Tiesler and Feinberg (loc. cit.).

From a diagnostic point of view, neuritis is distinguished from neuralgia by the continued character of the pains, which rarely present remissions or intermissions, by the absence of circumscribed puncta dolorosa, by the peculiar sensibility of the nerves to electrical irritation (especially to the induced current), and by the secondary phenomena of muscular atrophy and motor and sensory paralysis. As a rule, neuritis is only detected after long and careful observation.

Muscular rheumatism, which is often very painful, is recognized by its diffuse character, by the absence of other peripheral symptoms, and by the fact that the pains are intensified rather by movements than by pressure. The diseases of the vessels which accompany the nerves are characterized by the sudden pain, absence of pulsation, depression of temperature, abolition of sensibility and nutrition (arterial embolism), the appreciable induration of the veins, the extensive œdema and concomitant venous stasis (venous thrombosis). These phenomena are, therefore, not readily mistaken for neuritis.

The *etiology* of inflammation of the nerves is variable. An intense rheumatic influence, traumatic lesions, compression, and inflammation and suppuration in the vicinity of the nerves may give rise to neuritis. At a later period the neuritis may terminate by prompt absorption of the exudation. In the unfavorable cases, in which it pursues a chronic course, it terminates in more or less severe disturbances of motion and sensation.

In the *treatment* of inflammation of the nerves, it is advisable to resort, from the beginning, to the employment of antiphlogistics. Good results are often obtained from local bleeding, cold compresses, prolonged tepid baths (with the necessary precautions upon entering and leaving the bath). I can also recommend the use of moist packs, continued until the return of warmth to the body, and followed by half-baths of 24°–20° C. (five to eight minutes). When the pain is violent we may resort to hypodermic injections of morphine in remote parts. Iodide of potassium is prescribed in chronic cases, but iodated baths, the indifferent thermal waters, and mud-baths have a much more positive action in producing absorption of the inflammatory products. The secondary disorders of motion and sensation are best combated by means of electricity (galvanization of the nerves and faradization of the muscles). This can be advantageously combined with hydrotherapeutic or thermal treatment.

d. *Neuralgia.*

The term neuralgia includes those pains which appear in the various segments of the nerves, from their origin to the periphery, and which usually develop in paroxysms, either spontaneously or after pressure upon certain points. The production of pain requires that a feeble stimulus should react very quickly upon the nerve-fibres, though a violent irritation may, by its intensity, replace the slowness of propagation. Nutritive disturbances in the myeline (sometimes secondary to disorders of circulation) may also cause painful sensations. The latter are usually regulated by the primary intensity or the increase of the exciting cause, by the duration of the irritation, and by the degree of exhaustion of the nerves. According to Schiff's experiments, the receptivity to stimuli, but not the conducting power, is increased in hyperæmic nerves. The periodical return of neuralgia may be due to the fact that the internal organic stimuli act at intervals. The exhaustion of the exaggerated nervous activity may be caused by a diminution either in the receptivity of the irritated point, of the conductibility of the fibres, or of the central perception.

As the nerve-fibres which are distributed to the skin enter the nerve-trunks from the exterior at different heights, compression or other irritations of the nerves will affect the external fibres earlier than the internal.

It therefore follows that the pain appears to run along the course of the nerves from above downwards. The lancinating pains along the nerve-trunks are especially produced under the influence of rapidly acting, strong stimuli, such as occur in sudden shocks to the elbow, or from the effects of intense cold.

The arrangement of the central mosaic determines the law of peripheral manifestations. An irritation of the intra-medullary sensory fibres in the gray columns will be transformed into painful sensations in the terminal expansions of the nerves. The posterior roots of the spinal nerves, the numerous sensory filaments situated between the external integument and the aponeuroses, and penetrating, in part, into the muscles, also furnish weak points which may give rise to neuralgias in the vast network of the peripheral nervous system.

When the irritation is situated centrally, we can readily understand why the terminal nervous apparatus, which is affected with intermittent pains, does not present any morbid change. Tissue changes are some-times observed in peripheral affections of the sensory nerves. Under this head we may mention : swelling of the nerves and granular opacity of the myeline, with periostitis of the osseous orifices (supra-orbital, infra-orbital, inferior alveolar, mental nerves, etc.); thickening of the sheaths of the nerves from inflammation of the surrounding parts; proliferation of the connective tissue between the nerve-bundles, and of cancer-cells be-tween the nerve-fibres (as in a case which I shall report under the head of sciatica); the nodular swellings of the nerves in amputation stumps, which may give rise to neuralgia; finally, to this category belong the neuralgias dependent upon the compression exercised by adjacent tumors, vertebral affections, and venous stases in the nervous tissues. We shall again refer to these particulars in treating of special neuralgias.

Pain constitutes the chief phenomenon among the symptoms of neural-gia. In the majority of cases it follows the anatomical course of the nerves, and appears under the form of paroxysms, which may be separated from one another by complete intermissions, or merely by remissions. The patients describe the pain as shooting (with or without cutaneous hyper-æsthesia), tearing, piercing, pricking, burning, etc. Facial neuralgia and ataxia dolorosa are the forms which give rise to the most violent paroxysms. Certain points frequently constitute the site of the pains from which the patients suffer. They may also be propagated to other branches of the nerve-roots, and almost always radiate from the centre to the periphery, though sometimes in the opposite direction.

Valleix first discovered the *puncta dolorosa* which form such an impor-tant characteristic of neuralgia. They are most frequently found at the points at which the nerves emerge from their bony canals in order to spread over the surface of bones, when they pass through aponeurotic or muscular orifices, or in the regions in which important cutaneous nerves anastomose with one another. As a rule, they constitute circumscribed painful spots, which may be discovered by careful exploration upon press-ing with the finger along the course of the nerves; they are present in the majority of neuralgias. But there are some cases (and I have fre-quently observed such) in which the puncta dolorosa only appear during the paroxysms and are absent at other times. In doubtful cases I have often discovered, by means of electrical exploration, certain points along the nerves which were very sensitive to the electrical current (continuous or induced), while other portions of the same nerve or corresponding parts on the healthy side, were not especially affected by the current. The pains in neuralgia may also extend, secondarily, to other nerve-filaments (originating in the same roots), or may even be propagated by irradiation to remote parts in cases of extreme irritability of the nervous system.

Tuerck had observed hyperæsthesia or anæsthesia in certain neuralgias, and Noth-nagel (Virch. Arch., 54. Bd.) has more recently shown that these phenomena habitu-ally accompany neuralgias of the limbs and of the superficial nerves of the trunk and head. Cutaneous hyperalgesia is found at the onset of the attack (from two to eight weeks), but later the sensibility of the skin is diminished. Both symptoms are ob-served upon all the corresponding nerve-fibres, or they may extend to the entire half of the body (Tuerck), and disappear during the course of recovery. According to Nothnagel, the hyperæsthesia results from an irradiation of the stimuli to a large number of sensory nerve-cells; the anæsthesia is caused by the exhaustion of the nerve-cells, following excessive stimulation. In many of my cases these sensory dis-orders were evidently due to vaso-motor irritation.

Neuralgias are not infrequently accompanied by peculiar reflex symp-toms, which are explained by the numerous communications of the pos-terior root-fibres with the gray substance of the cord. In facial neural-gia we will find that contractions of the muscles of the face follow the sensory irritation ; in neuralgia of the limbs the latter are the seat of more or less extensive muscular spasms. The rhythm of the movements of the heart and of respiration may also be changed. In rare cases, pre-existing muscular spasms are replaced by neuralgia (as sometimes occurs in the irritative stage of ataxia). The depression of the reflex power may thus lead to the absence of Goltz's phenomenon, when the irritation of the intestines (which, under other circumstances, will produce arrest of the heart's action through the medium of the pneumogastric) is com-bined with intense irritation of the sensory nerves of the limbs. Finally, we must also classify, among the reflex acts, the vaso-motor disturbances produced by irritation of the sympathetic nerve-fibres (which are inter-mingled with sensory fibres). These include the anomalies of circulation and secretion which are observed in neuralgias, the cutaneous eruptions, and the disorders of nutrition (as in prosopalgia).

The *etiology* of neuralgia is involved in considerable obscurity. Its causes vary considerably, being sometimes general, sometimes local. Among the general causes the most important is the abnormal excitabil-ity of the nervous system, either in the central organs or in the periph-eral expansions; it may be hereditary or produced by external influences. Experience has shown that fathers, suffering from nervous affections, frequently transmit to their sons a certain predisposition to nervous dis-orders and to neuralgia. In the same manner, mothers, who are affected with neuralgias of the head, rachialgia, cardialgia, etc., transmit this pre-disposition to their daughters. But I do not believe that we can admit the hypothesis hazarded by Anstie (Neuralgia and Diseases that Resem-ble It, London, 1871), who presupposes an hereditary weakness of the nerve-cells of the posterior columns, which, after prolonged centripetal irritation, leads to interstitial atrophy of these cells, terminating either in recovery (?) or in degeneration.

Sex possesses a certain influence, in the sense that some neuralgias (intercostal, lumbo-abdominal) are most frequently observed in females, while sciatica is most fre-quent in men. Until the age of thirty years, women are usually more exposed to neuralgia than men, a fact which may be attributed, in great part, to the sexual con-ditions (menstruation, chlorosis, pregnancy).

The season of the year and changes in temperature have a positive influence upon the appearance of neuralgias. In a third of the cases collected by Valleix and other authors, the invasion of the disease occurred during the cold or changeable months of the year. Wind, moist cold, chilling of the body while perspiring, may only affect the peripheral nerve terminations, or may transmit their action to the central fibres along the trunks and nerve-roots, thus giving rise to excentric neuralgias. The development or return of neuralgias is frequently caused by residence in moist, cold houses, and living in a locality which is exposed to the winds. Finally, the neuralgias observed by Guensburg and Leudet (Arch. Gén., fév., 1864), in certain cases of phthisis and chlorosis, result from the effect of vitiated blood upon the nervous system.

The local causes of neuralgia are either central or peripheral. The central causes proceed from the brain or cord. Among the cerebral affections, certain congestive conditions (those, for example, which precede apoplexy) may be attended with neuralgias; or the latter may form a concomitant symptom of inflammation, tumors, sclerosis, or softening. Spinal affections very often assume, at the onset, the appearances of vague neuralgias. Lancinating pains with cutaneous hyperæsthesia are a frequent initial symptom of ataxia. Spondylitis of the upper segment of the vertebral column is also accompanied, at the onset, by neuralgia of the cervical and brachial plexuses and of the intercostal spaces. A large number of hysterical, dyscrasic, and toxic neuralgias may also be ranged in this category.

Among the peripheral causes may be mentioned : local lesions of the nerves or of their sheaths, following traumatism, compression, laceration, inflammation; periostitis and caries of the adjacent bones, and especially of the bony orifices through which the nerves pass; rheumatic affections of the articular and muscular nerve-fibres; stases in the venous channels adjoining the nerves, and atheroma of the arteries; compression of the nerves by aneurisms, degenerated glands, neoplasms, syphilitic gummata, inflammation and enlargement of internal organs, and foreign bodies. In all these cases the character of the inflammatory or mechanical irritation, and the nature of the tumors, influence the neuralgic phenomena. At a later period we will discuss the neuralgias which develop from reflex agencies and from irradiation.

The *diagnosis* of neuralgias is usually less difficult than their localization. Pains which follow the course of the nerves, which recur paroxysmally, and which present certain *puncta dolorosa*, point to the neuralgic character of the affection. In the absence of these various conditions, we can only diagnose neuralgia with more or less probability.

As neuralgia is almost always symptomatic of various morbid conditions, the most important question, from a clinical stand-point, is to discover the primary source of the neuralgic symptoms. In this respect we may state that it is a useless labor to divide neuralgias, as do some authors of the present day, into artificial groups, which rest more upon personal views than upon real objective signs.

In dealing with neuralgia, the physician should, above all, determine, both with regard to prognosis and treatment, whether it is merely the expression of a local irritation, or the peripheral indication of central morbid processes. In the majority of cases it is possible, by a careful consideration of the other morbid phenomena, to form an opinion concerning the nature of the neuralgia. It is sometimes necessary to observe for a long time the manner of development of the disease in order to collect sufficient data; it is only in very rare cases, however, that the primary cause of the neuralgia completely escapes us during life. We shall now point out the most striking and characteristic symptoms of this affection.

Neuralgias of cerebral origin are accompanied by headache (especially in the forehead and temples); they develop upon one-half of the body, and appear as tearing pains along the course of certain nerves (as in prosopalgia), with reflex contractions in the face, and general hyperæsthesia or psychical symptoms. The neuralgias which are symptomatic of cerebral tumors (facial neuralgia, fixed or wandering pains in the neck, pains in the limbs) are characterized by periodical cephalalgia, vertigo, trigeminal neuralgia, followed by anæsthesia, by the appearance of convulsions, early signs of neuroretinitis, paresis of various cranial nerves, and, at a later period, paralysis in the extremities. Spinal neuralgias are almost always preceded by early paræsthesiæ (sensations of cold, formication in the fingers and toes, numbness). Periodical brachialgia or rachialgia, with painful sensations in the back, and in one or the other leg (lancinating pains in the sciatic nerve, with cutaneous hyperæsthesia at the beginning or during the course of the ataxia); intercurrent diplopia, marked inequality of the pupils; ready fatigue; coexisting genital irritation; extreme sensibility to winds and moisture; abnormal excitability to the galvanic current in certain definite spots: these are the symptoms which evidence the spinal origin of neuralgias

Hysterical neuralgias usually appear after mental excitement or hysterical convulsions. They are recognized by their rapid modifications as regards situation and intensity, and by the coexistence of other motor and sensory disturbances (for further details, *vide* page 41, Vol. I.). Hysterical neuralgias are of cerebral or spinal origin, but rarely of a peripheral nature. Mercurial and lead neuralgias are almost always of peripheral origin, and are recognized by the other symptoms and by the antecedents of the patient. Anæmic neuralgias which sometimes develop in tuberculosis, chlorosis, and intermittent fever are due to the influence of the vitiated blood upon the nervous system, and are readily recognized by the ensemble of the disease.

Arthritic neuralgias are only observed in old people, and are accompanied by swelling and stiffness of the joints; the influence of neuritis nodosa upon this class of affections has not been hitherto well determined. Syphilitic neuralgias are attributable to periostitis or osteitis. For the consideration of traumatic neuralgias we refer to page 170, Vol. II. Rheumatic neuralgias are usually limited to the final nerve ramifications in the skin, aponeuroses, muscles, and joints, and they result from the effects of cold. Neuralgias of mucous membranes, such as the urethra, rectum, stomach (gastralgia), intestine, abdominal walls (simulating peritonitis) are almost always concomitant phenomena of central affections or of hysterical seizures. Finally, pains of peripheral origin may radiate to remote sensory nerves, and may give rise, in case of abnormal excitability (in nervous individuals and especially in females), to irradiated neuralgias. To this category belong the pain in the shoulder in hepatic colic, the dorsal pain in cancer of the stomach, the femoral pains in renal calculi, etc.

The *prognosis* of neuralgia depends upon the primary affection to which it is due. The peripheral forms may recover, in certain cases, if the patients are placed under appropriate treatment. At other times, on the contrary (as in certain cerebral and spinal affections), they offer an obstinate resistance to treatment, and we are forced to resort to mere palliative measures. Hysterical and toxic neuralgias, and those which are due to anæmia, grow better with the improvement in the general condition. Neuralgia, caused by peripheral diseases, will disappear when the source of irritation to which they are due has disappeared. As a rule, recent neuralgias, developing in young subjects, are more susceptible of recovery than the chronic, complicated forms affecting old people. The frequency of relapses in neuralgia is universally known, and the persistence of *puncta dolorosa* is premonitory of a return of the disease.

In the *treatment* of neuralgias especial attention must be paid to the removal of the cause. But, as a rule, it is much easier to discover the cause than to effect its removal. In the majority of cases we must endeavor to relieve the morbid excitability of the nerves as much as possible, or to suppress their conducting power (as in prosopalgia). Frequently this purpose is but partially effected, and it only remains for the physician to procure for his patient at least some relief, some moments. of repose in the midst of the despairing monotony of his pains. In rheumatic neuralgias, rapid improvement is obtained by the immediate use of antiphlogistics, diaphoretics, vapor-baths, moist packs (a half hour to an hour), followed by cool half-baths and the electrical current. When the disease assumes a chronic course, we must continue the employment. of the latter measures methodically and for a long time, as well as the different thermal waters. If the affection is due to anæmia, resort may be had to tonic treatment and to ferruginous waters (Franzenbad, Spa, Pyrmont, etc.); iodide of potassium may be administered, if periostitis. is suspected. In toxic neuralgias we may prescribe warm baths and nutritious diet, and stimulate the secretions.

Palliative treatment consists in the endeavor to diminish the abnormal excitability of the nerves. Among the new remedies employed for this purpose, bromide of potassium (two to four grammes daily) sometimes. renders good service. In periodical neuralgia, quinine is prescribed in large doses (alone or combined with opiates), or Fowler's solution. Opium internally and preparations of hydrocyanic acid are poorly tolerated by many patients; they very often produce severe gastralgic symptoms, and their sedative action is very slow. In such cases preference must be given to subcutaneous injections of morphine, extract of opium, atropine, etc., although they usually possess only temporary efficacy, and permanent recoveries are exceptional.

If we desire to combine morphine and quinine for hypodermic use, we must employ aqueous solutions of the hydrochlorate of morphine and bisulphate of quinine. I have shown (Med. Presse, 22, 1867) that a mixture of concentrated solutions of acetate of morphia and bisulphate of quinia will give rise to a cheesy precipitate of the insoluble neutral sulphate of quinia, with the formation of the sulphate of morphia and hydrated acetic acid (according to the law of double substitutions). The severe accidents which Nussbaum has observed upon himself from the use of these injections (intense pruritus over the entire body, redness of the face, tinnitus aurium, flashes of light, pulse of one hundred and fifty to one hundred and seventy) are exceedingly rare occurrences.

The endermic administration of opiates is little used on account of the numerous inconveniences connected with it; ointments containing veratrine and aconitine (0.05–0.15 mixed with fat) are sometimes useful. Flying blisters (Valleix) are especially successful in acute rheumatic neuralgias. Local anæsthesia (Richardson) and inhalations of chloroform only produce an effect during the period of application. Bernatzik's liquid (chloroform eighteen grammes, acetate of morphia 0.2 grammes, rectified alcohol 0.8 grammes) acts favorably in neuralgia. of the dental nerves (prolonged friction over the painful points), but only for a certain length of time.

Electricity has been largely employed in recent times, and has proved

successful in a considerable number of cases. But complicated, extensive, and old central affections sometimes resist all electrical treatment.
In practising faradization, the secondary current is most frequently employed, the electrical brush being placed along the course of the nerves.
In using the continuous current (which merits the preference on account
of its less tension) the anode is applied as closely as possible to the centres, and the cathode upon the painful points (sittings of three to four
minutes with moderate currents, the intensity of which may be gradually
increased). In spinal neuralgias, galvanic currents are passed through
the vertebral column, and stabile currents through the nerve-trunks. In
cerebral forms, weak currents are applied locally, or they are made to
traverse the head through the medium of the mastoid processes. In basilar and arthritic neuralgias, certain authors recommend the galvanization
of the cervical sympathetic nerves.

By means of hydrotherapeutic treatment we endeavor to diminish the
excess of local or general sensibility, and to soothe the erethism of the
nerves or of their centres, by acting upon the vast sensory network of the
skin. In the beginning we prescribe half-baths at 24°–22° C., and gradually
lower their temperature. If the pains are intense, we may combine the
baths with moist packs of a half hour's duration and with dorsal affusions;
local douches should only be employed if the neuralgia is known to be
peripheral. In neuralgias of central origin, care must be taken to diminish the exciting action of cold, and we should avoid all stimulating measures, taking into consideration the individual conditions.

Surgical interference frequently constitutes the only refuge to which
the patients can resort for the relief of their torments. The majority of
surgeons favor excision of a considerable portion of the nerve (neurectomy) in order to prevent the reunion of the two ends ; according to
Bruns, at least one centimetre of the nerve must be excised. Only a few
modern authors (Stromeyer and O. Weber) advocate simple section (neurotomy) of the nerves. The operation is indicated when the neuralgia
occupies a circumscribed region, when it is due to compression, or
the pains are very intense and rebellious (as in trigeminal neuralgia).
Although excision of the nerves often possesses merely a temporary utility, and the neuralgia may return in other branches, nevertheless a long
suspension of the pains is a benefit, the value of which the patient is in a
better condition to recognize than others.

I.—DISEASES OF THE CRANIAL NERVES.

In studying the affections of the cranial nerves, we shall, at first, make a summary review of certain central forms, and shall then pay special attention to the disorders occurring in the peripheral course of the nerves. The following clinical exposé of the disorders affecting the nerves of special sense, the motor and the mixed cranial nerves, will correspond to the three fundamental types expressive of their physiological functions.

CHAPTER XLIV.

A.—AFFECTIONS OF THE NERVES OF SPECIAL SENSE.

FOLLOWING the anatomical order, we shall refer to neuroses of the olfactory, optic, acoustic, and glosso-pharyngeal nerves. In order to avoid repetition, we will merely call attention to the part which the sensorial nerves assume in the central affections of which we have previously spoken, and will direct our attention chiefly to the peripheral diseases of these nerves.

a. *Diseases of the Olfactory Nerve.*

The principal disorders which occur on the part of these nerves are hyperæsthesia (hyperosmia) and anæsthesia (anosmia). Temporary hyperæsthesia may be observed in certain patients who have become extremely nervous after prolonged diseases, but it is most frequently noticed in hysterical patients and in the insane. In the latter case, in which subjective olfactory sensations exist, softening of the olfactory nerve, neoplasms of the base of the brain extending to the anterior lobe, softening or discoloration of the olfactory bulb, and adhesions of the olfactory nerves to the dura mater, have been discovered. In a case reported by Bérard, olfactory sensations had existed during life, despite the absence of the first pair of nerves (anomaly of central perception or of conductibility). In an observation recently published by Sander (Arch. f. Psych., 1873), epileptiform attacks occurred with subjective sensations of taste, and the left olfactory nerve was found to have been destroyed by a tumor. In hyperosmia, it is always necessary to treat the primary affection.

Anosmia is much more frequent and important. In exceptional cases it may be congenital or it may be hereditary, as in Cloquet's case, in which the filaments of the olfactory nerves were imperfectly developed. Temporary anosmia occurs in coryza, in which the swelling of the nasal mucous membrane and the accumulation of mucus abolish the perception of olfactory impressions, or as in facial paralysis, in which the application of the alæ nasi against the septum of the nasal fossæ presents an obstacle to the penetration of air charged with odoriferous particles. Anosmia is also produced in tumors at the base of the brain (*vide* p. 102), in abscess of the pituitary gland (Oppert), rarely in syphilitic thickening of the periosteum and mucous membrane (in Romberg's patient, mercurial treatment caused the disappearance of the affection); finally, it occurs in hysteria, in which disease it is almost always accompanied by trigeminal anæsthesia. Partial or total abolition of the sense of smell may also result from chronic rhinitis, from peripheral lesions (blow upon the face and nose), or from the prolonged use of irritating injections. It is also sometimes observed in the course of typhoid fever and meningitis, and the loss of smell is then usually spontaneously restored. Anæsthesia of the first pair may be combined with that of the trigeminus (as in hysterical or certain insane patients), and the mucous membrane then loses its reflex excitability. At other times, the anosmia is simple, and the nasal fossæ preserve their normal sensibility despite the loss of smell. In a case of this kind reported by Pressat, the olfactory nerves and the foramina of the cribriform plate of the ethmoid bone were wanting, but the orifices intended for the ethmoid nerves were preserved. In the diseases to which we have just referred, the return of olfactory perceptions follows general tonic treatment. In the anosmia due to chronic rheumatism, traumatism, or hysteria, benefit is derived from faradization of the nasal mucous membrane (Duchenne, Beard and Rockwell). In the other cases, it is almost hopeless to expect any improvement.

b. *Diseases of the Optic Nerve.*

The sensations of light and color, and the illusions produced by an abnormal irritation of the optic nerve, are regarded as evidences of hyperæsthesia. The latter may follow a direct or indirect irritation of the optic nerves in their central course.

Congestive conditions of the brain, the development of cerebral tumors, of certain mental diseases (hypochondria, ecstasy), hysteria, chorea magna, chronic alcoholism and narcotism, and the inhalation of toxic gases, may also act as causes of optic hyperæsthesia. Among the local causes, we may mention diseases and atrophy of the optic nerves at their periphery (compression, extravasation), congestive and inflammatory conditions of the retina, the sudden perception of a bright light, and application to delicate work. Hyperæsthesia of the optic nerves usually follows a chronic course, and may constitute a threatening symptom, especially in central affections, in which it is very frequently the forerunner of optic anæsthesia. The *treatment* consists of the application of leeches to the mastoid processes, of cold compresses to the head, cool half-baths, stimulating enemata, tartar emetic in divided doses, prolonged rest for the eyes, and a trip to the country. These measures sometimes prove successful at the onset of the affection.

Anæsthesia of the optic nerve is called amblyopia or amaurosis, according as the visual faculty is partially or completely lost.

Among the central alterations of the chiasm or optic nerves, we must especially refer to the connective tissue thickenings of the sheath of the optic nerve, and to optic neuritis and its sequences (*vide* p. 101). In addition, more or less advanced atrophy of the nerve, changes in the neuroglia, an abundant formation of connective tissue in the interior of the bundles, frequent increase of the cellular elements, and development of granular cells and amyloid corpuscles, are also found (as Virchow and Leber have shown). In a case of paralytic dementia with unilateral amaurosis, Meynert found the external geniculate body on the same side, and the internal geniculate body on the opposite side, atrophied and sclerosed.

The *diagnosis* is confirmed by the ophthalmoscopic examination; the diminution or complete abolition of the movements of the pupils is due to the absence of retinal reflexes. As Tuerck first discovered, pressure upon the cervical vertebræ or mastoid processes in optic anæsthesia, may have a momentary favorable or unfavorable influence upon the visual faculty (by reflex action through the trigeminal nerve). The central causes of optic anæsthesia include: neuroretinitis following cerebral tumors, softening, hæmorrhages, dropsy of the ventricles, optic atrophy in ataxia, hysterical cerebral disorders, malarial cachexia, Bright's disease, lead poisoning, syphilis. In the latter case, the disease assumes the ordinary appearances of cerebral amaurosis (atrophy of the optic nerves), while in ocular syphilis the ophthalmoscope reveals the symptoms of retinitis or retino-choroiditis (Sichel). The affection is of peripheral origin in traumatism of the eyeball, inflammation and hæmorrhage of the retina and adjacent parts, retinal tumors, glaucomatous compression, tumors of the base of the brain, or thickening of the meninges extending to the chiasm. The course of the disease is usually chronic and its prognosis is almost always unfavorable. The malarial, hysterical, saturnine, syphilitic, and hæmorrhagic forms may recover after appropriate treatment.

Before the discovery of the ophthalmoscope, strychnia had been employed in atrophy of the optic nerves, and Nagel, Woinow, Hippel, etc., have again advocated its employment more recently (under the form of hypodermic injections). But further observations, to which I may add my personal experience, have not confirmed the efficacy of this remedy. Santonine has been recently used (Schoen), but we do not know as yet whether better results are to be expected from this drug.

c. Neuroses of the Acoustic Nerve.

Acoustic neuroses, which are naturally more obscure and much more inaccessible to our investigations than those of the optic nerve, have had considerable light thrown upon them by new means of investigation and especially by Brenner's galvanic method. When the acoustic nerve is healthy, if one of the poles is applied to the previously moistened auditory meatus or to the tragus (Erb), and the other pole to the neck or inner side of the arm, and the intensity of the current be regulated by means of the rheostat, the nerve will respond to the galvanic exploration with the normal formula of reaction viz.: at the closure of the cathode (KaF), during the permanent action of the cathode (KaD), and at the opening of the anode (AO).

Modifications of the normal reactions will be observed, however, if the acoustic nerve manifests symptoms of irritation or depression.

Acoustic hyperæsthesia may be of central origin, as in chronic cephalalgia, cerebral hyperæmia, irritative conditions of the brain and cord, hysteria, insanity (most frequently with hallucinations of hearing), etc. The peripheral causes include an exaggerated tension of the muscles and bones of the ear, with secondary compression of the labyrinth. According to Lucae's recent experiments (Berl. Klin. Wschr., 1874), the tensor tympani muscle presides over the accommodation for musical tones, and the stapedius over the accommodation for shriller and non-musical auditory sensations. When the stapedius is paralyzed, we observe an abnormal acuteness of hearing for tones and noises, i.e. hyperæsthesia. This symptom is also observed at times in facial paralysis.

Simple acoustic hyperæsthesia, following disorders in conductibility and intracranial lesions of the acoustic nerves, or combined with paralysis of the ocular muscles, mydriasis, etc., is manifested, according to Brenner, by abnormal excitability of hearing to weak currents, and by much greater intensity and duration of auditory sensations (intense ringing produced by closure of the cathode and persisting until opening). These reactions may be formulated as follows:

KaF (loud ringing).   AF (no reaction).
KaD (continuous ringing).   AD ("   ").
KaO (no reaction).   AO (ringing becomes weaker).

When the affection is more pronounced, the hyperæsthesia is accompanied by qualitative changes in the reactions in question. We most frequently observe, in addition to perverted auditory sensations, an abnormal reaction (only in the affected ear) at the closure of the cathode, during continuous action at the anode (AD), and more rarely at the opening of the cathode. The following are the pathological reactions:

KaF (increased ringing).   AF (loud hissing).
KaD (continuous ringing).   AD (continuous hissing).
KaO (hissing).   AO (ringing becomes weaker).

When the morbid excitability of audition, combined with simple hyperæsthesia, has existed for a long time, the normal reactions grow weaker and weaker, until finally only the abnormal reactions persist. According to Brenner, the reverse of the phenomena produced in simple hyperæsthesia (reversal of the reactions) then occur, and the reactions observed in the diseased ear may be expressed as follows :

KaF (no reaction).   AF (ringing loud).
KaD ("   ").   AD (ringing continuous).
KaO (ringing grows weaker).   AO (no reaction).

According to Brenner, there is a peculiar form of exaggerated auditory irritability, consisting of hyperæsthesia with an inverse formula to that of the non-irritated ear in old and severe auditory affections. This condition is characterized by the remarkable fact, that upon applying the current to one ear, there is a reaction not only on the part of the auditory nerve of this side, but also on that of the opposite side.

Galvanized Ear.   *Non-Galvanized Ear.*

KaF (ringing).   (No reaction).
KaD (ringing continuous).   ("   ").
KaO (no reaction).   (Ringing grows weaker).
AF ("   ").   (Ringing loud).
AD ("   ").   (Ringing grows weaker).
AO (ringing grows weaker).   (No reaction).

Finally, the abnormal excitability of the acoustic nerve may disappear although the reversal of the formula persists, and there is then a modification of the reactions without coexisting hyperæsthesia. According to Brenner, we may also observe modifications of the formula without co-existing hyperæsthesia (as in facial paralysis).

The galvanic treatment of acoustic hyperæsthesia has met with a certain amount of success. This is especially true of the nervous ringing in the ears which, according to Brenner, diminishes at the closure of the anode and during the continuous action at the anode, while, on the other hand, it is increased by opening of the anode and closing of the cathode. It is also necessary, in order to avoid any persistent cause of irritation, to employ very gentle currents at the opening and closing or the circuit. In hyperæsthesia with an inverse formula in the non-irritated ear and subjective acoustic sensations, it is necessary, according to Brenner, to apply the anode, divided into two branches, to both ears. Benedikt recommends the employment of alternate currents (modification of the excitability by reversing the direction of the current) in tinnitus aurium. In some cases, I have seen the symptoms improve after galvanization, but sooner or later relapses usually occur. In these cases, good effects are sometimes obtained from a prolonged stay in an Alpine region or at the sea-shore.

Anæsthesia of the acoustic nerve or torpor (reactions feeble or completely absent at closure of the cathode, during constant action of the cathode, opening of the anode or reversal of the current, Brenner) is almost always accompanied by severe and persistent disorders of the faculty of audition, and is caused by disturbances of conductibility in the central or peripheral fibres of the acoustic nerve. Independently of the poorly understood changes which the acoustic nucleus may undergo in medullary processes, and of certain localized affections in the mesocephalon, posterior regions and cerebellum, we must also take into consideration neoplasms at the base of the brain, increase of intra-cranial pressure (on account of the communications, demonstrated by E. Weber, between the arachnoid space and the labyrinth), organic affections of the labyrinth itself, and probably also certain forms of neuritis of the acoustic nerve which have been hitherto but little studied. In two cases of nervous deafness, Hiebrich has recently noted (Arch. f. Psych., V. Bd., 1874) the integrity of the labyrinth and of the cavity of the tympanum, and traced an amyloid degeneration of the acoustic nerve into the medulla oblongata. The deafness observed in ataxia, hysteria, typhoid fever and the acute exanthemata, is due either to profound disturbances or, in curable forms, to slight changes in the meninges. *Deaf-mutism* is caused by malformation of the middle and internal ear, either congenital or acquired during childhood after cerebral diseases.

We can only expect slight results from *treatment*. Acoustic hyperæsthesia is sometimes improved by galvanization (Brenner), strong but not painful currents being employed, and the current being alternated from the anode to the cathode. Duchenne, Erdmann, etc., have obtained benefit from faradization of the ear in nervous deafness; Duchenne met with similar success in a case of deaf-mutism.

d. *Neuroses of the Gustatory Nerves.*

In concluding our consideration of the pathology of the nerves of special sensibility, we shall examine the most striking facts in the normal and pathological history of the organs of taste, although the nerves which are distributed to these organs belong in reality to the mixed nerves. The most important of the gustatory nerves of the tongue is the glosso-pharyngeal, which is chiefly distributed to the posterior third of the organ, but also in part to its anterior third, by means of a filament discovered by Hirschfeld. According to the experiments of Stannius, it presides exclusively over the sensation of bitterness in the corresponding parts of the tongue. The other gustatory perceptions are determined by nerve-fibres of different orders. These consist of the fibres of the chorda tympani and lingual nerves, which subserve the gustatory functions of the anterior region of the tongue. Section or lesion of the chorda tympani within the middle ear (Bernard, Lussana, Neumann) abolishes gustation in the anterior third of the tongue, in the same manner as section of this nerve before its reunion with the lingual at the base of the brain. In man, resection of the lingual nerve deprives the anterior part of the tongue of all gustatory function (Busch, Inzoni, Vanzetti, etc.).

According to Schiff's experiments (Molesch. Unters., X. Bd., and Il Morgagni, 1870), the fibres of the chorda tympani leave the facial nerve at the ganglion geniculata, unite with the large and small superficial petrosal nerves, pass through the otic and spheno-palatine ganglia to the trigeminus and reach the brain in the second branch of this nerve. On the other hand, according to Lussana (Arch. de Physiol., 1869 and 1872), the fibres of the chorda tympani arrive at the brain with the facial, and the trunk of the trigeminus does not contain any gustatory fibres. The pathological data tend to support Schiff's opinion. In trigeminal paralysis from lesions at the base of the brain, with integrity of the facial, taste is affected in the anterior half of the tongue. Erb has collected and carefully analyzed the observations which point to this conclusion (Arch. f. Klin. Med., XV. Bd., 1874). On the other hand, according to the results of the autopsies reported by Ziemssen, Wachsmuth, etc. (excluding the cases complicated with lesions of the fifth pair), it is not probable that the trunk of the facial, at the base of the brain, contains the gustatory fibres of the anterior part of the tongue. In certain cases of isolated facial paralysis, an alteration or loss of taste is observed in the corresponding part of the tongue, a phenomenon which is due to the simultaneous affection of the fibres of the chorda tympani contained in the facial nerve.

All the preceding questions must be cleared up by physiology, clinical observation, and pathological anatomy. It now remains for us to discuss the interesting phenomena of hyperæsthesia and anæsthesia of the gustatory nerves. Hyperæsthesia of taste (hypergeusia) or the abnormally exaggerated excitability of the gustatory perceptions, is sometimes observed in marked neuropathic conditions, such as hysteria and melancholia. In order to obtain a scientific conception of this hyperæsthesia of taste, we must take into consideration Valentin's experiments (Lehrb. d. Physiol., II. Bd.) upon the minimum conditions of gustatory excitability, and also the degrees of sensibility recently established by Keppler, according to the different concentration of the solutions employed. I have recognized for a long time that in irritative conditions of the centres in very nervous, anæmic, and hysterical individuals, the application of weak ascending galvanic currents (especially upon closure and during constant action of the cathode) to the cervical or upper dorsal vertebræ, will produce a gustatory sensation of electrical origin. The current may exercise, in these cases, an exciting action upon the corresponding centres.

Anæsthesia of taste (ageusia) is observed after surgical section of the lingual nerve in neuralgias, and after traumatic or intra-cranial paralysis of the trigeminus (Hirschberg). I have also reported cases of basilar tumors (p. 102), in which, in addition to unilateral anosmia, abolition of taste was observed upon the left half of the tongue. In Boettcher's observation reported in the same chapter, the patient complained of a sensation of burning and bitterness in the mouth, and upon autopsy a tumor was found at the base of the brain, compressing the glosso-pharyngeal and pneumogastric nerves, which were in a condition of fatty degeneration. Loss of taste has also been noticed in atrophy of the glosso-pharyngeal nerve from compression by tumors situated at the jugular foramen. But in the cases reported by Longet (in his Physiologie nerveuse), the affection was complicated by lesions of the trigeminal, pneumogastric, and spinal accessory nerves. Finally, in anæsthesia, there is usually an incomplete or complete abolition of taste, according as one or both halves of the buccal cavity and tongue are anæsthetic. As a rule, we usually find, at the same time, anæsthesia of other nerves of special sense (olfactory, optic, acoustic) and of the skin, mucous membranes, and articulations.

The *prognosis* of anæsthesia of taste depends upon the nature of the primary disease. In gustatory disturbances from rheumatic facial paralysis recovery occurs spontaneously; anæsthesiæ of central origin (cerebral or spinal) present an unfavorable prognosis, but it is more favorable in hysterical ageusia. We do not as yet possess sufficient clinical data with regard to the re-establishment of the gustatory functions after surgical excision of the lingual or facial nerves to aid us in forming a prognosis. In hysterical anæsthesia of taste Duchenne has obtained good results from faradization of the tongue.

CHAPTER XLV.

B.—Diseases of the Motor Cranial Nerves (Ocular, Facial, and Hypoglossal Nerves).

a. *Diseases of the Ocular Muscles.*

The symptoms of motor irritation on the part of the ocular muscles are almost exclusively observed in cerebral and spinal affections attended with convulsions and in hysteria. Contractures of the ocular muscles may result from direct irritation originating in some pathological process, or from prolonged paralysis of the antagonists. Spasm of the muscular fibres of the iris are secondary, in rare cases, to irritative conditions of the cerebro-spinal system, which have involved the cilio-spinal centre (further details upon this point will be found in preceding chapters). Clonic spasms of the external muscles of the eye, attended either with simple oscillations or with involuntary rotatory movements, constitute the phenomenon known as nystagmus. It is always double and may be produced by central causes (meningitis, hydrocephalus), by peripheral causes, such as uterine disease, worms, dental caries, or by a disease of the refracting media of the eye or of the retina. According to Adamueck's and Ferrier's experiments, the starting-point of nystagmus is situated in the anterior tubercula quadrigemina.

The *prognosis* of these symptoms depends upon the intensity of the central causes, though, as a rule, it is not favorable. In adopting any plan of treatment, we must endeavor to relieve the irritation of the central nervous system. The relatively best results are furnished by the use of atropine, quinine, bromide of potassium, mild hydrotherapeutic measures, and by the electrical treatment to which we shall refer in discussing paralysis of the ocular muscles.

Paralysis of these muscles may be either a complication or an initial symptom of central affections, or may result from peripheral causes. Paralysis of the motor oculi communis is most frequent and is observed under the following circumstances: exposure, syphilis (affecting the nerve in its central or peripheral portions), orbital tumors, circumscribed meningeal processes at the base of the skull, tumors of the cerebral peduncles (paralysis of the oculo-motor on the side of the tumor, with a tendency to extension to the nerve on the opposite side), hæmorrhages and softening of the cerebral ganglia, the cerebral peduncles and adjacent parts, ataxia (sometimes with simultaneous paralysis of other cranial nerves), finally, diphtheria, and aneurisms of the carotid (Lebert). Paralysis of the external motor oculi, either single or double, occurs in central affections, and in rheumatism, syphilis, orbital lesions, traumatism and cerebral tumors; this also holds good of paralysis of the patheticus.

Ocular paralysis of cerebral origin may affect the muscles partially or in their totality, exists symmetrically upon both sides, or extends progressively to other ocular nerves. These paralyses very often constitute (under the form of insufficiency and diplopia) the first signs of chronic cerebral affections (tumors, basilar inflammations, cerebral aneurisms) and their true character is then recognized by the following conditions: co-existence of cephalalgia and vertigo, early appearance of neuro-retinitis (hyperæmia and swelling), more or less circumscribed or general convul-sive movements, feeling of heaviness in the limbs (usually of the hemi-plegic type); disturbance of speech, disorders of the intellectual facul-ties; later, symptoms on the part of other cranial nerves; paresis or paralysis of the limbs.

Ocular paralyses of spinal origin (frequent prodromata of ataxia) are accompanied by vague neuralgias in the branches of the cervical and brachial plexuses, and in the sciatic nerves; they are complicated by ab-normal sensations in the back, knees, or soles of the feet, by sexual irritability (pollutions, frequent erections, diminution of virile power), a tendency to fatigue, sometimes manifested upon rising from bed, extreme sensitiveness to wind and moisture, and increase of the galvanic excita-bility of the nerve-trunks. Ocular paralyses of bulbar origin (motor oculi communis and externus) result from an affection of the correspond-ing nerve nuclei in glosso-labio-pharyngeal paralysis and ataxia, and are accompanied by other characteristic signs of these affections. Ocular paralyses of a peripheral nature are usually of rheumatic origin; they develop without other symptoms of a central affection, and chiefly affect the motor oculi communis and externus. According to E. H. Weber's experiments, the ocular region, especially at the inner and outer angles, is very sensitive to heat and cold.

The *diagnosis* presents no especial difficulties in the majority of ocu-lar paralyses. In complete paralysis of the motor oculi communis the upper lid droops, and the eyeball is only moved by the external rectus and superior oblique muscles. External strabismus is therefore produced, and the eye does not accompany the unaffected one in its movements; these are supplemented by the movements of the head. The pupil is moderately dilated (paralysis of the sphincter of the iris), and the eye only accommodates itself for a single visual distance (paralysis of the tensor of the choroid). In isolated paralysis of the upper branch, ptosis is pro-duced, but the eye preserves its lateral movements. In paralysis of the inferior branch, there is no ptosis, but external strabismus (paralysis of the internal rectus) and pupillary dilatation occur. The rotatory move-ments of the eye and accommodation are equally disturbed.

Paralysis of the external oculo-motor is characterized by internal strabismus, diplopia in the outer part of the field of vision, and preserva-tion of the other movements of the eye. In paralysis of the patheticus, the position of the eye is but little modified, but sight is disturbed by the formation of two images, which are situated obliquely above one another. When the head is inclined to the sound side, the two images become con-fused; they grow clearer, on the other hand, when the head is inclined to the paralyzed side. In the beginning, the head is carried forwards (in order to command the upper part of the field of vision), but later the head is turned around the vertical axis (towards the sound side) in order to place the objects in the two symmetrical halves of the visual field. For the subtle signs of these affections, especially in complicated para-lyses, we refer to the investigations of Graefe (Arch., I. Bd., 1854) and to the clinical labors of Arlt (Krankh. d. Auges, III. Bd., 1856).

The consideration of ocular paralyses is especially interesting with reference to the clinical study of paralysis in general. The most significant fact in the delicate and harmonious play of the ocular muscles, is that the various forms and degrees of functional disturbances are due to different causes. Diplopia and strabismus may result from an inequality in the energy of the ocular muscles on both sides. One of these muscles is more readily fatigued in the various movements of one or both eyes, furnishes less force than its associate, and cannot maintain, as in the normal condition, the maximum point in its course, although the absolute amount of its mobility may not be compromised. This unilateral enfeeblement of the muscular energy may be merely temporary, as in slight cerebral irritations; it may also present alternations, corresponding to the modifications in the cerebral condition. It is especially manifested in accommodation, and in very marked convergence or divergence of the visual axes. A slight diminution in the tonicity of an ocular muscle may not be revealed by any pathological signs. If its energy diminishes markedly, we will perceive, in excursions of the eye, an abnormal position of the globe and the action of the antagonists then reveals a want of harmony in a certain direction. When the paresis is even more marked, the antagonist will maintain the upper hand even in a condition of repose, and the eye sometimes assumes persistent pathognomonic positions, which may terminate, in certain cases, in true paralysis. Finally, there are certain disorders in the associated movements of both eyes, which, in binocular vision, cause secondary functional affections on the part of the muscles.

Among *the anatomical lesions* in disorders of the ocular movements, alterations in the muscular substance are much more rarely observed than changes in the nerve-fibres and in their central origins. In fact, certain slight and initial disorders of innervation (first period of cerebral disorders or ataxia) are manifested by diplopia and strabismus, before the other parts of the muscular system have become affected. These phenomena frequently present a spontaneous retrogression, but may then return with symptoms of sensory irritation (paræsthesia, neuralgia), a fact which proves that morbid processes are slowly developing in the nerve-centres. For the same reason, tenotomy, which is sometimes performed by oculists in diplopia of this character, only furnishes incomplete results. The operation may diminish but will not cause the entire disappearance of the difference in the height of both images, since the latter vary according to the visual angle, and according to the side to which the movements are directed. In correcting the error in one direction, an aggravation of the symptom in the opposite direction is produced, and we cannot entirely compensate those disorders which are produced by insufficient innervation.

The *prognosis* of ocular paralyses is more or less unfavorable according to the nature and intensity of the affection which gives rise to them. In severe cerebral diseases (tumor, softening) there is no hope of improvement; in circumscribed meningeal processes and in hæmorrhages into the cerebral peduncle, the paralysis (of the motor oculi communis) may retrocede. The ocular paralysis in ataxia often disappears spontaneously during the first periods, though we cannot, therefore, draw any favorable conclusions with regard to the progress of the central affection. Peripheral paralysis usually presents a favorable prognosis, but the chronic forms (with atrophy and fatty degeneration of the muscles) are almost always incurable.

The *treatment* of ocular paralyses should be begun as soon as possible. Electrotherapeutics renders relatively the best services. On account of the deep situation of the ocular muscles and their slight motor irritability, faradization is less indicated than galvanization. According to Benedikt, an application of half a minute's duration should be made daily, from five to fifteen Siemens' elements being employed, according to the sensibility of the skin. The anode is placed upon the forehead. The cathode, in paralysis of the eyelid, internal rectus and superior oblique muscles, is placed in the neighborhood of the inner angle of the eye; in paralysis of the superior rectus, upon the upper border of the orbit; in paralysis of the external rectus, upon the malar bone. In mydriasis, the anode is applied over the closed lid. Eulenburg and myself have also applied the constant current directly to the sclerotic, in cases of ocular paralyses. For this purpose, very weak currents are employed (one to two Siemens' elements) with a curved electrode as thick as a knitting-needle, which is applied to the sclerotic for one or two minutes, as near as possible to the insertions of the muscles. Faradic currents are apt to produce a local hyperæmia, which, however, soon disappears.

b. *Diseases of the Facial Nerve.*

1. SPASMS OF THE MUSCLES OF THE FACE.

We frequently observe an irritable condition of the facial nerve which gives rise to mimic spasm of the face or convulsive tic, and which may result from an irritation of the nerve in the brain, from reflex irritation, or from causes which act upon the peripheral course of the nerve. In rare cases, the affection is hereditary in its nature. I am acquainted with a family in which the mother, son, daughter, and two other relatives on the maternal side, are affected with more or less extensive facial spasm. In excitement, mental diseases, affections of the brain and its envelopes, and in general neuroses (epilepsy, eclampsia, tetanus, chorea, hysteria), tonic or clonic spasms which are of central origin, occur in the face; to them we have referred, in discussing these various diseases. In the following remarks, we shall only consider the facial spasm due to reflex action or to direct irritation along the course of the nerve.

Cases of this character are due to exposure, wounds of the face, and compression of the peripheral nerve filaments. Thus, in Schuh's patient, the facial spasm (with prosopalgia) was caused by a cholesteatoma at the base of the brain; in Romberg's case, by an inflammation of the lymphatic glands along the trunk of the facial nerve; in Oppolzer's patient, by caries of the temporal bone. Remak and myself have observed several instances of peripheral facial paralysis following an otitis (probably with destruction of the Fallopian canal), in which spasms developed in the facial muscles.

Facial spasms are much more frequently of a reflex nature, from irritation of the trigeminus, dental caries, periostitis, irritation, or inflammation of the eyeball, the lids, and conjunctiva. The spasm described by Graefe, with painful points upon pressure along the peripheral course of the sensory branches, may be due to swelling of the nerves in the interior of their osseous canals. We may here mention an observation made by Remak in a case of cervico-brachial neuritis (with nodosities along the course of the nerves), of a spasm starting from the hand and arm, and extending to the neck and face on the same side. Finally, we may refer to the reflex facial spasms which are secondary to intestinal irritation (worms) and to diseases of the female sexual organs.

Facial spasms may be tonic; the rigidity of the features, the furrowing of the face, and the muscular tension observed in tetanus, after exposure, in facial paralysis, or too intense faradization, are of this character; or they may be clonic, with grimacing movements of the forehead, and eyebrows, and contractions in the lids, lips, nose, cheeks, tongue, and muscles of the neck, causing a profound change in the expression of the features and the position of the head. The contractions are then separated by intervals of relaxation, and often reappear in the muscles according to a certain rhythm, although the patients do not complain of fatigue.   Excitement and effort favor the appearance of these convulsive movements and increase their intensity.

From a *diagnostic* point of view, we must, above all, eliminate the facial spasms dependent on central affections; the latter are usually accompanied by convulsions of the limbs, and by disorders of the mental faculties and special senses.   Careful observation will determine whether the facial nerve is exposed to a direct irritation along some point of its course, or whether the spasm is produced by reflex means, in which event we will sometimes find an irritation of the sensory nerves in the neighborhood of the eye, in the branches of the trigeminus, or in the buccal cavity.

The *prognosis* is not unfavorable in cases which are recent or of slight duration, in circumscribed spasms, or in those due to rheumatic influences.   But in chronic, severe and extensive forms of convulsive tic, which have extended to the motor portions of the trigeminus and spinal accessory, positive improvement and, still less, recovery are rarely obtained.

The *treatment* of facial spasm varies according to its causation.   The cases which are due to exposure, recover from the use of active cutaneous revulsives, vapor-baths, facial douches (the water at first of a medium temperature and then gradually cooled).   Moist packs continued until the return of warmth, followed by affusions to the head in a cool half-bath, are also useful in these, and even in somewhat older and more extensive cases, in order to diminish the reflex excitability.   The same end can be obtained by subcutaneous injections of atropine and morphine, and by large doses of bromide of potassium.   In one rebellious case, Sander obtained complete relief by the hypodermic administration of strychnine; Gualla obtained similar results from the use of curare.   In two cases of facial spasms with intense blepharospasm, Romberg procured permanent recovery by section of the supra-orbital nerve.   Graefe found good results from tenotomy in cases of irritation of the eye and its annexes.   Dieffenbach cured a patient by a subcutaneous section of the muscles affected with spasm.

Remak claims to have cured facial spasm on several occasions by galvanization of the sympathetic.   Lately, Frommhold and Erb have completely relieved this affection by means of induction currents which were gradually made stronger and stronger (application of the positive pole to the neck and of the negative pole to the affected muscles).

2. PARALYSIS OF THE MUSCLES OF THE FACE.

After having discussed, in previous sections, the varieties of facial paralysis due to lesions of the facial nucleus and of the nerve during its course at the base or in the interior of the brain, we shall consider the paralyses of the seventh pair which are secondary to processes acting upon the peripheral terminations.   According to the nature and intensity of the cause, the symptomatology of facial paralysis presents important differences, the distinctions between which were first pointed out by Charles Bell and then by Romberg.   Continual progress in this direction is being made at the present time through the aid furnished by experimentation.

In order to facilitate matters, we shall classify peripheral facial paralysis according to its causes, and shall divide it into six groups, furnishing examples of each class (in the Wien. Med. Presse, 1868, I have given a detailed account of the various forms of facial paralysis, with twenty personal observations).

1. We shall first refer to facial paralysis from diseases at the base of the brain. In basilar tumors and in compression of the roots of the facial nerve at the pons varolii the nerve is affected with paralysis in the first portion of its peripheral course. In these intra-cranial forms of facial paralyses the paralysis is total, and its peripheral origin is shown by the different reactions to the galvanic and faradic currents, to which I have previously referred. Observations of this kind have been reported in detail upon pages 118 and 126, 127.

2. In facial paralysis from suppuration or hæmorrhage in the interior of the auditory apparatus, a diminution or abolition of electro-muscular contractility, and of the galvanic and faradic excitability of the nerve, is observed; these symptoms vary according to the intensity and chronicity of the facial lesion. In an observation by Erb (tubercular caries of the temporal bone, paralysis of the left facial with partial abolition of faradic excitability), the facial nerve floated free in a cavity filled with pus, and was surrounded by a mass which was intimately adherent to the neurilemma (connective tissue with scattered round cells). Fibrillary connective tissue with oval nuclei was also found between the nerve-fibres and, in a portion of the fibres, there was destruction of the myeline and production of fat granules. Some branches of the facial and of the pes anserinus presented a similar degeneration. In the muscles there was increase of the interfibrillary connective tissue, formation of nuclei and atrophy of the muscular fibres, a portion of which were in a condition of waxy degeneration.

In the chronic cases which I have observed in adults, I have always obtained some improvement. One case of acute facial paralysis, following otitis, recovered completely by the use of weak astringent injections and iodide of potassium. In children, I have seen the facial hemiplegia soon disappear, after the auricular affection (intense hyperæmia or transudation into the Fallopian aqueduct) has improved. The fibres of the facial are affected in otitis to a variable degree. I have published one case in which the paralysis, which had lasted for twenty-two years, followed a purulent catarrh of the middle ear, with perforation of the tympanum, from which the patient had suffered during childhood (the centre of the tympanum was occupied by a thick cicatrix, Politzer). The faradic and galvanic excitability were abolished in the upper muscles of the face, but were still present, to a slight extent, in the lower muscles. The trunk of the nerve was completely insensible to galvanization; when the temporal region was touched, contractions of the lips were produced. Galvanic treatment merely improved the play of the features.

Facial paralysis from hæmorrhage into the Fallopian aqueduct (usually after a blow upon the ear) is accompanied at the onset by loss of consciousness, a sanguineous discharge from the ear, followed by enfeeblement of hearing and often by deviation of the uvula and palate towards the paralyzed side. In lesions of the petrosus superficialis major there is obliquity of the uvula and pillars of the palate (which also happens in other facial paralyses); but simple deviation of the uvula, especially when the latter is very long and touches the base of the tongue, is very often observed in a condition of health.

3. Rheumatic facial paralyses are the most numerous and extended of all varieties due to external causes (the ocular branch is almost always affected at the same time). According to E. H. Weber's experiments, the cheeks, as well as the eyelids, are also remarkable for their sensitiveness to cold and heat. We meet with patients who have several times

suffered from rheumatic paralysis of both halves of the face, but very rarely upon one side alone.

According to Wachsmuth, irritation from cold will affect the vaso-motor-fibres, which are very much exposed at their entrance into the stylo-mastoid foramen. This causes a retardation, perhaps even suppression of the flow of blood to the facial nerve, with rapid abolition of excitability, formication and metallic taste. According to Cl. Bernard's experiments, these phenomena are dependent upon the fibres of the sympathetic, which unite with the chorda tympani at various points.

The symptoms of unilateral facial paralysis are evident, to a certain extent, at the first glance. The paralyzed cheek is sunken, flaccid, and expressionless, the characteristic grooves and ridges are effaced. The forehead, upon the paralyzed side, appears smoother and higher, cannot be made to frown, and the eyebrows cannot approach one another. On account of the paralysis of the orbicularis palpebrærum, the lids cannot be closed voluntarily; the lower lid droops, the palpebral fissure is open (lagophthalmos), the eye weeps freely; the wing of the nose is flattened, the labio-nasal fold is effaced, the labial commissure drawn towards the sound side; on account of the unilateral paralysis of the orbicularis oris, the mouth is only partially closed, so that the saliva and liquids flow out at the side. The movements of the lips in whistling, blowing, sucking, or expectorating, and the pronunciation of labials, are embarrassed or rendered entirely impossible. On account of the relaxation of the buccinator, food readily lodges between the cheek and teeth, and the patient is then obliged to remove it with the fingers (cats also perform this movement with the paws after section of the facial). Every marked effort of the facial muscles, as in laughing and talking, causes a more decided appearance of deformity.

Facial paralysis, like peripheral paralysis in general, presents great variations in the symptoms, which have been studied by Ziemssen (in his work upon Electricity, 1866), and more recently by Erb (Arch. f. klin. Med., XV. Bd., 1 H., 1874).

The peculiarities and modifications of the electrical phenomena in rheumatic facial paralysis are interesting, not only from a theoretical but also from a practical point of view.

Electrical exploration in rheumatic facial paralysis enables us to determine various degrees of change in the nerves and muscles. In mild forms (from simple swelling of the periosteum in the Fallopian aqueduct), the muscles and nerve-fibres do not present, even after the lapse of a week, any appreciable modification of their faradic and galvanic excitability. In moderately severe forms, the electrical excitability of the nerve-fibres is simply diminished, the farado-muscular contractility is abolished, and the galvano-muscular contractility increased; in all these cases, there are slight changes in the nerves, which affect their electrical excitability but slightly, while in the muscles profound changes develop with which we are already acquainted. In severe forms (with facial neuritis), both nerves and muscles present very marked changes. In the nerves, the faradic and galvanic excitability diminish from the beginning of the paralysis until they completely disappear; the nerve may, nevertheless, preserve its galvanic excitability in some branches. The return of the excitability of the nerves occupies a longer or shorter period, irrespective of their excitability to the will. In the muscles, the faradic and galvanic reactions diminish at the beginning of the paralysis. From the end of the second week, the faradic excitability disappears, while the galvanic excitability increases (Baierlacher, Schulz, Neumann, Ziemssen, Rosenthal, Erb, Eulenburg). According to Erb, the mechanical excitability is also increased. In proportion as improvement progresses, the effects of the galvanic current diminish, and the reactions of the muscles to the faradic current and to the will usually increase.

Neumann and Koenigsberg first pointed out the following facts with regard to the physiological reason of these peculiar electrical phenomena (they are also produced in lead and traumatic paralyses,: if there is absence of farado-muscular with preservation of galvano-muscular excitability, this peculiar phenomenon is recognized in a definite manner, not by currents of different direction which rapidly follow one another, nor by reversal of the current, but only by one of a certain duration, such as the constant galvanic current. If the galvanic current is rendered almost instantaneous by means of any mechanism, no contractions will be produced. Similar peculiarities were then observed by Neumann upon exhausted muscles and by Bruecke upon frogs poisoned with curare. Much weaker induction currents were required in a foot which had been previously tied, than in one which had been subjected to the action of the poison, while the latter, on the other hand, reacted to weak currents of a galvanic pile. The galvanic current of a rapidly rotated Volta's wheel produced tetanus of the intact limb while the poisoned limb remained quiet.

The *prognosis* of rheumatic facial paralyses is usually favorable. In children and in young, healthy individuals, facial paralysis from exposure often recovers spontaneously. In these forms, no marked modification of faradic and galvanic contractility, or of the excitability of the nerve-fibres, is observed during the first and second weeks. The moderate forms (with slight diminution of the excitability of the nerves, abolition of the faradic reaction of the muscles, increase of their galvanic reaction) terminated favorably at the end of four or six weeks. In severe cases (with complete abolition of the excitability of the nerves and abnormal electrical reactions in the paralyzed muscles), there are serious disturbances of nutrition (neuritis), the repair of which demands weeks or even months (six to nine months). Certain facial paralyses of the latter class pass into a chronic stage and become incurable. Electrical treatment will then merely improve the play of the features and diminish the distressing sensation of muscular tension. The *treatment* consists, in recent cases, of vapor baths followed by a facial douche of moderate temperature, and the internal administration of iodide of potassium. In old forms, strychnia, administered with the necessary precautions, gives good results (endermic or hypodermic method, doses of two to five milligrammes in adults, and less in children). But electrical treatment constitutes the most efficient remedy at our command.

In recent cases, we may employ the secondary induction current, for three to five minutes at a sitting, to the paralyzed muscles or nerve-fibres. We must avoid the use of currents with strong tension and rapid interruptions, since they may produce electrical muscular stiffness from over-stimulation. In order to relieve deformities which may have been acquired during treatment, we may use, according to Remak, stabile constant currents of ten to twenty Siemens' elements. Recent contractures may disappear under the use of this measure, but old ones can only be corrected by myotomy or by producing faradic contracture of the homologous muscle (Duchenne). In applying the galvanic current, the anode is placed upon the cervical vertebræ and the cathode upon the paralyzed muscles. In order to stimulate the facial nerve or its branches the anode is placed in the mastoid fossa and the cathode is moved over the pes anserinus or the other nerve-fibres (upon the temple for the superior muscles, outside of the zygomatic arch for the lids and upper lip, upon the ramus of the jaw for the chin and lower lip. (Fig. 20.)

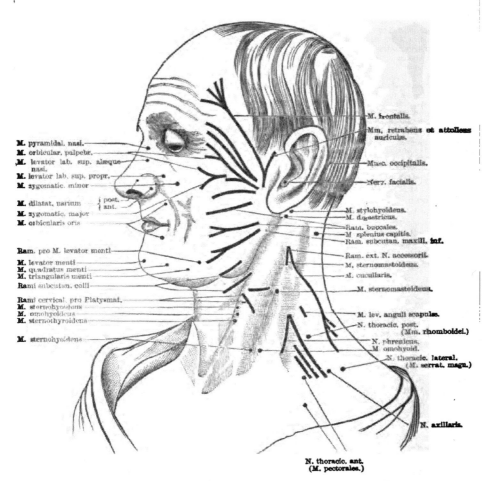

M. frontalis.

Mm. retrahens et attollens
auriculæ.

M. pyramidal. nasi.

M. orbicular. palpebr.

M. levator lab. sup. alæque
nasi.

M. levator lab. sup. propr.

M. zygomatic. minor

M. dilatat. narium { post. ant.

M. zygomatic. major

M. orbicularis oris

Musc. occipitalis.

Nerv. facialis.

M. stylohyoideus.

M. digastricus.

Ram. buccales.

M. splenius capitis.

Ram. subcutan. maxill. inf.

Ram. pro M. levator menti

M. levator menti

M. quadratus menti

M. triangularis menti

Rami subcutan. colli

Ram. ext. N. accessorii.

M. sternomastoideus.

M. cucullaris.

M. sternomastoideus.

Rami cervical. pro Platysmat.

M. sternohyoideus

M. omohyoideus

M. sternothyroideus

M. lev. anguli scapulæ.

N. thoracic. post.
(Mm. rhomboidei.)

M. sternohyoideus

N. phrenicus.

M. omohyoid.

N. thoracic. lateral.
(M. serrat. magn.)

N. axillaris.

N. thoracic. ant.
(M. pectorales.)

Fig. 20.—Motor points of face, showing the position of the electrodes in electrization of the facial
nerves and muscles. The anode is placed in the mastoid fossa, and the cathode upon the part indicated in
the figure.

Galvanic stimulation of the buccal cavity (the anode upon the mucous membrane of the cheek, the cathode upon the paralyzed muscles) recommends itself, according to my observations, on account of the more ready penetration of the current into the muscular layers, and because it requires a smaller number of elements to produce contractions, a matter of importance in the neighborhood of the eye. In obstinate cases, which are complicated by deformities of the face, it is advisable to alternate galvanization of the nerves with faradization of the muscles. Landois and Mosler cured one of these cases (Berl. klin. Wschr., 1868) by simultaneously applying a descending galvanic current, and an induced current at the negative pole (electro-tonic faradization).

4. Traumatic facial paralysis results from various lesions, such as puncture, sword-cut, gunshot wound, blows upon the cheeks (Brodie), compression by forceps, section of the nerve in operations, compression by tumors and deep cicatrices (as in suppurations of the parotid). According to the intensity of the traumatic cause, there will be complete facial paralysis or merely paralysis of certain branches and of the corresponding muscles.

In the anthropoid apes, in whom the mouth is also closed by a sphincter, facial paralysis acts as in man (Shaw and Bell), while in dogs, cats, and rabbits, section of the facial nerve causes a deviation of the face towards the paralyzed side. Schiff explains this by the fact that there is a solution of continuity in the sphincter of the upper lip, which thus forms a sort of natural hare-lip. In two half-grown rabbits, in whom Bruecke (Vorles. u. Physiol., II. Bd., 1873) had extirpated the facial nerve at its exit from the Fallopian aqueduct, Schauta found, at the end of several months, a paralysis of the corresponding half of the face with loss of faradic and increase of galvanic excitability. In one of these animals, the paralyzed muscles were found atrophied with disappearance of the transverse striæ and production of connective tissue.

To judge from two of my observations, and from a case published by Ziemssen, the voluntary movements and faradic excitability disappear in those muscles to which the injured nerve-fibres are distributed, with preservation and often with increase of the galvanic excitability in the first weeks which follow section of the facial.

These remarks are confirmed by Erb's observations upon beginning muscular degenerations following section of the nerves.

The nerve-fibres lose their irritability to both currents. Stimulation of the nerve-trunk only produces contractions in those muscles which respond to the faradic current; some muscles react to the will but not to electrical stimulation.

As the conducting power of the nerves is gradually re-established, their electrical irritability usually reappears more quickly in the trunk than in its branches. In the beginning, there may be increase of reaction to the galvanic current and of electro-muscular sensibility.

Pathological data agree with the results of experimentation. After killing the nerves with curare or the vapor of conicine, we also find the nervous irritability disappear, although the muscles preserve their electrical reactions (Schiff, Wundt, Fick, Bruecke).

Traumatic facial paralyses are very rebellious and require months for the completion of recovery, voluntary motion being re-established more rapidly than the electrical excitability. The best method of treatment is the alternate use of the constant and induced currents.

5. Syphilitic facial paralyses, when they result from an affection of the

cerebral substance, assume the characteristics of intra-cerebral paralyses. On the other hand, specific lesions of the facial nerve at the base of the brain are of a peripheral nature, according to the electrical investigations of Ziemssen (Virch. Arch., 13 Bd., 1858).

In the patient in question, after the appearance of secondary syphilis, diplopia developed, followed by complete paralysis of the right facial nerve, the patheticus, both external motor-oculi, incomplete paralysis of the facial and motor oculi communis on the left side, and of the majority of the flexors and extensors of the hand. Faradic exploration showed an abolition of electrical contractility in the paralyzed muscles, and a considerable diminution in the muscles which were merely paretic (this confirmed the diagnosis of an extra-cerebral syphilitic affection). At the autopsy, the remains of a chronic inflammation of the pia mater were found at the base of the brain, attended with exudation and formation of connective tissue, the retraction of which had strangulated the facial nerve ; in the central end there was a moderate accumulation of fatty granules, and. in the peripheral portion a degeneration corresponding to the compression ; the paralyzed muscles had undergone fatty degeneration.

In one of my observations, after several relapses of syphilis, periostitis occurred in the tibia and in the mastoid process of the left temporal bone; the left facial nerve was paralyzed, with the exception of its upper branch. The nerve-trunk did not respond to the faradic current, and the muscles only contracted feebly. Davaine published a case which was similar to this in several respects.

In another case observed at Prof. Sigmund's clinic, the faradic excitability of the nerve-trunk, like that of the muscles, was abolished in the paralyzed half of the face. Although the galvanic current produced muscular contractions, the irritability of the nerve-trunks had, on the other hand, considerably diminished, and was only manifested with a very strong current (twenty-four Siemens' elements). These facts led me to diagnose a morbid process compressing the nerve-trunk itself (probably in the bony canal of the nerve). The examination of the ear had been previously made by a specialist, Dr. Gruber, who determined the existence of syphilitic otitis with exudation into the Fallopian aqueduct, but without lesion of the tympanum.

6. I have seen one case of diphtheritic facial paralysis (*vide* p. 149, Vol. I.), in which electrical exploration gave the same results as in peripheral paralysis.

We shall now mention the principal complications which may occur in the various kinds of peripheral facial paralysis, and which are important in diagnosing the position at which the nerve-fibres are affected.

a. Paralysis of the posterior auricular nerve, with abolition of the functions of the occipital nerve and of the retractor muscles of the ear on the paralyzed side. Erb has recently discovered (loc. cit.) a much more characteristic sign of this paralysis, viz.: abolition of faradic and increase of the galvanic excitability of the muscles. This paralysis indicates that the lesion is situated outside of the Fallopian aqueduct.

b. Paralysis of the chorda tympani: According to the views expressed in the preceding chapters, the fibres of the chorda tympani, contained in the facial, furnish the sense of taste to the anterior portion of the tongue. Numerous examples of facial hemiplegia attended with abolition or diminution of taste in the corresponding half of the tongue, are found in old and recent medical literature.

I have reported (W. Med. Presse, 1868, obs. 7) a case of rheumatic facial paralysis on the left side, with cephalalgia, noises in the ears, and tingling in the tongue; upon rubbing the left half of the tongue with powdered sugar, or upon smearing it with syrup, the patient perceived an acid taste; crystals of sulphate of magnesia appeared acid and bitter, and the tincture of opium also tasted bitter; on the right side, gustation was normal. The salivary secretion is sometimes diminished (with a sensation of unilateral dryness), a fact which is explained by the simultaneous implication of the secretory nerves which the facial sends to the parotid and submaxillary glands. The preceding symptoms indicate that the lesion is situated in the Fallopian canal, above the point of emergence of the chorda tympani.

c. The paralysis of the nerve supplying the stapedius below the geniculate ganglion produces hyperakusia (Willis) or hyperæsthesia of hearing, and has been observed by Roux, Wolf, and Landouzy, and more recently by Hitzig and Lucae. The subject was discussed in detail in a preceding chapter on neuroses of the acoustic nerve.

d. Paralysis of the nervus petrosus superficialis major: In addition to the paralysis of the external muscles of the face, a deviation of the velum palati with difficulty of movement in it has been observed, together with an alteration in taste. The site of the lesion is at the intumescentia gangliformis, at the entrance of the gustatory fibres and exit of the motor fibres of the pillars of the palate. Mere deviation of the uvula is unimportant, as we have previously shown.

e. We may finally mention difficulty of hearing with abnormal acoustic reactions. Acoustic hyperæsthesia with abnormal reactions is also observed at times.

In conclusion, it only remains for us to discuss double facial paralysis.

Bilateral paralysis, which was recognized by Bell, Sanders, Grisolle, and Romberg, has been more thoroughly investigated by Davaine, Trousseau, and Wachsmuth. According to Schiff, if both facial nerves are divided, the animals are unable to close the mouth, the cheeks remain flaccid even during the movements of mastication, the food introduced into the mouth in part falls outside, while another part lodges between the cheeks and gums. Hence arises great difficulty in the formation of the alimentary bolus and in deglutition. In man, facial diplegia causes immobility of the face and fixity of the features; the cheeks and labial commissures are drooping; the alæ nasi, deprived of mobility, collapse mechanically during deep inspirations, together with the cheeks, which are also puffed out by the expired air. The nasal character of the voice and the defective pronunciation of the labials render speech almost unintelligible; when the head is slightly bent forwards, the salvia trickles out between the opened lips. Mastication and deglutition are greatly interfered with, the food is arrested in its passage and the patients are obliged to push it into the pharynx with the fingers.

The central form of facial diplegia is sometimes observed in labio-glosso-pharyngeal paralysis (from implication of the facial nuclei); it may exist to a less marked extent in certain chronic cerebral diseases. The paralysis may also be peripheral and due to various intra-cranial, but extra-cerebral, affections of the facial nerves. Thus, basilar tumors, exostoses of the basilar process, aneurisms, and meningeal exudations, may produce atrophic degeneration of the facial nerves from compression, and the adjacent nerves do not always escape. According to Jaccoud and Pierreson (Arch. Gen., II. Bd., 1867) the facial, like other nerves, sometimes atrophies spontaneously from hyperplasia of the connective-tissue and development of amyloid corpuscles. Peripheral facial diplegia may also be due to disease of the petrous portion of the temporal bone (inflammation, caries, necrosis, or syphilitic otitis).

In a case observed by Ehrmann, double facial paralysis followed bilateral tubercular otitis. The autopsy revealed simply caries of the middle ear, the Fallopian canals being perfectly intact; the neurilemma of the nerves contained a large number of pus globules (participation of the sheath of the nerve in the inflammation of the middle ear). Finally, facial diplegia may be of rheumatic origin, the cold either acting at the same time upon both halves of the face, or the paralysis involving first one side and then the other.

The diagnosis of peripheral facial diplegia does not present any difficulties, if we are able to eliminate central causes. In double facial paralysis of rheumatic origin, the movements of the tongue and the timbre of the voice are unaltered, and the disturbances of deglutition diminish when the nares are closed. The *prognosis* depends upon the nature of the disease. *Treatment* may be ineffectual in certain peripheral forms. In a case of double paralysis of the face published by Baerwinkel (Arch. f. Heilk., I. Bd., 1867), the paralyzed muscles on the right side were insensible to the faradic, but sensible to the galvanic current; on the left side, the electrical reactions were normal. Cephalalgia, diplopia, and uncertainty of gait were also present. After ten months of electrical treatment, recovery was almost complete.

c. *Diseases of the Hypoglossal Nerve.*

Spasms involving the territory of the hypoglossal nerve are very rarely of a peripheral nature. As a rule, they accompany serious disorders, such as epilepsy, hysteria, chorea, meningitis. Partial clonic spasms (fibrillary tremor) sometimes occur in progressive muscular atrophy, neuralgias of the lingual nerve and convulsive tic. The spasms of the tongue are, therefore, due either to central or peripheral causes.

Paralysis of the hypoglossal nerve is also rarely of peripheral origin, as in tumors at the base of the brain, compression of the hypoglossus at its point of emergence, and in extirpation of tumors of the tongue, when some fibres of the nerve have been injured in the operation. Paralysis of the tongue is usually unilateral, of central origin, and is observed in hæmorrhage, embolism, softening, cerebral tumors, progressive paralysis of the insane; in labio-glosso-pharyngeal paralysis, it may present various stages up to complete abolition of motion; in progressive muscular atrophy, it is accompanied by signs of atrophy.

After section of the hypoglossus in animals and in unilateral glossoplegia in man, the tongue when protruded deviates to the diseased side. Schiff attributes this fact to the predominance of the genio-glossus on the sound side, which directs the tip of the tongue towards the opposite side. When the tongue is drawn backwards, the action of the stylo-glossus draws it towards the sound side.

Paralysis of the tongue, in its various forms, should not be mistaken for those cases in which language is affected by disorders of co-ordination, or by disturbance of the centrifugal conducting power, as in localized affections of the motor ganglia, pons and floor of the fourth ventricle (lesions of the nucleus of the hypoglossus or of its ascending root-fibres).

The *prognosis* is unfavorable in the majority of cases. The *treatment* of lingual paralysis consists in the restoration of the energy of the nerve-centres. The functions of the tongue may sometimes be improved by the prudent application of the galvanic current through the head, or by combining local faradization or galvanization of the tongue and hypoglossus with invigorating hydro-therapeutic measures.

CHAPTER XLVI.

C.—DISEASES OF THE MIXED CRANIAL NERVES.

(Trigeminus, Pneumogastric, Spinal Accessory.)

a. *Diseases of the Trigeminal Nerve.*

THE various affections of the fifth pair of nerves include neuralgia or anæsthesia of the sensory branches, and tonic or clonic spasms, and paralysis of the third branch.

1. NEURALGIA OF THE TRIGEMINUS.

Neuralgia of the different branches of the trigeminal nerve (prosopalgia, facial pain of Fothergill, tic-douloureux) has attracted the attention of physicians since a very early period.

The *anatomical changes* in the nerve or its surrounding tissues in prosopalgia, embrace the following lesions : chronic hyperæmia and redness of the neurilemma, thickening of the neurilemma following neuritis, partial granular degeneration of the myeline, enlargements and nodosities upon resected branches of the nerve (connective tissue enclosing the nerve fibres as in the enlargement of the nerves in amputation stumps), periostitis, concentric hypertrophy (Gross), osteophytes or caries of the osseous canals, exostoses upon the roots of the wisdom tooth (Thompson, Glasgow Med. Journ., 1867), very rarely exostoses in the cranial cavity or upon the petrous portion of the temporal bone, which penetrate into the Gasserian ganglion (Chouppe). Finally, inflammatory changes may be found in the various ganglia of the trigeminus: the spheno-palatine ganglion (Carnochan), Gasserian ganglion (Wedl's case, with calcareous degeneration and considerable development of vessels), neuroma of the Gasserian ganglion with a prolongation through the dilated foramen ovale, finally, compression of the trigeminus by cerebral neoplasms. In many cases of prosopalgia, no organic changes were found in the nerves, but the number of these cases will diminish as microscopical examinations are more frequently made.

Among the *symptoms* of tic-douloureux, pain is the most important. Very frequently, a more or less disagreeable sensation may exist for a long time before the development of a true paroxysm. In some cases, however, the paroxysm develops suddenly. The pain is usually extremely violent, and the patients describe it as burning, piercing, shooting, or compare it to a concussion of the brain. The pains often appear spontaneously or they are produced by excitement, slight friction, or pricking of the cheeks, a gentle current of air, or even by speaking. One of the most distressing forms is that in which the pains are called forth by the movements of mastication and deglutition. The patients hardly dare swallow a little fluid food and neglect cleansing the mouth, thus causing a bad odor from the accumulation of tartar.

The pain of prosopalgia may be continuous, in which event it is manifested with less violence, and by a sensation of compression or burning, or it may appear in the form of dreaded paroxysms, increasing in intensity and frequency, and very frequently radiating from certain points towards the centre, more rarely towards the periphery. The continuous pains are usually found in certain situations which have been called *puncta dolorosa* by Valleix. These include, in the course of the first branch: a frontal point at the emergence of the frontal nerve, a palpebral point upon the upper lid, a supraorbital point, corresponding to the nerve of the same name, a point at the outer angle of the eye, pertaining to the lachrymal nerve, and two points upon the lateral surface of the nose, an upper one, corresponding to the inner angle of the eye and along the subtrochlear nerve, and a lower one, at the union of the nasal bone and triangular cartilage, corresponding to the ethmoidal nerve. In the territory of the second branch are found: the infraorbital point (for the nerve of the same name), a malar point over the zygomatic arch, a maxillary point at the anterior border of the masseter muscle (corresponding to a filament of the pterygo-palatine nerve), a palatine point for the descending palatine nerve, and a gengival point upon the anterior or posterior surface of the gums, corresponding to the anterior, median, or posterior branches of the superior dental nerve. In the course of the third branch are found the following: a temporal point in front of the tragus, a parietal point at the union of the frontal, superficial temporal and occipital nerves, a maxillary point in the region of the temporo-maxillary articulation, a lingual point for the lingual nerve, and a mental point upon the chin.

Frequently, the patients indicate of their own accord these painful points, pressure over which causes excessive sensibility, which may increase until a paroxysm appears. Painful points are also found upon pressure over the spinous and transverse processes of the upper cervical vertebræ (Trousseau's "point apophysaire"). The attacks of pain usually start from the *puncta dolorosa*, which we have mentioned, and then extend in a centripetal or centrifugal direction. In certain cases, however, these points are not noticed by the patients, nor can they be detected in the intervals between the paroxysms. These forms of neuralgia are usually of central origin.

The motor and vaso-motor complications of prosopalgia consist of reflex facial spasms upon the affected side (more rarely on the healthy side), and of irradiated sensations in the occiput, neck, shoulder, thorax, and limbs. Prosopalgia is also accompanied by disorders of secretion, in consequence of the relations of the branches of the trigeminus with the vaso-motor fibres. In neuralgia of the first branch, they consist of an increase in the lachrymal secretion, especially at the close of the paroxysm, from relaxation of the vessels of the lachrymal gland; in affections of the second and third branches, of a hypersecretion of nasal mucus and saliva, the vessels of the Schneiderian membrane being innervated by the vaso-motor fibres of the trigeminus, and the latter stimulating, by reflex means, the submaxillary gland (according to Ludwig's and Rahn's experiments). A secretion of sweat also occurs upon the affected side of the face, the trigeminus containing nerve-fibres going to the cutaneous vessels.

Other vaso-motor disturbances may also occur in neuralgias of the fifth pair, such as swelling, redness, elevation of temperature upon the affected side (Schuh), and a tendency to erysipelatous inflammations (Anstie). Zona, discoloration of the face, and roughening or falling out of the hairs, are sometimes observed. Ophthalmia, due to an affection of the trigeminus, has been discussed in the chapter on tumors of the base of the brain, but we shall again recur to this subject in detail. Among trophic disorders Romberg, Notta, Brodie, and Niemeyer have observed an hypertrophy of the affected cheek. Unilateral atrophy of the face, which rarely accompanies neuralgia, will be discussed in the chapter on trophoneuroses.

The *causes* of the disease are as follows: tumors of the middle cerebral fossa and of the base of the brain (with neuralgia in case of prolonged irritation, and anæsthesia in degeneration of the nerves), foci of suppuration, tumors of the pons, aneurisms of the carotid in the sella turcica (Romberg), and morbid processes around the Gasserian ganglion. While I was a student I saw, at Schuh's clinic, a case of prosopalgia of nine years' duration; the mylo-hyoid nerve was resected, but the internal maxillary artery was cut during the operation and the hæmorrhage necessitated the ligature of the primary carotid. The patient died at the end of four months from purulent infection, and, upon autopsy, a steatoma was found as large as a hazel-nut at the point of emergence of the trigeminus, which the tumor surrounded like a ring. Facial neuralgias sometimes occur in diseases of the cervical cord, ataxia and hysteria (irritation of the fibres of the trigeminus which originate in the posterior column and most inferior portion of the medulla oblongata). A frequent cause of neuralgia is periostitis of the bony orifices traversed by the trigeminus. According to Hyrtl, the branches which pass through narrow osseous canals (supraorbital, infraorbital, zygomatic, superior and inferior dental) are often affected with neuralgia, while those which have free exit through the spheno-palatine fissure are rarely involved. We have previously referred to exostoses of the cranial bones and maxillæ as causes of this affection; tumors of the jaw may also act in the same manner. Exposure constitutes the most frequent among the occasional causes.

The greatest number of neuralgias and their relapses occur in the cold months. Next to sciatica, neuralgia of the trigeminus is most frequently produced by cold. Traumatism (foreign bodies, cicatrices following wounds of the face) is a very rare cause of this affection.

Women, especially in early life, are more subject to tic-douloureux than men. The largest number of cases occur between the ages of thirty and fifty years. Nervous individuals of an irritable temperament possess an especial predisposition. Examples of heredity are very rare. We sometimes observe at an advanced age intense facial neuralgias, accompanied by reflex symptoms and an abnormal mental irritability (Trousseau's epileptiform neuralgia). Several times, also, I have seen old men (sixty to seventy years of age) suffering from melancholia, complicated with neuralgia of the dental branches; these cases must be attributed to senile changes in the tissues (osseous canals or arteries). In malarial districts supraorbital neuralgia (metapodynia) is often observed, running the course of intermittent fever, and is regarded by physicians as a latent fever. But the enlargement of the spleen is almost always wanting in these cases, and when it exists, may be due to a previous attack of intermittent fever. Furthermore, the effects of quinine do not establish the identity of these neuralgias with intermittent fever, but the drug merely acts as in periodical affections in general. It is more proper, therefore, to admit that the influence of malaria may give rise to certain neuralgias which, by their febrile and intermittent course, present analogies with intermittent fever, but do not constitute a latent form of the latter disease.

The course of trigeminal neuralgias is extremely variable. The acute forms present a very regular type; on the other hand the chronic forms have an irregular course and are composed of a series of attacks following one another rapidly, varying from thirty seconds to one minute in duration, and forming in reality a very long paroxysm. The patients may be thus tormented for days or weeks, then the pains disappear for a period which is often quite long, to reappear again under the influence of change of weather, a draught of air or mental excitement. Not infrequently the disease is followed by general excessive hyperæsthesia or by psychical disorders. The patient is often a veritable martyr and is sometimes led to commit suicide.

The *diagnosis* of tic-douloureux frequently offers great difficulties, less to detect the neuralgia than to determine its nature and origin. The pains correspond to the anatomical distribution of the trigeminus, occur in paroxysms, and often present (but not always) certain painful points. Its intra-cerebral origin is chiefly recognized by the following signs: absence of the *puncta dolorosa* in the intervals between the paroxysms, appearance of these points during the paroxysms, general excessive hyperæsthesia, extensive reflex muscular contractions (in the face and limbs) during and after the attacks, psychical excitement or depression. When the lesion is extra-cranial, the nerve-fibres accessible to exploration usually present, outside of the paroxysms, some point which is peculiarly sensitive, and pressure upon which may even produce a paroxysm; the pain usually occupies the distribution of a certain nerve-fibre and examination sometimes reveals a peripheral affection. In many cases, the diagnosis is merely possible with a greater or less amount of probability, and we can only arrive at greater certainty after prolonged observation.

A certain amount of attention is often necessary in order to avoid mistaking prosopalgia for other analogous affections. It is most frequently mistaken for the pain arising from decayed teeth, but a careful exploration of the teeth by means of a sound or cold water will soon disclose the diseased tooth or root. If the latter is removed, the pains will disappear, while true trigeminal neuralgia is aggravated by extraction of the teeth. Inflammation of the temporo-maxillary joint, or of the antrum of Highmore during an attack of coryza, may give rise to acute pains in the face, but they are not situated along definite nerve-fibres. Their origin is furthermore recognized by the detection of swelling or distention of the inflamed parts, and the pains disappear after spontaneous or artificial opening of the abscess. Migraine (hemicrania) is distinguished from tic-douloureux by the gradual increase of the pains, the shorter duration of the attacks, their much rarer appearance, their renewal at the menses, the frequent coexistence of vaso-motor disturbances, the unilateral dilatation of the pupil, by the frequent appearance of vomiting, and finally by the absence of painful points which are usually replaced by circumscribed hyperæsthesia. The pains which radiate into the face and are sometimes observed in chronic leucorrhœa and uterine diseases, are readily distinguished from prosopalgia by the character of the local phenomena, the absence of *puncta dolorosa*, and by the general hyperæsthesia. In Cerise's case (Annal. Med. Psychol., May, 1845), the facial pain disappeared after the extirpation of a fibroid tumor of the uterus.

Neuralgias of the fifth pair, due to cerebral tumors, are complicated by diplopia, vertigo, chronic cephalalgia, symptoms of neuro-retinitis, spasms and paralyses in the limbs; there are no *puncta dolorosa* in the face. In basilar tumors, in which trigeminal neuralgia usually terminates in anæsthesia, other adjacent nerves are affected at the same time, and we observe the tumor symptoms with which we are already acquainted. Facial pains in spinal affections are accompanied by vague neuralgias in the arms or legs, genital irritation, motor exhaustion, etc. Hysterical facial neuralgias occur in company with other characteristic symptoms of hysteria, and saturnine pains are combined with other signs of lead poisoning.

The *prognosis* varies according to the nature, intensity, and chronicity of the neuralgia. The central forms will not yield spontaneously unless the nerve undergoes destruction. Acute, periodical facial neuralgias offer the best chances of recovery. Among the chronic cases of an irregular type, those in which the pain occupies a circumscribed region and in which there are *puncta dolorosa*, may be improved or cured by a surgical operation. In the absence of these symptoms and especially when the affection has lasted for a long time, the chances of recovery diminish, and many of these cases continue for life. As a rule, the proportion of recoveries is greater in young than in old people.

A fatal termination is extremely rare, but the pain, insomnia, and insufficient alimentation may sometimes give rise to a serious diminution of the vital energies. In certain cases in which surgical interference has been resorted to, death has been due to gangrene of the wound after operation, to metastatic abscesses, or to erysipelas with meningitis.

In the *treatment* of prosopalgia we must pay especial attention to the nature of the affection. In recent and periodical neuralgias, benefit is usually derived from large doses of quinine. If good results are not obtained after this treatment has been continued for three or four days, it is useless to continue it. Sometimes the combination of quinine and opium succeeds better; finally, if this also fails, we may prescribe five or six drops of Fowler's solution every three hours. If there are signs of periostitis, resort must be had to iodide of potassium and to local bleedings. Iron is preferable in chlorotic patients, in whom facial neuralgia is merely a radiated pain. Metallic preparations have almost entirely lost their former repute. Ointments of veratrine (Turnbull, 0.10–0.20 to four grammes) or of aconitine (Watson, 0.07–0.15 to four grammes), applied for several minutes over the seat of pain, merely produce momentary relief. Fumigations with substances rich in essential oils, practised daily for several months upon the affected side of the face, have a soothing effect. I saw one case recover after this treatment had been continued for nine months.

In chronic forms of an irregular course, derivatives are still frequently employed (revulsive plasters, Valleix' flying blisters, Jobert's transverse cauterization, frictions with croton oil). Subcutaneous injections of a strong solution of nitrate of silver are also employed in the neighborhood of the affected nerve; their effects are nil or only of short duration. In the majority of cases, hypodermic injections of morphine constitute a useful palliative measure. They promptly relieve the violence of the pains and may be repeated two or three times daily for months without the disturbances of digestion, which are almost always produced by the internal administration of opium in large doses. But, after a certain length of time, the subcutaneous injections also lose their efficacy. I have seen two cases of frontal and supraorbital neuralgia, lasting for several months, which yielded after the use of subcutaneous injections of morphine for a few weeks. The disease has not reappeared at the end of two years.

Among the newer remedies, electricity and hydrotherapeutics are most frequently employed. The induced current must be applied with caution, on account of its great tension; the painful points are touched with an electrode in the form of a brush, until a slight erythema appears. In using the less irritating constant current, the anode is applied over the cervical vertebræ or under the mastoid processes, and the thinner cathode is placed over the *puncta dolorosa* (with an increasing current). The influence of the galvanic current upon the circulatory and trophic phenomena is sometimes successful even in inveterate forms, as I have observed in several cases and as has been confirmed by Niemeyer, Wiesner, etc. In the majority of cases, we at least obtain some improvement; the attacks become less frequent and intense and, if a relapse occurs, the patients demand a renewal of the treatment. But, in certain chronic forms, electrical treatment fails completely. Hydrotherapeutic measures (daily moist packs from fifteen to thirty minutes' duration, followed by cool half baths with affusions) have often furnished good results in relieving the morbid excitability of the nerves of the face. But irritant measures (cold-water douches, etc.) should be completely proscribed.

If all these methods of treatment have failed, surgical interference constitutes the only means left at our command. The uselessness of simple neurotomy has caused it to be almost entirely abandoned. At present, the only operation resorted to is excision of the nerves (neurectomy), and the portion removed should measure, according to Bruns, at least a centimetre in length. As trigeminal neuralgia generally involves the second branch, this nerve is most frequently operated upon, and in order to approach the source of the neuralgia, the nerve is often excised at its exit from the foramen rotundum, with the object of separating its branches from all communication with the brain.

According to Bruns, the operation is indicated when the pain occupies a fixed position and a small extent of surface; when the paroxysms are provoked by external causes acting upon the peripheral terminations of the nerves; in those cases in which the cause of the disease is situated at a point beyond which the nerve is accessible to the bistoury; in cases attended with intolerable pains, which threaten to destroy the vital energies of the patient. The possibility of relapse should not militate against resection.

Although its curative action may only extend over a period varying from a few months to two or three years, the resection prolongs life for several years without presenting, in the majority of cases, any serious dangers.

According to the latest statistics of Bruns and A. Wagner, among one hundred and thirty-five cases of neurectomy, the operation failed nine times; death occurred in six cases, relapses at the end of several months thirty-two times, at the end of several years (up to the third year) twenty times; no relapse at the end of several months eighteen times, at the end of several years twenty-three times; the duration of recovery was not mentioned in twenty-four cases.

We may finally mention ligature of the carotid, the impetus to the performance of this operation being due to the diminution of the pains observed upon compression of the carotid. It was proposed by Nussbaum and performed successfully eleven times. Patruban had six recoveries among seven cases, one case terminating fatally. Further surgical observations are necessary in order to enable us to determine the value of ligature of the carotid as a radical operation.

2. SPASMS OF THE TRIGEMINUS.

After having considered the phenomena of morbid irritation in the sensory portions of the fifth pair, it remains for us to discuss those which affect the motor portion of the trigeminus. They are known as masseteric spasm, or tonic or clonic spasm of the masseter.

Tonic spasm of the elevators of the lower jaw (temporal and masseter) constitutes trismus, of which we have previously spoken; clonic spasm alternating between these two muscles and the depressors of the lower jaw (anterior belly of the digastric and mylo-hyoid) constitutes the chattering of the teeth in fever; I have also seen these spasms of the jaw in hysteria, combined with other clonic spasms.

Tonic spasm of the depressors of the lower jaw is rarer and is manifested by the mouth being continually kept open (divaricatio maxillæ inf.). Tonic spasm of the lateral muscles of the jaw (external and internal pterygoids) produces an automatic movement of the maxilla and grinding of the teeth. Leube reports a case (Arch. f. Klin. Med., I. Bd.) of tonic spasm of these muscles in an hysterical patient; the contraction of the right pterygoids carried the lower jaw to the left, and the lower teeth passed in front of the upper. The case recovered in three days by the employment of the induced current and the internal administration of arsenic.

The *causes* of these spasms may be central, such as apoplexy, cerebral softening, meningitis, localized affections of the pons or medulla oblongata, hysteria, epilepsy, tetanus, and hydrophobia, or they may be of peripheral origin, following exposure, basilar meningitis, or tumors irritating the motor portion of the Gasserian ganglion. The spasms are sometimes of a reflex nature and may be produced by dental pains, teething, and intestinal or uterine irritation. By careful examination, we will avoid mistaking trismus for inflammation or ankylosis of the temporomaxillary joint. In rheumatic trismus, the excessive reflex excitability peculiar to tetanus is wanting. Trismus and tetanus of the new-born have been discussed on page 92, Vol. II.

The *prognosis* is favorable when the spasms are of peripheral origin, but doubtful in the central forms.

The *treatment* of spasms of the jaw in the central forms must be antiphlogistic and derivative; in the reflex varieties, we should endeavor to remove the cause of irritation. Subcutaneous injections of morphine or atropine and enemata of laudanum or chloroform, sometimes prove successful. In rheumatic trismus, recourse may be had to vapor baths, to the application of progressive increasing faradic currents to the muscles, or to stabile galvanic currents.

3. TRIGEMINAL PARALYSIS.

The motor and sensory portions of the trigeminus may be separately affected with paralysis; they are rarely affected at the same time. Trigeminal anæsthesia, as we have shown above, may be of central origin, as in apoplexy, ataxia, hysteria, and in the diseases involving the large root of the fifth pair between the pons and olivary bodies. We have discussed these conditions with the necessary detail in preceding chapters.

At the present time, we have special reference to peripheral anæsthesia, which may be caused by disturbances of conduction or by abolition of the local irritability of the trigeminus. The causes of this affection are as follows: exposure, traumatism, surgical operations, caries of the osseous canals, suppuration of the soft parts, tumors or exudations at the base of the brain; it also exists in the Norwegian leprosy, described by Daniellsen and Boeck, and in which sclerosis of the peripheral nerves has been found.

The anæsthesia may be complete and attended with abolition of sensibility to contact, pain, and temperature ; or it may be incomplete, strong impressions are still perceived, or some forms of sensibility may be differentiated. As each portion of the integument of the face is supplied by the nerve filaments of different branches, a careful examination of the patient requires the use of a needle, compass, or electrical brush.

Paralysis of the first branch gives rise to contraction of the pupil, insensibility of the conjunctiva, upper lid and integument of the forehead, a diminution in the sensibility of the skin of the inferior and external parts of the nose, and an abolition of the tactile sense in the anterior portion of the nasal mucous membrane.

Paralysis of the second branch causes a disappearance of sensibility in the lower lid, in the corresponding portions of the cheek and nose, in half of the upper lip, in the middle and posterior regions of the nasal mucous membrane, in the mucous membrane of the roof of the palate, velum palati, uvula, and in the teeth and gums of the upper jaw.

In paralysis of the third branch, there is loss of cutaneous sensibility in front of the temporo-maxillary articulation, upon the outer surface of the ear, in the temporal region, in a portion of the external auditory meatus, in half of the lower lip (internally and externally), in the tongue, buccal mucous membrane, tonsils, teeth and gums of the lower jaw. In lesions of small nerve filaments, the paralysis only affects the corresponding cutaneous surface.

Patients affected by anæsthesia are very much exposed to wounds, inflammations and abscesses of the peripheral parts. The gums are hyperæmic and ulcerated, bleed readily, and may even gangrene in certain places, under the influence of unfavorable causes. In rabbits, in whom the trigeminus has been cut within the cranial cavity, ulcerations readily occur upon the nose, lips, palate, and sometimes upon the tongue, which presents white spots, or upon other parts exposed to pressure.

The most characteristic and serious symptoms are the disturbances in the nutrition of the eye, which Magendie (Journ. de physiol. experiment., t. IV., 1824) first observed after destruction of the trigeminus (within the skull) in rabbits. The symptoms previously mentioned were followed, at the end of eight days, by redness of the conjunctiva and iris, by cloudiness, discoloration and central ulceration of the cornea, and then by rupture and atrophy of the eye. The first observations of this character in man were published by Landmann and Charles Bell, and since then various other cases of purulent destruction of the eye, especially in tumors compressing the trigeminus in the vicinity of the Gasserian ganglion, have been reported. I have referred to two personal cases on p. 118 (with anæsthesia dolorosa) and p. 127.

The later researches of Snellen (Arch. f. hollaend. Beitr. z. Nat. u. Heilk., 1858) seemed to show that ocular suppuration is merely the result of mechanical lesions, the anæsthetic conjunctiva being deprived of its reflexes and its rôle as protector. In recent observations by Baerwinkel (Arch. f. klin. Med., XII. Bd., 1874) and Spencer Watson (Med. Times,

1874), in patients presenting tumor symptoms, ulceration of the cornea was cured by artificial closure of the lids, without any change occurring in the facial paralysis and anæsthesia.

Other observations prove that the disturbances of ocular nutrition are not dependent upon anæsthesia. Bock (Mueller's Arch., 1844) and Friedreich (Beitr. z. Lehre v. den Schaedelgeschw., 1853) have seen cases in which ophthalmia developed (in patients suffering from tumor) despite the preservation of sensibility. We may also refer to the experiment performed by Samuel (Die trophischen Nerven, 1860, p. 61) who, after having produced a violent irritation of the Gasserian ganglion in rabbits by means of the induced current, observed the development of acute ophthalmia, accompanied by hyperæsthesia of the eye.

Meissner has deduced from his experiments (Zschr. f. rat. Med., XXIX. Bd.) a different interpretation of the symptoms following section of the trigeminus. In animals in whom the eye remained sensitive but had nevertheless become inflamed, the nerve was wounded in its median portion. In three other cases of incomplete neurotomy, in which the most internal fibres had escaped, the eye was insensible, but, although exposed, did not become the seat of nutritive disturbances. Neuro-paralytic ocular inflammations are therefore due to section of the trophic fibres contained in the central portion of the nerve. This view is confirmed by Schiff's experiments (Centralbl., 1867) upon lesions of the trigeminus with preservation of sensibility. Sinitzin has more recently undertaken some extremely interesting experiments (Med. Centralbl., II., 1871). He observed that extirpation of the upper cervical ganglion of the sympathetic system caused the disappearance of trigeminal ophthalmia if the latter were not too far advanced. If the extirpation of the ganglion was performed previous to section of the trigeminus, the ocular inflammation was not produced. After section of the sympathetic, the eye upon the operated side acquired a greater resistance to external irritation; the introduction of small bits of glass produced less serious disorders than upon the sound side, in which the eye became readily inflamed. After excision of the upper cervical ganglion, there was an increased supply of blood to the eye, visible to the ophthalmoscope, and the temperature became elevated.

A great diversity of opinions has resulted from these numerous experiments. While some authors attribute the ophthalmia to traumatic iritation, others regard it as chiefly due to the trophic fibres of the fifth pair, which originate in the Gasserian ganglion. Finally, according to Charcot and Friedreich, the trophic disturbances in the eye are caused by an inflammatory irritation (descending neuritis). In an experiment performed by Buettner, after multiple incisions into the Gasserian ganglion and a purulent ophthalmia of rapid course (despite the immediate application of a protecting apparatus), the ganglion was found in a condition of traumatic inflammation, extending into the ophthalmic branch. According to the recent experiments by Feuer (Wien. Med. Jahrb., t. II., 1877), keratitis after section of the trigeminus is due to the cessation of the movements of the lids; the portion of the cornea situated in the fissure of the lids first becomes necrotic, and this source of irritation causes a reactive inflammation of the surrounding tissues, in order to eliminate the necrosed part. The artificial protection of the operated eye prevents the development of keratitis. We still require a careful study of experimental data and of human pathology in order to decide this question definitely.

In forming a *diagnosis* we must endeavor to distinguish the central or peripheral origin of the trigeminal anæsthesia. In the central forms, the third branch is usually alone affected; we must also pay attention, in addition to the previous history, and to the co-existence of paresis or paralysis, of the face, tongue jaws, or limbs. Anæsthesia from tumors at the base of the brain are characterized by cephalic symptoms, the simultaneous affection of adjacent cranial nerves, the frequent transformation of facial neuralgia into anæsthesia, the electrical reactions of the facial paralysis, and the previously mentioned trophic disturbances. The previous existence of periostitis, abscess, local tumefaction, and pain, enable us to attribute the anæsthesia to periostitis or caries of the osseous canals. Syphilitic, traumatic, or rheumatic agencies are readily recognized in individuals who are otherwise healthy.

With the exception of anæsthesia due to the latter affections, the *prognosis* is usually unfavorable, because we are incapable of reaching the cause of the disease. Anæsthesia of long duration is almost always accompanied by persistent changes in the texture of the nerves.

In trigeminal anæthesia of central origin we can expect little good from treatment. Surgical interference may be resorted to in accessible tumors or foreign bodies. Iodide of potassium is indicated if periostitis is present. When the disease is of peripheral origin, we may prescribe frictions with volatile substances, cutaneous revulsives, and cold douches to the face; one of the most efficient measures of treatment consists of the electrical brush with a progressively increasing secondary current.

In a case of syphilitic anæsthesia of the posterior half of the cheek, (with circumscribed necrosis of the maxilla and vault of the palate), I obtained recovery by the use of iodide of potassium, followed by faradization.

Motor paralysis of the small root of the trigeminus produces paralysis of the muscles of the jaw, with the exception of the buccinator, which is innervated by the facial. In paralysis of the masticators, the healthy muscles push the jaw to the opposite side during mastication. The cause of this paralysis is frequently central (meningitis, extravasations, tumors); morbid processes at the base of the brain may at first affect the sensory and then the motor portion of the trigeminus, and in these cases we find other symptoms peculiar to basilar affections. The prognosis is usually unfavorable. Electrical treatment (faradization of the muscles of the jaw) may perhaps produce improvement in some cases.

b. *Diseases of the Pneumogastric Nerve.*

Despite the anastomoses which establish intimate relations between the pneumogastric and spinal accessory nerves, and thus prevent us from obtaining a precise knowledge of the functions of each, we shall, nevertheless, endeavor from a clinical standpoint to trace separately, as far as possible, the physiological and pathological history of these two nerves. We shall begin with the affections of the pneumogastric, which, with Volkmann, Hyrtl and Valentin, we regard as a mixed nerve, as its motor branches are too numerous to be derived from its slight anastomoses with the spinal accessory.

The pharyngeal branch of the pneumogastric is both motor and sensory. Irritation of the vagus at its exit from the jugular foramen produces contractions of the pharynx and œsophagus; in favorable cases, contractions are also noticed in certain muscles of the velum palati (Valentin). As an irritative phenomenon in the course of the pharyngeal nerves, we may mention the globus hystericus, which is not usually of a spasmodic nature, since it does not prevent the patients from swallowing. In paralysis of the pharyngeal branches of the pneumogastric, deglutition is very much embarrassed and becomes almost impossible when the affec- tion is bilateral.

The superior laryngeal nerve is extremely sensitive. Irritation of the central por- tion and especially of its inner branch, produces, according to J. Rosenthal (Die Ath- embewegungen und ihre Beziehungen zum Vagus, Berlin, 1862) an arrest of inspiration and contraction of the expiratory muscles, with simultaneous relaxation of the dia- phragm. The internal branch presides over the reflex movements of cough, when a foreign body irritates the laryngeal mucous membrane. Irritation of the superior laryngeal nerve also gives rise to cough. Section of both superior laryngeal nerves causes slowing of the respiratory rhythm ; and, since paralysis of the crico-thyroid arrests the rotatory movements of the cricoid cartilage and diminishes the tension of the vocal cords, the voice of the animal becomes very hoarse.

The superior laryngeal nerve is subject to peculiar conditions of irrita- tion, although it is rarely paralyzed. Among the former, we may mention spasm of the glottis and whooping-cough. Spasm of the glottis (stridu- lous laryngitis, Kopp's asthma) is an asphyxial disorder peculiar to child- hood, occurring almost always at night in children otherwise perfectly healthy, and attended with pallor or turgidity of the face, retraction of the head, and sibilant inspiration which is often terminated by a cry. General eclamptic spasms frequently occur after the paroxysms. The first three years of life, infantile rickets, anæmia and the digestive disorders which accompany it, are the factors which furnish the greatest contingent to this disease. It is much more frequent in winter than in summer. It is sometimes observed in adults after exposure, and in hys- teria.

Stridulous laryngitis is supposed to be due to a spasm of the constric- tors of the glottis, although this has not been directly observed during an attack, by means of the laryngoscope. The disease is usually chronic, but possesses no gravity; death from asphyxia is a rare termination. *Treat- ment:* During the attack, cold injections, inhalations of ether or chloro- form, drawing the base of the tongue upwards and forwards with the finger, and raising the epiglottis (Krahner) are indicated. In the intervals of the attacks, employ moist frictions, bromide of potassium (in large doses), and tonic preparations.

Whooping-cough (tussis convulsiva) and the spasmodic cough of hys- teria are also included in this category. They consist of spasmodic con- vulsions of the expiratory muscles, with spasm of the glottis and inter- mittent suspension of inspiration. According to Rosenthal's experiments (l. c.), irritation of the superior laryngeal nerve produces analogous symptoms. The contagious, catarrhal secretion of whooping-cough pro- duces an increasing irritation of the nerve-fibres in the laryngeal mucous membrane, attended with the characteristic paroxysms. In the hysterical forms, the irritation undoubtedly starts from the spinal centre. *Treat- ment:* The most efficient remedies consist of belladonna, bromide of po- tassium, inhalations of chloroform, the use of a spray of tincture of hy- oscyamus or belladonna, and of nitrate of silver.

The recurrent nerve is the true nerve of phonation, for, with the ex- ception of the crico-thyroid, it innervates all the other laryngeal muscles. Section of both inferior laryngeal branches causes paralysis of the dilators of the glottis and the tensors of the vocal cords. In this condition, the inspired air may cause, in young animals, collapse of the walls of the glottis and asphyxia, while, during repose, adult animals, who possess a larger glottis, may compensate for the diminution of the air supply by more frequent respiration. In forced respiration, however, the relaxed vocal cords become applied to one another and give rise to asphyxial phenomena.

In man, the paralyses of the vocal cord have only been thoroughly understood since the introduction of the laryngoscope. The primary central causes of paralysis of the recurrent nerve include the following : apoplexy, cerebral tumors, multiple paralyses of the cranial nerves, hysteria, diphtheria, typhoid fever, and diseases of the genital apparatus. The peripheral causes include : inflammations, traumatism, cancer, sarcoma, tumors of the lymphatic glands, goitre, aneurism of the aorta, innominata and subclavian arteries, pericardial exudations, lesions of the larynx or œsophagus, pulmonary tuberculosis or induration. Atrophy of the recurrent nerve and atrophy and fatty degeneration of the paralyzed muscles have been observed upon autopsy.

Paralysis of the recurrent nerve may be complete or incomplete, unilateral or bilateral. In complete double paralysis, the laryngoscope discloses, according to Ziemssen, the following appearances : cadaveric relaxation of both vocal cords and of the arytenoid cartilages, absolute aphonia, expulsion of an enormous quantity of air when the patient wishes to speak or cough. There is inability to cough strongly and to expectorate, but no dyspnœa in adults, except after exertion. When the paralysis is incomplete or unequal on both sides, the appearances are analogous, but the movements of the vocal cords and phonation are still possible to a slight extent.

In forming a *diagnosis*, we can frequently determine the nature of the paralysis, by ascertaining its cause. But, in certain cases it is impossible to determine whether the paralysis is traumatic, rheumatic, neuropathic, or myopathic. The *prognosis* varies according to the nature of the case, and in great part also according to the integrity or abolition of the excitability of the paralyzed muscles and nerves to both currents.

With regard to *treatment*, the early employment of the electrical current furnishes the best results, but this is not true of all hysterical paralyses. Faradization of the larynx is practised through the skin by means of secondary currents of increasing intensity, or an electrode of the proper shape is introduced into the interior of the larynx, by the aid of a mirror, while the other pole, applied to the thyroid cartilage, is connected with an induced or galvanic current of moderate intensity. Galvanization of the inferior laryngeal nerve may also be practised by firmly pressing a thin electrode into the groove which separates the trachea from the œsophagus.

The pulmonary plexus of the vagus, formed by the bronchial nerves and the branches of the sympathetic, may cause (either from irritation of the pneumogastric or by reflex means) a spasm of the bronchial muscles, a result which is also obtained experimentally after irritation of the vagus or of the mucous membrane. The older authors termed this affection nervous asthma. It may be produced by a mental influence acting upon the cerebral origin of the pneumogastric, by tumors compressing the trunk of the nerve, by reflex means as in hysteria (uterine asthma), by exposure, and by the inhalation of irritating powders (very small quantities of ipecacuanha in nervous females). Bronchial asthma occurs in paroxysms separated by longer or shorter intervals.

The attack often begins at night; the patient, wakened by a feeling of oppression, is compelled to sit up in bed and the respiration becomes sibilant and noisy. The patient becomes terrified, the face is pale, the forehead covered with a cold sweat, the head thrown backwards, the arms are fixed and all the inspiratory muscles act convulsively in order to raise the thoracic walls. The cardiac impulse is violent and irregular, the pulse small and feeble, the temperature lowered. This condition lasts fifteen minutes (rarely longer). Sometimes, when the respiratory passages are again free, the air penetrates violently and noisily, or the dyspnœa may cease gradually with the expectoration of a thick, frothy mucus.

The *prognosis* is not unfavorable, especially in recent cases, and even in chronic forms life is rarely endangered.

The treatment, during the paroxysms, consists in energetic friction of the chest and lower limbs, the admission of plenty of fresh air, and the application of cutaneous revulsives. The patient should take small mouthfuls of strong coffee, tea or ice (Romberg). Subcutaneous injections of morphine, inhalations of chloroform, and emetics are only indicated in grave cases. During the periods of remission, we may prescribe with advantage the continuous use of belladonna, Fowler's solution, or iodide of potassium. I have also obtained good effects from the method-ical employment of compressed air, from change of air, and especially from prolonged residence in southern climates and in a marine atmosphere. In young and nervous people or in hysterical patients, the best treatment is the adoption of moist frictions over the entire body (the water should not be too cold) during the intervals between the paroxysms. Even in inveterate forms, the attacks disappear or become more infrequent and milder under this plan of treatment.

Among the paralytic symptoms affecting the pulmonary function of the vagus, we must first mention the neuroparalytic hyperæmia and its sequences, due to section of the nerve. As the vascular nerves of the lung enter the organ with the trunk of the pneumogastric, a lesion of this nerve produces dilatation of the pulmonary vessels and a serous infiltration into the parenchyma. Valentin has observed a phenomenon which proves that this hyperæmia is not of mechanical origin. During the hybernating period, marmots do not swallow or secrete any buccal fluid, and their respiration is not markedly changed. Section of the vagus will nevertheless produce in them pulmonary congestion. Similar disturbances in the lungs may be caused by surgical lesions, compression of the nerve by tubercular or cancerous degenerations of the glands (especially those which are situated at the bifurcation of the bronchi), aneurisms of the thoracic vessels, etc.

Arrest of the heart's action is caused much more rarely by irritation than by paralysis of the pneumogastric. Czermak experimented upon himself (Prag. Vjschr., 1868) by producing prolonged digital compression of the right pneumogastric, and thus caused arrest of the heart's action with a feeling of oppression. In a case observed at Skoda's clinic and published by Heine (Mueller's Arch. f. Physiol., 1841), the symptoms were those of angina pectoris. At the autopsy, Rokitansky found the cardiac plexus thickened and surrounded by a black tumor as large as a hazel nut; lower down, the fibres of the left pneumogastric going to the pulmonary plexus were also compressed by a bluish-black, hypertrophied lymphatic gland. More recently, Concato and Rossbach have also observed retardation and an unrhythmical condition of the pulse from compression of the pneumogastric nerve.

Angina pectoris (cardiac neuralgia) is a neurosis of the heart, occurring paroxysmally and accompanied by radiating pains into the neck or arm, and is attributed either to a hyperæsthesia of the cardiac plexus or to motor disorders of the cardiac nerves. The disease almost always begins suddenly by a painful constriction of the chest, with a distressing sense of exhaustion, which is of very short duration. Angina pectoris may accompany various cardiac affections (hypertrophy, fatty degeneration, lesions of the aortic valves, ossification of the coronary arteries) or may follow excitement or depressing emotions. The *prognosis* is very bad. The *treatment* during the attack consists of the careful administration of ether by inhalations, and of small doses of opium. During the intervals, quinine and increasing doses of Fowler's solution may be administered.

Ludwig and Cyon have discovered the depressor nerve (Saechs. akad. Berichte, 1868), a sensory cardiac branch of the pneumogastric, the central irritation of which diminishes vascular tonus. We are too little acquainted with the functions of this nerve in man to study its pathological history with any degree of success.

In conclusion, we will examine the disorders of the abdominal portion of the pneumogastrics. This category includes nervous cardialgia, boulimia, polydipsia, nervous vomiting, and paralysis of the functions of the stomach. Cardialgia (gastrodynia) is a neuralgia of the sensory fibres of the stomach, manifesting itself by periodical attacks attended with a constricting pain in the pit of the stomach and with irradiations into the back and thorax. As the pain increases, the patient groans and writhes and is obliged to lie down. There is reflex irritation of the vascular and cardiac nerves, pallor of the face, coldness of the limbs, small, irregular pulse, and usually retraction of the epigastric region. The attacks last from a few minutes to a half hour and terminate by eructations, slight vomiting, and perspiration.

Nervous cardialgia is most frequently observed in anæmic and hysterical individuals, in diseases of the uterus and ovaries, and sometimes in cerebral and spinal affections and in dyscrasiæ. In the majority of cases it is readily distinguished from organic affections of the stomach. *Treatment:* In the intervals between the paroxysms we may employ ferruginous preparations, valerianate of zinc, belladonna, bismuth, local treatment of the uterus, or methodical hydrotherapeutic measures (cool sitz-baths, frictions, then moist packs and half-baths), according to the peculiarities of each individual case. During the attacks themselves, subcutaneous injections of morphine constitute the most efficient remedy.

Morbid sensations of hunger and thirst may also be attributed to an irritation of the sensory fibres of the stomach. Boulimia consists of a painful sensation of hunger, occurring with unusual frequency, appeased by very slight nourishment, more rarely by strange articles of diet, and returning at short intervals with intolerable violence, either during the day or even during sleep. Boulimia is observed in hysteria, in extreme neuropathic conditions, in insanity, diabetes, and after severe fevers and syphilis (Fournier). *Treatment:* Prolonged hydrotherapeutic measures, according to the principles previously laid down; the internal administration of Fowler's solution, opium (preferably as hypodermic injections), codeine (Emminghaus, 0.01 three times a day). The morbid sensation of thirst or polydipsia is also a form of hyperæsthesia of the pneumogastric, in which the sensory fibres of the buccal and pharyngeal mucous membranes participate. Polydipsia is observed in the diseases mentioned above, and its treatment is similar to that of boulimia.

Polyphagia constitutes another morbid condition in which the patient is only satiated after eating an enormous quantity of food. Experimental facts and pathological observations serve to demonstrate an anæsthesia of the gastric fibres of the vagus in these cases. According to Legallois, Brachet, etc., animals also manifest an insatiable appetite after section of the pneumogastric in the neck. In Swan's patient (affected with dyspnœa, polyphagia and frequent vomiting) both pneumogastrics were found atrophied; in Bignardi's case the nerves were strewn with small, reddish neuromata. In Johnson's patient (complete absence of the sensations of hunger and thirst) the medulla oblongata was softened, and the roots of the left pneumogastric nerve were compressed by an aneurismal dilatation of the vertebral artery. Polyphagia is also observed in hysteria, epilepsy, and insanity. *Treatment:* Opiates, especially subcutaneously, and Fowler's solution. In a hypochondriac, who had been benefited by the Carlsbad waters, though only during the first two weeks of treatment, I obtained complete recovery from the polyphagic symptoms after the continued employment of hydrotherapeutic measures.

Finally, nervous vomiting should also find a place in this category. Independently of its central causes, the vomiting may occur from peripheral, reflex irritation of the sensory fibres of the pneumogastric, as in irritation of the auricular branch, of the respiratory fibres, etc. Nervous vomiting is observed especially in pregnancy, hysteria, and chlorosis, and frequently accompanies digestive disorders, cardialgia, and gastric pneumatosis. The nutrition of hysterical patients does not suffer, even after repeated vomiting, as a portion of the food is retained. As a rule, there is little difficulty in distinguishing these cases from the vomiting due to tissue changes in the stomach (chronic catarrh, ulcer, etc.). *Treatment:* Anti-hysterical remedies, faradization of the gastric region, subcutaneous injections of morphine, valerianate of cafeine, etc.

Paralysis of the stomach must be attributed in great part to a diminution in the energy of the pneumogastric nerves. The stomach then becomes considerably enlarged from the accumulation of gaseous, solid, or liquid contents, as is sometimes observed in typhoid fever, cholera, and gastric degenerations. *Treatment* must consist in the attempt to restore the energy of the nervous system as much as possible.

c. *Diseases of the Spinal Accessory Nerves.*

Although the spinal accessory nerve is composed almost exclusively of motor fibres, we are, nevertheless, able to produce painful sensations by exercising traction upon its roots. Hyrtl discovered upon the spinal accessory, unilateral ganglia into which a portion of its fibres enter, and which thus demonstrate its sensory properties. If the external branch of the spinal accessory is extirpated near the base of the skull upon both sides, and before its junction with the pneumogastric, paralysis of the movements of the larynx (in addition to paralysis of the sterno-mastoid and trapezius muscles) will be produced in the same manner as if the recurrent nerve is cut. According to Schiff, the roots which preside over the movements of the glottis originate in the medulla oblongata above the calamus. After extirpation of the twelfth pair, tetanization of the pneumogastric nerve in the neck will not produce arrest of the heart's action.

Affections of the external branch of the spinal accessory will give rise to symptoms of spasm or of paralysis. Exposure, diseases of the upper cervical vertebræ, forced movements of the head, and reflex irritations originating in remote viscera (as in hysteria), may act as causes of muscular spasms. These spasms may be tonic (torticollis, collum obstipum), and are then always unilateral, or they may be clonic and occur upon one or both sides. In tonic spasm of the sterno-mastoid muscle, the head is turned to the side and forwards, the occiput approaches the shoulder, the ear the clavicle, and the chin is directed towards the opposite side. In the chronic forms there is very marked obliquity of the neck and vertebral column, the cervical portion of which describes a convexity towards the sound side, with compensatory deformity in the thoracic and lumbar regions. In tonic spasm of the trapezius, the head as a whole is drawn strongly backwards and to the side, without rotation of the chin, the scapula is drawn upwards, and the trapezius becomes rigid and sensitive if an attempt is made to restore the position of the head.

In the diagnosis of tonic spasms depending upon the spinal accessory nerve, especial attention must be paid to the etiological conditions, to reflex irritation, and to diseases of the vertebræ, and the *treatment* must vary accordingly. Acute rheumatic or traumatic forms often yield to warm baths, or to vapor-baths followed by tepid douches. Chronic cases are sometimes relieved by means of secondary currents, which are gradually intensified, or by the passage of stabile galvanic currents through the nerves and muscles (sittings of five to eight minutes).

Unilateral clonic spasm appears in rare instances as isolated convulsions of the sterno-mastoid muscles with a corresponding position of the head; the adjacent muscles (jaw, face, and arm) are also subject to spasm. When the convulsions are prolonged and increase in frequency, true paroxysms develop, the intensity of which is enormously increased by mental excitement and prevents the patient from pursuing his occupation. When the scaleni are affected, stiffness, anæsthesia, and œdema of the arm may also develop, according to Romberg, from compression of the brachial plexus and veins.

Bilateral clonic spasm of the sterno-mastoids (salaam convulsion of Newnham) is rarely observed in adults; in Brodie's patient, it alternated with insanity. In the majority of cases paroxysms of this affection (of a longer or shorter duration, sometimes lasting several days) are observed in children from the period of dentition until the age of puberty. They are attended with convulsions of the face and strabismus, and perhaps even with general spasms and disordered consciousness. Hitherto it has not been determined by autopsy whether these extraordinary, and happily rare, spasmodic forms are due to exudations at the base of the brain, or to a hyperæmic irritation of the roots of the spinal accessory (as in some cases of indigestion or intestinal worms). At times the affection has been known to terminate in epilepsy, paralysis, or insanity. The spasms in question may also be due to other causes, such as exposure, traumatism, tumors, caries of the cervical vertebræ, lesions of the cervical cord, uterine affections, and hysteria.

The disease does not always terminate favorably in children. The *treatment* of clonic spasm of the sterno-mastoid muscle is rarely attended with permanent results, whether resort is had to hydrotherapeutics, preparations of zinc, iron, bromide of potassium or inhalations of chloroform. M. Meyer cured a case of spasm of the face and of the sterno-mastoid by faradization. The constant current has also proved beneficial at times, when applied to the spinal accessory nerves and to the muscles, or under the form of longitudinal and transverse currents through the head. In severe spasms of reflex origin, electricity proves as useless as the injections of morphine, atropine, derivatives, and orthopædic appliances, which are sometimes employed. In three obstinate cases, Busch (Ber. Klin. Wschr., 1873) obtained good results from the application of moxæ to each side of the vertebral column, suppuration from which was kept up for a long time. Myotomy and neurotomy (Busch) have not proven successful.

Paralysis of all the muscles of the neck (sterno-mastoids and trapezii) is very rarely observed. I have never observed its occurrence except in one case of very marked progressive muscular atrophy. All the muscles in question were reduced to the thickness of a sheet of paper, and, in order to prevent the head from falling forward, the patient was obliged to support it with a pasteboard collar. The movements of the muscles of the neck were reduced to a minimum, and were only performed very feebly after great exertion. Peripheral paralysis of the spinal accessory nerve may be caused by exposure, traumatic lesions, fractures of the cervical vertebræ, tumors, degenerations of the lymphatic glands, etc. One or both pairs of muscles innervated by the spinal accessory may be affected.

In unilateral paralysis of the sterno-mastoid, voluntary rotation towards the opposite side is performed with difficulty, and the muscles during these movements do not project so strongly as in the normal condition. If the unilateral paralysis is prolonged, torticollis becomes established from contracture of the healthy muscle. In bilateral paralysis of the sterno-mastoids, the power of rotation of the head is markedly diminished, the projection of the muscles is lost, and the lateral region of the neck is visibly flattened.

The trapezius is often affected with partial paralysis, especially in progressive muscular atrophy. In paralysis of the lower fibres, the scapula recedes from the median line of the back, and the shoulder may become lower. But if the scapulæ are brought very close together, the rhomboids will raise the shoulder and draw it around its outer angle. In paralysis of the middle fibres, the scapula is lowered and its anterior border and inner angle are separated from the vertebral column. In paralysis of the clavicular portion there is considerable difficulty in the elevation of the arm to the horizontal. In paralysis of both trapezii, the scapulæ are lowered to the outside and forwards, and the back appears larger and more strongly arched.

II. DISEASES OF THE SPINAL NERVES.

CHAPTER XLVII.

A.—Nervous Disorders in the Branches of the Cervical and Brachial Plexuses.

The first four pairs of cervical nerves, which form the cervical plexus, furnish sensory filaments to the occiput and to the neck as far as the shoulder. Among its branches, the occipitalis major, the cervical cutaneous, and the phrenic nerves are most frequently the seat of disease.

1. CERVICO-OCCIPITAL NEURALGIA.

This neuralgia, which had been recognized by the elder Bérard but was first established clinically by Valleix, is a rare affection. It is most frequently due to exposure, much more rarely to cervical spondylitis or periostitis, irritation of the cervical cord, wounds of the cervical nerves, foreign bodies, adenitis, tumors, neuromata. In this neuralgia, the pains are sometimes continuous, dull and circumscribed, sometimes lancinating and paroxysmal, extending from the occiput to the neck and shoulder, and rendering the movements of the head, or even of mastication and speech, impossible.

The *puncta dolorosa* indicated by Valleix are: 1, an occipital point between the mastoid process and the first cervical vertebra, at the exit of the occipitalis major (in one of my cases, this point corresponded to the articulation of the occipital and parietal bones); 2, a cervical point between the sterno-mastoid and trapezius, a little above the median plane of the neck, at the emergence of the nerves of the cervical plexus (this point is not constant); 3, a mastoid point behind the mastoid process, corresponding to the occipitalis minor and auricularis major nerves; 4, a parietal point at the circumference of the parietal protuberance, in which the branches of the frontal, occipital, and auricularis major nerves meet; 5, an auricular point (not constant) upon the concha of the ear. Cervico-occipital neuralgia is sometimes associated with neuralgia of the trigeminus or brachial plexus. Among the nutritive disturbances, I have observed falling out of the hairs in the occipital region. The *diagnosis* is founded on the existence of circumscribed painful points and of paroxysms starting from these points. These data also distinguish neuralgia from muscular rheumatism of the neck, which is of very frequent occurrence. In the latter affection the pains, instead of being limited to certain positions, occupy all the muscles and are greatly intensified by movement. Irritation of the cervical cord is characterized by associated symptoms; in cervical spondylitis there are pains in the cervical column upon pressure and during movements, deflection of the head and creaking of the joints; the head is raised with greater facility if the occiput is supported.

The *prognosis* of simple neuralgia is favorable; recovery generally requires several weeks or months, more rarely years. The *treatment*, in symptomatic neuralgia, must be directed against the primary disease. In the rheumatic form, vapor-baths and flying blisters are employed with advantage; large doses of quinine are recommended in the intermittent forms. I cured one case of this kind in six weeks by galvanization with stabile currents of gradually increasing intensity (the anode upon the neck, the cathode upon the occipital point). In a second case, subcutaneous injections of morphine produced prompt improvement, but recovery was only obtained at the end of several months by the employment of hydrotherapeutics (moist packs of the entire body, including the head, until the return of warmth, and followed by cool half-baths and affusions to the head).

2. NERVOUS DISORDERS IN THE DISTRIBUTION OF THE PHRENIC.

The phenomena of irritation include neuralgia of the phrenic, clonic spasm of the diaphragm (hiccough), and tonic spasm of the same muscle, the latter being exceedingly rare; among the symptoms of depression is paralysis of the diaphragm. Under the term neuralgia of the phrenic nerve (Luschka and Henle regard it as a mixed nerve), Falet (Montpel. Méd., 1866) and Peter (Arch. Gén., t. XVII., 1872) have described a painful disease, affecting the base of the thorax at the insertion of the diaphragm, and radiating upwards to the neck and shoulder into the territory of the cervical plexus. Upon careful examination, painful points will be found upon the spinous processes of the second to the sixth cervical vertebræ, upon the phrenic nerve at its passage into the subclavicular fossa, and at the anterior insertions of the diaphragm, which correspond to the seventh to the tenth ribs (more rarely at the posterior insertion).

Diaphragmatic neuralgia accompanies continuous movements of the diaphragm, is aggravated at times, predominates usually upon the left side, and is observed as a primary affection after exposure and in anæmic nervous individuals. As a secondary affection, this neuralgia follows diseases of the heart and vessels, Basedow's disease, angina pectoris, diseases of the liver, etc. The diagnostic signs are furnished by the symptoms previously mentioned and by the puncta dolorosa. The *treatment* must be directed towards the primary disease, combined with wet cups, blisters, and subcutaneous injections of morphine.

Clonic spasm of the diaphragm (hiccough) consists of violent, spasmodic contractions of this muscle, which are accompanied by an inspiratory sound, interrupted by momentary spasm of the constrictors of the glottis; the attack terminates in a short expiration. According to the intensity and duration of these different phenomena, the paroxysm may be accompanied by pains, retraction of the epigastrium, embarrassment of speech, and symptoms of dyspnœa. Hiccough may result from direct irritation of the phrenic nerve by tumors of the mediastinum, aneurisms, pneumonia, and pleuritic effusions (if the mediastinal pleura is also involved). It is also of a reflex nature, as in irritations of the pharynx, œsophagus, stomach, intestines, peritoneum, in biliary and renal calculi, and in diseases of the prostate (Loquet) and uterus. Hiccough is of central origin in hysteria, after emotional excitement, hæmorrhages, in cholera, severe dysentery, etc. Its appearance is an ominous symptom, as it usually occurs in the later stages of severe diseases.

In order to combat this spasm, which often constitutes a distressing and very obstinate condition (especially in hysteria), the *treatment* must be principally directed against its causes. Slight forms are relieved by swallowing cold water, pieces of ice, or acid drinks. In hysterical hiccough we may prescribe enemata of asafœtida, hypodermic injections of morphine, atropine internally or hypodermically, or small doses of chloroform in inhalation. I have several times arrested the hiccough by prolonged galvanization of the phrenic nerve (daily sittings of three to five minutes). The paroxysms are also relieved by moist frictions, half-baths with affusions to the head and neck, and circling douches around the base of the thorax. A simple remedy in rebellious cases is circular compression of the base of the thorax, with forced flexion of the head upon the chest for five to ten minutes. Relaxation of the diaphragm is almost always obtained in this manner. In obstinate forms, good effects are also obtained from the use of musk, combined with alkaline baths (Klein) and from catheterism of the œsophagus (Carcassonne). Coexisting affections of the genital apparatus demand appropriate treatment.

Tonic spasm of the diaphragm (tetanus of the diaphragm) is a very grave, but fortunately extremely rare, disease. Its symptomatology has been described by Duchenne from his experiments upon animals, in whom contracture of the diaphragm was produced by vigorous and prolonged faradization of the phrenic nerve. The results thus obtained have been since confirmed in man by the observations of Valette, Duchenne, Vigla, Oppolzer, Nesbit-Chapman (upon himself), and Fischl. These cases were secondary to exposure, intercostal rheumatism, and violent concussion of the body. Spasm of the diaphragm may also occur as a partial symptom in tetanus and in epileptic and hysterical attacks.

The spasm is evidenced by severe asphyxial phenomena. The patient rapidly sinks into collapse ; immobility and considerable enlargement of the lower half of the thorax and of the abdominal walls, with sinking of the liver, very short inspiration, and prolonged and noisy expiration are noticed. The face is cyanotic and anxious, the pulse is very small and slow, the voice is monotonous and often interrupted ; there are acute pains in the lower thoracic and epigastric regions. In Valette's observation, which terminated fatally in twenty-four hours, autopsy only revealed general cyanosis and repletion of the veins. All the other known cases have rapidly recovered.

The *diagnosis* rests upon the symptoms which we have mentioned and upon the acute character of the disease. According to Bamberger (Wuerzb. Zeitschr., VI. Bd., 1865), cases of this character should be regarded as a form of nervous asthma. But in bronchial spasm there is no manifest depression or immobility of the diaphragm, and the affection assumes a periodical character. The *prognosis* is not absolutely unfavorable if the patient receives prompt and active assistance. Vigla applied compresses soaked in boiling water to the lower half of the thorax. This produced intense pain in the skin, but without vesiculation, and respiration soon became free. Oppolzer saved his vigorous patient by a venesection amounting to one pound; at the same time he covered the entire thorax and epigastric region with a mustard poultice and administered 0.12 of morphine internally. We may also employ inhalations of chloroform and hypodermic injections of a concentrated solution of morphine. Duchenne employed active faradization by means of dry metallic conductors or the electrical brush, applied around the nipples or to the base of the thorax. It would appear preferable to pass a constant current through both phrenic nerves.

Paralysis of the diaphragm sometimes appears as part symptom in paralysis of the bulbar nuclei, in progressive muscular atrophy, hysteria, and lead paralysis. Inflammation of the adjacent structures (peritoneum or pleura) may also give rise to partial paralysis of the diaphragm. Exudation and suppuration then occur into the muscular tissue of the diaphragm, and the longitudinal and transverse striæ disappear in part and are replaced by granulations. This partial disorganization is shown during life by the signs of a unilateral paralysis of the diaphragm.

The following are the pathognomonic symptoms of paralysis of the diaphragm: retraction of the abdominal walls during inspiration, with dilatation of the lower part of the thorax; in expiration, however, the epigastrium and hypochondria sink in and the thorax is narrowed. In beginning paralysis, the respiration is more or less embarrassed, and becomes especially slow when the patient speaks or performs any movements. The patient is orthopnœic, and the intestines appear to mount into the chest during inspiration; the voice is feeble or completely abolished.

The causes of the paralysis may be determined from the history and previous pathological condition. The prognosis is unfavorable, especially in severe forms of bulbar paralysis and progressive muscular atrophy, in which the diaphragm is usually affected towards the last. Paralysis of the diaphragm from hysteria or lead-poisoning frequently terminates in recovery. Treatment consists of faradization of the diaphragm or galvanization of the phrenic nerves. These measures are successful in the beginning of the paralysis, but in old cases they merely diminish the intensity of the respiratory disturbances.

3. CERVICO-BRACHIAL NEURALGIA.

Neuralgia of the cervico-brachial plexus may occupy the entire plexus and thus involve the larger portion of the upper limb, or it may be confined to a few of the nerves of the arm. Neuralgia of the brachial plexus had been recognized by Cotugno towards the middle of the last century, but Valleix first called attention to the "painful points," and the investigations of Cruveilhier, Martinet, Neucourt, and Notta have still further increased our knowledge of this affection.

Neuralgia of the cervico-brachial plexus is much more common than that of the cervico-occipital. It usually occurs upon one side (most frequently on the left), rarely on both, as in diseases of the vertebræ.

We may mention the following causes: the action of cold or of water upon the arm, excessive exertion, compression exercised by tumors upon the plexus or in the axillary space, wounds of the nerves by foreign bodies or in bleeding, aneurisms of the arch of the aorta (Hasse), formation of callus after fracture of the first rib (Canstatt), diseases of the vertebral column (inflammation, tuberculosis, cancer), inflammatory irritation of the upper portion of the cord, chronic lead-poisoning. Pains which radiate into the arm are frequently present in cardiac stenosis and in diseases of the liver and spleen.

The pain sometimes develops suddenly in paroxysms of variable duration. But, even in the intervals, pressure over the brachial plexus in the supra-clavicular fossa will produce pain, and we can recognize, in addition, certain circumscribed points, which are the seat of a dull pain, and pressure upon which gives rise to extreme sensitiveness. These *puncta dolorosa* are : 1, the cervical point, situated outside of the lower cervical vertebræ at the point of emergence of the lower cervical nerves; 2, the suprascapular point, within the angle formed by the acromial portion of the clavicle and the acromion; 3, the deltoid point, at the inferior third of the deltoid, corresponding to the circumflex nerve; 4, the axillary point, in the axillary space near the articulation of the humerus, at which the six nerves composing the brachial plexus are accessible; 5, the superior median point, at the inner border of the biceps; 6, the superior radial point, between the middle and lower thirds of the arm, where the radial nerve winds around the humerus to pass outwards; 7, the superior ulnar point, at the elbow between the inner condyle and olecranon process; 8, the elbow point, corresponding to the musculo-cutaneous nerve; 9, the inferior radial point, upon the dorsal surface of the forearm, at the place where the superficial branch of the radial nerve passes between the supinator long. and brachialis int.; 10, the inferior median point (carpomedian), where the median nerve becomes superficial between the tendons of the radialis int. and palmaris long.; 11, the inferior ulnar point (carpoulnar), opposite the former, near the styloid process of the ulnar; 12, the palmar and digital points, corresponding to the digital nerves in the palm of the hand.

The other symptoms of these neuralgias consist of painful muscular spasms, caused by an irritation of the mixed nerves or by reflex action, and of vaso-motor disturbances, under the form of herpes in the neck or arm, pemphigus, urticaria, and panaritia. At the onset of vertebral and spinal affections, the brachialgia is sometimes complicated with intercostal and sciatic neuralgia.

The *diagnosis* is determined from the history, the local lesions, the existence of painful points along the course of the nerves, and the periodical return of the pain. In those cases in which it is symptomatic, as in affections of the vertebræ, we are guided by the modifications in the position and in the movements of the vertebral column; in diseases of the cord, by the well-known symptoms of spinal irritation. Neuralgia of individual nerve-fibres (circumflex, musculo-cutaneous, median, radial, ulnar, internal and middle cutaneous), are characterized by the existence of painful foci along the course of these nerves.

The *prognosis* varies with the etiology, the duration, and the extent of the neuralgia. As a rule, it will disappear so much the more readily, the slighter its intensity and extent, and the more rapidly the peripheral causes can be removed. The central forms are sometimes very rebellious, but sooner or later the attacks usually terminate.

Treatment: Flying blisters, hypodermic injections of morphine, warm baths, mineral waters, moist packs of the entire body (the arm being packed separately) until the return of warmth, and followed by half-baths of 24°–20° C. I have obtained good results on several occasions by passing descending stabile galvanic currents from the cervical vertebræ to the plexus and to the various *puncta dolorosa* along the nerves. Neurotomy of the superficial nerves, especially in peripheral lesions, has been recently employed by Bruns, Langenbeck, Nélaton, Schuh, Gherini, etc. In the majority of cases it has produced recovery or at least cessation of pain for several years. Sometimes, also, the excision of retracted cicatrices yields good results.

The nerves of the brachial plexus also present other sensory disturbances, such as neuritis, hyperæsthesia, and anæsthesia. Neuritis (which sometimes terminates in nodosities and thickening of the nerve) may follow cómpression, wounds, exposure, typhoid fever, or febrile diseases. For the symptoms and treatment of neuritis we refer to pages 179, 180.

The hyperæsthesia may be of peripheral origin and accompany brachial neuralgia, or it is due to some central cause, as in hysteria or lesions of the cervical cord.

Anæsthesia is observed much more frequently in the course of the brachial nerves. It is produced by the following causes: solutions of continuity after operations, crushing or tearing of the nerves, destruction of the nerves by adjacent foci of suppuration; compression by tumors, or the fractured or dislocated ends of bones; obstruction to the circulation, as in embolism of the brachial arteries; finally, anæsthesia is sometimes due to the action of cold, moisture, or to a former neuritis. Among its central causes may be mentioned hysteria, and the cerebral, spinal, and saturnine affections previously discussed. The various methods of treatment have been referred to in preceding chapters.

4. SPASMS AND PARALYSIS OF THE MUSCLES OF THE ARM AND TRUNK.

As our knowledge of spasmodic affections in general still presents considerable gaps, we are very frequently left in doubt as to the real origin of the spasms which may occur in the upper limbs. Here, as in all other analogous diseases, the chief rôle is played, not by the violence of the irritation, but by the increase in the motor excitability.

The disproportion between the intensity of the irritation and the motor effects may result, in spasmodic affections, from an abnormal receptivity of the peripheral motor apparatus. This may originate in the reflex systems which, in the gray substance, unite the sensory fibres and cells to the cells into which the motor fibres are inserted. But the principal cause of these phenomena is the exaggerated excitability of the nervous centres.

The abnormal receptivity of the peripheral motor apparatus is usually due to local inflammations or traumatic lesions. In such cases the spasms are almost always circumscribed and tonic in character. Reflex action is the most frequent cause of these spasmodic phenomena. It is extremely difficult, if not impossible, to determine the real point of departure of reflex spasms. We may, nevertheless, state that the morbid increase of excitability is due to one of the following causes: diminution of the inhibitory action discovered by Setschenow in the brain of animals; increased irritability of the reflex apparatus contained in the medulla oblongata and spinal cord; excessive receptivity of the central fibres which terminate in the reflex cells.

Apart from psychical irritation, which predisposes to reflex spasms by irritation of the centres, they are generally produced by peripheral irritation of parts rich in nerves, such as the integument, mucous membrane of the digestive apparatus, genital organs, articulations, etc. The causes of the spasms may consist of rheumatic, traumatic, and more rarely chemical irritations, of circulatory disturbances, and of vaso-motor irritation starting from the sensory nerves. Finally, the predisposition to spasms, known as convulsibility, may be due to nutritive disturbances (anæmia, cachexia), or to an hereditary perversion of excitability.

Rheumatic muscular spasms (tonic) usually affect the muscles of the neck and shoulder, the sterno-mastoid, the clavicular portion of the trapezius, the scaleni, the splenius, and the oblique muscles of the head. Torticollis, secondary to spasm of the first of these muscles, has been studied under the diseases of the spinal accessory. Contracture of the rhomboid is a rare disease (the inferior angle of the scapula is elevated and drawn nearer to the median line, the border of the scapula presents a projection which is prolonged towards the neck, and the deformity is effaced during voluntary movements of elevation of the arm, Duchenne).

Treatment: Faradization of the opposing muscle, and passage of a stabile galvanic current through the nerves and muscles. In recent cases we may prescribe with advantage warm baths or 'vapor-baths in addition to rest of the affected muscle.

Traumatic contracture consists, as we have shown above (page 170), of a contracture of certain muscles secondary to paralysis of their antagonists. It is sometimes of reflex origin. Artisan's spasm (which occurs usually in the hands, more rarely in the feet, in shoemakers, tailors, carpenters, locksmiths, etc.) is a painful spasm of the flexors, produced by hard labor. In the majority of the cases which I have observed, the patients had attained the age of puberty, a period in which the sexual development is accompanied by a peculiar excitability of the nervous system. In acute cases the spasms are quieted by enveloping the hand in warm, moist cloths, together with rest in bed. In combating the pains, we may employ warm baths, tartar emetic in divided doses, and subcutaneous injections of morphine. The faradic current does not act well in such cases; on the other hand, it is used with success in chronic cases, in which partial pareses and anæsthesias have developed secondary to relapses. During the last few years Nussbaum has observed some very interesting facts in this connection (Aerztl. Intelligenzbl., 9, 1872). He has succeeded in curing muscular contractures and rebellious anæsthesias by traction of the nerves of the brachial plexus which had been laid bare. In another case he relieved ankylosis of the elbow, with contracture of the fourth and fifth fingers, by extension of the ulnar nerve, which had contracted.

Idiopathic spasms are partial, occur usually in the flexors, especially in children, and may be regarded at first sight as a symptom of a central affection. Analogous phenomena are also observed in adults after exposure or severe diseases, in the course of typhoid fever, cholera, acute exanthemata, renal affections, and in pregnant and parturient women. These spasms are probably, in great part, of reflex origin. The treatment is the same as in the spasmodic affections previously referred to. Moist packs (until the return of an agreeable warmth), followed by half-baths at 24°–20° C., will almost always cause the disappearance of the spasmodic phenomena.

Writer's spasm is placed in this category by the majority of authors. We have previously maintained, however (page 127), that it is a disturbance of co-ordination in the muscles innervated by the brachial plexus.

Paralyses of the brachial plexus and of the trunk.—These paralyses are usually limited to the territory of certain nerves, and are produced by lesions of the nerve-trunks or by myopathic processes.

The obstacles to nervous action are accompanied by abolition of voluntary or even of reflex movements, by disorders of sensibility, retardation of the circulation, low temperature, more or less rapid loss of muscular nutrition and of the faradic reaction of the muscles, often with retention of galvanic excitability. Among the causes of these paralyses we may mention the rheumatic diathesis, traumatic lesions, luxations, the compression produced by tumors, periostitis, and neuritis.

Duchenne (Electris. local., 3ᵉ édit.) and Seeligmueller (Ber. Klin. Wschr., 1874) have called attention to paralysis in infants after obstetrical operations (forceps, version, traction).

They especially involve the muscles of the shoulder and arm, and may be complicated with fractures or dislocations. These congenital paralyses, which are usually due to a contusion limited to the plexuses, recover if faradic or galvanic treatment is promptly instituted. The prognosis is less favorable in severe, inveterate forms. Thus, I have seen a case of

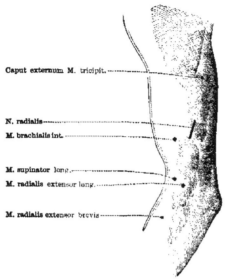

Caput externum M. tricipit.

N. radialis
M. brachialis int.

M. supinator long.
M. radialis extensor long.

M. radialis extensor brevis

FIG. 21.—Motor points of outer aspect of arm.

hemiplegia following the employment of the forceps, in which only slight improvement was obtained after the lapse of ten years.

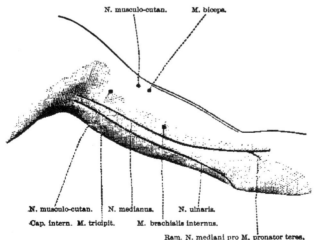

N. musculo-cutan.   M. biceps.

N. musculo-cutan.   N. medianus.   N. ulnaris.
Cap. intern. M. tricipit.   M. brachialis internus.

Ram. N. mediani pro M. pronator teres.

FIG. 22.—Motor points of inner aspect of arm.

Among the paralyses of the muscles of the arm, the most frequent and important is that of the deltoid, attended with abolition of motion forwards, outwards, or backwards, according as it affects the anterior, middle (most frequent), or posterior parts of the muscle (progressive muscular atrophy). In total paralysis of the deltoid, the arm is immobile and pendent, and the patient can only grasp the hand after throwing it forwards by means of the pectoralis major.

The infraspinatus is often affected at the same time (both muscles are supplied by the circumflex nerve), and rotation outwards, elevation and abduction of the arm, and the formation of straight lines in writing and drawing (Duchenne) are then rendered difficult or impossible. In paralysis of the teres major, supraspinatus, and subscapularis, the arm is turned outwards, with abolition of the power of inward rotation.

Paralysis of the sterno-mastoid and trapezius has been referred to in the preceding chapter. In paralysis of the rhomboid (which is extremely rare) the inner border of the scapula is not maintained in its position against the thoracic wall, the scapula is separated from the trunk at its inner border and inferior angle, and the movements of translation of the shoulder towards the median line, and the movements of the arm backwards, are very limited.

Paralysis of the serratus magnus is not very rare. During repose the scapula see-saws around its axis and approaches the vertebral column at its inferior angle, and the anterior border is lowered. The inner border is directed obliquely outwards and upwards in the form of a wing. The extended arm can only be raised to the horizontal plane; in order to raise it completely, it must obtain a *point d'appui* externally and be turned forwards. When the arm is raised and directed forwards, the inner border of the scapula separates itself very sharply from the chest (scapula alata). This paralysis is due to traumatism, the rheumatic diathesis, and to overwork of the shoulder muscles. Simple or double paralysis of the serratus magnus is also observed in progressive muscular atrophy, cerebral or spinal paralyses, and after typhoid fever.

Paralysis of the extensors of the back (sacro-lumbalus and longissimus dorsi), following traumatism, rheumatism, cerebral or spinal lesions, progressive muscular atrophy, etc., is characterized by unilateral scoliosis, and, when double, by paralytic kyphosis, with inflexion of the trunk. The vertebral column cannot be restored spontaneously, but can be retained passively in the erect position. Electricity may prove useful in these cases.

According to Londe's statistics, the radial and median nerves are, on account of their position, more exposed to traumatic lesions than the other nerves of the arm. In paralysis of the radial nerve and of the extensors of the forearm to which it is distributed, the hand and fingers are pendent and flexed, the thumb is adducted and flexed. Elevation of the arm, extension of the fingers, and abduction of the thumb are impossible

On account of the loss of the movements of extension the flexors also contract more feebly. Peripheral paralysis of the radial nerve may be of rheumatic or traumatic origin (blow upon the forearm, compression by crutches, gun-shot wounds, compression of the arm during a prolonged sleep). Paralysis of the radial nerve has also been observed in hysteria, progressive muscular atrophy, lead palsy, typhoid fever (small hæmorrhages into the extensor muscles, with degeneration of their fibres and nerve-filaments, Friedberg). We refer to the remarks on page, 166, for the differential diagnosis.

Paralysis of the median nerve is very rare in rheumatism; it is more frequently produced by traumatism, luxations of the shoulder, tumors compressing the brachial plexus, neuritis (typhoid fever and acute diseases), or central affections (progressive muscular atrophy). In paralysis of the median the movements of pronation of the forearm are markedly embarrassed, and flexion of the hand towards the radial side and of the two last phalanges is more or less compromised. The supinator longus then acts as pronator and flexor. When the muscles of the thumb are paralyzed, the latter is extended and abducted and directed with the other fin-

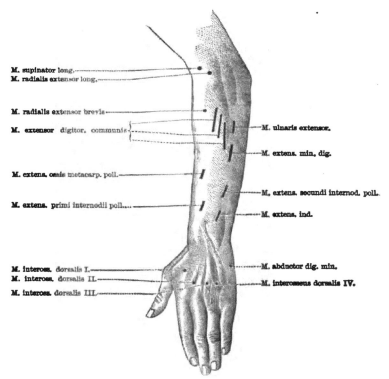

M. supinator long,
M. radialis extensor long,

M. radialis extensor brevis

M. extensor digitor. communis

M. extens. ossis metacarp. poll.

M. extens. primi internodii poll....

M. inteross. dorsalis I.
M. inteross. dorsalis II.
M. inteross. dorsalis III.

M. ulnaris extensor.

M. extens. min. dig.

M. extens. secundi internod. poll.

M. extens. ind.

M. abductor dig. min.

M. interosseus dorsalis IV.

FIG. 28.—Motor points of extensor aspect of forearm.

gers towards the palm of the hand. In isolated paralysis of the opponens, the thumb loses the power of opposition. In paralysis of the flexor and short adductor of the thumb, the latter cannot be brought in contact with the tips of the other fingers, and prehension and delicate work are rendered impossible.

Paralysis of the ulnar nerve is usually secondary to traumatism (vide p. 174), fractures, dislocations, and is more rarely of rheumatic origin. It may be also due to neuritis (after typhoid fever or acute diseases), or may constitute one of the symptoms of progressive muscular atrophy. In paralysis of the ulnar, the hand is abducted, and has lost the power of adduction and flexion at the wrist. Paralysis of the adductor of the thumb renders writing, and the fixation of objects in general, difficult; paralysis of the muscles of the little finger entails the loss of its individual movements.

Paralysis of the interossei is characterized by extension at the meta-carpo-phalangeal joints, with simultaneous flexion of inter-phalangeal

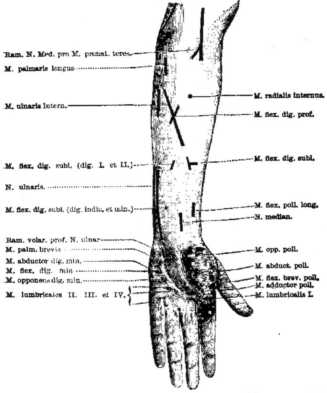

Ram. N. Med. pro M. pronat. teres.

M. palmaris longus

M. ulnaris intern.

M. radialis internus.

M. flex. dig. prof.

M. flex. dig. subl. (dig. I. ct II.)

M. flex. dig. subl.

N. ulnaris.

M. flex. dig. subl. (dig. indic. et min.)

M. flex. poll. long.

N. median.

Ram. volar. prof. N. ulnar
M. palm. brevis
M. abductor dig. min.
M. flex. dig. min.
M. opponens dig. min.
M. lumbricalis II. III. et IV.

M. opp. poll.
M. abduct. poll.
M. flex. brev. poll.
M. adductor poll.
M. lumbricalis I.

FIG. 24.—Motor points of flexor aspect of forearm.

articulations from predominance of the flexors. At a later period the dorsal surface of the hand becomes furrowed, and subluxation and incurvation of the fingers towards the palm of the hand (en griffe) occurs (the deformity is especially marked in progressive muscular atrophy).

Galvanization of the nerves, alternating with faradization of the paralyzed muscles, furnishes the best results in the treatment of paralysis of the upper limbs. Persistent gymnastics and hydrotherapeutics may also aid in restoring the motor power.

CHAPTER XLVIII.

B.—Nervous Disorders in the Branches furnished by the Dorsal Cord and Lumbar Plexus.

1. DORSO-INTERCOSTAL NEURALGIA.

UNDER the term intercostal neuralgia are classed those pains which are situated in the intercostal branches distributed by the dorsal nerves to the sternum and epigastrium.

This is the most frequent of all neuralgias. It is much more common on the left side than on the right, and is usually situated in one or more of the intercostal spaces comprised between the fifth and ninth ribs. As a rule, it begins slowly, increases little by little in intensity, and presents, like other neuralgias, exacerbations and remissions. The patients complain of a painful tension around the trunk and of intermittent lancinating pains darting from the back to the thorax. All movements which present a certain degree of violence, deep respirations, coughing, mastication, perhaps even the simple contact of the clothes, may give rise to the pain. Intercostal neuralgia is especially observed from the twentieth to the forty-fifth years of life, and chiefly in nervous females (Valleix).

We know little concerning the anatomical changes in the nerves in intercostal neuralgia. Nicod, and especially Beau, found the nerves inflamed or atrophied and in a condition of fatty degeneration in cases of intercostal pains occurring in pleurisy and phthisis. Neuromata and thickening of the sheaths of the nerves have also been observed. An opportunity of making necroscopic investigations is rarely afforded in ordinary cases. The following are the exciting causes: exposure, traumatism, over-exertion, vertebral affections (inflammation, caries, cancer), diseases of the ribs, adenitis, aortic aneurism, tuberculosis, exudations upon and thickening of the pleura. Stasis in the intercostal veins may also act as a cause of the neuralgia. This occurs more readily on the left side, and must be attributed, according to Henle, to the sinuosities and longer curves of the vena azygos minor, which receives the blood from the inferior intercostal spaces. The repletion of the venous plexuses on the left side may thus cause compression of the nerve-roots.

According to Bassereau, intercostal neuralgia is almost always accompanied by some uterine affection (congestion, abnormal sensibility, catarrh, and menstrual disorders), but it appears that he has also ranged cases of lumbo-abdominal neuralgia in this category. Finally, intercostal neuralgia occurs frequently in hysteria and diseases of the cord.

The *puncta dolorosa* in dorso-intercostal neuralgia are: a dorsal point, a little outside the spinous process at the intervertebral foramen; a lateral point, in the middle of the intercostal space at the bifurcation of the intercostal nerve (this point is not constant); a sternal or epigastric point, outside of the sternum for the superior intercostal nerves, and outside the median line in the epigastrium for the inferior nerves.

Circumscribed anæsthesia and zona (which is readily explained by the presence of vaso-motor fibres in the dorsal nerves) are sometimes observed as complications. The appearance of zona may be attributed, as we have seen above, to the existence of a neuritis. The neuralgia often precedes the eruption, but at other times follows it, and may last for a long time afterwards.

The *diagnosis* does not present, as a rule, any especial difficulty. In intercostal rheumatism, which is most readily mistaken for neuralgia, the pain is more widespread, increases more upon motion and deep respirations than upon pressure, and is very frequently accompanied by febrile symptoms. No circumscribed painful spots are observed in the lancinating intercostal pains of pleurisy, pneumonia and pericarditis, and physical examination reveals other characteristic signs. This is also true of tuberculosis, in which the pain is usually situated in the superior intercostal spaces near the sternum. Angina pectoris is characterized by a sensation of faintness, irregularity of the heart's action, and absence of *puncta dolorosa*. The intercostal pains, which are symptomatic of spinal affections, are complicated by other neuralgias of the arms and legs, and by symptoms of loss of power. In vertebral affections the nature of the co-existing neuralgias is recognized by the pathognomonic signs previously referred to.

As a rule, the *prognosis* of intercostal neuralgia is not unfavorable, but it very often pursues a slow course. In rebellious cases the disease may continue for an indefinite period.

Treatment: This should be directed, above all, against the primary disease, especially the anæmia, hysteria, or uterine affection which may be present. More or less ready relief is obtained by the employment of flying blisters, the endermic or hypodermic administration of morphine, and stabile galvanic currents passed through the vertebral column and along the course of the intercostal nerves. According to Anstie, the application of a blister over the posterior nerve-fibres will also act favorably upon neuralgia of the anterior branches, and will even prevent the secondary development of herpes. Benefit is also frequently derived from moist packs, followed by half-baths at 24°–22° C., local douches, sea-bathing, the waters of Gastein, Teplitz, Tueffer, Voeslau, Tobelbad, Wiesbaden, Baden-Baden, etc.

Mastodynia (*irritable breast* of Cooper).—Neuralgia of the mammary gland should be regarded as a variety of intercostal neuralgia (pectoral cutaneous nerves). This view is supported by the following circumstances: complication with brachialgia (the superior branch of the first intercostal nerve takes part in the formation of the brachial plexus); the appearance of analogous pains in the inner wall of the axilla, in the back and shoulder, parts to which the pectoral cutaneous branches are distributed; finally, the accidental complication with neuralgia of the abdominal walls (some filaments of the fifth intercostal nerve are distributed to the abdominal muscles).

In mammary neuralgia, which is observed most frequently from the period of puberty to the age of thirty, the mammary gland is, in some places, the seat of lancinating pains, which radiate towards the shoulder, arm, loins, and abdomen. The pains increase before menstruation, and diminish in intensity during the menses. Cooper has found in the mammary gland movable nodosities from the size of a pea to that of a hazel-nut, which, like neuromata, are extremely sensitive to contact. They have been regarded as connective-tissue formations. In a case reported by Franque (Med. Halle, 1864), the mastodynia was due to a carcinoma of the liver and stomach (probably a radiated neuralgia). Beigel published the case (Virch. Arch., XLII. Bd., 1868) of a girl, nineteen years of age, who had never been pregnant, and who suffered, at the age of seventeen, from galactorrhœa, followed by pains in both mammæ. In Fr. Schultze's case (Ber. klin. Wschr., 42, 1874) a secretion of colostrum with double mastodynia was observed (reflex irritation of the secretory nerves from neuralgia of the cutaneous nerves of the breast).

Treatment: Support the painful breast and cover it with a fine fur; employ frictions with belladonna ointment; administer opium and calomel (Cooper's method) internally. The treatment indicated for intercostal neuralgia will also apply here in great part.

2. LUMBO-ABDOMINAL NEURALGIA.

Under this term are included all neuralgias occurring in the branches of the lumbar plexus. According as the disease affects the anterior or the posterior branches of the five lumbar nerves, the pains radiate into the back and loins, or into the abdomen and external genital organs. Over such a large surface the neuralgic affections may be situated in various nerve-fibres, and we accordingly distinguish lumbo-abdominal neuralgia, properly speaking, neuralgia of the testis, hysteralgia, neuralgia of the obturator nerve, and crural neuralgia.

a. *Lumbo-abdominal neuralgia.*—This is most frequently produced by affections of the lumbar portion of the vertebral column or the neighborhood of the lumbar plexus, by pelvic diseases, or by exudations upon the ilio-psoas muscle. Strains, contusions, exposure, and hysteria are regarded as pathogenic factors. The pains occur in paroxysms. They are usually lancinating in character, and follow the course of the nerves towards the posterior portion of the trunk or the hypogastric region, or are manifested upon pressure over certain parts of these regions. The *puncta dolorosa* are: 1, a lumbar point, a little to the outside of the spinous processes of the upper lumbar vertebræ; 2, an iliac point, above the middle of the crest of the ilium, where the ilio-hypogastric nerve penetrates the transversalis abdominis muscle; 3, a hypogastric point, above the inguinal canal, a little outside of the linea alba, where the ilio-hypogastric nerve traverses the aponeurosis of the external oblique muscle; 4, an inguinal point; 5, a scrotal or labial point, upon the scrotum or labium major. Spasm of the cremaster and increase of sexual appetite (priapism and ejaculation, Notta) sometimes occur as complications.

Lumbo-abdominal neuralgia may be mistaken for rheumatic myalgia (of the sacro-lumbalis and longissimus dorsi). But in the latter affection sufficient diagnostic data are found in the pathognomonic position of the vertebral column (convexity towards the affected side), in the sensibility of the entire muscle to pressure, and especially during motion, and in the absence of circumscribed *puncta dolorosa*. Uterine affections (chronic infarctus, cancer), which are sometimes accompanied by pains in the back, hips, and groins, are readily recognized by a vaginal examination. *Prognosis* and *treatment* are the same as in intercostal neuralgia.

b. *Neuralgia of the testis.*—This exceedingly distressing affection (irritable testis of Cooper; neuralgia of the spermatic plexus, according to Romberg) is characterized by painful sensations in the testicle, spermatic cord and perineum, which, without any visible change, become extremely sensitive to pressure over certain parts. It is due to venereal excesses, onanism, unsatisfied sexual excitement, chronic urethritis, and irritation of the spinal cord. In a case under my observation (Wien. Med. Zeit., 9, 1864), the urethra was hyperæsthetic, and a fluid like the white of egg was discharged after micturition. The microscope showed the presence of filaments of mucus, but no spermatozoa (gonorrhœal secretion furnished by the follicles of the prostate, Cowper's glands, or the seminal vesicles).

The theory of an inflammatory affection is contradicted by the normal appearance of the testicle. Nephritic colic, in which the pains radiate into the groin and testis, is distinguished from neuralgia of the testis by the disorders in the urinary secretion and the appearance of concretions, gravel, and blood in the urine. Beginning spinal affections are characterized by coexisting motor and sensory disturbances. The acute cases run a much more favorable course than the chronic ones. The latter often continue for years, are apt to return, and the pains sometimes become so intense that the patients demand castration. This operation has been performed several times by surgeons, but has not always resulted successfully. *Treatment :* In acute cases benefit is obtained from frictions with belladonna ointment upon the testis and along the cord (two or three times daily) and from warm baths. In chronic cases we may prescribe flying blisters, and pass a descending constant current through the lumbar spine and spermatic cord. Resort is also had to cool sitz-baths, moist packs, half-baths, cool dorsal affusions, fine douches to the vertebral column and perineum, and, finally, sea-baths—sexual indulgence being limited as much as possible.

c. *Hysteralgia.*—Uterine neuralgia (irritable uterus of Gooch) is also an extremely distressing and rebellious affection. The uterus, although maintaining its normal volume, mobility, and temperature, becomes the seat of extremely violent spontaneous pains, and is usually so sensitive to pressure that examination is rendered impossible. Narcotics and nervines have proved useless in the cases observed by Scanzoni. Thermal waters, hydrotherapeutics, and sea-baths are probably the measures which will give the best results in this affection.

d. *Neuralgia of the obturator nerve,* a very rare form, has been observed in cases of strangulated obturator hernia. It consists of acute pains upon the inner surface of the thigh, with abolition of the power of abduction, and comes on after the symptoms of strangulation.

e. *Crural neuralgia.*—This neuralgia is manifested by paroxysms of pain upon the anterior and inner surfaces of the thigh and leg, extending to the inner border of the dorsal surface of the foot and large toe. As a pure neuralgia it is much rarer than the analogous affection upon the posterior surface of the leg; both forms are often associated. The causes of this affection include exposure, traumatism, compression of the lumbar plexus in the pelvis by degenerated lymphatic glands, exudations upon the iliac muscle, aneurisms of the iliac artery, strangulated crural herniæ, dislocations of the thigh, coxalgia, etc.

The *puncta dolorosa* are: 1, a crural point, at the exit of the crural nerve below Poupart's ligament; 2, an anterior femoral point, where the small saphenous nerve perforates the fascia lata in the middle of the thigh; 3, an articular point, at the inner surface of the knee, where the nerve divides; 4, a plantar point, at the inner side of the sole of the foot; 5, a point upon the tuberosity of the great toe: the two latter points belong to the anterior saphenous major nerve. Hyperæsthesia or partial anæsthesia and formication are sometimes observed along the course of the small saphenous nerve. With regard to prognosis and treatment, we refer to the remarks on sciatica.

CHAPTER XLIX.

C.—NERVOUS DISORDERS IN THE BRANCHES OF THE SACRO-COCCYGEAL PLEXUS.

a. Sciatic Neuralgia.

SCIATICA affects the sciatic plexus, which is formed by the fourth and fifth lumbar and the first two sacral pairs of nerves. The neuralgia, starting from the lower lumbar region, occupies the buttock and thigh, and also extends to the popliteal fold and the adjacent part of the calf of the leg; it sometimes extends to the external malleolus, the heel, and the outer surface of the foot. In the majority of cases the neuralgia is limited either to the upper or lower segment of the course of the nerve.

The *anatomical lesions* of sciatica are very imperfectly known. In one case, Cotugno found a dropsical enlargement of the nerve, which was very probably due to the general anasarca from which the patient was suffering. Andral, Gendrin, and Martinet have several times seen the nerve red and injected and the neurilemma infiltrated with serum or pus. Béclard found the nerve of a yellowish color, strewn with small hæmorrhages, and thickened in places, and Bichat found it coursed by dilated vessels. Dupuytren, in a case of cancer, and Noegelé, in a case of elephantiasis of the thigh, have observed the formation of nodosities and cysts upon the tibial nerve. At the point of emergence of the nerves belonging to the sciatic plexus, Hasse has seen the neurilemma inflamed by a deposit of tubercular granulations, although no tubercles could be discovered in the spinal canal or nerves.

In a case of sciatica, caused by an ulcerated cancer of the uterus (Med. Zeit., 12–13, 1864), I found the neurilemma of the sciatic nerve ecchymosed and even sclerosed, and drawn towards the neoplasm, the latter extending to the sheath of the nerve. Microscopical examination of the nerve, after hardening in chromic acid, gave the following results : considerable development of interstitial connective tissue around the transverse sections of the nerve-fibres, with infiltration of large cancer-cells of various shapes, and provided with one or two nuclei. In a second case of sciatica, which had continued for a year, and had developed after confinement, an abscess finally formed in the sacral region. Upon opening it, fœtid pus escaped and the bone was found roughened. The patient died of pyæmia, and autopsy showed caries of the sacro-iliac symphysis; in the pelvis an abscess was found around the left sciatic nerve, the sheath of which was uneven and thickened and the nerve-fibres red and surrounded by dilated vessels.

Sciatica rarely begins with suddenness and violence, but, in the majority of cases, the pains develop gradually. As in other neuralgias, there is usually a dull pain in the deeper parts, especially in the buttock, which, from time to time, radiates upwards or downwards, either spontaneously or from an external cause, under the form of burning or lancinating pains.

The following are the *puncta dolorosa* found in sciatica: 1, the lumbar point, upon the lateral portion of the last lumbar vertebræ (according to Romberg, this is an associated sensation situated in the posterior branches of the sacral nerves); 2, the posterior iliac point, at the posterior superior spinous process of the ilium; 3, the sacral point (of Trousseau), over the sacral vertebræ; 4, the superior iliac point, upon the middle of the crest of the ilium; 5, the median iliac point, at the summit of the sciatic foramen; 6, the inferior iliac or trochanteric point, at the posterior border of the great trochanter; 7, the superior femoral point, upon the tuber ischii; 8, the middle femoral point, corresponding to the posterior cutaneous nerve; 9, the inferior femoral point, at the inferior and inner part of the biceps (the two latter are inconstant); 10, the popliteal point, at the division of the sciatic nerve; 11, a point at the head of the fibula, where the bone is encircled by the peroneal nerve; 12, the deep fibular point, at which the pains extend for a certain distance; 13, the sural point, upon the calf; 14, the tibial point, at the edge of the tibia; 15, the external malleolar point; 16, the internal malleolar point (much rarer); 17, the dorsal point, at the toes; 18, the plantar point, upon certain parts of the sole of the foot.

The most frequent and marked of these painful points are those of the lumbar region, the great trochanter, the tuber ischii, the popliteal space, the head of the fibula, and the external malleolus.   Nevertheless one or the other of these points is often wanting, and in certain sciaticas (especially those of spinal origin) no painful point can be discovered upon pressure.

In acute cases the patients are compelled to remain in bed, and are most comfortable when the thigh is brought closer to the trunk and the knee is slightly flexed.   Every forcible movement, such as turning in bed, and coughing or sneezing, and prolonged decubitus upon the affected side, increase the pain.   At first the pain prevents the patient from using the affected limb in walking.   After a while locomotion again becomes possible, but it is attended with a peculiar one-sidedness and lameness, as the patients bear the weight of the body upon the healthy limb and walk upon the toes of the affected leg.   The patients are bent somewhat backwards and advance by inclining forwards slightly at each step.

The accompanying motor symptoms and complications consist of reflex muscular spasms, and sometimes of persistent contractures (of the biceps) and pareses, especially in neuralgias of central origin.   The sensory disturbances consist of hyperæsthesia (over circumscribed spots, especially in the lancinating sciatica of beginning ataxia) or anæsthesia. I observed one case of severe sciatica (Wien. Med. Zeit., 12, 1863), attended with hyperæsthesia of the calf and anæsthesia of the anterior surface of the thigh.

Among the vaso-motor disorders we may observe, in addition to subjective sensations of cold in the affected leg, a diminution of temperature (1.5–2°C. in chronic cases), diminution of the perspiration, and atrophy of the affected side.   In acute cases the absence of movement may undoubtedly be looked upon as the cause of the atrophy.   But in severe and chronic forms in which the atrophy chiefly involves the diseased limb, we must admit that the irritated sensory fibres act by reflex means upon the vaso-motor apparatus, and that the atrophy is due to the prolonged contraction of the vessels. The low temperature and the diminution in the secretions also favor this view. Graves reported a case in which the affected limb presented a considerable hypertrophy, which disappeared after a month's treatment with the actual cautery. Braun (in his Balneotherapeutics) has several times observed sugar in the urine of patients suffering from sciatica.

Exposure plays the most important part in the etiology of sciatica. The largest number of cases occur in those months which are accompanied by strong winds and low barometric pressure.

Exposure to winds and moisture, contact with the damp ground, insufficient clothing, and living in damp places are the most frequent causes of sciatica, especially in artisans. The disease is much more infrequent among the better classes. Injuries, wounds, over-exertion, and sudden movements may also lead to the development of sciatica.

Symptomatic sciatica may occur under the following conditions; inflammation of the sciatic nerve, diseases of the sacrum (caries, cancer), pelvic tumors, periostitis of the ilium, perimetritis, uterine and ovarian tumors, pregnancy, displacements of the uterus (compression of the sacral plexus), hypertrophy of the retro-peritoneal glands, peritoneal exudations and abscesses (Niemeyer), concretions of solid fæcal matter, accumulation of cherry-pits in the sigmoid flexure, tumors along the course of the nerves of the thigh and leg, popliteal aneurisms. Sciatica may also be due to spinal affections, hysteria, and metallic poisoning, and may follow the puerperal condition, typhoid fever, syphilis, and gonorrhœa. Finally, it may occur as a reflex phenomenon in dental and facial neuralgias. (Brown-Séquard and Piorry).

The male sex, being more exposed to vicissitudes than the female, is also more liable to sciatica. In the large majority of my cases the patients were between the ages of twenty-five and thirty-three years; the youngest patient was a girl twelve years of age, the oldest was a man of seventy. The neuralgia is usually limited to one side, but Valleix, Leubuscher, Romberg, etc., have observed the bilateral form. All my cases of double sciatica were accompanied by spinal symptoms.

As a rule, the *diagnosis* of sciatica does not present any serious difficulties. Neuritis of the sciatic nerve is usually characterized by febrile movement and continuous pains along the course of the nerves without any circumscribed painful points, and terminates, in severe cases, with symptoms of motor and sensory paralysis.

In rheumatism of the muscles of the hip (rheumatic myalgia) the symptoms consist of swelling, elevation of temperature, and widespread pains, with absence of the characteristic puncta dolorosa. The pains are more readily produced by movement than by pressure. Psoas abscess is accompanied, like sciatica, by pains in the hip and lumbar region; but the flexion and retraction of the thigh, the acute pains upon forced extension, the fever of suppuration, the œdema of the limb, the swelling, and the fluctuation upon the inner side of the thigh, constitute distinctive signs of the former affection.

Among the osseous affections, periostitis of the femur and coxalgia may be mistaken, in the beginning, for sciatica. But periostitis of the femur begins with elevation of temperature, and this is followed by swelling and a deep pain, which is only increased upon active pressure. In coxalgia the beginning of the articular inflammation is shown by the pain upon motion (especially upon rotation of the thigh), and also by striking upon the heel and thus acting upon the head of the femur. At a later period the enlargement of the hip, the effaced gluteal fold, the dissimilar position of the lower limbs, and the communication of movements of the thigh (in the horizontal position) to the pelvis, prevent a mistake.

Certain vascular affections, such as embolism and thrombosis, are also accompanied by pains in the thigh. In embolism of the crural artery the character of the disease is shown by the absence of pulsation below the obliterated point, by the absence of puncta dolorosa, and by the coolness of the limb.

Phlyctenulæ, filled with a reddish fluid, and the signs of gangrene soon make their appearance. Thrombosis of the crural veins is recognized by the cyanosis and œdema and by the distention of the lower veins, especially upon the dorsal surface of the foot. If the patients are not obese, we will be able to detect the cord formed by the obliterated vein.

When sciatica is symptomatic of spinal affections, it involves both sides, at least at intervals. The puncta dolorosa are often wanting, and the pain is combined with other symptoms of motor and sensory irritation. The sciatic pains which sometimes occur in hysterical and saturnine affections are almost always accompanied by other characteristic signs. It is often much more difficult to determine whether a sciatica of recent date is of rheumatic or spinal origin. When the sciatica is accompanied by shooting pains or some points of cutaneous hyperæsthesia, or when it is combined with ocular paralyses, and with diplopia; when it occurs with other vague neuralgias, after long-continued masturbation or obstinate pollution; when it develops in the midst of phenomena indicative of genital irritation (frequent seminal losses with increase of the neuralgic pains, precipitate ejaculations, incomplete erections, disagreeable sensations in the back or legs after coitus), or is accompanied by abnormal sensitiveness to lower temperature or electrical stimulation,—it should be regarded as indicative of an irritation in the cord (especially of beginning ataxia).

The *prognosis* of sciatica depends upon the character of the affection. The idiopathic, rheumatic, or traumatic forms, those which follow the puerperal condition, typhoid fever, or syphilis, and those in which an existing compression of the nerves may be removed by an operation, are susceptible of recovery. In the same manner the sciatic pains, which sometimes occur in hysteria and lead-poisoning, may be relieved by treating the primary disease.

As a rule, the recovery of idiopathic forms occupies weeks or even months. Recent cases, in young and previously healthy individuals, terminate more rapidly than chronic neuralgias occurring in old people, although the latter are not hopeless. Inveterate sciaticas, which readily relapse and resist all treatment, the bilateral forms and those which are symptomatic of spinal affections, almost always present an unfavorable prognosis.

Treatment.—Local bleeding is indicated (wet-cups, leeches; in case of hæmorrhoids, leeches to the anus) in very painful, acute cases, and in robust individuals. But we are frequently compelled to resort to subcutaneous injections of morphine in order to diminish the violence of the pain and to enable the patient to obtain rest. Rapid improvement is sometimes obtained by applying, for several successive days, flying blisters to the painful points, especially over the posterior branches upon the sacrum (Anstie), and by rubbing the blistered parts with a little morphine mixed with olive oil or fat. Betz has recently advised the prolonged application, behind the trochanter, of a nitrate of silver ointment until it drops off spontaneously (powdered nitrate of silver, 1–1.50 grains; adipis, 15 grains).

Turpentine has been highly recommended by Romberg, Récamier, and Trousseau. It is prescribed with honey (one to five grammes of turpentine to thirty-five grammes of honey, one teaspoonful morning and evening) in capsules or in pills, to which magnesia has been added (Oppolzer). It is not well tolerated by many patients, and in such cases can only be employed externally.

Frictions with croton oil upon the posterior surface of the thigh and leg are also employed, but it must usually be applied several times before eczema and pustules are produced. In order to diminish the burning sensation produced by these eruptions, the limb may be covered with moist compresses and then with powdered starch. In the Vienna General Hospital I have obtained good results from the use of croton oil, even in obstinate cases.

One of the best revulsive measures consists of linear cauterization with a thin cautery. But the employment of this measure meets with an almost insurmountable obstacle in the fears of the patient, and a second application is rarely permitted. We may then resort to cauterization with sulphuric acid along the course of the painful nerves. Kollas (Harless Annalen, X. Bd.) and Malgaigne have advocated a measure which is made use of in veterinary medicine, viz.: the cauterization of the lobe of the ear upon the anterior surface of the helix on the affected side. Section of the peripheral nerves is only applicable to small nerve-fibres, and has not given very good results in the majority of cases in which it has been hitherto performed. As a rule, the operation causes quite extensive paralysis of motion and sensation. In one of Dieffenbach's cases, which was published by Romberg (excision of a neuroma of the sciatic nerve), persistent ulceration of the heel occurred together with osseous suppuration (trophic disorders from traumatic nerve lesions). In many instances the patients died of pyæmia. We may finally add, with regard to surgical treatment, that Patruban (Allg. Wien. Med. Zeit., 43–53, 1872) cured a rebellious case of sciatica by exposing and stretching the nerve (Nussbaum's operation).

Combining derivative treatment with narcotics, Trousseau prescribed, in obstinate sciatica, narcotic boluses (equal parts of extract of belladonna and opium, with powdered guaiac and mucilag. gum tragacanth), which were introduced at night in an incision made above the sciatic notch. During the day the premature closure of the wound was prevented by the introduction of two or three peas. In the sciatica following confinement, Basedow has several times obtained recovery by bandaging the leg from the toes to the knee.

As thermal treatment we may prescribe, especially in chronic sciatica, the sulphur waters of Wiesbaden, Aix-la-Chapelle, Baden (near Vienna), Gastein, Pistyan, Teplitz, Trentsin, etc. In those cases which are accompanied by symptoms of irritation on the part of the cord, mineral waters of high temperature are usually tolerated poorly, and are apt to increase the medullary symptoms.

In peripheral sciatica good results are obtained from faradic treatment (secondary current applied to the painful points for five to ten minutes by means of dry electrodes), and from the descending stabile current (the anode upon the lumbar plexus and nerve-roots, the cathode upon the painful points). Weak currents are used in the beginning, and their intensity may then be increased. In some cases in which electricity is not well borne, its use may be preceded, for a certain length of time, by sub-cutaneous injections and baths. In sciatica of central origin, electricity often produces merely palliative effects, and the relapses demand long-continued thermal or hydrotherapeutic treatment.

The hydrotherapeutic treatment of sciatica includes various procedures. In Fleury's method the patient, wrapped in woollen cloths, is placed in a sweating apparatus, heated by an alcohol lamp; the head, covered with moist compresses, protrudes from the sweat-chest. The patient remains in this position from ten to twenty minutes until he perspires profusely, and then takes a cool bath or douche. The "douche écossaise" consists of a shower-bath in which warm and cold water are used alter-nately. When the warm douche has been applied to the affected leg to the limit of the patient's endurance, it is followed by a local or general cold douche. Recent cases are also benefited by vapor-baths followed by moist frictions. Some physicians prescribe the application of ice-bags to the painful points, cold douches and dry frictions to the diseased limb, or the filiform douche (Fleury), which constitutes a form of high-pressure atomizer.

Although these measures may undoubtedly prove successful, especially in robust individuals and in the peripheral forms (as is shown by Lagre-lette's statistics), we must nevertheless, in a large number of cases of sciatica, avoid all extremes of temperature. A much milder plan and one that is applicable to all cases, consists of the use of moist packs (until the return of warmth over the entire body and especially in the legs), followed by cool affusions or half-baths at 22°–18° C., with frictions to the limbs.

b. *Spasms and Paralyses of the Lower Limbs.*

Spasms (tonic or clonic) of the lower limbs may constitute a part symptom of central spasmodic neuroses (hysteria, epilepsy, tetanus, chorea, etc.). At other times they are manifested directly under the influence of the will, or indirectly by reflex action.

Spasm of the muscles of the hip (spasmodic contracture, Stromeyer) is a tonic spasm of the ilio-psoas, the quadratus lumborum, and the adja-cent muscles upon the anterior surface of the thigh. It is due to inflamma-tion and neuralgia of the coxo-femoral articulation, to psoas abscess, or to diseases of the lumbar segment of the vertebral column. The thigh is then strongly flexed upon the hip, the pelvis tilted up, the limb shortened, active flexion difficult or impossible, and passive extension painful and accompanied by a deviation of the body towards the affected side. Spasm of the extensors or adductors of the thigh is a rare affection. The tonic and clonic forms are observed in central spasmodic neuroses and in neu-ralgia of the knee-joint. Spasm of the flexors of the leg may be of central origin (hysteria, spinal affections), or it may be secondary to diseases of the knee or muscles. Spasms of the anterior muscles of the leg (region of the peroneal nerve) are rare, and are caused by exposure and over-exer-tion or by paralysis of the antagonists. Spasms of the muscles of the calf and of the sole of the foot (region of the tibial nerve) are much more frequent. They include the contractures from spinal affections, joint diseases, and paralysis of the peroneal nerve, which give rise to talipes equinus. Rapid and painful tonic spasms of the calf and sole of the foot are caused by exertion in certain occupations, by forced marches, chilling of the foot, or by reflex action, as in cholera. Schulz has observed very

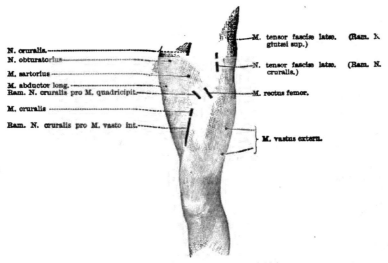

N. cruralis.
N. obturatorius
M. sartorius
M. abductor long.
Ram. N. cruralis pro M. quadricipit.
M. cruralis
Ram. N. cruralis pro M. vasto int.

M. tensor fasciæ latæ.   (Ram. N. glutæi sup.)
N. tensor fasciæ latæ.   (Ram. N. cruralis.)
M. rectus femor.
M. vastus extern.

FIG. 25.—Motor points of anterior region of thigh.

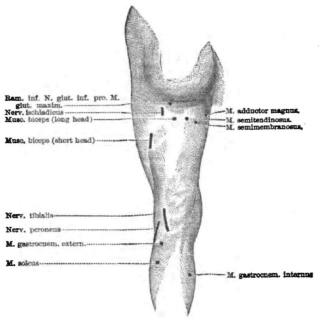

Ram. inf. N. glut. inf. pro M. glut. maxim.
Nerv. ischiadicus
Musc. biceps (long head)
Musc. biceps (short head)

Nerv. tibialis
Nerv. peroneus
M. gastrocnem. extern.
M. soleus

M. adductor magnus.
M. semitendinosus.
M. semimembranosus.

M. gastrocnem. internus

FIG. 26.—Motor points of posterior region of thigh.

violent spasms, commencing in the soles and extending to the dorsal surface of the foot and to the calf (region of the posterior tibial nerve), in
danseuses, after dancing upon tip-toe. They recovered after treatment
with electricity.

The saltatory spasms, which have been referred to on page 385, are
probably of central origin. The nature of the tonic rheumatic spasms of
the lower limbs attended with albuminuria, which were described by
Kussmaul (Ber. Klin. Wschr., 42–44, 1871), has not been thoroughly
determined.

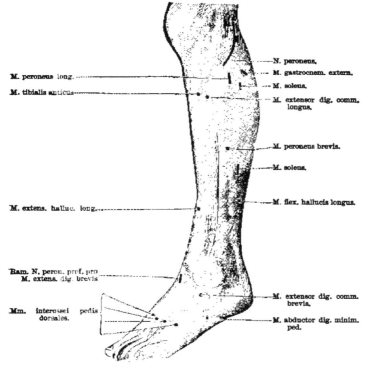

M. peroneus long.
M. tibialis anticus
N. peroneus.
M. gastrocnem. extern.
M. soleus.
M. extensor dig. comm. longus.
M. peroneus brevis.
M. soleus.
M. flex. hallucis longus.
M. extens. halluc. long.
Ram. N. peron. prof. pro M. extens. dig. brevis
Mm. interossei pedis dorsales.
M. extensor dig. comm. brevis.
M. abductor dig. minim. ped.

FIG. 27.—Motor points of outer side of leg.

The *treatment* of all the spasms in question is determined by the
principles which we have previously laid down; careful attention must be
paid to the primary disease. Cupping along the spinal column, galvanic
or faradic treatment, anti-spasmodics, subcutaneous injections of morphine, tenotomy, or orthopedic apparatus in old and obstinate cases, are
the principal measures employed.

Paralysis of the crural nerve and of the extensors of the leg which
are innervated by it, is observed after traumatism, pressure upon the lumbar plexus during delivery, acute diseases, neuritis, progressive muscular
atrophy, infantile paralysis, and myelitis. Electrical contractility is al-

most always affected to a greater or less extent. Not alone is extension of the leg compromised in severe forms, but the paralysis of the ilio-psoas muscles also causes the loss of the power of flexion of the leg upon the pelvis. In bilateral forms (after difficult labor) the patients are compelled to remain abed.

Paralysis of the obturator nerve (with loss of the power of adducting the thigh) and of the gluteal nerves (loss of the movements of abduction and rotation of the thigh) is rarely observed, and only as a part symptom of central lesions or of general paralysis after acute diseases.

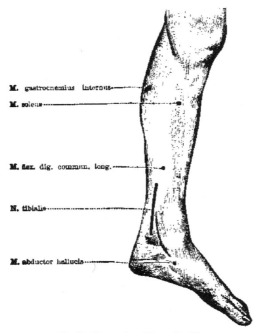

M. gastrocnemius internus
M. soleus

M. flex. dig. commun. long.

N. tibialis

M. abductor hallucis

FIG. 28.—Motor points of inner side of leg.

Paralyses of the lower limbs occur most frequently in the distribution of the sciatic nerve and its branches. The superior segment of the sciatic nerve is much more rarely involved than the lower, which corresponds to the peroneal and tibial nerves. These forms of paralysis are chiefly attributable to rheumatic and traumatic influences (delivery, operations, pelvic tumors). Upon page 172, we have reported a case of simultaneous paralysis of the tibial and peroneal nerves, from a gunshot wound of the sciatic at its bifurcation. The nerves in question are also the seat of more or less extensive paralysis in various cerebral and spinal lesions, after febrile diseases, and in infantile spinal paralysis and progressive muscular atrophy. Paralysis of the flexors of the thigh is extremely rare.

Among the paralyses occurring in the distribution of the peroneal nerve, that of the anterior tibial muscle is characterized by dropping of the toes, by the abduction which occurs during attempts at flexion, and by the prominence formed by the extensor proprius pollicis. In paralysis of the peroneus longus, the foot is adducted; when standing, it assumes the position of talipes valgus, but in attempts at extension this changes to varus, and is accompanied by pain; the foot readily tires, and is the seat of acute pain in the external malleolar region. At a more advanced stage the secondary contractions of the peroneus brevis and the extensor communis produce complete rotation of the foot outwards. In paralysis of the common extensor of the toes, active extension of the first phalanges is abolished, the foot is abducted, and is flexed with difficulty.

Among the paralyses in the distribution of the tibial nerve, that of the muscles of the calf produces what is known as talipes cavus, consisting of valgus with forced extension of the heel, exaggerated excavation of the plantar arch, and secondary deformities in the articulations of the foot. Paralysis of the flexors of the toes abolishes the power of flexing the first two phalanges. In paralysis of the interossei, the lateral movements of the toes, flexion of the first joint, and extension of the last two joints of the toes, are rendered impossible.

The *diagnosis* of these various motor disturbances is rendered easy if we are able to exclude primary contracture and if passive movements are preserved. The *prognosis* depends upon the etiology, the duration of the disease, and the secondary changes in the muscles and joints. The most efficient therapeutic measures consist of galvanization of the nerves, combined with faradic stimulation of the muscles, and rational gymnastics and orthopedics.

c. Coccygodynia.

Krukenberg, Nott, Simpson, Erichsen, and Scanzoni have applied the term coccygodynia to neuralgia of the branches of the coccygeal plexus. The disease is characterized by acute pain in the coccyx, especially in the sitting or vertical position, the pain usually radiating into the perineum, the vesical region, and even into the hips. This distressing sensation forces the patient to sit sideways upon the edge of a chair or to place the hand underneath the buttocks while sitting. Some patients experience extreme difficulty in walking and in going to stool. The pains increase upon slight concussion, as upon coughing and sneezing, and upon pressure, especially from below upwards.

Among the *causes* of coccygodynia, we may enumerate the following conditions: inflammation of the coccyx and its ligaments, diseases of the periosteum, caries of the last coccygeal vertebra (Nott), displacement of the coccyx in consequence of muscular contractions, fracture or ankylosis, and perhaps inflammation of the coccygeal gland. This affection occurs most frequently in women after difficult labors, in uterine affections, hysteria, and after injury.

As regards treatment, Scanzoni prescribes leeches, warm-baths, compresses, and subcutaneous injections of morphine. In Gosselin's case the neuralgia disappeared after the prolonged use of an air-cushion (to avoid pressure) and mild purgatives. Surgical intervention is the only resource left in rebellious and very painful cases. Nott, of Alabama, who first resorted to surgical interference, extirpated the coccyx (Amer.

Journ. of Med. Science, III., 1832). Simpson performed subcutaneous section of the muscles and ligaments inserted into the coccyx; in severe cases he resorted to excision of the bone. Seeligmueller (Neuropath. Beob., Jena, 1873) cured a coccygodynia of twelve years' standing by faradization (the negative pole in the cervical canal, the positive upon the sacrum). Amann merely obtained a certain amount of improvement by the employment of galvanization.

Neuralgias of the Joints (Articular Neuralgia).

These were first described by Brodie (Pathol. and Surg. Observ. on Diseases of the Joints, London, 1818), and were investigated at a later period by Stromeyer (Handb. d. Chir., 1844, and Erfahr. u. Localneurosen, 1873), Esmarch (Ueber Gelenkneurosen, 1872), Wernher (Ueber nerv. Coxalgia, Deutsch. Zeitschr. f. Chir., Bd. I., 1872), and O. Berger (Ber. Klin. Wschr., 1873, and Deutsch. Zeitschr. f. prak. Med., 1874).

Ruedinger (Die Gelenksnerven des menschlichen Koerpers. 1867) discovered that a large number of nerve-fibres are distributed to the ligaments, fibrous capsule, and especially to the synovial membrane of the large and small joints of the limbs (and also to the vertebral articulations). The articular nerves originate partly from the spinal, partly from the sympathetic system.

The abundance of nerves in the larger and smaller joints and in the surrounding skin enables us to understand why these parts are the seat of irritative phenomena, which Esmarch and especially Berger regard as true neuralgias.

Among the etiological factors, the chief importance must be attached to a neuropathic condition, which is either congenital or acquired by the habits of life and diet, and in consequence of anæmia and hysteria. It is for this reason that women and girls suffer so frequently from various forms of articular neuralgia. Upon several occasions, also, I have observed neuralgia of the shoulder, elbow, and knee, in young boys who have been addicted to masturbation for a long time. The exciting causes include emotional excitement, traumatism, contusions, pressure upon the joints, fatigue, and more rarely rheumatic influences. At times articular neuralgias are induced by gastric disturbances, irritations of the sexual apparatus (the abdominal sympathetic has numerous relations with the sacro-coccygeal plexus), and, finally, by acute diseases and central affections (hemiplegia and ataxia, according to Berger).

The symptoms develop gradually, but they may also appear suddenly. Pain is the chief symptom; it appears in certain joints with periodical exacerbations, radiates into the surrounding parts, and usually increases towards evening and diminishes at night. The pain sometimes disappears if the patient immediately begins to walk. Menstruation may either diminish or increase the neuralgic phenomena.

Examination of the affected joint does not reveal any especial changes. Certain signs, which are found in the majority of neuralgias, are nevertheless present. These include the *puncta dolorosa*, for the hip, between the trochanter major and ischium, and in the vicinity of the anterior superior spinous process of the ilium; for the knee, upon the inner border of the patella, in the popliteal space and above the head of the fibula; for the ankle-joint, behind the two malleoli; for the shoulder, over the nerves of the brachial plexus and in the axillary space; for the elbow, over the epitrochlea and head of the radius; for the wrist, over the styloid process of the ulna. According to my experience, certain forms of rachialgia and so-called spinal irritation should be attributed to neuralgias of the vertebral articulations. They are characterized by lancinating or pricking pains, which recur periodically, and exacerbate either spontaneously or after excitement, effort, or forced movements. The pains extend along the vertebral column, with painful points over the spinous and transverse processes, between the shoulders or upon the scapulæ, and are accompanied by circumscribed cutaneous hyperæsthesia, local sensations of heat or cold, and sometimes by other arthralgias. We rarely find other positive signs of hysteria in these cases. Superficial pressure over certain portions of the dorsal region do not give rise, as in hysteria, to the characteristic attacks which are accompanied by sensations of dread, constriction of the neck or epigastrium, etc.

In addition to the puncta dolorosa, articular neuralgias are accompanied by diffuse hyperæsthesia of the surrounding integument (Brodie), and, in cases of long duration, by irradiated anæsthesia and paræsthesia (formication, burning). The vaso-motor disorders consist of periodical alterations in the color and temperature of the skin, diffuse œdema around the joint from time to time, considerable swelling, and urticaria (Brodie). Wernher and others have published cases of emaciation of the limb and atrophy of the muscles around the articulation. The motor disorders include muscular spasms (frequently combined with immobility of the limb in extension or pseudo-ankylosis, which disappears under the influence of chloroform) and paralytic weakness, even in the intervals between the neuralgic attacks.

Among eighty cases of articular neuroses collected by Esmarch, thirty-eight occurred in the knee, eighteen in the hip, eight in the wrist, seven in the ankle, four in the shoulder and elbow, and one in the fingers. This leaves out of consideration the neuralgias of the vertebral articulations which, in our opinion, are of frequent occurrence.

The *diagnosis* may be surrounded with great difficulties from the fact that articular inflammations or caries sometimes present at the outset all the appearances of neuralgic arthritis. In such cases continued observation will enable us to recognize the true character of the affection. A marked neuropathic condition and positive signs of hysteria are of great assistance in forming a diagnosis. But the chief sign, as Esmarch has shown, is the striking disproportion between the intensity and persistence of the affection and the slight importance of the articular changes. The following phenomena speak in favor of articular neuralgia: paroxysms of pain, which usually grow milder during the night, puncta dolorosa, cutaneous hyperæsthesia, vaso-motor disorders, slight pain upon bringing the articular extremities in contact, slight emaciation even after absolute rest for several months. In articular inflammations, on the other hand, there is persistent tumefaction, spasmodic flexion of the limb, and increase of the pain upon pressing the ends of the joints; rest and the use of fixation apparatus exert a favorable influence. Careful examination will enable us to avoid the serious diagnostic and therapeutic mistake which was committed in a case reported by Brodie. For a relapsing neuralgia of the knee, the unfortunate patient was subjected to amputation of the thigh, then to section of the sciatic nerve, and, finally, to disarticulation of the hip-joint.

The *prognosis* is favorable in young patients who suffer from simple nervousness; it is more doubtful in old and obstinate forms of hysteria. In the *treatment* we may employ cool affusions and douches to the joint, followed by massage and passive movements (Esmarch), and may also apply the faradic brush or galvanize the joint. Mountain air, sea-baths, mild hydrotherapeutics, simple gymnastic exercises, the administration of arsenic, and an appropriate moral treatment, also furnish good results.

CLASS X.

VASO-MOTOR AND TROPHIC NEUROSES.

—————◆—————

CHAPTER L.

VASO-MOTOR AND TROPHIC DISORDERS.

VASO-MOTOR and trophic neuroses form the last chapter in our study of the diseases of the nervous system. The vaso-motor disorders which occur in cerebral and spinal affections, in hysteria, epilepsy, and peripheral traumatisms, have been previously discussed.

We have also referred to the fact that the latest experimental investigations of Goltz (Pflueg. Arch., Bd. IX., 1874) and Vulpian (Arch. de Physiol.), upon the vaso-dilator nerves, have led to radical modifications of the views hitherto entertained. According to Goltz, vascular dilatation and elevation of temperature are not attributable to paralysis of the vaso-motor nerves, but to an active process, viz., to functional over-stimulation of the vaso-dilator nerves. The vaso-dilator fibres of the nerves proceed directly from the cord or may be brought into play by reflex means, from irritation of the centripetal fibres of other nerves. These experimental data require confirmation and elucidation by new investigations. Nevertheless they afford a more satisfactory explanation of certain contradictory symptoms in hysteria (*vide* page 31) and in Basedow's disease.

The theory of the existence of trophic nerves and the disorders dependent upon them, is still under discussion, and its solution will, perhaps, occupy a long time. According to some authors, the vaso-motor elements contained in the mixed nerve-trunks become paralyzed when central innervation is arrested, and thus give rise to retardation of the circulation and passive hyperæmia, with disturbances in the nutrition of the muscles. Nevertheless, observation teaches us that motor paralysis may continue for a long time with marked functional and circulatory disturbances, but without any appreciable alteration of nutrition. Conyba and Charcot attribute the trophic disorders occurring after injuries to the nerves to a neuritis, and the same interpretation has been more recently applied by Friedreich to the pathogeny of progressive muscular atrophy, which he attributes to an inflammatory process in the muscles and an intra-muscular neuritis that is propagated along the nerve-trunks and roots to the spinal cord. We have analyzed and refuted this theory in the chapter on progressive muscular atrophy (pages 17–19).

The view that the principal source of trophic disorders is situated in the spinal cord, is gaining ground more and more. As we previously showed, a large number of clinical and anatomical observations have proven that in central myelitis, whether primary or secondary, and in bulbar foyers, in cerebro-spinal sclerosis, in sclerosis of the posterior columns, in symmetrical sclerosis of the lateral columns, in meningo-myelitis and hypertrophic pachymeningitis, in a word, in all lesions of the anterior gray columns of the cord, marked trophic disturbances occur in the muscles, joints, and skin. Secondary sclerosis of the lateral columns in cerebral apoplexy, when it is propagated forwards, and central myelitis with inflammatory degeneration of the anterior horns, give rise to progressive muscular atrophy. The multipolar cells of the anterior horns of gray matter contain, therefore, important trophic centres (Charcot). But the trophic influence of the cord can only act upon the peripheral parts by passing along certain paths of transmission, and solutions of continuity in these trophic conductors in traumatic lesions of the peripheral nerve-trunks will produce considerable disturbances in the nutrition of the muscles and other tissues.

In the following section we shall discuss those diseases of the vaso-motor and trophic nerves which, thanks to the discoveries of pathological anatomy, are better understood at the present time. We refer, for further details, to the works of Eulenburg and Guttmann upon the pathology of the sympathetic system (Berlin, 1873).

1. MIGRAINE (HEMICRANIA).

This term refers to a paroxysmal headache which was known to the older physicians (Tissot, J. Frank, etc.), but was not distinguished by them from prosopalgia. Romberg and Leubuscher were the first to recognize the fact that migraine is a cerebral neuralgia. Nearly twenty years ago, Du Bois-Reymond (Arch. f. Anat. u. Phys., 1860) observed certain phenomena in his own person (the temporal artery forming a hard cord upon the affected side, anæmia of the face, sinking in of the eye, dilatation of the pupil, and, finally, redness of the ear), which led him to believe that migraine consists of a condition of tetanus of the vascular muscles on the affected side or of tetanus of the vessels in the distribution of the cervical sympathetic (sympathico-tonic migraine).

The spasm of the vascular muscles, and the compression of the sensory nerves which traverse the vessels, were regarded as the immediate causes of the pain, as they are in cramps in the calves, colic, and labor pains. According to Eulenburg and Landois, the fluctuations in the current of arterial blood, the temporary hyperæmia and anæmia of one-half of the head, will suffice to irritate the sensory nerves of the scalp, pericranium, cranial meninges, or sensitive parts of the brain, and to produce the paroxysms of pain.

According to Moellendorf (Virch. Arch., Jan., 1868), migraine is due to a lack of energy (occurring either with or without periodical manifestations) in the vaso-motor nerves of one of the carotids, with secondary relaxation of the vessel and arterial fluxion to the brain. According to Goltz's experiments, however, there is active irritation of the vaso-dilator nerves. The secondary symptoms include hyperæsthesia of the senses and of the scalp, nausea and vomiting. Dimness of vision, difficulty in the movements of the eyeballs, and dulled sensibility, are observed among the symptoms of compression. In support of his theory, Moellendorf refers to the entire suppression of the pain which follows compression of the carotid on the affected side, to the return of the pain when the compression ceases, and its increase by compression of the carotid on the healthy side; to the dilatation of the central vessels which was observed in one case with the ophthalmoscope (scarlet redness of the fundus of the eye, dilatation of the central retinal artery and vein, the latter being knotted and sinuous), the eye upon the healthy side being in a normal condition; finally, to the marked slowness of the pulse, the small size and contraction of the radial arteries contrasting with the ample pulsation in the carotid and temporal arteries (sympathico-paralytic migraine).

Two of my cases of migraine were very characteristic. In one of these patients, whom I examined several times at the close of the attacks, the seat of the affection was readily recognized by the bright redness of the left cheek and ear. In the second case I could note the transition from the first stage, that of vascular spasm, to the second or angio-paralytic period. This occurred in a young hysterical girl in whom the migraine began with a sensation of cold in the fingers and toes of both sides (the tips of the fingers became cold in the intense heat of midsummer). In a little while the face became pale and the pulse fell to sixty. After the paroxysm, the hands became very warm and perspired freely, and the cheeks reddened, especially on the right side. The pupil of the affected side was dilated.

The vaso-motor cephalalgia of Eulenburg (with fronto-temporal pain, redness and heat of the face and ear) is probably merely a variety of migraine attended with vascular spasm. The latter is not a neuralgia of the brain or trigeminus, but a disease of the cervical or cephalic portion of the sympathetic or of the vaso-motor centres themselves. The slow pulse observed in the angio-paralytic form must be attributed (according to Landois' experiments upon artificial cerebral hyperæmia) to irritation of the medulla oblongata and pneumogastric nerves. This variety of migraine also presents the signs of paralysis of the sympathetic. Enteralgia and diarrhœa are sometimes observed as complications, and are due to paralysis of the abdominal vaso-motor nerves. In the tonic form, ptosis and myosis (Berger) sometimes occur, probably from paralysis of the muscular fibres of Mueller, which are innervated by the sympathetic and are distributed to the orbicularis palpebrærum. The salivation has been attributed by Gruetzner to irritation of the salivary centre in the medulla oblongata.

Migraine occurs chiefly in women, who present, for the most part, a morbid excitability due to anæmia or hysteria. It is a very distressing affection, and is often accompanied by vomiting. I have observed it in girls ten to twelve years of age, whose mothers also suffered from migraine or from extreme nervousness. The disease is also frequent in men under similar conditions. Migraine disappears at the menopause, when the vascular system becomes calmer.

Treatment.—In the periodical forms: quinine and Fowler's solution (in increasing doses); in irregular forms: valerianate of caffeine, paulinia sorbilis (two to four grains per diem), large doses of bromide of potassium; in chlorotic patients: ferruginous preparations, mineral waters, country air. Nitrite of amyl has been recently recommended in migraine attended with vascular spasm (the patient inhales two to five drops). Filehne (Pflueger's Arch., Bd. IX., 1874) believes that this drug especially paralyzes the vaso-motor centres and the origin of the pneumogastrics (it is attended with considerable slowing of the pulse). Eulenburg and Berger highly recommend the extract of ergot (internally or subcutaneously) in angio-paralytic migraine. According to my observations, these various drugs do not possess a permanent influence upon irritation of the vaso-motor apparatus. Better results are obtained by stimulating the energy of the vascular nerve-centres by means of hydrotherapeutics, sea-baths, mountain air, and rational and moderate gymnastics. Electrotherapeutics also prove successful in some cases. Frommhold employs the primary induced current, the positive pole being applied to the neck, the negative pole to the orbit, forehead, temple or top of the sagittal suture, for three to five minutes. Holst, with more propriety, resorts to galvanic treatment, with a large electrode over the cervical sympathetic at the outer border of the sterno-mastoid muscle, and the other electrode in the palm of the hand. In the spasmodic form, the anode is placed over the sympathetic in order to diminish the excitability. In the varieties which are attended with depression, the cathode is placed over the sympathetic, and, in order to obtain increased stimulation, it is provided with a commutator.

2. UNILATERAL ATROPHY OF THE FACE (FACIAL HEMIATROPHY).

This peculiar affection, which is characterized by atrophy of the soft parts, bones, and cartilages upon one-half of the face, has been called prosopodysmorphia by Bergson, nervous atrophy of the face by Samuel and Baerwinkel, progressive laminar aplasia of the face by Lande, and progressive facial hemiatrophy by Eulenburg.

The disease begins with the appearance of white spots upon one-half of the face, followed, in a short time, by extreme rarefaction of the subcutaneous adipose tissue and atrophy of the different layers of the skin, with circumscribed discoloration of the hairs or alopecia (head, beard and eyebrows), and diminution or complete abolition of the cutaneous secretions, especially of the sebum. In very marked forms, the skin is rough, puffy, or squamous; its sensibility is sometimes increased, and it is the seat of neuralgic sensations and circumscribed paræsthesias. For a long time the muscles present no appreciable change in volume or in the electrical reactions. But, in the very advanced forms; the face is often drawn slightly away from the atrophied side, and the masseters, the muscular tissue of the lips (Hueter, Lande, Hitzig, Guttmann), of the tongue, and the pillars of the soft palate are found atrophied. Excitement sometimes produces redness of the affected cheek, but, in other cases, this phenomenon is not produced. Finally, extreme atrophy also occurs in the osseous and cartilaginous skeleton of the face (nasal cartilages, malar bone, superior and inferior maxillæ), with displacement of the teeth. Sight remains intact.

The following etiological conditions have been noted: acute exanthemata (diphtheria, Emminghaus), exposure, traumatism, syphilis (Graefe's case with paralysis of the left oculo-motor externus and trigeminus), epileptiform convulsions (M. Meyer, Brunner), cerebral affections with hemiplegia (Parry), with neuralgia of the trigeminus and keratomalacia (Pissling), symptoms of irritation of the cord (personal observation, Wien. Med. Presse, 1868). Unilateral atrophy of the face is much more frequent in females, and the largest number of cases occur in early life until the age of twenty. The disease manifests a predilection for the eft side of the face.

In a case published by Brunner (Petersb. Med. Zschr., Bd. II., 1871), a woman, twenty-seven years of age, who had previously suffered from epileptiform attacks, was affected with left facial atrophy. The brows and hair were blanched, and yellowish-gray spots formed, which then changed to brown. She suffered from pains in the left cheek and eye, which darted into the neck and thorax as far as the epigastric region. Upon examining the patient, complete atrophy of the left frontal and temporal muscles was noted, and less pronounced atrophy in the muscles of the ala nasi, zygomatic arch and lips. The faradic and galvanic contractility and the electro-muscular sensibility were normal, and the stimulus of the will was readily transmitted to those fibres of the facial muscles which were still intact.

In addition, the left pupil was dilated and reacted slowly to light, there was a slight degree of exophthalmia, and the temperature was lowered upon the affected side of the face. The secretion of perspiration was suppressed, and the cardiac impulses were irregular and usually accelerated. Galvanization of the sympathetic produced immediate slowing of the heart's action and slight dilatation of the pupil; the atrophied half of the face then became bright red, and covered with profuse perspiration. Epileptic attacks appeared after the employment of weak induction currents, but no convulsions could be produced by the use of the constant current.

In a case of atrophy of the left side of the face reported by Guttmann (Arch. f. Psych., Bd. I., 1868), galvanization produced redness of the affected side which persisted for an hour.

According to Brunner, his case was due to permanent irritation of the sympathetic (following an inflammatory process or a tumor), such as was obtained in the experiments of Biffi and Claude Bernard. In the latter investigations, galvanization of the cervical sympathetic, after section of the nerve, produced dilatation and sluggishness of the pupil, exophthalmia, fall of temperature, and pallor of the conjunctiva, ear, and nose. When the galvanization was interrupted, the reverse symptoms, due to section of the sympathetic, made their appearance. In the complete absence of anatomical data, which will enable us to explain unilateral atrophy of the face, we are compelled to resort to mere hypotheses. Certain authors consider it an affection of the vaso-motor nerves of the face which are contained in the branches of the trigeminus. Others regard it as due to a lesion of the trophic fibres or of the cervical sympathetic, traumatic lesions of which have given rise to a slight amount of facial atrophy. In one case of facial atrophy, limited to the distribution of the infra-orbital nerve, Baerwinkel diagnosticated disease of the spheno-palatine ganglion. It is not unreasonable to suspect a neuritis of the facial nerves corresponding to the atrophied parts.

The *prognosis* is unfavorable, as there is no hope of a cessation of the disease except from spontaneous arrest of the atrophy. Medicinal, hydrotherapeutic, and electrical treatment have hitherto proved useless.

3. BASEDOW'S DISEASE.

This symptomatic triad (cardiac irritation, goitre, and exophthalmia) had been recognized by Stokes, but its distinct character was only established by Graves (1835) and Basedow.

During the last twenty years it has been observed more frequently and carefully. The first pathognomonic sign of the disease is usually intense cardiac irritation, appearing at first under the influence of exciting causes, and then in a condition of repose. It is characterized by acceleration of the pulse (120–160 per minute), irregularity of the heart, strong pulsation and "bruit" in the carotids, in the usually dilated vessels of the thymoid gland, and often also in the abdominal aorta. Physical exploration of the heart frequently reveals nothing abnormal. At other times a systolic murmur and cardiac hypertrophy are observed after the disease has lasted for a certain length of time.

Enlargement of the thyroid gland makes its appearance after the lapse of several weeks and months. Only one of the lobes is usually enlarged, and it is sometimes traversed by arteries which give rise to a blowing murmur. After the lapse of several years it assumes a harder consistence and is lifted rhythmically by the pulsation of its vessels. Either at the same time, or a little sooner or later, both eyes, or at times only one, become more and more prominent, and finally assume the peculiar fixed look characteristic of a bull's eye. The palpebral fissure is widely opened, closure of the lids is infrequent and incomplete, and, as Graefe first showed, the upper lid takes but little part in the movements of elevation and depression of the eyeball. Stellwag observed abolition of the lateral movements of both eyes with preservation of the convergence of the optic axes (Wien. Med. Jahrb., Bd. XVII., 1869); O. Becker noticed, as a new symptom, spontaneous arterial pulsations in the retina (Wien. Med. Wschr., 1873). In many cases the cornea loses its sensibility and its surface becomes dry and opaque. Graefe has seen ulcerations of the eye in fourteen cases (Ber. Klin. Wschr., Aug., 1867). The pupils are sometimes dilated, sometimes contracted or normal. The conjunctiva is red, and chemosis is observed at times; the secretion of tears is often very abundant. By means of the ophthalmoscope, Graefe has found in some cases dilatation and sinuosity of the retinal veins.

The attendant symptoms of exophthalmic goitre consist of paresis of the upper lid, partial paralysis of the face, and double paralysis of the motor-oculi externus (Stellwag). The following sensory and vaso-motor disorders have been observed: partial anæsthesia or neuralgic pains in the distribution of the trigeminus ; circumscribed vascular dilatations upon the integument (production of erythema upon contact with the scalp, "taches cérébrales" of Trousseau), unilateral or bilateral, and sometimes recurring paroxysmally (Stellwag); redness of one-half of the face, with abnormal pallor of the other side; elevation of temperature (Teisier, Cheadle, Eulenburg, Guttmann), with a sensation of heat and hypersecretion of sweat; œdematous swelling of the lids, conjunctiva, lips, or integument of the face; in one of Stellwag's patients there was swelling of the entire cervical region, and periodical attacks of asthma. Geigel, Solbrig, and Andrews have observed psychical disturbances (exaltation, melancholia, and even mania), which diminished in intensity as the primary affection improved.

The symptomatology of exophthalmic goitre may be varied by the absence of one or the other of the clinical signs. Thus, among fifty-eight cases collected by Busch (Lehrb. d. Herzkrankh., 1868), the cardiac phenomena were absent three times, and goitre four times. In Prael's and Fischer's cases, Basedow's disease was limited to a double exophthalmos. But the diagnosis was confirmed by the want of harmony between the movements of the eyes and those of the lids, and by other general phenomena.

The anatomical examinations which were made in a certain number of cases have revealed, as local lesions, a serous infiltration or proliferation of the retro-ocular adipose tissue. Naumann found atheromatous degeneration of the ophthalmic artery; Recklinghausen and Schoch, fatty degeneration of the ocular muscles. In Schnitzler's case (Med. Halle, 1864) Rokitansky found the inner wall of the orbital cavity, formed by the ethmoid, of unusual firmness, convex, projecting into the orbital cavity, and narrowing it very markedly behind; the ethmoidal sinuses were enormously dilated, gorged with muco-pus, and their walls very much thickened. In many cases the thyroid gland presented hyperæmic swelling and vascular hyperplasia or dilatation. The heart was often free of abnormalities. But, at other times, it presented waxy degeneration of the cardiac muscles, dilatation or hypertrophy, valvular lesions, or atheroma of the large vessels (of the ascending aorta, in Prael's case).

The following changes have been observed in the nervous system : spots of softening at the base of the anterior cerebral lobe, softening of the optic thalamus, tubercula quadrigemina and cerebellum (Prael's observation, lesions probably of embolic origin), and various changes in the sympathetic nerves. Trousseau and Lancereaux, and more recently Knight, have found an increase of the connective tissue, and atrophy and diminution of the nerve-cells in the cervical sympathetic. Beveridge observed thickening and tubercular degeneration of the sympathetic system, and of the fibres supplying the inferior thyroid and vertebral arteries; in addition, hypertrophy and induration of the middle and inferior cervical ganglia, which were filled with a granular mass and looked like tuberculous lymphatic glands. In Moore's case the inferior cervical ganglion was almost entirely destroyed and replaced by connective and adipose tissue. Recklinghausen and Biermer found atrophy, Virchow, on the other hand, hypertrophy and interstitial thickening of the cervical sympathetic. In Geigel's case the cervical sympathetic on both sides was surrounded by a sheath of thickened, fatty connective tissue, but no change was discovered with the microscope in the nerves themselves and in the ganglia, apart from the intense brown pigmentation of the latter. In addition, the central canal of the spinal cord was obliterated, and the adjacent parts of the cord presented an increased consistence, with slight proliferation of the neuroglia and marked fulness of the capillaries. On the other hand, the microscope showed no changes in the sympathetic system in cases published by Paul, Fournier, Ollivier, Rabejac, and Wilks.

The etiological factors which are regarded as occurring most frequently are intense psychical excitement and physical or mental over-exertion. Bouillaud saw the disease develop under the influence of onanism, and Graefe found it attain its maximum of intensity within a few days after unusual sexual irritation. In two cases reported by Begbie and Graefe, the first symptoms appeared after a violent blow upon the head. Among the predisposing causes we may mention anæmia (severe diseases, confinement, hæmorrhages), extreme nervousness, and hysteria. The much greater liability of the female sex to this affection under the influence of these causes is readily understood. Twenty-four among twenty-seven of Romberg's and Henoch's cases were females, and twenty among twenty-five of Taylor's observations. Among nine cases, Prael only found one in a male ; according to Graefe, the proportion is about one to seven. The much larger number of cases occur from the twentieth to the fortieth years of life. Stokes and Trousseau have, in exceptional instances, seen the disease in childhood and in women past the age of sixty.

The most diverse opinions have been entertained concerning the nature of this peculiar disease. Basedow, and more recently Hiffelsheim and Beau, considered the primary phenomenon to be a modification of the blood analogous to chlorosis. But experience disproves this view, as there is no manifestation of this disease in the vast majority of chlorotic patients, and exophthalmic goitre also develops as an acute affection in patients who are otherwise healthy, in men and children, and from various causes (traumatic, psychical, and sexual influences). Nor can we entertain the theory proposed by Piorry, Bouillaud, etc., who attributed the pathognomonic symptoms of the disease to the compression exercised by the hypertrophied thyroid gland upon the vessels and nerves of the neck, or upon the cervical sympathetic (Koeben), as the thyroid enlargement does not appear primarily, and even very large goitres or tumors compressing the sympathetic do not give rise to similar morbid phenomena.

Stokes' hypothesis which attributes the goitre and exophthalmia to hypertrophy of the heart, is also unsatisfactory, for physical exploration of the heart frequently reveals nothing abnormal in Basedow's disease, and, on the other hand, very marked organic affections of the heart are unaccompanied by any of these symptoms.

The theory which is most in unison with physiology and with the clinical data, is that which attributes Basedow's disease to an affection of the sympathetic system. This view numbers among its adherents Aran, Trousseau, Charcot, Friedreich, Geigel, Graefe, etc. We know from the experiments of Biffi and Claude Bernard that section of the cervical sympathetic causes dilatation of the vessels of the head and neck, and an elevation of temperature in the corresponding ear. The cornea then becomes flattened, the pupil contracts and the eyeball sinks into the orbit; galvanization of the central end of the sympathetic causes enlargement of the palpebral fissure, the restoration of the corneal convexity and the protrusion of the eyeball from the orbit. In accordance with these experimental data, Geigel (Wuerz. Med. Zschr., Bd. VII., 1866) believes that exophthalmic goitre is due to paralysis of the cephalic and cervical vascular nerves contained in the cervical sympathetic, and to the simultaneous irritation of its oculo-pupillary fibres.

Many clinical signs appear to confirm the theory of paralysis of the sympathetic in Basedow's disease. Paralysis of the sympathetic vascular fibres of the neck and head produces primarily a congestion of the vessels, the persistence of which causes the accumulation of adipose tissue in the orbit, and of colloid or connective-tissue elements in the thyroid gland; the enfeeblement of nervous action in the cardiac vaso-motor fibres of the sympathetic causes the increase in the intensity of the cardiac pulsations.

This interpretation is also supported by other facts, such as the rise of temperature observed in many patients; the ulcerations of the cornea, which were regarded by Graefe as neuroparalytic in character; the unilateral or bilateral redness and heat of the face observed by Stellwag and Geigel; the circumscribed vascular dilatations of the skin and the partial œdema of the mucous membranes; Graefe's observation, in which the disease developed within several days after intense sexual excitement, that had been followed, for half an hour, by very marked vaso-motor disturbances, etc.

In order to explain, according to the preceding theory, the contradictory manifestations of exophthalmic goitre, we are forced to admit a simultaneous irritation and paralysis of the sympathetic nerve, whereas we can arrive at a much more natural and simple view of the vaso-motor disorders by interpreting the symptoms in the light of the recent experiments of Goltz (loc. cit.). If we admit that the vascular dilatation is not due to paralysis, but is an active process, caused by exaggerated function of the vaso-dilator nerves, we can understand why the vascular dilatation and prolonged hyperæmia in the thyroid gland and in the orbits will give rise to connective-tissue proliferation, to the formation of goitre, and the protrusion of the eyeball. The increased blood-supply will also explain the irritation of the cardiac ganglia, the elevation of temperature which has been observed on several occasions, and the phenomena of psychical excitement. We have to deal, therefore, in Basedow's disease, with a neurosis due to irritation of the vaso-motor apparatus. The opposing actions of the nerves which pass through the sympathetic system must be attributed to irritation of their respective medullary centres.

Basedow's disease almost always pursues a chronic course, lasting months or even years. Recovery is possible in recent cases and in young subjects (as is shown by the observations of Prael and others). A certain amount of improvement is obtained in most cases, but relapses are not infrequent.

Treatment.—Milk, whey, or grape cures in the country (Graefe), small doses of iron, or iodide of iron; in palpitation, applications of ice to the præcordial region (Aran); Trousseau obtained good results in some cases by mild hydrotherapeutic treatment. By means of galvanization, Dusch, Guttmann, Wietfeld, and Chvostek have obtained marked improvement, with diminution in the frequency of the pulse, and in the goitre and other symptoms. The ascending stabile galvanic current, from one to ten elements, is passed through the cervical sympathetic (the anode in the mastoid fossa and the cathode upon the upper cervical ganglion) for eight to ten minutes at a time. The current is also directed transversely across the thyroid tumor, or an ascending current may be applied to the cervical and upper dorsal vertebræ.

4. TRAUMATIC AND RHEUMATIC NERVOUS DISORDERS OF THE SYMPATHETIC SYSTEM.

Traumatic lesions of the sympathetic are characterized by symptoms of irritation and depression of the vaso-motor nerves when the sympathetic system is compressed by tumors or has been injured in any manner. We may regard these phenomena, as Goltz does, as the results of a functional irritation of the vaso-constrictor or vaso-dilator nerves, similar to the effects produced by experimental irritation or section of the cervical sympathetic.

In tumors of the lateral region of the neck or superior orifice of the thoracic cavity, we frequently find the so-called symptoms of depression predominate. Thus contraction of the pupils has been observed in neoplasms or lymphatic enlargements in the neck (Heineke, Ogle, Willebrand), and in aneurisms of the aorta and innominate artery (Gairdner, Coates). In one of the latter cases a cold sweat appeared upon the face on the affected side, alternating with flashes of heat.

In Verneuil's patient, upon whom ligature of the carotid was performed for a tumor of the parotid gland, persistent contraction of the pupil developed shortly afterwards, with rise of temperature and vascular dilatation upon the temple and gums, and abundant perspiration upon the side of the face corresponding to the operation. All these symptoms can be produced experimentally upon animals by dividing the cervical sympathetic.

Tumors of the cervical ganglia and aneurisms of the aorta, like electrical irritation of the cervical sympathetic, often produce dilatation of the pupils. Upon page 217, Vol. I., I have reported certain observations, some personal, others taken from various authors, of caries, tuberculosis, and cancer of the upper cervical vertebræ, with unilateral dilatation of the pupil.

In Kidd's patient the right pupil was sometimes dilated, sometimes contracted, during the development of a suppurating phlegmon of the neck, and did not return to its normal condition until the abscess was opened.

In a patient who had suffered from a cystic goitre, with mydriasis and slight exophthalmia, Demme found, upon autopsy, well-marked redness of the left cervical sympathetic with serous infiltration of the adjacent tissues. In Eulenburg's case a vascular goitre of the right lobe was accompanied by mydriasis, paresis of accommodation, and a reduction of temperature in the right ear. Basedow's patient presented no pupillary symptoms, the exophthalmia was double, and the temperature was increased in both auditory canals. Gerhardt and Rossbach have observed mechanical irritation of the pneumogastric (with slow pulse) and sympathetic nerves (with pupillary dilatation) by supraclavicular and mediastinal tumors.

Examples of isolated traumatic lesions of the cervical sympathetic are extremely rare, and hitherto only a very small number have been collected. During the American Rebellion, Mitchell, Morehouse, and Keen (loc. cit.) observed a soldier who had received a bullet-wound upon the right side, behind the lower jaw, and at the anterior border of the sterno-mastoid muscle. The ball, after having partially traversed the neck, made its exit on the left side, below and about an inch from the angle of the lower jaw; the wound had healed after the lapse of six weeks The examination of the patient, made during the tenth week, showed that the right pupil (especially when the eye was shaded) was extremely small; myopia, slight ptosis, redness of the conjunctiva, and frontal pains were also present upon this side. On several occasions an unusual redness of the left half of the face was observed after exertion. During repose the temperature was normal in the mouth and both ears. This group of symptoms agrees entirely with the effects of experimental section of the sympathetic in animals and with the pathological observations reported above. Kaempf reported the case of a soldier (Ges. d. Wien. Aerzte, Mar. 8, 1872) who had received an injury of the right sympathetic from a wound in the cervical region, and who presented right paralytic myosis, repeated galvanization of which proved ineffectual.

Wounds of the cervical region of the cord and of the brachial plexus also give rise to disturbances in the distribution of the cervical sympathetic. The oculo-pupillary disorders produced in these cases, and their anatomical relations, have been discussed on page 211, Vol. I. I have also reported an example of lesion of the cervical cord with persistent slowness of the pulse and very marked dilatation of the left pupil.

Rendu has since published some observations upon fracture of the cervical vertebræ, in which unilateral mydriasis was accompanied by other symptoms of irritation. Myosis was observed, however, in luxations of the vertebræ with symptoms of paralysis and in my two cases of caries of the odontoid process, reported on page 216, Vol. I. Considerable contraction of the pupil is also observed in progressive muscular atrophy and in certain forms of ataxia, upon the side which is most affected. In these cases periodical attacks of sciatica sometimes occur (usually combined with cutaneous hyperæsthesia), during which spasmodic mydriasis appears at times upon the same side as the neuralgia. I have also observed spasmodic dilatation of the pupils in attacks of chorea (vide page 119).

In traumatic lesions of the brachial plexus, Hutchinson has observed unilateral myosis, narrowing of the palpebral fissure, and elevation of temperature upon the corresponding side of the face. Seeligmueller (Ber. Klin. Wschr., 1870 and 1872) has noted, in addition, emaciation and atrophy of the cheek upon the side of the wound.

Among the nervous disturbances, dependent on the cervical sympathetic, we must also mention unilateral hypersecretion of sweat (unilateral hyperhidrosis or ephidrosis). In the cases of unilateral compression of the sympathetic, referred to above, we have already alluded to the exaggerated production of sweat. Nitzelnadel, Chvostek, etc., have published some cases of unilateral ephidrosis due to Basedow's disease or diabetes. The pupil was contracted, the skin red, and the temperature elevated upon the side of the face which was the seat of the hypersecretion. As a result of suppurative parotiditis, Botkin has observed an elevation of temperature upon the same side with increase in the vigor of the pulsations of the temporal and facial arteries. In Chvostek's patient, galvanization of the cervical sympathetic caused profuse sweating upon the corresponding half of the face, while the opposite result was obtained in Nitzelnadel's case. In Fraenkel's patient (Inaug. Diss., Breslau, 1874), who was suffering from hypertrophy of the heart and thyroid gland, with attacks of dyspnœa and hyperhidrosis of the left half of the face, Ebstein found upon autopsy that the left cervical sympathetic was covered with rounded nodules, as large as grains of sand, and of a blackish-brown color. Under the microscope they were found to consist of varicose dilatations of the vessels, with formation of fusiform-cells in the vascular walls ; the ganglion-cells were markedly pigmented and filled with dark cells.

Seguin's patient (Amer. Journ. of Med. Sciences, Oct., 1872) presented a suppression of perspiration upon the right side of the face and neck, even when the left side sweated profusely.

At the autopsy the right cervical sympathetic was found adherent to the sheath of the vessels and of the pneumogastric, with injection of the superior ganglion and adjacent parts.

We are already acquainted (*vide* page 163) with the phenomena of vascular spasm and dilatation which are produced experimentally by the action of cold upon the cutaneous vascular nerves. Nothnagel has published (Arch. f. klin. Med., Bd. II., 1867) some observations relative to the influence of cold upon the development of vaso-motor nervous disorders. In all these cases the affection appeared in women, especially upon the forearms and hands after washing in cold water. The symptoms consisted of numbness and stiffness of the limbs, neuralgic pains, manifest diminution of sensibility, difficulty in performing delicate movements, pallor of the fingers, and a reduction of temperature. The local anæmia and all the other disorders of innervation are due to the arterial spasm caused by cold. In vasculo-nervous affections, Chapman has acted upon the vascular nerves by making warm or cold applications along the vertebral column.

In a case reported by Eulenburg and Landois (Wien. Med. Wschr., 56, 1868), the vascular spasm occurred in paroxysms, especially in the distribution of the right median nerve, and was accompanied by motor disturbances (tremor with flexion of the fingers and opposition of the thumb). While galvanic treatment was being carried out, an eruption of urticaria developed, as an intercurrent phenomenon, upon the palm of the hand and the palmar surface of the forearm. In the *treatment* of these rheumatic vascular neuroses we must endeavor to procure relaxation of the spasm of the vessels; this may be done by energetic friction, volatile liniments and especially the continuous current. A stabile current is passed from the cervical vertebræ to the brachial plexus for three to five minutes (Nothnagel).

We have previously remarked that, in fever, the stage of chill is accompanied by vascular spasm, with secondary pallor of the superficial parts of the body. In the hot stage there is dilatation of the vessels, with redness of the skin and active perspiration. The point of departure of these phenomena must be in the spinal centres of vascular innervation, especially in those of the medulla oblongata. According to Claude Bernard, fever results from paresis of the sympathetic system. He bases this opinion upon the fact that irritation of the central end of a sensory nerve, in an animal suffering from fever, will cause an abolition of the rise of temperature.

5. VASO-MOTOR ANGINA PECTORIS.

We have previously remarked that the imperfection of our actual knowledge concerning cardiac innervation, and the absence of sufficient anatomo-pathological data, prevent us from obtaining a clear clinical interpretation of the disorders of the nervous system of the heart. We refer to page 219, for the symptoms of angina pectoris, but, in order to render·the subject complete, shall here mention a certain number of facts which tend to demonstrate the participation (at least partial) of the sympathetic system in the symptomatology of this affection. According to Bezold's experiments (Travaux du Laboratoire de Wuerzbourg, 1867), the heart receives sympathetic fibres, some of which are contained in the cervical sympathetic, while others originate in the brain, and pass to the inferior cervical ganglion and cardiac plexuses through the cervical and dorsal portions of the cord. These fibres transmit to the heart the central stimuli which cause its contractions. to become slower. An observation, made by Lancereaux (Gaz. Méd., 1864), shows that changes in the cardiac plexus may give rise to symptoms of angina pectoris. The patient died in an attack of stenocardia (to which he had been subject), and the autopsy showed the existence of lesions in the aorta, considerable narrowing of the coronary arteries, injection of the vascular walls and of the cardiac plexus, and an accumulation of nuclei in the nerve-fibres and ganglia between the more or less compressed nerve-tubes.

As the vascular nerves of the heart are contained in the sympathetic, it is conceivable, from the experiments of Ludwig, Thiry, and the Cyon brothers, that the pressure in the aortic system and the cardiac action should be increased or diminished, according to irritation or relaxation of the vaso-motor apparatus. Finally, the observations of Landois (Corresp.-Blatt. f. Psych., 1866) and Nothnagel (Arch. f. klin. Med., Bd. III., 1867) also tend to demonstrate the sympathetic origin of a large number of cases of stenocardia. The latter author has published, under the term vaso-motor angina pectoris, some cases in which the symptoms of stenocardia had followed spasm of the arteries, usually from cold.

The attack is manifested by the following subjective symptoms : heaviness, formication, numbness, and a sensation of cold in the limbs, followed by præcordial anxiety and palpitation of the heart, terminating even in syncope. Dull pain in the region of the heart, dyspnœa, and vertigo are also observed at times. The list of objective symptoms comprises extreme pallor of the face, ears, and limbs, cyanosis of the finger and toe nails, marked diminution of sensibility, fall of temperature, and the presence of a cold, viscid sweat upon the skin. The cardiac pulsations are often more rapid, at other times regular, and rarely diminished, the heart-sounds are normal, the radial pulse tense, but seldom slow; in one case a large quantity of clear urine (nervous urine) was discharged. According to Nothnagel and Eichwald, palpitation of the heart is caused by the increased resistance which the heart meets with on all sides from the contracted vessels; the dread and præcordial pains are caused by the overexertion to which the heart is subjected. Paroxysms of this nature may occur, with variable intensity and duration, either daily or at the end of certain intervals, during which the health remains satisfactory, or the patient suffers from persistent headache (Cordes).

The affection only appears in adults, in men and women of all classes and pursuits. The action of cold (washing in cold water, damp feet, moist dwellings) is the chief etiological factor. The disease is most frequent in winter and in rigorous climates; it usually disappears in the mild season, and returns in the following winter. The prognosis is almost always favorable. Old cases are very intractable to treatment, but even in these instances the paroxysms terminate after a certain length of time. The *treatment* aims to diminish the vascular spasm and to favor the flow of blood to the integument. Warm full-baths and foot-baths, friction of the limbs, stimulating liniments, etc., are the remedies employed. We should avoid the action of cold upon the limbs, and endeavor to counteract the anæmia. Frictions with moderately cold water serve to prevent a relapse.

6. NEUROSES OF THE ABDOMINAL SYMPATHETIC.

This category includes certain peculiar nervous disorders which are observed in the abdominal viscera, within the distribution of the abdominal sympathetic and of the cerebro-spinal nerves with which it communicates.

Enteralgia (colic), caused by rheumatic influences, psychical excitement, or hysteria, and which is also called hyperæsthesia or neuralgia of the mesenteric plexus, had been recognized by the older writers as an affection of the sympathetic system. Tanquerel des Planches, the distinguished writer on saturnine affections, regarded lead colic as dependent on the sympathetic system (Traité des Maladies de Plomb., 1839). Nevertheless, among forty-nine autopsies on patients who had suffered from this disease, only one was found in which the abdominal ganglia of the sympathetic were changed (increased to two or three times their normal volume, and colored yellowish gray as compared with the corresponding ganglia in two other subjects). Ségond also found the ganglia and some fibres of the sympathetic hypertrophied and indurated (Essai sur la névralgie du grand sympathique, colique de Poitou, 1837). Within recent times, Kussmaul and Maier have published an example of sclerosis of the cœliac and superior cervical ganglia, in a case of chronic lead-poisoning. We have referred to this case in detail on page 141.

We are taught by physiologists that the motor nerves, which the sympathetic system distributes to the muscular fibres of the viscera and vessels, are chiefly contained in the anterior roots, the posterior roots serving for the transmission of sensory stimulation or centripetal impressions received by the same sympathetic fibres. The abdominal vascular nerves terminate centrally in the brain. Lesions of the corona radiata, optic thalamus, and even of the corpus callosum give rise, according to Valentin and others, to hyperæmia of the abdominal viscera, especially of the small intestines, and to softening and ulceration of the mucous membrane. We can frequently notice, in recently killed animals, that irritation of the optic thalamus or cerebral peduncle does not affect the striated muscles, but causes contraction of the muscular fibres of the intestines and other abdominal viscera.

It follows from these considerations (which are also applicable, in large part, to man) that central irritation (excitement) may give rise to enteralgia, especially in very impressionable patients. On the other hand, the abnormal irritation of the intestinal muscular fibres or intra-muscular nerve-fibres (perhaps from the lead which has been detected by Devergie, Meurer, and Orfila in the intestinal walls of patients suffering from lead-poisoning) may reach the nerve-centres through the paths of transmission mentioned above, and may thus give rise to reflex movements in the muscular apparatus of the intestines. Colic cannot therefore be regarded as a mere hyperæsthesia of the mesenteric plexus.

The remaining symptoms of lead colic, such as pallor and coolness of the face and limbs, the slow, small, and hard pulse, and irregular respiration, must be attributed (as Eulenburg and Landois have emphasized, loc. cit.) to irritation of the medullary centre of the pneumogastric and to reflex arrest of the cardiac and respiratory movements, as in Goltz's experiments upon percussion of the intestines. The fibres which act in a reflex manner upon the pneumogastric are contained, according to Bernstein (Centralbl., 52, 1864), in the sympathetic system and reach the cord through the anastomotic branches. Section of the sympathetic above this point will interfere with Goltz's percussion experiment. In frogs, according to Bernstein, the nerve-fibre which accompanies the mesenteric artery transmits the reflex fibres of the abdominal viscera to the sympathetic system, and stimulation of this nerve produces arrest of the heart's action. According to Asp's recent experiments, stimulation of the central end of the splanchnic nerve causes retardation of the pulse and an elevation of the arterial pressure. We cannot state with certainty, however, that the syncopal attacks observed by Romberg in lead colic are due to a reflex arrest of the heart's action. The severe and obstinate constipation, which almost always accompanies lead colic, may be attributed to the prolonged irritation of the splanchnic nerve, which acts as the inhibitory nerve of intestinal movements (Pflueger). The recent experiments of Basch and S. Mayer (Wien. Akad. Sitz.-Berichte, 1870 and 1873) and of Hougkest van Braam (Pflueg. Arch., 1873) have shown that the inhibitory action of the pneumogastric results from the vaso-motor functions of this nerve. The vaso-motor fibres of the pneumogastric originate in the medulla oblongata.

Autenrieth and Romberg have described a hyperæsthesia of the solar plexus (cœliac neuralgia) with pains in the epigastrium (as in neuralgic gastrodynia) which radiate into the thorax and towards the back. In the absence of material lesions and of a sufficient physiological foundation, we are not entirely justified in attributing these phenomena to an affection of the sympathetic.

Gastralgias, like the "crises gastriques," which are sometimes observed in the irritation-stage of ataxia, are explained more readily by the sensory fibres recently discovered in the pneumogastric.

Extirpation of the solar plexus merely produces trophic disorders in the stomach and upper part of the small intestine. Hyperæsthesia of the hypogastric plexus (painful sensations in the hypogastric and sacral regions, radiating towards the thighs and hæmorrhoidal nerves) has also been recognized, but the actual condition of our physiological knowledge will not sanction the expression of an opinion as to its character. Hyperæsthesia of the spermatic plexus constitutes the neuralgia of the testis, which we discussed in connection with the neuralgias of the cerebro-spinal branches of the lumbar plexus.

This category also includes the neuralgia of the urethral canal (which is almost always accompanied by local hyperæsthesia and other symptoms of irritation of the cord), the acute pains at the neck of the bladder (with frequent desire to urinate) and in the rectum (with tenesmus, constipation, sensation of great heat), which Duchenne observed in a physician who was suffering from beginning ataxia. The pains recurred at intervals of two or three months, and continued for twenty-four hours; they disappeared after the use of purgatives or the appearance of diarrhœa. At a later period lancinating pains occurred with cutaneous hyperæsthesia, unilateral amblyopia, and mydriasis without diplopia; ejaculation during coitus occurred precipitately. Nevertheless no marked disturbance was noticeable in the gait.

The neuroses of the urethra, neck of the bladder, and of the rectum, which sometimes develop in the irritation-stage of ataxia, must be regarded as symptoms of irritation of the lumbar cord, and especially of the genito-spinal and ano-spinal centres. The hypothesis of a functional disorder of the abdominal sympathetic is here entirely superfluous. We refer, for further details, to the remarks made on pages 247,–249, Vol. I.

Some writers have also described anæsthesiæ of the sympathetic system. Although, according to Hasse's recent experiments, certain poisons (such as opium and curare) greatly increase the reflex excitability of the intestines, it is none the less true, in a general sense, that all portions of the sympathetic normally present but a very slight degree of sensibility. Neither anatomical nor physiological data enable us to entertain a decided opinion concerning the anæsthesiæ under consideration. The suppression of movements (those of the intestines, for example) may be due to the abolition of the direct excitability of the peripheral ganglia as well as to disturbances of conduction in the reflex paths.

Our information with regard to atrophy of the abdominal portion of the sympathetic is still extremely meagre. In a case of diabetes mellitus, reported by Munk (Naturforscherversammlung, Innsbruck, 1869), Klebs found atrophy of the solar ganglion, the nerve-filaments supplying the hepatic artery being intact. Experiments have been made in dogs upon the part played by the solar ganglion in the development of diabetes. Partial extirpation of the ganglion gave rise to glycosuria, which either lasted until death (one to two weeks) or was merely temporary. In the latter case the diabetes returned temporarily, after its previous disappearance, under the influence of an exclusively animal diet. Under a vegetable diet it returned for a few days, and then disappeared entirely. Upon making an autopsy in these cases, Klebs found a marked degeneration of the elements of the nervous tissue. Neither section of the hepatic nerves nor of the pneumogastrics is sufficient, in itself, to give rise to diabetes. Lubimoff found sclerosis of the cells of the cœliac ganglion in diabetes mellitus (Virch. Arch., Bd. LXI).

7. ADDISON'S DISEASE.

The peculiar symptomatology which is characteristic of degeneration of the suprarenal capsules was first described by Thomas Addison (On the Constitutional and Local Effects of Disease of the Suprarenal Capsules, London, 1855). The clinical signs of the disease in question are: deposit of a dark, bronze-colored pigment in the rete Malpighii, more rarely in the internal organs; symptoms of irritation on the part of the digestive canal (vomiting, abdominal or lumbar pains, etc.); great muscular weakness; anæmia almost always terminating in death.

The most frequent anatomical lesion is a chronic inflammation of the suprarenal capsules, the exudation into which is usually cheesy (tubercularization). A bronzed coloration of the skin is seen during life in very exceptional cases of cancer and echinococci of the suprarenal capsules (Huber). Arerbeck has published a complete monograph, comprising all the cases reported prior to 1867 (Die Addison'sche Krankheit, Erlangen, 1869).

Experimental investigations have not hitherto contributed much towards clearing up the pathology of the suprarenal capsules. According to Brown-Séquard, animals succumb more rapidly after extirpation of these organs than after removal of the kidneys or wounds of the peritoneum. Nevertheless some of the larger or smaller animals thus operated upon may survive.

With regard to the accumulation of pigment in the blood after extirpation of the suprarenal capsules, Brown-Séquard has seen injection of this blood rapidly produce death in an animal in whom only one capsule had been removed, while animals deprived of both organs could be kept alive for several hours by injecting the blood of a healthy animal. The accumulation of pigment in the blood causes its elimination by the capillaries and congestion of the latter, with circulatory disturbances terminating in death. Nevertheless the experiments of Philippeaux, Harley, Berruti, and Perusino have shown that, after extirpation of both suprarenal capsules, large as well as small animals may survive for months without presenting pigmentary anomalies in the skin or internal organs. According to Schiff, extirpation of the suprarenal capsules, or of the nerves distributed to them, does not give rise to any change of color either in pigmented animals or in albinos.

As experimentation merely furnishes us with negative results, other facts, such as the great abundance of nervous elements in the parenchyma of the suprarenal capsules, and the relations of these elements with the sympathetic system, assume a so much greater importance. According to recent investigations by Ecker, Koelliker, and J. Arnold, the semi-lunar ganglion furnishes the suprarenal capsules with numerous nerve-fibres, which are provided with ganglia and form a kind of network in the interior of these organs. Virchow has also found, in their parenchyma, large nerve-cells, furnished with prolongations, and Holm has described a second variety of cells much smaller and destitute of prolongations. This abundance of afferent nerves, compared with the small size of the organs, and the considerable number of ganglion-cells, which must be regarded as origins of nerves, prove that the suprarenal capsules possess intimate relations with the abdominal sympathetic plexuses. On the other hand, the absence of all secretory function and the structure of the capsules will not justify us in regarding them as glandular organs.

Although the experiments performed upon the abdominal sympathetic plexus by Pincus, Samuel, Budge, and Adrian have not given rise to any of the changes characteristic of Addison's disease, anatomical investigations have revealed, in a large number of cases, degenerations in the sympathetic system. In addition to the changes in the suprarenal capsules (retraction of the cells and nuclei, with fatty detritus), the following lesions have been found: bright redness and enlargement of the cœliac ganglion and of the sympathetic nerves (Monro, Recklinghausen), fatty degeneration of the solar plexus and semi-lunar ganglia (Quekett, Meinhardt, Bartsch, Southey), atrophy of the abdominal sympathetic and of the solar plexus (J. Schmidt, Van Audel), hypertrophy of the solar plexus, semi-lunar ganglia, and efferent nerve-fibres (Virchow, Greenhow, Wolff, Burresi), adenoid degeneration of the semi-lunar ganglia and of their nerve-filaments (Sanderson), purulent softening of a part of the solar plexus, starting from the suprarenal capsules (A. Fraenkel).

Among twenty-nine autopsies, anatomical lesions were found in nineteen; but in ten cases the sympathetic nerves remained intact. But all parts of the sympathetic were not examined in these cases, and in the future this examination should be carefully performed. We refer, for further details, to the investigations of Eulenburg and Guttmann (Pathologie des Sympathicus, Berlin, 1873).

The *clinical symptoms* of Addison's disease are evidence of a serious affection of the entire nervous system. Apart from the characteristic pigmentation of the integument of the trunk and of the accessible mucous membranes (with the exception of the conjunctiva and of the nails), we find the following indications of a nervous affection: frequent cephalalgia, vertigo, syncopal attacks, neuralgic pains in the limbs, shoulders, sacrum, and epigastrium; later, dyspepsia and vomiting, diarrhœa, mental depression, hallucinations, and great muscular weakness. The convulsions which are sometimes observed must be regarded as due to cerebral anæmia; the anæmia of the nerve-centres ends in cachexia, exhaustion, and somnolence, which terminate in death.

According to Risel, Addison's disease consists of a paralysis of the abdominal sympathetic plexuses from a propagation of the inflammatory processes developed in the suprarenal capsules; this gives rise to general anæmia on account of the stasis of blood in the abdominal viscera. According to Rossbach, the symptomatology depends upon a functional disturbance of the entire nervous system, which cannot be demonstrated anatomically, and which is presided over in a direct, though not indispensable, manner by the suprarenal capsules.

The *diagnosis* of Addison's disease is based chiefly on the discoloration of the skin, varying from a clear brown to a bronze tint, and upon the feeling of intense weakness which is very often accompanied by profound moral depression. When the discoloration of the skin is less marked or the pigment has not been deposited on account of the rapid progress of the disease (Gull's observation with degeneration of both suprarenal capsules and of the right semi-lunar ganglion), the adynamia and diarrhœa may lead us to suspect typhoid fever or acute miliary tuberculosis. But the absence of a rise of temperature, of enlargement of the spleen and of meteorism, enables us to exclude typhoid fever in these cases. The slight importance of the fever, and the trifling increase in the number of the respiratory movements, preclude the idea of miliary tuberculosis. When it is possible to examine the patient for any length of time, we should especially direct our attention to the discoloration of the skin and to the nervous disorders to which we have referred.

The disease almost always pursues a chronic course, and lasts months or even years. The affection was acute in two cases reported by Virchow (with recent hæmorrhagic inflammation of the suprarenal capsules), but it was found that the patients had died in the midst of typhoid symptoms. The *prognosis* is usually unfavorable. Temporary improvement and periods of arrest in the course of the symptoms are to be looked for rather than recovery. In the majority, if not in all the cases, the disease terminates in death, which is frequently hastened by the invasion of an acute or chronic pulmonary tuberculosis. The *treatment* should be invigorating and sedative.

8. MUSCULAR PSEUDO-HYPERTROPHY.

This affection, which had been described in 1838 by Coste and Gioja, and more carefully investigated by Duchenne, has been called lipomatosis musculorum luxurians (Heller), atropia musculorum lipomatosis (Seidel), myosclerotic paralysis (Duchenne). We are much better acquainted with its clinical history than with the anatomical lesions. If we examine cases of this disease, reports of which have become very numerous during the last few years (Friedreich, in his work upon progressive atrophy, has collected all the known examples of true and false muscular hypertrophy), we will find that the male sex, childhood, and morbid hereditary predisposition play an extremely important part from an etiological point of view. The proportion in females is only seventeen to one hundred: the cases are most numerous from the fifth to the tenth years of life, much rarer towards the period of puberty, and exceptional in adults.

Heredity is one of the most active predisposing causes. In the same manner that the male sex presents in progressive muscular atrophy a congenital diathesis, which appears to consist of a diminution in the resistance of the motor and trophic nervous system to exertion and fatigue, so there is a congenital predisposition, in muscular pseudo-hypertrophy, to nutritive disturbances and hyperplasia of the muscular tissue.

In a large number of instances several brothers and sisters, or several members of the same family, fall victims to the disease. Bad hygienic conditions, fatigue, exposure, and febrile diseases have sometimes appeared to favor its development.

The clinical history of muscular pseudo-hypertrophy is very characteristic. It almost always occurs in sickly children, who develop slowly and begin to walk very late and with great difficulty. In the beginning the movements are only slowed, the walk becomes slower and more fatiguing, and the child becomes rapidly tired, even from standing. The legs are separated from one another, and the gait is staggering and uncertain.

The sacro-lumbar region is often saddle-backed from paralysis of the extensors of the vertebral column (Duchenne). At a more advanced period (at the end of several months or a year) a considerable increase occurs in the volume of the thighs, which is often accompanied by talipes equinus and flexion of the toes *en griffe*. Little by little the other muscles are affected in their turn, and the hypertrophy extends by preference to the buttocks, the extensors of the vertebral column, and to the muscles of the shoulder and thorax. As this hypertrophy is often combined with atrophy of the trunk and upper limbs, the body of a sickly infant appears to be placed upon the legs of a vigorous adult.

At a still later period, fibrillary contractions are often observed in the hypertrophied muscles (Wagner, Eulenburg, etc.). The skin of the diseased parts is tracked by large veins, and is as white as marble. The temperature is sometimes markedly lowered; sensibility presents no special modifications.

Electrical exploration gives various results according to the degree of intensity of the muscular degenerations and the functional disorders. The best-preserved muscles and the nerve-trunks of these parts react normally to the faradic and galvanic currents. The faradic contractility is visibly weakened in those nerves and muscles which are moderately affected.

According to Eulenburg (Virch. Archiv, Bd. LIII.), the contractions are stronger at the closure of the anode than at the closure of the cathode, and the "opening" contractions are sometimes entirely wanting. Barth (Arch. f. Heilk., Bd. XII., 1871) also found the farado-muscular contractility abolished, and only slow and feeble contractions produced by strong galvanic currents. All electrical excitability disappears in the muscles in which the paralysis and degeneration have attained their maximum. Electro-muscular sensibility has been found to be either increased or diminished.

After longer or shorter stationary periods, the last vestiges of voluntary motion disappear, and the child is entirely helpless and unable to leave the bed. In the prone position the hypertrophied lower limbs present slight contractures at the hip and knee, the thigh is rotated outwards, and the contraction of the muscles of the leg gives rise to talipes equinus and varo-equinus. The muscles, which are at first increased in size, then become atrophied, and certain groups of muscles, especially in the upper limbs, present very pronounced atrophy, although the legs are still entirely misshapen. Other complications are sometimes observed, such as diminution of intelligence, slowness of speech, and convulsions. The patients often succumb to diseases of the respiratory organs.

The anatomical changes in the muscles have been studied either in the living subject (by excision or harpooning) or only after death.

The pale, discolored, and enlarged muscles show atrophy of the fibrillæ, even to complete disappearance, and an abundant development of interstitial adipose tissue. Many cases present hyperplasia of the interstitial connective tissue, with simple atrophy of the muscular fibres, which Billroth, Charcot, Knoll, etc., regard as the primary disease. The accumulation of fat in the proliferated connective tissue, which has developed at the expense of the internal perimysium, only occurs secondarily after the progressive atrophy and the final disappearance of the muscular tissue. Waxy, tubular atrophy, with formation of fissures in the primitive fibres, has hitherto been observed only by Martini. On the other hand, granular infiltration of some muscular fibres (parenchymatous exudation) and proliferation of muscular nuclei have been several times noted by Charcot, Cohnheim, and Friedreich.

Cohnheim was the first to discover in the muscles, which were increased in size, hypertrophied muscular fibres (two or three times larger than the normal primitive fibres) between the atrophied elements, and this observation has been confirmed by Eulenburg, Barth, Mueller, and Knoll. Within recent times, Auerbach (Virch. Arch., LIII. Bd.), Berger (Deutsch. Arch. f. klin. Med., 1872), and Hitzig (Ber. Klin. Wschr., 1872) have observed some cases of true hypertrophy of the muscular fibres, without proliferation of the interstitial connective tissue, and the two first-mentioned authors have noticed this in the initial stage of muscular pseudo-hypertrophy, which terminated, at a later period, in atrophy of the hypertrophied fibres and hyperplasia of the interstitial tissue. The case of true muscular hypertrophy of the left upper limb, described by Friedreich (loc. cit.) was a congenital condition, with which we are not concerned at the present time.

The examination of the nervous system, which has been made in a small number of cases of muscular pseudo-hypertrophy, has furnished negative results. In Meryon's two patients, and in the cases examined by Cohnheim and Charcot, no pathological changes were found in the sympathetic system, in the columns of the cord, in the anterior gray horns, which were studied with especial care, or in the roots of the nerves and peripheral nerve-trunks. On the other hand, Barth's case (Arch. f. Heilk., Bd. XII., 1871) presented sclerosis of the antero-lateral columns, with considerable vascular dilatation and partial atrophy of the cells in the anterior horns. In W. Mueller's case (Beitr. z. path. Anat. u. Phys. d. menschl. Rueckenm., Leipzig, 1871) the cord presented very extensive degeneration, especially in the lateral columns, with atrophy of the cells of the anterior horns and obliteration of the central canal. But in Charcot's opinion, Barth's case was one of symmetrical sclerosis of the lateral columns (lateral amyotrophic sclerosis, *vide* page 262, Vol. I.) accompanied by degeneration of the anterior horns, and, in Mueller's case, the gray degeneration of the spinal columns, with atrophy of the cells of the anterior horns, the chronic meningitis, ependymitis, and cellular infiltration of the vessels of the brain and cord, must be attributed to the general paralysis from which the patient was suffering. L. Schlesinger (Wien. Med. Presse, 49 and 51, 1873) also observed a patient affected with hypertrophy of the left lower limb (which had lasted for nine years), with normal electrical reactions and very slight functional weakness; this patient also presented the symptoms of dementia paralytica.

On account of our ignorance of the true nature of muscular pseudo-hypertrophy, we are compelled to resort to hypotheses. Fatty degeneration of the muscles sometimes accompanies certain central affections, such as progressive muscular atrophy, amyotrophic lateral sclerosis (Charcot), and general paralysis of the insane. But even in well-marked cases, which were examined by the most competent histologists, the muscular degeneration was found to be independent of any appreciable change in the cord, nerve-roots, or sympathetic system.

We must conclude, therefore, that the muscular hypertrophy, which complicates certain spinal affections, plays merely a secondary and accessory part. In addition to the absence of lesions in the nerve-centres, there are other important reasons for assigning a peripheral origin to the disease in question. In traumatic lesions of the nerves (as in the previously quoted experiments of Mantegazza and Vulpian, and in the more recent ones of Bizzozero and Golgi), increase of the interstitial connective tissue and an abundant accumulation of adipose cells between the muscular fibres, advancing even to complete transformation of the muscles into adipose tissue, have been observed in addition to the atrophy of the muscular fibres. It is easier to discourse upon than to demonstrate the relations which exist between suppression of the trophic functions of the nerves and the retrogressive processes of muscular hypertrophy. The diagnosis of muscular pseudo-hypertrophy is based upon a certain number of important signs, viz. : the striking disproportion between the volume of the limbs and their motor functions, the peculiar modifications in the position of the body and in movements, the appearance of these symptoms during childhood or puberty, the hereditary antecedents, and the examination of the muscles after excision or harpooning. For the differential diagnosis from amyotrophic lateral sclerosis and spinal infantile paralysis, we refer to the details given on page 262, Vol. I., and page 4, Vol. II.

The *prognosis* of fatty degeneration of the muscles is not absolutely unfavorable during the first period of the disease. Recovery may follow the early employment of electricty, hydrotherapeutics, and massage. At a more advanced stage these measures may give rise to a certain period of arrest or to temporary improvement of the paralysis, but will not prevent the fatal issue of the affection. Hereditary predisposition and severity of the initial manifestations render the prognosis much more serious.

Tonic remedies have not been shown to produce any positive action upon the progress of fatty degeneration of the muscles. Galvanization of the sympathetic, which was recommended by Benedikt, has proven unsuccessful in the hands of Erb, Roquette, Guttmann, and Berger. Duchenne obtained recovery by the application of local faradization continued for months, and combined with hydrotherapeutics and massage. In one case I observed very marked improvement in the motor power by the application of the galvanic current, for several weeks, to the nerves of the hypertrophied limbs, in addition to the daily use of moist frictions and cool baths. The action of these various measures is also furthered by rational gymnastics and by the exhilarating air of the mountains.

9. TROPHIC AFFECTIONS OF THE SKIN.

Danielssen and Boeck (Recueil d'Observations sur les Maladies de la Peau, 1856) first called attention to the cutaneous eruptions occurring along the course of the nerves in neuralgia. In a patient who had suffered for two months from left intercostal neuralgia, complicated with zona, and who died of pneumonia, the autopsy revealed intense redness and swelling of a large number of the cutaneous filaments of the sixth left intercostal nerve, with infiltration of the neurilemma. Baerensprung (Annal. d. Charité zu Berlin, 1861-'63) then endeavored to establish, from a large number of observations, that the irritation of the trophic fibres in zona occurs at their point of origin in the intervertebral ganglia and in the Gasserian ganglion (in facial zona). Autopsy showed injection and swelling of several intercostal nerves and of the corresponding intervertebral ganglia. Under the microscope a granular substance of a brownish color (disintegrated blood-globules) was discovered in the sheaths and in the interior of these organs, with nuclear proliferation in the connective tissue and varicose nerve-fibres at some points.

Brown-Séquard (Quart. Journ. of Med., May, 1865) has observed cutaneous eruptions upon the arms in spinal meningo-neuritis of the lower cervical region. Charcot and Cotard (Gaz. Méd., 1866) found intense redness and enlargement of the ganglia and nerve-trunks within the intervertebral foramina, in cancer of the cervical vertebræ, which had been attended with zona along the course of the compressed nerve-plexuses. Bahrdt (Zur. Ætiol. des Herpes Zoster, Diss., Leipzig, 1866) and E. Wagner (Arch. d. Heilk., 1870) have seen tubercular pachymeningitis propagated, in vertebral caries, to the spinal nerves and ganglia (with degeneration of the nerve-cells). In one of Weidner's cases (Ber. Klin. Wschr., 1870) the posterior root of the thoracic nerve contained connective-tissue new growths, containing particles of calcareous matter. In a second case, reported by the same author, the patient suffered from painful herpes along the course of the first branch of the trigeminus, with relapses of neuralgia and ophthalmia of the right eye. Five years later the autopsy showed : hyperæmia and cicatricial retraction at the origin of the right fifth pair in the medulla oblongata and atrophy of the large root, with exudation of a reddish fluid between the fibres; the nerve-cells of the Gasserian ganglion were imbedded in connective tissue, rich in nuclei, the interior of the cells containing a finely granular and highly pigmented substance (traces of an old inflammation). Haight (Wien. Akad. Sitz.-Ber., Bd. 57, 1868) found the connective tissue, in the deeper layers of the skin, softened, infiltrated with cells (which were especially abundant around the nerves of the subcutaneous connective tissue), and the nerve-fibres swollen. We may finally refer to the important facts reported by O. Wyss (Arch. d. Heilk., Bd. XII., 1871). In a case of herpes in the distribution of the first branch of the trigeminus, attended with inflammation of the conjunctiva and cornea, this author found purulent inflammation of a portion of the Gasserian ganglion and of the nerve, extending even to the small nerve-filaments of the face, with numerous pus globules between the nerve-cells and some extravasations within and around the ganglion.

The interpretation of these data, as explanatory of the trophic disturbances, presents great difficulties. Eulenburg and Landois (loc. cit.) regard them as due to vaso-motor paralysis, with increased pressure in the capillaries, and the development of vesicles with serous contents. This theory is far from being satisfactory, since very marked paralysis of the vascular nerves, from division of the sympathetic, is unaccompanied by similar transudations into the integument. American military surgeons (Mitchell and others) and Charcot, having found that trophic disorders of the skin appear especially after incomplete nerve lesions, regard them as due to inflammatory irritation of the nerves. The latter author calls attention to Paget's case of fracture of the lower end of the radius, with compression of the median nerve during the formation of callus, and inflammatory lesions in the corresponding fingers. The ulcerations only disappeared after the compression of the nerve had ceased.

According to Friedreich (loc. cit.) the trophic disturbances are caused by a neuritis which is propagated from the irritated point even into the cutaneous filaments through the medium of the nerve branches.

Although the anatomical data as well as the clinical signs (fever, hyperæsthesia, then cutaneous anæsthesia) favor the theory of the inflammatory origin of the trophic disorders in question, there are many other considerations which prevent us from always attributing them to a neuritis or to an inflammation of the ganglia. Perfectly well-marked neuritis may develop without any trophic disturbances, while, on the other hand, herpetic eruptions make their appearance without any symptoms of irritation in the nerves, especially in young subjects. In cases of this nature, in addition to the very frequent propagation of inflammation to the skin, we must admit an irritation of the trophic nerves, which will also serve to explain other alterations in the tissues, such as changes in the hairs and pigmentary hyperplasiæ and anomalies. Further anatomical and experimental investigations are necessary in order to clear up these questions.

Herpes zona of the face usually appears upon one side, although double zona has been observed by Hebra, Moers (along the course of all the branches of the trigeminus), and Thomas. Zona may also appear upon other parts of the body, and Esmarch (Schmidt's Jahrb., Bd. 95) has seen a case extending over the entire posterior surface of the left leg, from the buttock to the foot. The anatomical examination showed the presence of neuritis of the sciatic nerve. Zona is accompanied by fever, and Trousseau and M'Crea (Brit. Med. Journ., 647, 1873) have observed hyperæsthesia and, later, anæmia and anæsthesia of the skin. In addition to zona, other trophic changes may occur in the skin, such as erythema, erysipelatous inflammation of the face (in prosopalgia, Anstie), urticaria, and bullæ of pemphigus. We have previously mentioned the hypertrophy of the skin and the peculiar shining appearance (glossy skin) which follow in the wake of traumatic lesions of the nerves. The acute eschars (acute decubitus) of cerebral and spinal diseases have been discussed in various preceding chapters.

From an etiological point of view, we may add that cutaneous trophic disturbances are generally observed after traumatic nerve-lesions, especially when the latter are incomplete, and remain absent after complete division of the nerves. Herpetic eruptions also appear in neuralgias, febrile diseases, intermittent fever, and true neuritis. These exanthemata are rarer in diseases of the cord, although zona may be present in cerebro-spinal meningitis, in cancer, contusions and fractures of the vertebral column, and in acute and chronic myelitis. I have also seen, as I have previously stated, herpes vesicles along the course of the radial nerve in progressive muscular atrophy.

10. TROPHIC AFFECTIONS OF THE BONES AND JOINTS.

Schiff first demonstrated experimentally the influence of the nerves upon trophic changes in the bones. Division of the nerves of the limbs in mammalia and destruction of the lumbar cord produce dilatation of the blood-vessels, not only in the soft parts and muscles, but also in the periosteum and bones. In an adult animal the limb remains paralyzed and the diameter of the bones diminishes considerably. The surfaces and apophyses are rounded, the medullary cavities are enlarged, the periosteum thickened, and the proportion of calcareous matter diminished. Young animals develop poorly, and present hypertrophy of the bones in the first few weeks after section of the nerves. Even in adult animals, section of the inferior dental nerve has produced, at the end of several weeks, hypertrophy of the corresponding half of the jaw. Schiff explains this fact by the remark that the preservation of the movements of the jaw prevents atrophy, while the persistence of the vascular dilatation gives rise to hypertrophy.

Within the domain of pathology there are numerous examples of osseous and articular lesions developing under the influence of the nervous system. In spinal infantile paralysis there is atrophy of the bones, narrowing of the vessels, diminution of temperature, and a livid discoloration of the skin. Virchow (Gesam. Abh., 1858) has described a case of progressive paralysis and atrophy of the bones after typhoid fever. The autopsy revealed a chronic myelomeningitis and hydrorachis of the cervical region. Chambers' observation (Med. Chir. Trans., Vol. XXXVII., 1854) of very marked muscular atrophy, complicated with osteomalacia, must undoubtedly be classed among trophic disorders of central origin. In Le Gendre's and Friedreich's case the progressive muscular atrophy presented the extremely rare complication of concentric osseous atrophy, the latter extending to the iliac bones, the ribs, and to the epiphyseal cartilages. We have referred, in a preceding chapter, to the osseous atrophy and other characteristic disturbances of nutrition which occur in unilateral atrophy of the face. The periostitis, and hypertrophy of the bones and articulations observed after traumatic nerve-lesions, whether experimental or accidental, have been mentioned on pages 169–174. Profound changes in the bones have also been noticed in surgical division of the large nerve-trunks in man. In a case reported by Romberg (excision of a portion of the sciatic nerve for a neuroma, by Dieffenbach) motor and sensory paralysis at first occurred in the right leg. At a later period ulcerations developed upon the toe and outer surface of the foot, pieces of necrosed bone escaped, the skin desquamated, the nails exfoliated, and the temperature of the paralyzed leg was considerably increased.

Charcot, Fournier, and others have observed arthropathies and enlargement of the metacarpo-phalangeal articulations and of the extensor tendons of the fingers in cerebral apoplexy. The same class of phenomena includes the forms of spinal arthropathy recently described by Charcot (loc. cit.). According to Ball, eleven analogous cases have been hitherto observed in progressive locomotor ataxia. In these cases an enlargement, which almost always occupies one of the large joints, develops without any external cause during the period of shooting-pains and the initial motor disturbances. Hydrarthrosis of the knee occurred in Ball's case, and an explorative puncture showed the presence of a serous fluid containing blood-globules. Revulsive measures and galvanization (loco dolenti and upon the dorsal spine) proved ineffectual. In a patient who presented an enlargement of the shoulder with hydrarthrosis and creaking during movements, and who died of choleraic diarrhœa, the autopsy showed: roughness and erosions upon the head of the humerus, which presented no trace of cartilage, resorption of a portion of the osseous substance, formation of osteophytes; the surface of the glenoid cavity was also destitute of cartilage, and the joint was filled with a yellowish fluid, but without any signs of inflammation. The synovial capsule was merely thickened and contained a deposit of some osseous lamellæ. The spinal cord presented gray degeneration of the posterior columns and atrophy of the posterior roots.

The differential diagnosis of these joint affections was discussed upon page 251, Vol. I., and we then stated that Charcot and his pupils regarded atrophy of the cells of the anterior gray columns as their anatomical cause. In the only case in which this lesion was absent, the spinal ganglia were very much swollen and otherwise changed. As the limbs which are the seat of these arthropathies often present muscular atrophy, and as progressive muscular atrophy is sometimes complicated with similar arthropathies (Remak, Patruban, and myself), we must conclude that the trophic centres of the articulations are in close proximity to those of the muscles in the cells of the anterior horns. We may state, in conclusion, that Brown-Séquard has seen arthritis of the knee develop upon the corresponding side after unilateral incision of the lumbar cord.

The thickening of the articular extremities in certain forms of arthritis has been attributed by Remak to an affection of the sympathetic ganglia. In such cases galvanization of the sympathetic in the neck will cause diminution of the articular enlargement and of the pains, while local treatment is useless. The thickening of the ·heads of the metacarpal bones in progressive muscular atrophy was first noticed by Remak, and I have also met with two examples. In another case I observed a very similar deformity of the hand in a painter who was suffering from lead palsy. Hysterical arthritis (Brodie), with hyperæsthesia, swelling, and œdema, is regarded by Cohen (Névroses vaso-motrices, Arch. Gén., 1863) as a vaso-motor hyperæmia of the articulations.

Inflammations of the nerves, after central or peripheral affections, are sometimes accompanied by enlargement, redness, and tenderness of the joints. In lead paralysis Gubler and Nicaise have observed circumscribed swellings of the extensor tendons, which attained the size of hazel-nuts and were painful during movement. The influence of nerve lesions upon these nutritive disorders is rendered probable by the appearance of similar phenomena in apoplectic and traumatic paralyses, in which the articulations of the hand and fingers are very frequently involved.

This is the actual condition of our knowledge concerning vaso-motor neuroses. They form the first stones of an edifice which future discoveries must finish and consolidate.

INDEX.